Further praise for

delta blues

"Ted [Gioia] comprehends with outstanding aesthetic sympathy and compassionate awe the human qualities that make these men and what they produced so important to us all. In that sense, this book is something almost as imperishable as its subjects." —Stanley Crouch

"Tremendously useful. . . . Gioia uses original research, interviews with reliable sources, and his own calm, argument-closing incantations to draw a line through a century of Delta blues. . . . He's in favor of the blues retaining some mystery, but only highly informed mystery."
—Ben Ratliff, *New York Times*

"A book we've needed for a long time. [Gioia] is one of the outstanding music historians in America. His 1997 *The History of Jazz* is as near definitive as a one-volume work can be. In *Delta Blues* he has written an equally excellent work as meticulously researched and lucidly written as its predecessor." —Bryan Woolley, *Dallas Morning News*

"The rare combination of a tome that is both deeply informative and enjoyable to read." —*Publishers Weekly*, starred review

"Bringing the same clear-eyed musical analysis and commonsense empathy to bear on the subject as he's long brought to bear on jazz, Ted Gioia has given us one of the best books we have on the Delta blues."
—Francis Davis, author of *The History of the Blues*

"A contemporary classic in its field. . . . This is a remarkable book, full of insights, and full of intriguing data. It is a book that any reader who enjoys the blues will savor and enjoy reading often." —Lee Prosser, *Jazz Review*

"Unlike recent books on the blues where writers revel in spinning controversy, Gioia delivers the straight goods without a polemic agenda. Throughout the 400-plus pages of *Delta Blues*, he tells the blues story with clarity and depth. . . . Rather than continuing with one reasoned insight after another, potentially setting up logjams for non-academic readers, he shifts into a smooth narrative flow that makes for pleasurable reading the rest of the way."   —Frank-John Hadley, *Downbeat*

"No matter how much you may think you know about the blues, you will learn much more from this authoritative and insightful work."
                                    —Dan Morgenstern, author of *Living with Jazz*

"Here we have in one volume just about everything you need to know about America's greatest blues artists. . . . This is a rich and deeply satisfying book about blues musicians and those who loved them. This book smells like a classic."   —William McKeen, author of *Highway 61*

"Ted Gioia travels the highways and back roads of the blues with no agenda. He neither romanticizes nor demystifies the music. He just sees and hears the blues clearly and lets the truths of the music he loves emerge and speak eloquently to his readers."
                                    —Anthony DeCurtis, contributing editor, *Rolling Stone*

"Very, very cool. This is history that's alive . . . as deep and full of passion as the men and women who first made this music I love. This is history you can taste and smell. Rich, deep, and funky as a juke on Saturday night. Did I mention I learned a lot too?"   —Shemekia Copeland

delta blues

delta blues

the life and times of the mississippi masters
who revolutionized american music

---

ted gioia

artwork by Neil Harpe

W. W. NORTON & COMPANY   NEW YORK · LONDON

For my sons, Michael and Thomas

For information about permission to reproduce selections from this book, write to
Permissions, W. W. Norton & Company, Inc., 500 Fifth Avenue, New York, NY 10110

For information about special discounts for bulk purchases, please contact
W. W. Norton Special Sales at specialsales@wwnorton.com or 800-233-4830

Manufacturing by RR Donnelley, Bloomsburg
Book design by Chris Welch
Production manager: Julia Druskin

Library of Congress Cataloging-in-Publication Data
Gioia, Ted.
Delta blues / Ted Gioia ; artwork by Neil Harpe. — 1st ed.
p.   cm.
Includes bibliographical references (p.   ) and index.
ISBN 978-0-393-06258-8 (hardcover)
1. Blues (Music)—Mississippi—History and criticism. I. Title.
ML3521.G56 2008
781.64309762′4—dc22
2008009412

ISBN 978-0-393-33750-1 pbk.

W. W. Norton & Company Inc., 500 Fifth Avenue, New York, N.Y. 10110
www.wwnorton.com
W. W. Norton & Company Ltd., Castle House, 75/76 Wells Street, London W1T 3QT

5 6 7 8 9 0

contents

contents

preface and acknowledgments

At the age of twenty, I naïvely believed I had a deep understanding of the blues. Schooled as a modern jazz pianist, I had studied the chord patterns and substitute harmonies, the rhythmic devices, the standard melodic licks and the more convoluted bebop or modal reconfigurations of blues music. I could play the blues in every key and in various time signatures. I even composed my own blues, drawing on the trendiest musical notions of the day.

Yet my knowledge, as I see now in retrospect, began and ended with the structure of the blues. Of its meaning and inner vitality, I understood very little at the time. In a very real sense, I was ignorant of the most essential aspects of the music I was attempting to assimilate and perform.

Only gradually did I come to appreciate the deeper essence of the blues. The process took place so slowly that I was often only dimly aware of how my perspectives and preconceptions were being transformed. But in time

I found myself listening to the same blues music I had heard in my youth with much different ears, and certainly no longer with the glib assurance that I had plumbed its depths. On the contrary, the music now seemed multilayered, otherworldly, elusive. I sensed a richness to these songs, especially the older blues from the Delta tradition, that I had missed before.

Of course, the music itself had not changed during the intervening years, but I had altered considerably. Partly, this newfound appreciation stemmed from (I would like to think) a growing maturity on my part. But equally my attraction to traditional blues was no doubt fueled by my growing dissatisfaction with the overpowering commercialization and commoditization I encountered elsewhere in the music world. Traditional blues' stubborn allegiance to its own guiding lights, its resistance to corporate interference, its blissful ignorance of music videos and trendy radio formats, its affirmation of its own inexpressibly rich heritage—these all sharpened my sense of its value.

My research into traditional styles of music during much of the 1990s further stirred my interest and appreciation of early African-American performances styles. At first this research was conducted from afar, but my move to Texas five years ago, after a lifetime mostly spent in California or overseas, gave me an exciting opportunity to study traditional music in the locales where it had once flourished. Here I settled in a neighborhood where Skip James had spent much of the 1930s, and a few miles away from the site of Robert Johnson's final recording session, but also within walking distance of the old Chisholm Trail. After decades of passionate, almost obsessive, interest in modern jazz, I now found many of my most satisfying moments of musical discovery coming from a much different body of work. I researched and wrote on cowboy music, work songs, Native American traditions, and other neglected facets of our nation's aural history. But above all, the early blues captivated my imagination, and as I began undertaking research trips into the Mississippi Delta region, I felt myself confronted by what I now felt was perhaps the most influential musical tradition America had produced, yet one still poorly understood and insufficiently appreciated.

All my assumptions about music now seemed under attack and constant revision. After several decades of playing the piano, I began learning the traditional instruments of the Delta. I returned to the harmonica, an instrument I had played with enthusiasm in my teens. On a Delta trip, I acquired a diddley bow, the one-string instrument that had been the starting point for many blues guitarists, and began learning how to play it with a knife—quite a change, and challenge, after years of having the eighty-eight notes of the piano keyboard at my disposal. I next returned to the guitar, an instrument I had hardly picked up since I was sixteen years old, and taught myself how to read tablature notation. I studied the transcriptions of Delta blues guitar recordings, and also began developing blues figures and patterns of my own, inspired by the music of the masters of the idiom. To some extent, I felt like a child again, discovering music for the first time.

In this book, I have tried to take an expansive view of the Delta tradition, not only focusing on the musicians native to the region, but also pausing to explore the careers of those who lived in close vicinity to the Delta, and thus absorbed its influences, or who resided in the Delta for shorter or longer periods, and brought the experiences of these years to other parts of the world. This is a rich and complex story. As the careers of Muddy Waters, Howlin' Wolf, John Lee Hooker, and B.B. King make clear, the sounds of the Delta have traveled far over the decades, impacting other styles of music, and changing the sonic landscape of our times. These far-reaching reverberations are, I believe, a proper part of my account of the Delta blues. But I also wanted to take time to focus on the almost forgotten figures, large if little known talents such as Geeshie Wiley or Kid Bailey or Mattie May Thomas and others, who might have developed into well known stars, but whose brilliance is obscured because they recorded so little and their biographies are so sketchy. My hope is that a far-reaching study of this sort will inspire readers to open up their ears to riches from the Delta heritage that they may have previously missed or ignored.

And, as always has been the case for me, researching and writing gave me a grand excuse to knock on doors, meet people, and initiate conversations. The resulting dialogues are often referred to in the following pages, but this book gives only the barest indication of the full scope of these encounters. My debts in this regard are many, especially since my studies were not solitary ones, but enriched by daily exchanges with many people. My acknowledgments are due, first and foremost, to the blues researchers who made the pioneering field trips into the Delta when I was just a youngster. Almost without exception, these individuals took an interest in my project, and were generous in sharing their expertise and ideas, or in reviewing sections of my book and offering their feedback. David Evans, who began his fieldwork in the Delta, in the mid-1960s, responded graciously to my frequent queries and provided invaluable advice at many points during my work on this book. Gayle Dean Wardlow, a native Mississippian who has been researching this music for more than forty years, also gave generously of his time and firsthand knowledge. Mack McCormick, another indefatigable researcher, is often said to be reclusive and unapproachable, but I found him extremely helpful and a great repository of insights and experiences. My several encounters with him left me all the more saddened that so few of his writings have been published—a great loss to blues lovers and future researchers. Stephen Calt, another pioneering blues researcher and incisive writer, helped me out in innumerable ways. Steve and I exchanged several hundred e-mails during the period I was writing this work—the correspondence would be longer than the book itself—and his frank, penetrating thoughts on the Delta tradition frequently forced me to reexamine my own assumptions and attitudes.

I also benefited from the recollections of the individuals who had "rediscovered" many of the Delta musicians, or served in other areas of blues advocacy during the 1960s and 1970s. I was helped by Dick Waterman, who tracked down Son House during the summer of 1964, and later worked tirelessly to advance the careers of many important blues players. Phil Spiro, who had accompanied Waterman on the trip to find House, also answered my many questions, and cleared up many previously confusing details of this historic encounter. ED Denson told me about his similar rediscovery of Booker White. George Mitchell shared with me his recollections of his fieldwork in Mississippi in the 1960s, and his recordings of R. L. Burnside and others. Steve LaVere discussed his efforts in promoting and researching early blues music, and bringing to light biographical information on Robert Johnson and others. Samuel Charters recounted his own experiences in reclaiming the history of the Delta blues. I am greatly indebted to each of these individuals for their contributions to my own Delta blues project.

Lori Thornton is a skilled genealogist, and she guided me through databases and information sources on the early Delta blues musicians that I would never have discovered on my own. Dr. Philip R. Ratcliffe, Ronald Cohen, James Segrest, Mark Hoffman, Robert Gordon, Paul Garon, David McGee, Bob Groom, and Fernando Benadon also shared the insights gathered from their own researches and areas of expertise. In other instances, I was helped by Anna Lomax Wood, Jay Kirgis, Larry Cohn, Ellen Harold, Don Fleming, Paul Pedersen, Sherry Robinson, Viken Minassian, Ed Leimbacher, Gordon Keane, Andy Karp, Alan Kurtz, Alain Recaborde, Jay Sieleman, Alex Andreas, Herbert Wiley, and Johnny Winter.

I also want to thank Todd Harvey and Michael Taft of the American Folklife Center at the Library of Congress; Richard Ramsey of the Howlin' Wolf Blues Museum in West Point, Mississippi; and the staffs at the Mississippi Department of Archives and the Blues Archive at Ole Miss. I must express my gratitude too to Hubert Sagnières for his support on this project, and to my agent Brettne Bloom. In addition, I would like to thank my editor Maribeth Payne, her assistants Graham Norwood and Imogen Howes, and the others at Norton who contributed to this book. I also owe a great debt to Neil Harpe, whose artwork illustrates these pages. From the very start, I had envisioned Neil's images as an integral part of this project, and have been delighted by the results of our collaboration.

None of these individuals, I must add, bears any responsibility for the limitations or oversights of the present work.

Finally, I must thank my wife Tara, and our two sons, Michael and Thomas, without whose constant support this book would not be possible.

—TG

chapter one

the blues and the old kingdoms

1. from catfish row to graceland

The Delta region of Mississippi is an expansive alluvial plain, shaped like the leaf of a pecan tree hanging lazily over the rest of the state. Stretching some two hundred and twenty miles from Vicksburg to Memphis, it is bounded on the west by the Mississippi River, and extends eastward for an average of sixty-five miles, terminating in hill country, with its poorer soil and different ways of life, and the Yazoo River, which eventually joins the Mississippi at Vicksburg. For blues fans, this is *the* Delta, although geologists will remind us that it is not the proper delta of the Mississippi River, which is found where the mighty currents flow into the Gulf of Mexico south of New Orleans.

No U.S. president has hailed from the Delta region, or indeed from anywhere in Mississippi. Nor has a vice president. No Chief Justice of the Supreme Court was born here. No Secretary of State. The region's contributions to the fields of chemistry and physics are practically nil. The same can be said for economics, psychology, sociology, and a college course catalog full of other academic disciplines. None of the Dow Jones Industrial companies have their headquarters here. In fact, not a single member of the Fortune 500 calls Mississippi its home.

Yet music the world over was transformed by the songs made here. The influence of the Delta on the sound of our musical lives is so pervasive today that it is almost impossible to take full measure of its impact. One might as well try to imagine cooking without herbs and spices, or medicine before the arrival of penicillin. Our soundscapes were revitalized by the blues tonality, which found rich deposits by mining the cracks between the notes of our Western scales. New modes of musical expression were made possible by the blues way of phrasing, the crisp bite of its distinctive harmonies, and its penetrating melodies. Without the blues, much of the music we hear every day would be fundamentally different, eviscerated and tepid. And without the Delta, we can hardly imagine the blues exerting such a powerful influence.

During the 1920s and 1930s, when the first great recordings of the Delta blues were made, the level of poverty among the people who created this music was staggering. Mississippi had the lowest per capita income of any state, less than half of the average for the country as a whole. It ranked dead last in per capita retail sales; last in the percentage of its residents who owned telephones and radios; last in the proportion who registered motor vehicles; last in the percentage whose homes were wired for electricity. Indeed, for the Delta residents, electricity might as well have not existed; as late as 1937, fewer than 1 percent of the farms had use of it. Here it seemed as if a Third World country had been abandoned in the heart of the United States, left to fend for itself, with its simple rural staples of cotton and catfish, in the midst of a booming, modern economy whose benefits it did not share.

But the poverty of the people stood in stark contrast to the richness of the soil—declared by an expert at the dawn of the twentieth century to be the most fertile to be found anywhere on the globe. Even so, cultivation of this land did not come easily. Thick forests of cypress and gum, oak and ash, planted their roots here, and were home to deer and wolf, bear and panther. What little space remained was crowded with impenetrable vines and dense canebrakes, which sometimes stood taller than a man on horseback. During the Civil War, Grant twice failed in his attempts to mount an attack on

Vicksburg from the north by way of the Delta region, and he finally gave up in despair at bringing his troops through such an impassable combination of swamp and cane, trees and wild animals.

Yet visitors today see wide open land, and a terrain so flat that the bumps on Highway 61 are often the highest elevation in sight, and the center line of the road stretches on for miles without deviating more than a few inches to left or right. The deforestation started by the loggers was continued by the planters, until only the mounds left behind by the region's first settlers, the Choctaw—puzzling protuberances sometimes containing graves or artifacts, at other times empty of any remains or objects—resisted the leveling impulse. But even these last elevations in the landscape have been forced to give way, removed one after another until only a few still stand. Like the trees and cane, the mounds fell victim to zealous grading, planting, or building, the new civilization of land levelers replacing the mound builders of a previous age. Today, the eye searches in vain for elevation on the Delta landscapes, and quickly reaches the horizon at almost every point on the compass.

As the ground was leveled, the social strata became more steeply separated. Census figures from antebellum Mississippi reveal the sharp racial divide between town and country. Whites outnumbered blacks two to one in cities such as Vicksburg and Natchez; but the reverse held true in the surrounding countryside, and especially in the Delta region where, by 1850, there were five slaves for every white resident. As a result, the slave experience was seldom touched by the varied influences of town life. The white artisans and tradesmen of the city worked hard to retain this state of affairs. Records have preserved the response of one white mechanic, who was offered the assistance of several slaves for six years, provided he taught them his craft: he angrily responded that he would rather starve than teach the mechanical arts to a black man. And even the few slaves who managed to find places within the city economy failed to mitigate this great divide between town and country; they tended to hold themselves apart from the field slaves and the associations of plantation life.

But if city ways were dictated by the white power structure, the sheer impact of numbers ensured that the cultural tone of rural Mississippi would be shaped by black realities. The repression, even the brutality, of daily life could not prevent the black population from dominating the musicmaking, the storytelling, the values and priorities of the Delta region. The emergence of the blues depended, one suspects, in no small part on this pervasiveness of the black experience and its relative isolation from the formalities of city life. We have seen this same pattern elsewhere in the New World—in Bahia, in Haiti, in Jamaica—where black populations achieved a critical mass that shaped the culture, despite tremendous poverty and a general absence of opportunities for social or individual betterment. It is interesting to note that these same settings have produced some of the most vibrant musical traditions of the last hundred years. If music were a fungible commodity, like gold or oil, perhaps these pauperized economies might form an OPEC of song, demanding monopoly pricing for their sole treasure. But as it stands, these riches have spread freely, crossing borders in ways that no tariff or customs agent can hinder, a duty-free gift to the world.

Today, the blues remains the Delta region's most lasting legacy, still potent after so many other dreams here have faded away. Most of our cotton now comes from Asia—China is the leading producer in the world, while India has also surpassed the United States in annual output, and Pakistan may soon do the same. Delta farmers are hard-pressed to survive in this global marketplace, and double-digit unemployment rates are endemic. Although some hope for manufacturing jobs to take up the slack, even these are disappearing in the face of more aggressive competitors overseas. In this harsh environment, the promise of tourism beguiles with its potential for easy dollars from those anxious to experience, in the language of marketing, "the land where the blues began." But not everyone shares in this dream. "Some of us in Mississippi don't like to be too closely associated with the blues," a music professor at one of the state's universities confided to me. "People tend to think that it is all we've got." Yet the blues music, so despised by the masters of the region in earlier years, looms larger and larger in the region's self-identity and economy with each passing decade, until it has come to represent the most promising substitute for the riches no longer given up freely by the soil.

We cannot prove that the blues began here—the assertions of tourism brochures notwithstanding—although the Delta's claim as its birthplace is as strong as any other region's. Yet the music thrived here with a special intensity that demands our attention and earns our respect. The blues, by its nature, is a raw, roughshod music, with few frills, but especially on this stretch of land. The music here often lacks the surface polish of other regional blues styles—the elaborate finger-picking virtuosity of the Piedmont blues, the rapid-fire single note lines of the Chicago guitarists, or the engaging banter of the Texas songsters—but in its searing emotional fire, the Delta holds second place to none. If, as some have suggested, there are "blues" and there are "deep blues," a gradation marked by an emotional scale more easily felt than defined, then the homegrown variety in this part of the world leaves little doubt about where it stands in the pecking order. The Delta blues possess the deepest roots of all.

Simplicity and starkness are defining qualities of the Delta idiom, especially in the choice of instruments and how they are played. Other cities—Chicago or Memphis or Detroit—might pride themselves on their blues *bands*, but here in the Delta, a band is a rare luxury. A single instrument, the guitar, mostly stands self-sufficient, cradled by the singer, who treats it with tough love, sometimes slapping it in percussive accompaniment, or playing it with a knife or the neck of a broken bottle or some other *objet trouvé* unknown to Parkening or Segovia. Every once in a while, a piano or a fiddle enters our story, but only at the widest intervals; and as for *horns*, they are as rare as the legendary walking catfish in this Delta landscape, unless you admit the harmonica or kazoo under this stately rubric. But the guitar—inexpensive, portable, suitable for dances or street corners or isolated musicmaking—was perfectly adapted to the needs and limitations of the people who made this music.

Although the guitar is undisputed king of the Delta, it is a much ill-treated one. Chords are not so much strummed as torn from the instrument: clusters of notes—drawn from a pentatonic scale, or colored with wry dissonances—a willy-nilly school of harmony where one seeks in vain for the "voice leading" or textbook resolutions taught in music schools. Harmonic variety is not a virtue here; sometimes a single chord, with just a few modifications, suffices for an entire song, a throbbing texture of sound, insistent and unrelenting. Often compositions are built around a simple riff, a repeated figure, perhaps only a few notes that serve as anchor, compass, and engine room, all put together, for a blues performance. Melodies are no more ornate than the harmonies, a wail or a growl counting for as much as a coloratura. At times the voice seems to want to blend into the guitar, and the guitar aspires to be a voice—one completing a phrase started by the other.

This is strange, wonderful music, no less peculiar for having eventually achieved lasting appeal and commercial success. Especially in its earliest days, the Delta blues tended to defy all the common expectations of popular art forms. Nowhere is this more evident than in the lyrics to these songs. On a superficial level, the Delta music dealt with the familiar themes of love and courtship, travels and adventures, but the psychological aspects of these encounters almost always overwhelmed the incidents related. Indeed, these songs almost never told a complete story, but merely sketched enough detail to communicate a charged and turbulent state of mind. Odder still was the propensity of the Delta blues singers to address these secular topics with a fervor more typical of religious music. Sometimes the songs explicitly talked about fall and redemption, about the devil in hot pursuit, or anticipated some coming apocalypse in language more resonant of the Book of Revelation than the Book of Love. But even when the time-honored topics of romance or wanderlust figure in this music, they are regularly filtered through an anguished soul-searching rarely broached by any commercial tunesmith.

We are blessed to have inherited these songs as a key part of our American—and now our global—cultural legacy. Around the time Robert Johnson recorded his first blues, a Mississippi writer quipped that the Delta region "begins in the lobby of the Peabody Hotel in Memphis and ends on Catfish Row in Vicksburg." A music historian today might reverse the order: starting on Catfish Row, then migrating across the lands that gave us Robert Johnson, Son House, Charlie Patton, Muddy Waters, Howlin' Wolf, and so many others, and ending not at the Peabody, but eight miles away at Graceland, the spiritual home of the rock music that drew its life force from the Delta blues. Here is the true final destination of the Delta sound, the gateway through which it entered the genetic code of contemporary song, changing how we play, hear, and even move to the music of our modern lives. Critic Nat Hentoff likes to tell how, when he first heard Elvis Presley on the radio, he was certain that the singer was the Delta bluesman Arthur "Big Boy" Crudup, who refined his distinctive style in Clarksdale in the late 1930s. The first stirrings of rock, in those early days, merely extended by the shortest of intervals the musical roots that had germinated decades before in the receptive soil of the Delta region. As Muddy Waters would later sing: "The blues had a baby and they named the baby rock and roll." As for the grandchildren . . . they are literally too many to name. In a very real sense, the rough and insistent Delta sound now pulsates as the underlying heartbeat of virtually all styles of popular music.

2. on being blue

Where do we begin in plumbing the depths of the blues? William Gass, in his eccentric philosophical treatise *On Being Blue*, has attempted to circumscribe this melancholy color and concept, aiming to establish its eminence among the hues—no, not as found in objects of the natural world, where it is relatively rare, but within our psyches. Blue, he argues, conveys an extraordinary emotional range and, as such, is "most suitable as the color of the interior life." Gass focuses primarily on painters and poets, the visual image and the written word, and seems blissfully unaware of flatted thirds and bent fifths. His preferred blue is the "blue for blue's sake" of Jackson Pollock or "the overcast blue / Of the air" as described by Wallace Stevens. Yet his comments apply with even greater validity to the blue spectrum of the musical arts. We will never know the sage who christened the distinctive music of the Mississippi Delta, who perhaps also linked it to the low-down melancholy that shares its name. But the choice was inspired. Call it what you will. The blue devils. The blue funk. Or merely the blues (is it concrete noun or abstract noun? singular or plural?). If ever sound could map the dark night of the soul, the churning waters within, it would be these heartfelt strains.

Yet where should we begin in telling its story? With the great Mississippi flood of 1927 and the first traditional blues recordings of the 1920s? With the first published sheet music in 1912? In the Delta land of the turn of the century? Among the plantations and cotton fields of the antebellum South? On the slave ships with their doleful commerce in human misery? Or in the rich musical traditions of mother Africa? Every beginning seems to point back to an earlier reference point, every tradition to a previous one. No consensus view guides us on this matter. Some hear the birth of the blues in the field hollers of the nineteenth century. Others find its counterpart in the songs of the griots of West Africa, or the bardic practices of East Africa, or the music of the Yoruba priests, or the calls to prayer of the Islamic tradition. We know the finished product, the genealogy eludes us.

This constant seeking backward in time, this quest for more and more distant roots of the blues, is also a part of the distinctive culture of the music. Just as blues fans prize the oldest musicians as being closer to the "source," more in touch with primal springs from whence blue-ness came; just so, do they also seek antecedents for the art form as a whole, convinced that it must arise from deep in the abyss of time. The very words and phrases associated with the blues convey this pervasive view. In recent years, fans have taken to referring to the blues as "roots music," the horticultural analogy suggesting an origin before all other styles, a first sprouting from which all other branches derive. Others call it "the Devil's music"—sometimes as denunciation, just as often as praise—implying an antediluvian origin just beyond the gates of Eden. The history of the music as documented may be brief, when measured in years. But the emotional truths, the wisdom of the blues, are dimly felt to have required the accumulation of centuries before appearing in recording studios and on acetate disks.

In seeking first causes and earliest influences, our study of this music inevitably draws us back to Africa. But this lineage, as we shall see, raises far more questions than answers. Our historical information is scanty, but tantalizing. An account of slave ships from 1793 is indicative: "In the intervals between their meals they [the slaves] are encouraged to divert themselves with music and dancing; for which purpose such rude and uncouth instruments as are used in Africa, are collected before their departure." No benevolent spirit inspired this indulgence. The high mortality rate on board slave ships motivated traders to encourage exercise and recreation among their captive passengers in hopes of preserving their health and energy. In some instances, flogging was ordered for those who refused to dance. Put simply, mercenary considerations facilitated the export of African music to the New World, and such practices can be documented for a period of over one hundred fifty years, from 1693 to 1859. The tolerance of slave traders was not always matched by slaveowners once the dismal cargo was landed, and many instances of prohibition or repression of music and dancing, public or private, could be provided. The reasons given were various: some slaveowners feared any occasion for large numbers of slaves to gather together; others found the dancing sinful and lascivious; still others may have been driven merely by cruelty or a tyrannical disposition. But whatever the motives, the results were invariably the same. The various steps taken merely hindered, and never eliminated or significantly impoverished the musical life of African-Americans, which continued to be distinguished by its abundance and vitality.

As one might expect, the music of black Americans bore the unmistakable stamp of their African heritage, but tracing the linkages is a far more complicated endeavor than might appear at first glance. First, African music is not a monolithic construct but itself a composite of many different cultural traditions. Recall that even today there are more than fifty countries in Africa, and over one thousand tribes and spoken languages. Just so, song and dance, instruments and performance styles, related rituals and social practices, show extraordinary variety and contrast. Isolating specific attributes as exemplary of African musical traditions from these diverse strands is a complicated task, and our path becomes even more difficult if we try to connect these common threads with the blues, since many of these practices were transformed on the soil of the New World. Some changes were small, others large, but the cumulative impact of the adaptations—in the instruments employed, the ways they were played, in the settings and social milieu, and so on—were substantial and are impossible to ignore. Finally, the blues on its arrival brought with it entirely new aspects, not derivative of either African or American precedents. A revolutionary new sound was born, forever changing the landscape of popular music, setting off reverberations still heard today. Even the most imaginative and resourceful historical sleuthing will fail to reduce it to a summation of preexisting influences. Just as a study of the rules of cricket, however thorough and painstaking, will never suffice for an understanding of the game of baseball, so the blues resists assimilation into its African prehistory.

A generation ago, the pioneering blues writer Samuel Charters confronted this chasm between new and old when he journeyed through Africa to uncover the roots of the blues. Packing microphones and tape recorder, bringing along as well decades of experience studying the American blues, Charters was like an explorer already familiar with the ebb and flow, the magnificent outpouring of a great river, but who now sought its hitherto hidden headwaters. But in this instance, our determined researcher found that tracing the upstream origins of the story he had uncovered on the Mississippi brought him to the crescent-shaped arc of the Niger. He wrote up the story of his trip in *The Roots of the Blues: An African Search*, and his descriptions of griots and street drummers, balafon players and other performers and dancers make for gripping reading. Yet though he found many fascinating musicians in West Africa, Charters did not discover the blues. As he concluded: "Things from the blues came from the tribal musicians of the old kingdoms, but as a style the blues represented something else. It was essentially a new kind of song that had begun with the new life in the American South." More recent scholars, such as Gerhard Kubik, Harriet

Joseph Ottenheimer, John Storm Roberts, and David Evans, among others, have expanded our knowledge of the African heritage of the blues and have enhanced our appreciation of the linkages between the old and the new, but they have been unable to bridge the gap identified by Charters.

Yet even if a study of African music fails to present us with the blues as a fait accompli, it remains our proper starting point, for here came much of the kindling, at least, that would contribute to the fiery ascendancy of blues music in later years. Who can experience the rich West African traditions of solo performance on string instruments and deny their spiritual affinities with the Delta blues style? The diversity of these African instruments is remarkable: the *bolon*, with its striking appearance of a hunter's bow married to a calabash drum; the harplike *kora*, with its twenty-one strings, perhaps the most expressive traditional instrument found in any part of the world; the two-string *konde* of Burkina Faso, with metal bells attached to its neck, so that it jingles when the strings are plucked; the lutelike *ngoni*, an ancestor of the banjo, often unfairly dismissed as a hillbilly novelty in the Americas, but in Africa the instrument of heroes and kings; the one-string *molo* of Senegal, played with a horsehair bow, inspiration to storytellers; and numerous other variants and hybrids. None of these is the precise equivalent of the American blues guitar, but the African and African-American traditions share many attributes, not just in the physical structure of the instruments, but even more strikingly in playing techniques. In the string music of West Africa as in the guitar work of the Delta, the rhythms and melodic material are primary, and merely imply—and sometimes not very clearly or precisely, by our Western standards—harmonic and compositional structures. In the Western tradition, the opposite is typically the case: the rules of harmony and compositional forms are far more codified and fundamental, akin to what engineering and architecture provide to a bridge or building. And if Western music is like a skyscraper, sharply delineated in meticulous and intricate scores, following rules of almost Euclidean precision, then the African sound is more akin to those rivers whose geography is so often intertwined with the history of the music, not pursuing a rigidly straight course or obeying perfect regularities in their progress, but no less powerful for these omissions.

If traditional blues music often resists our attempts to codify and analyze, it nonetheless opens itself up to more intuitive approaches. This, too, reminds us of many African performance styles. "After I returned to the United States, I tried to teach several people to play the Dagomba drums," John Chernoff has written in his seminal book *African Rhythm and African Sensibility*. "I found that if I tried to demonstrate how to enter with one drum by counting from another drum's beat, I could not do it. The only way to begin correctly was to listen a moment and then start right in." Good advice here: the master guides the beginner into the streaming currents of the music, not by imparting a series of discrete steps to be followed sequentially, rather by encouraging an immersion into the flow—much as a parent teaches the child to ride a bicycle. Pause, feel, do. Once again, blues fans will recognize the resemblance with their music, recognize the archetype for the Delta blues players who rarely counted "correctly" in their songs, adding or subtracting beats from the supposed twelve-bar structure, but who nonetheless maintained an ineffable rightness in their *feeling* for the music. Here was a process that transcended mathematical models of organization, and was for that reason doubly hard, for those trained in Western methods of musicmaking, to assimilate.

Blame it on Pythagoras, if you want. Western thinking on music was developed by scientists and philosophers, starting with Pythagoras and continuing with Ptolemy, Boethius, and others, who sought quantitative explanations for the art of plucking strings. What in Africa remained a matter of feeling and doing became, in the West, an area for thinking and counting. This profound difference impacts not just the structural basis of the two approaches to music, but even more the human element. To this day, the path to musicianship in the West builds from interaction with pieces of paper—written scores, lessons, songs to learn—driven by pedagogical systems, methodologies and arcane disciplines, scales, exercises, and the like. When African traditions entered the stream of American music, they challenged this hierarchy, almost to a scandalous degree. And here was the heart of the scandal: not just that there were no systems or scores; not just that it was played by the untutored and unlearned; not just that the music *wasn't* written down; the real rub here was that the music *couldn't* be written down, given the standard tools of Western notation. The African's achievement pointed to a weakness at the heart of the European system, an area of musical expression that eluded its grasp. The bent notes, the supreme inflections, the slipping, sliding tones and rule-breaking rhythms defied Pythagoras and his heirs, refused to be squeezed into the four-by-four boxes, stacked on high, of Western music. Music had bypassed mathematics and returned to an ethos of emotional immediacy and unmediated doing.

Eventually African and European paradigms came to terms with each other. The blues became more systematized: its form gravitated to a standard twelve-bar pattern; its harmonies and substitute chords were categorized and analyzed, codified by enthusiastic fans like axioms of a hieratic sect; method books appeared and teaching systems were developed; blues compositions were notated and arranged, played by big bands, symphonic orchestras, even school ensembles. New methods of musical notation and measurement were developed by scholars in order to capture on the page the nuances of a blues performance. True, a certain, ineluctable element remained unassimilated, beyond the scope of the systematizers, but for the most part blues became a part of the musical vocabulary of the West.

But the assimilators were transformed by their very receptivity to these alternative sounds. American music, for its part, would never be the same. Turn on the radio and listen. Whether your tastes gravitate toward country and western, or pop standards, or doo-wop, or heavy metal, or hip-hop, or jazz . . . the whole spectrum of popular music betrays the fingerprints of the blues. The lonesomest cowboys and the most impassioned Christian vocalists; neatly coiffured boy bands and pierced, tattooed renegade rockers; faceless commercial jingle singers and *American Idol* wannabes: all share the vocal inflections, the scalar ambiguity, the grit-in-the-throat silt accumulated at the intersection of the Mississippi and Yazoo rivers.

3. woke up this morning

Not only did African music change in the New World, but its social role was also transformed. And this metamorphosis was far greater than any alterations in rhythm or melody, musical form or content. Between African music and African-American performance styles we can trace many similarities and shared values, but the African musician and his New World counterpart play almost opposed roles in their respective societies. Many commentators have described the American blues musician as an extension of the West African griot or East African bard, yet one could hardly find two performers with less in common from a sociological perspective. The griot and bard were the historians of their communities, representatives of time-honored traditions, the preservers of cultural identity and accepted lore. They took these traditions and transformed them into song, and as a result often enjoyed great status in their communities. Paul Oliver tells of a Senegalese griot who earned more than the top officials of the country—and for good reason: in societies that lacked libraries and museums, official documents and archives, the griot's song filled many of the roles that these institutions serve in other times and places. The American blues musician, in contrast, honed a music of personal expression, often reflecting a lack of connection to the broader streams of society, evoking feelings of alienation and anomie. Slavery caused this terrible disjunction. Slavery destroyed in large part the social fabric, the communal values and manners, the historical continuities that made the griot's art possible. Blues music was, in many ways, a response to this deprivation.

And here we encounter the fundamental tragedy of the blues and one of the sources of its unparalleled symbolic power. For the music sings of small, everyday details of individual lives. But behind this façade always sits a larger catastrophe, invariably unspoken, but no less present for this silence. Torn asunder from the social institutions that gave life its meaning and resonance within their traditional societies, African-Americans struggled to find substitutes for what was lost within the smaller cosmos of their personal relationships and immediate surroundings. Blues music reflected this dynamic, gave it poetic expression. From this perspective, the perennial themes of blues music—broken relationships, heartache, hardships, rootlessness and restlessness—capture in a personal dimension the larger social truth. And here we perhaps can answer the puzzling question why blues music seems to strike so many listeners as enigmatic, mysterious, symbolic, even when its surface level meanings are concrete and specific almost to an extreme degree. Perhaps you think that symbolism exists only in *Moby-Dick*, or Wagnerian opera, in high art of a refined, rarefied nature, and is absent from the vernacular expressions of common people. Yet spend a few hours musing over the blues lyrics of Robert Johnson and Charley Patton—many of which take a considerable amount of deciphering and leaps of imagination to comprehend—and you will come away with a far different perspective. From a psychological point of view, the Delta blues has closer affinities to the French Symbolist poets of the nineteenth century than to the minstrel songs and medicine show ditties that are so often seen as anticipating its arrival on the scene. Even when the surface meanings of a blues song seem clear, the listener is often left with a vague, sometimes disquieting, sense that hidden layers of emotion and signification remain to be plumbed. The familiar "I woke up this morning"—the opening phrase of so many blues songs—is never *just* "I woke up this morning," never merely a nondescript response to the familiar ring of an alarm clock (or crowing of a rooster), but also brings with it half-remembered dreams and nightmares, and the sleepless anxieties, of many, many long and lonely nights. This submerged region is the true psychological terrain of the blues.

The same social forces that left the slave musician bereft of a larger societal role also severed and splintered the institutions and belief systems that imparted meaning to community life in the Old Kingdoms of Africa. Much has been made of the influence of Yoruban religious practices and their New World equivalents on African-American music. The Yoruban ceremonies and related rituals of West Africa involved drumming, dancing, call-and-response singing, and the use of symbols—such as the image of the crossroads, destined to become an important motif in blues culture—that survived in various degrees in African-American culture. We can easily identify these continuities and resonances in some of the popular belief systems of North and South America: with Candomblé in Brazil, Santeria in Cuba, Vodou in Haiti, and so on. The same survivals can be traced in African folklore, for example with the Anansi tales that mutated into the Aunt Nancy stories of the Americas.

Within the blues, we see echoes of some of these African traditions and institutions, but almost never in a straightforward manner. African ritual music typically involves larger groups, and often ignores the strict Western division between performer and audience. In contrast, blues music in the Delta evolved into a solo performance art (a process that would have been fascinating to observe firsthand and which, I believe, took place only gradually and in response to external, social pressures). By the same token, the call-and-response of communal African music now needed to adapt to the requirements of individual performance. Here, I believe, is the origin of the restatement of the first line in the blues: in essence, the Delta singer provided both the call and the response, which in the context of the blues sounded like mere repetition. A communal style of singing was replicated in the expression of a single person. Once again, a mutation in social situations shaped the ways in which music was performed, and by this very fact influenced how it sounded. Do similar exigencies also explain the relatively low profile of drums and percussion in traditional blues, despite their prominence in the rituals and communal musicmaking of Africa? Could the cumulative impact of restrictions on drumming in slave communities, or the attention they invariably attracted from white overseers, explain a preference for the quieter, more unobtrusive style of solo voice with guitar accompaniment that gained ascendancy on the Delta plantations? Probing the sociology of the blues as an extension of African practices, our questions are many, our answers at best tentative.

How can we ever hope to sift through the blues and determine with any precision what portion reflects African carryovers, and how much the constant imbibing of New World influences? Listen to a Robert Johnson record a hundred, a thousand times, and you will be unable to move beyond the vaguest generalization on this subject. Yet if one simply looks at the map, forgetting for a moment the music and those who made it, a compelling case can be made for the preponderance of the African elements. Put a pin in the map for every early citing of blues music in the United States before 1915, and you find a strange, almost unprecedented pattern. The blues came to life in the poorest parts of the country, in communities almost completely cut off from the hustle and bustle of city life, in groups largely untouched by outside influences. Tracing the early history of the blues takes us to places seldom visited by music historians . . . to plantations and prisons, and townships so small that even the mapmakers sometimes forgot they existed.

These are odd places for new art forms to emerge. We still know very little about how new cultural practices develop and spread, but the best predictors come to us (perhaps surprisingly to those unfamiliar with the ways of social scientists) from mathematical models employed to plot the spread of diseases. A cultural practice is much like a virus, and the best settings for both to propagate are in densely populated areas with a constant ebb and flow of human traffic. The dissemination of any innovation, when plotted on a chart measuring occurrences over time, follows a predictable S-shaped curve; once a critical mass develops, which invariably happens in the busiest centers of activity, the curve steepens, reflecting its spread and adoption. The blues—almost uniquely—violated this basic precept: it emerged in isolation and far from the well-traveled haunts. It emerged in settings that were almost perfectly suited for *halting*, not fostering, the spread of a new form of musical expression. One draws an important conclusion from this simple exercise: namely, that the essence of the blues was *not* innovation, was *not* the spread of a new way of making music, but stemmed primarily from the retention of traditional practices and perspectives. Jazz, in contrast, with its roots in New Orleans—perhaps the greatest cultural melting pot of its day (and, interesting to note, the American city perhaps most prone to the spread of virulent disease—the conditions again are the same!), reflects a more typical path of dissemination, and a more acculturated combination of influences. The earliest blues, we are forced to conclude, looked back to the past, not ahead to the future.

Yet the most fascinating questions—as always, with the blues—are more psychological than historical or statistical. Why has this music resonated so profoundly in the American consciousness? Why did the pain of the African-American, so often ignored in the political discourse of the day, evoke such a powerful response when translated into the sphere of popular music? How did the sensibility of the outcast, the outsider, the downtrodden find a musical path into the psyche of the mass public, creating a miniature alternative culture within the heart of the mainstream? What was it about the particularities of black-ness and blue-ness that let them modulate all other hues, reshaping the full spectrum of modern American self-identity? For in a very real sense, the blues released a new dominant strain into the DNA of American popular culture, one that has exhibited tremendous vitality, resilience, mutability over the passing decades, leaving its genetic imprints in bold relief on all later offspring. What was it about the blues that gave it such preternatural force?

Yes, there was a paradox here. But perhaps it reflected an equal contradiction in the American ethos. By the dawn of what would be called the American Century, the social cohesiveness of the communities that gave birth to the nation was already on the wane. American life had already begun its inevitable collapse into the hyper-individualism, the fluidity, the cultural tumult so characteristic of modern times. Perhaps the African-American musician, from the start torn asunder from the rich heritage and traditions of the Old Kingdoms, whose self-consciousness was permeated with a sense of loss from that very fact, was most sensitive to the essence of this situation. Perhaps the *outsider* was best capable of giving expression to what was destined to become the mainstream reality, to the emotional landscape of a world in which no ties held fast, no ground remained firm underfoot, no certainties stood unquestioned. Here all meanings were provisional, all relationships temporary. Only the particularities of the day-to-day—again the perennial "I woke up this morning" of so many blues lyrics—held sway. In essence, the blues—the stepchild of Africa; the legacy of slaves—had already plumbed the depths of these bracing new waters long before most Americans had even noticed a change in the currents. Its old-as-the-hills wisdom, as it turns out, would prove to be very much up-to-date.

chapter two

where the southern cross the dog

1. hard luck tales and love themes

The Delta soil can be as thick as tar in some parts. It will cling to your shoes—if you're fortunate enough to have a pair (not a given, hereabouts)—or to your feet, if you get by unshod, adhering below the ankle with the same tenacity that the humid air grabs onto everything above. It makes a few people rich, this gumbo mud, and a whole lot of folks "*dirt* poor," a fitting term given the soil's cruel dominion over people's pocketbooks in this land. And it's so deeply embedded in everything people say and think and do that even the music is said to rise out from it. When W. C. Handy first encountered the blues, at a Delta train station in 1903, he saw it as "an earth-born music," a term that would be later echoed in many similar phrases, linking these songs irrevocably to the land that gave them birth.

The musicians who defined the sound of the Delta blues worked the soil. Virtually all of them: Charley Patton, Son House, Tommy Johnson, Skip James, Robert Johnson, Muddy Waters, Howlin' Wolf, B.B. King, and so many, many others. Some for longer periods, like Howlin' Wolf, who devoted half a career to extracting his living from the land; others for shorter stints, like John Lee Hooker, who escaped from the Delta as soon as he could, and never looked back. Some with resentment and bitterness in their hearts; others with a degree of affection. B.B. King once estimated that he had journeyed some sixty thousand miles behind a plow before his music freed him from bondage to the land, but his memories were laced with a wistful nostalgia. "I did more than cope with the crop," King asserted. "I actually loved it. It was beautiful to live through the seasons, to break the ground in the chill of winter, plant the seeds against the winds of spring, and pick the blossoms in the heat of summer. There's a poetry to it, a feeling that I belonged and mattered."

But even those less enamored with farm life served their apprenticeships, one way or another, and the experience informed the music they made. And not just the musicians, also the patrons and audiences who supported it, the frivolous or world-weary who listened to the blues at jukehouses and fish fries, who sang along with its words, the dancers who moved to its irrepressible beat, even the bootleggers who, more often than not, paid for the music, cutting out a share of their take for the crowd-pleasing songs—they too worked the land, and the music adapted to their rhythms, the cycle of their seasons, the tenor of their lives. Little wonder that folks will still tell you that they can hear the call of the soil in the sound of the Delta blues.

Given the symbolic ties of these songs to the land that gave them birth, it is fitting that the first well-documented research into the music came from a group of folks who were digging into the ground. Charles Peabody, a Harvard archeologist, had no thoughts of discovering a new type of song when he arrived to undertake excavations in Coahoma County, Mississippi, on May 11, 1901. For the next seven weeks, he would lead a crew of workers in making successive cuttings in two of the enigmatic mounds left behind by the Choctaws long before the arrival of plantation owners or those who tilled their fields—one located on the Dorr Plantation in Clarksdale, and a second situated sixteen miles south of the city, at the Edwards Plantation in Oliver on the Sunflower River.

The digging continued until June 28, then resumed in May of 1902 and lasted until Independence Day. The thick, viscous soil made the work difficult. "The weight of the damp earth often crushed and broke the bones,"

Peabody later noted. "To excavate the skeletons even with a trowel was a matter of some difficulty and not always of success," he lamented, all because they were "buried in this so-called 'gumbo' or 'buckshot.'" But the end result was worth the considerable effort. The Edwards Plantation mound alone contained one hundred fifty-eight burials and sixty-eight vases. Turquoise beads, stone tools, seashells, bones of a dozen animals from bear to wildcat, brass bells, clay pipes, arrowheads, spearpoints, and a host of other objects also came to light during the weeks of digging. But as Peabody directed the efforts of his black laborers—the team varied in size from nine to fifteen individuals depending on the work—he soon found himself drawn less to what they found in the ground than what they did while engaged in their toils. The men sang, repetitively and at length, and the mesmerizing power of their music continued to haunt Peabody's imagination long after he returned to Cambridge.

Charles Peabody had little formal training in music, and the more he thought about it, he realized how incompetent he was to assess the songs that so deeply stirred his emotions. Yet at the conclusion of his dig, even before he had published the results of his archeological findings, he sketched out a formal academic paper on the music he had heard in Coahoma County, and submitted it for publication in the *Journal of American Folk-Lore.* "Busy archeologically, we had not very much time left for folk-lore, in itself of not easy excavation, but willy-nilly our ears were beset with an abundance of ethnological material in song," he wrote. He offered up his provisional "Notes on Negro Music" in hopes that they might be accepted as "suggestions for future study in classification."

If only some other researchers had taken up these "suggestions" at the time, and delved more deeply into the music Peabody highlighted in his essay! We cannot prove that the inquisitive visitor from Harvard heard the first strains of the Delta blues in 1901, yet his description of the songs, especially those performed by the workers at the conclusion of the day's labors, in their moments of leisure, rivet our attention. Here are all of the key ingredients of the Delta blues. Peabody remarks on the men's use of the guitar to accompany their singing when "at quarters or on the march"; he mentions the simple harmonies employed, referring explicitly to the use of "three chords"; he describes strange alterations of pitch, which could easily be mistaken for dissonances, but which we might recognize today as "blue" notes; he describes the topics of the songs, which invariably dealt with "hard luck tales" and "love themes," much like blues music does to this day.

But the final two paragraphs of Peabody's brief paper excite our curiosity even more than these preliminary observations. "I should not omit mention of a very old negro employed on the plantation of Mr. John Stovall of Stovall, Mississippi. He was asked to sing to us one very dark night as we sat on the gallery." Peabody had spent his career in classifying, labeling, documenting; but this music defied his best efforts at taxonomy. He tried desperately to find the right words: the song was like "a bagpipe played pianissimo," he suggested; or rather "a Jew's harp played legato"; or something "not far from Japanese"; or sounds with no cultural antecedent, merely "monotonous but weird." Witnessing his failure to convey what he heard, he simply sums up with a declaration of ignorance: "I have not heard that kind again nor of it." But of its purpose, he has no doubt. This music served the deeply felt need of the black residents "to throw off their sorrows in song."

Knowledgeable blues fans will immediately recognize the home of this anonymous singer. Forty years later, Alan Lomax and John Work would discover Muddy Waters at this very same Stovall Plantation. The possibility that one of the oldest black residents of the plantation was singing blues songs at the turn of the century forces us to wonder in awe at how long this music may have existed, at least in some embryonic form, before it came to the attention of the larger world.

2. workaday sorrow songs

If, in fact, Charles Peabody heard the Delta blues during his 1901 and 1902 archeological fieldwork in Coahoma County, the workaday trappings in which the music presented itself should not surprise us. As we have seen, researchers have offered many theories in their attempts to link the American blues to the earlier traditions of African and African-American music. But lay aside, for a moment, all the research, forget the various hypotheses and speculations, and just rely on your ears for guidance. They will tell you that the strongest aural connection, the most similar sound among all the styles that anticipated the blues, is found in the songs of work and everyday activities.

We cannot ignore the other connections—to the griots of West Africa, or the bards of East Africa, or the Islamic call to prayer, or the many drum traditions of the continent, to the religious or ritual music of the Old Kingdoms, or to the minstrel performances and medicine shows of nineteenth-century America. All these are also part of the family tree that led to blues music. But the very *sound* of the work song, with its long melis-matic phrases, its subject matter (in Peabody's words) of "hard luck tales" and "love themes," its repetitions and interjections, its emphatic delivery, its emotional intensity—these point to such an intimate connection with the blues that one sometimes is hard-pressed to say where the field holler ends and the blues begins.

"On the whole the work songs of any country are among the more African styles of that country," John Storm Roberts has instructed us, supporting his conclusion with examples drawn from North America, South America, and the Caribbean. Field hollers recorded by researchers in the American South could easily fool a careful listener, who might surmise that they came from Africa. Alan Lomax once spliced together a work holler he had recorded in a Mississippi penitentiary in the 1960s with a song David Sapir taped in a Senegal rice field around the same time. Lomax was so struck by the similar-ity in vocal style that he released the composite piece as the opening track of his *Roots of the Blues* compilation, concluding that the two performances sound "like a conversation between second cousins over a backyard fence." Here, in his opinion, was "positive aural evidence that, in spite of time and change of language and setting, the whole spirit of West Africa still flour-ishes in the United States and that the roots of the blues are African."

This continuity should not surprise us. Working was the one habit cul-tivated, encouraged, indeed brutally enforced among the Africans brought forcibly to the New World. Every other cultural carryover from Africa was, in the minds of many slaveowners, so much excess baggage to be tossed overboard at the slightest provocation or whim. But the work song enjoyed special status, not for its aesthetic qualities (although these were some-times admired), rather for its economic value, as a spur to productivity, an antidote to fatigue, a counter to potential dissent. Although most people associate work songs with the American South, they were in fact abundant throughout Africa, and linked to numerous occupations. Every African tribe or village had its storehouse of such songs—employed in hunting or herd-ing or grinding or gathering—and many must have been put to use on American soil in largely unchanged form.

If we could hear this music in its original form—what a fascinating mat-ter for speculation!—much of it would probably reflect characteristics now associated with traditional blues. The vocal timbre, the phrasing, the rhyth-mic feel, the infectious quality of this early African-American music were all ingredients that would eventually transform virtually all genres of popular music of the modern day. Yet the essence of the blues, its bitterness, its heartfelt lament, would have been harder to detect. "I have heard that many of the masters and overseers on these plantations prohibit melancholy tunes or words," actress and author Frances Kemble wrote during her residence on a Georgia plantation in 1839, "and encourage nothing but cheerful music and senseless words, deprecating the effect of sadder strains upon the slaves, whose peculiar musical sensibility might be expected to make them especially excitable by any songs of a plaintive character, and having any reference to their particular hardships." Only six years later, Frederick Douglass would denounce the view that the singing of slaves served as "evidence of their contentment and happiness"—further confirmation that the sensibility we now call the blues remained mostly hidden from view in the antebellum South. But its lack of visibility should not be confused with its absence. Black culture has long been rich in coded or buried meanings, inside jargon, double entendres, and other ways of communicating secretly while in full view. Fanny Kemble appends the following observation: "I have never heard the Negroes on Mr. [Butler]'s plantation sing any words that could be said to have any sense." Perhaps not to her. But make no mistake about it: bluesiness lived a subterranean life long before its appearance as a commercial product. Its ethos pervaded the African-American condition long before it was given a formal name.

"Very few of the Negro's ante-bellum secular songs have been preserved," Howard Odum and Guy Johnson lamented in their 1926 study *Negro Workaday Songs*, "but there is every reason to suppose that he had numerous melancholy songs aside from the spirituals. At any rate," the authors add, "the earliest authentic secular collections abound in the kind of songs which have come to be known as the blues." Odum and Johnson saw such strong connections between the blues and the work songs they had collected during decades of fieldwork, dating back to the early years of the century, that they preferred to refer to the blues as "workaday sorrow songs." And though they had found examples of this music throughout the South, even at this early stage—years before Charley Patton or Son House or Robert Johnson or any of the Delta blues legends had made a single record—these researchers had identified a geographical center for the most intense expressions of the blues sensibility. "Many of the most plaintive lines of blues yet recorded were gathered decades ago," write Odum and Johnson, "from the camp and road in Mississippi before the technique of the modern blues had ever been evolved. Eloquent successors to the old spirituals with their sorrow-feeling, these songs of the lonesome road have gathered power and number and artistic interpretation until they defy description and record."

The songs of work always coexisted with the music of leisure, and the latter would also exert a powerful influence on the later blues tradition. Descriptions of specific practices—the circular procession known as the ring shout; the festivities surrounding corn shucking; dances and other casual entertainments—have survived, with greater or lesser detail. Above all, the various accounts that have survived from letters, journals, and publications convey the extraordinary richness and inventiveness of this music. When deprived of instruments, the plantation slaves would rely on their bodies for an endless range of musical effects: striking their thighs, clapping, patting their feet, whistling, vocalizing, and so forth. Happenstance objects would be transformed into musicmaking devices. William Cullen Bryant, in an account from 1843, describes a slave who made music for other black residents by whistling and beating two sticks on the ground. We hear also of musicians playing bones, or panpipes fashioned from reeds, or other instruments constructed from gourds, jugs, cans, pie tins, shingles, pieces of wood, whatever might be at hand. When they had access to formal instruments, the black underclass mastered these as well, and the literature provides accounts of slaves playing everything from the piano to the bagpipes. But (prefiguring the later preference of blues musicians) string instruments were the most popular and the easiest to obtain. In particular, the banjo and violin held pride of place at plantation entertainments.

But even if we accept that the blues arose from the songs of everyday life, we still need to understand how the music evolved into a style of commercial performance. From this perspective, other genres—associated with minstrel acts, medicine shows, and other public entertainments—demand our attention. These later idioms are farther removed from the African roots of blues music, but they helped set the stage for black music as a form of popular mass entertainment. And here, at least, we have access to more detailed information. If the melancholy secular songs of the slaves and former slaves were mostly hidden or ignored during the nineteenth century, many details have been preserved about the minstrel shows that presented the happy, smiling face of black music to the American public in well-attended public settings. Around the same time Kemble and Douglass were writing, white entertainers began wearing burnt cork makeup to perform songs, dances, and skits in "blackface," at first as an interlude in a theatrical event or circus act, and later as stand-alone entertainments. In 1843, Dan

Emmett and his Virginia Minstrels established the first full-length minstrel show, in New York, to great success, spurring many imitators and rivals. These performances lampooned and ridiculed African-Americans, but ultimately depended on the vitality of black music and dance for much of their audience appeal. White minstrels visited plantations and studied slave music firsthand in order to get inspiration and material for their shows. Entertainer Thomas Rice created the most well known minstrel routine, "Jump Jim Crow," by imitating a black stable worker he had encountered in Louisville, Kentucky. In essence, these were the first "crossover" acts in American popular music, but with this critical difference: the black artists were rarely in a position to enjoy the success of the crossover, but merely served as unpaid, unacknowledged creative talent. Even worse, the finished product manipulated the source material to deride the slave culture that had brought it into existence.

To some extent, the minstrel shows anticipated, in their crude and contemptuous manner—and in some instances even influenced—the later generations of black entertainers who performed their own material. As such, they played a significant role in the evolution of African-American music, with many of the most influential black artists of the early twentieth century, such as Bert Williams and Bill "Bojangles" Robinson, adopting blackface upon occasion. A number of early blues performers joined minstrel troupes, but the influence of this popular style was relatively modest in shaping the Delta idiom, which mostly eschewed cornball humor and stage antics. Traditional blues were not *always* serious. Comic elements—especially ribald references—found their way into the music. Some Delta performers (such as Charley Patton) were slick entertainers. But, for the most part, the early Delta blues espoused a familiarity with the pathos and pain, a sensitivity to the emotional core of events, which would have been out of place in any minstrel show. Yet even if the essence of their music remained antithetical to the world of blackface, the minstrel companies provided valuable training grounds for many blues musicians, serving as a rare setting in which a black musician could tour safely throughout the South and gain experience entertaining large audiences. Moreover, the popularity of the pseudo-black entertainment of the blackface performers prepared American audiences, in some degree, for the more authentic African-American music of later years.

In many ways, the minstrel troupes were an extension of the much older tradition of traveling medicine shows, and during the middle years of the nineteenth century, these two forms of popular entertainment enjoyed a symbiotic relationship, often exchanging routines and performers, and following the same itineraries as they brought their carefully staged productions from town to town. We can trace the medicine shows back to the Old World, where mountebanks relied upon music, skits, jokes, and other forms of light entertainment to draw audiences who might purchase their pills and concoctions. No one knows when the first of these vendors arrived in the Americas, but the conjunction of buying power and credulous audiences made their appearance inevitable, and by the early eighteenth century they were common sights in all of the colonies. Even before the founding of the United States, local laws were passed to prohibit or limit these performances, but the traveling vendors continued to sell their dubious, and sometimes dangerous, cures, despite all attempts to restrict their activities. It is hard for the modern imagination, so skeptical and skilled in defusing the hype of incessant marketing messages, to comprehend the influence of these patent medicines in early America. In the days before the widespread adoption of vaccines and antibiotics, these products flooded the marketplace and captivated the minds of the American public. A catalog from 1804 includes no fewer than eighty patent tonics, but this was a small selection compared with the riches to come. A list from 1858 presents a stunning fifteen hundred patent medicines, offering remedies for "every disease, human and inhuman, between a hang-nail and natural death of two weeks standing." This institutionalized and unregulated celebration of the placebo effect, with its mishmash of wish-fulfillment and sheer quackery—and, one hopes, an occasional herbal tonic of some efficacy—persisted well into the twentieth century. Promotions for patent medicine account for around a quarter of the advertisements in many local newspapers from the Mississippi Delta during the 1920s, and a far from negligible portion of the local economy was devoted to supporting this mini-industry.

The name "medicine show," with its overtones of a hard-selling, infomercial-type pitch, does not do justice to the large-scale entertainment provided by these troupes. The more successful shows might encompass companies of thirty or forty workers, and were sometimes large enough to justify their own small train to take them from town to town. Repeat business was profitable, and the performers learned to vary their routines and acts: it was not unknown for a company to create a substantially different show for forty nights running. In addition to the standard music and comedy fare, and the inevitable promotion of a healing potion, the shows might present trapeze artists, circus acts, ventriloquism, dramatic skits, stage magic, vaudeville routines, or anything else that might hold an audience's attention for a few minutes at a time.

During the mid-nineteenth century, the medicine shows increasingly tried to present an exotic front to their audiences. Much of the allure of "Kickapoo Indian Sagwa" or "Mexican Mustang Liniment" or "Ka-Ton-Ka, the Great Indian Medicine" came from the elixir's very foreignness to everyday experience. The medicines, it seems, were all the more potent, the farther removed they were from the realities of small-town American life. In order to maintain the illusion, the entertainment presented by these traveling troupes also eschewed the familiar. Vanilla white performers would dress up like Indians or Turks or sorcerers in their attempts to present their audiences with the colorful and the curious, an escape from the here-and-now. Blackface performance fit in easily enough with this ethos, in which nothing was quite what it seemed, whether one looked at the black performer who was really white, or at the Indian medicine that was really sugar water dosed with alcohol.

Even before the Civil War, medicine shows had adopted most of the techniques of the minstrel troupes, offering banjo players, blackface entertainers, and plantation songs as part of their regular fare. But long after the end of slavery, the minstrel routines persisted. The blackface performer, addressed as "Sambo" or "Jake," and dressed in large, baggy pants held up by oversized suspenders, would often serve as master of ceremonies, comic, and musical performer all rolled into one. If a pitchman lacked a minstrel act, he might be forced to play both roles himself—putting on the burnt cork makeup while on stage, in the midst of his medical lecture, and switching into a dialect voice—rather than disappoint audiences who had become accustomed to this coarse entertainment.

The popularity and draw of these performers were enormous. In many communities, the medicine show might be the only traveling troupe to arrive during a period of months, or even years, and an audience of a thousand or more spectators was not uncommon. And some shows even journeyed to major cities, to Boston or Chicago or New York, competing head-to-head with the more bounteous theatrical and concert offerings of these large metropolitan areas. At a time when few black musicians had the means to present their music directly to the public, these surrogates took on undue influence. For many Americans, especially those outside of the South, their attitudes toward the country's growing slave population, their sense of

African-American vernacular speech, music, and behavior, were shaped as much by these vulgar routines as by any firsthand encounters with black culture. And the medicine show, seen as appropriate family fare in most communities, brought these stereotypes to audiences that would never have attended a minstrel performance—indeed, even the pious "Quaker Healers" included blackface comedians in their shows, imparting an aura of religious respectability to the base proceedings on stage.

The minstrel troupes and medicine shows lost much of their allure in the years following World War I. Perhaps a greater spirit of racial tolerance contributed in some small degree to this decline in popularity, yet the inroads of other, more technologically advanced forms of mass entertainment no doubt played a far more substantive role. There is some fitting justice in the curious fact that the blackface performance of Al Jolson in *The Jazz Singer*, the first "talking movie," set in motion the very shift in popular tastes that led to the marginalization, and eventually the disappearance, of the traveling minstrel troupes and medicine shows. The medicine show could hardly compete with the "all singing, all dancing" Hollywood spectacles of the era. A few of these troupes survived World War II; but the last documented performance by a minstrel group took place in Iowa in 1951, and the final touring medicine show folded its tents permanently in 1964.

Yet the blackface tradition left behind its peculiar aftertaste, long after its cheap jokes and routines had lost their piquant flavor for the general public. African-Americans, when they began performing their own music in earnest, were put in the strange, and perhaps unprecedented, situation of having to follow the ersatz entertainers who had already "educated" audiences about black song and dance. As a general rule, the copycats and parodists follow the trail blazed by the authentic innovator; but here it was the other way around. Many black performers found it expedient, or perhaps necessary, to imitate the imitators and, as we have seen, some even put on blackface themselves, in order to play by the rules established by their predecessors. A number of black minstrel troupes were organized in the years following the Civil War, but found themselves at a disadvantage in their business dealings. George Hicks, a black man who founded the Georgia Minstrels, ran into such constant problems with racist theater owners and promoters that he eventually sold out his company to George Callendar, a white manager. When W. C. Handy, sometimes lauded as the father of the blues, had served his apprenticeship with the Mahara Minstrels, he was quick to remind people that this group "was the genuine article, a real

Negro minstrel show." But the troupe, he was forced to add, "like most of the others of its type, was under white management." For better or worse, the opportunity to transform the tainted legacy of the minstrel show into an authentic presentation of black artistry was irretrievably lost long before the turn of the century. The more persistent black performers eventually rose above the imposed constraints, transcending the stereotypes of the minstrel tradition, and it is one of the great marvels of modern times that, in a half century, the roles were completely reversed: white musicians were mimicking the cultural patterns, on stage and off, of the black underclass. But it is, equally, one of the tragedies that almost two generations of musicmaking, encompassing all or most of the careers of the great blues pioneers, were compromised, at least in part, by the distortions and limitations of this all too gradual shift in the American popular imagination.

When black musicians finally gained access to the concert halls and performance spaces of mainstream America, their sacred music first opened the long barred doors. The tremendous success of the Fisk Jubilee Singers, who set out on the road in 1871 to raise money for the recently founded Fisk University in Nashville, revealed the commercial potential of black music even during these Reconstruction years. At first the singers did not include spirituals in their programs, and their initial concerts met with a lukewarm response, but with the—cautious and later more confident—addition of these heartfelt religious strains into their repertoire, the Jubilee Singers struck a responsive nerve in the American psyche. In New York, public demand kept the singers busy for six weeks; in Boston, they earned a stunning $1,235 for a single performance, at a time when U.S. per capita income was only $2,500 per year; and in the nation's capital, they performed for President Ulysses S. Grant. At the conclusion of the tour, they brought back more than twenty thousand dollars to Fisk University, enough to purchase a forty-five-acre tract of land that even today serves as home to that historic institution. A follow-up visit to Europe included a command performance for Queen Victoria, and raised an additional one hundred and fifty thousand dollars—an extraordinary figure at the time. A host of other singing groups, large and small, followed the groundbreaking example of the Fisk Singers, establishing, to any who doubted, the viability of black music as a moneymaking proposition.

But the formal presentation of sacred music in concert halls and theaters has never amounted to more than just the smallest portion of African-American religious music. And if we are seeking influential predecessors to the blues, we would do well to pay closer attention to the churches and con-gregations that served as bedrocks to the various communities where the Delta pioneers came of age. Although the blues has been called "the Devil's music," it has always remained on speaking terms with the ministers of the Lord. Many early blues artists made the switch, for shorter or longer peri-ods, to performing religious music, and some enjoyed alternative careers as preachers when not singing their suggestive secular songs. As we study the biographies, the recordings, the attitudes, of the performers who created the blues, we will constantly be reminded of the contrary pull of Christian-ity: with Son House, whose inability to resolve the conflicting demands of these forces haunted him throughout his life; with Robert Wilkins, Ishmon Bracey, Rube Lacy, and the many other bluesmen who actually became min-isters; with Skip James who, at the peak of his musical powers, left the blues behind to join his father's ministry in Texas; with the many Delta blues singers, from Charley Patton to B.B. King, who felt compelled at various junctures in their careers to record or perform sacred music; but perhaps most tellingly in the towering figure of Robert Johnson, whose life seemed to be lived in purely secular terms, yet whose music constantly returned to the most intense, soul-haunted themes, songs that have irrevocably shaped our image of him as a man at the crossroads between darkness and light.

Here, then, are the sounds that formed the blues. Songs of work. Songs of play. Music of the sinners. Music of the saints. And before them all, the rich, varied legacies of the Old Kingdoms of Africa, a residual energy field—halfway between collective memory and subconscious force—submerged undercurrents underpinning the whole enterprise, even today sending out tremors along so many hidden fault lines.

3. the sadness of the ages

In 1903, W. C. Handy needed to decide between two job offers. Handy, a tal-ented musician from Florence, Alabama, who would soon celebrate his thir-tieth birthday, had refined his performing and arranging skills while on the road with the Mahara Minstrels, but now a town in Michigan had offered him the chance to direct their municipal band. This orchestra consisted, moreover, of white musicians, and the position seemed to promise Handy entrée into spheres of society, and access to future opportunities, that few black musicians could enjoy at the dawn of the twentieth century.

But while he was contemplating this offer, a letter arrived from Clarksdale, Mississippi, inviting Handy to take charge of a black Knights of Pythias band. The choice between the two should have been an easy one. "There was little comparison between the two propositions, as I saw it," Handy would later write. "The Michigan thing was miles ahead, more money, more prestige, better opportunities for the future, better everything I thought. Yet, for no good reason that I could express, I turned my face southward and down the road that led inevitably to the blues."

In Clarksdale, Handy built his band into a nine-piece orchestra, and soon established it as one of the more popular ensembles in the Delta region—if we can believe his claims. Handy is a troubling figure in the history of the blues. No in-depth critical biography of this famous figure has yet been published, and most blues writers have taken at face value the celebratory account of Handy's life and times presented in his memoir *Father of the Blues*. Yet much of this entertaining book, starting with the title itself, is subject to question. Willie Moore, who met Handy in 1909 and worked for him for many years, recalled that Handy "didn't head up a band, but handled Jim Turner's band." According to this version of the story, Handy eventually inherited this ensemble, but how much Turner contributed to its success we may never know. In a 1941 interview, S. L. Mangham, who worked with Handy in Clarksdale, recalled that "when Handy came here his ambition was to write marches. . . . He said then that he was going to be the March King, another John Philip Sousa." But few can doubt Handy's shrewdness and perspicuity in quickly learning the lay of the land—both its physical contours and its less easily grasped cultural riches—in his new home. The March King evolved into the reputed Father of the Blues, and the new arrival later boasted of his intimate knowledge of everything the Delta contained. "I came to know by heart every foot of the Delta," Handy boasted, and he claimed he could call out each major and minor landmark on the different Delta train routes, even with his eyes closed.

But late one evening, at a railway station in Tutwiler, as he half nodded off to sleep while waiting for a train that had been delayed nine hours, W. C. Handy encountered a new aspect of the Delta, a different feature of the local landscape, hitherto unknown to him. This chance interaction would change his life decisively, and alter the course of American music. "A lean, loose-jointed Negro had commenced plunking a guitar beside me while I slept," Handy later recalled. "His clothes were rags; his feet peeped out of his shoes. His face had on it some of the sadness of the ages. As he played, he pressed a knife on the strings of the guitar in a manner popularized by Hawaiian guitarists who used steel bars." Handy did not yet recognize the local Delta tradition of tone-altering and bending with bottlenecks, knives, and other implements that would come to be known as "slide" or "bottleneck" guitar. But he was instantly spellbound by the sounds he heard. "The effect was unforgettable. His song, too, struck me instantly." The lyrics were simple and evocative. Three times the singer repeated "Goin' where the Southern cross' the Dog,"—all the time "accompanying himself on the guitar with the weirdest music I had ever heard." This three-line form would become a defining aspect of the blues, but at this point, Handy was less concerned with the formal structure of the lyrics he heard. He simply wanted to know what they meant. Unable to restrain his curiosity, Handy interrupted the singer and asked for an explanation.

With an expression of mild amusement, the musician told the story of his mournful refrain. The "Dog" referred to the Yazoo Delta rail line—the initials Y.D. had inspired some unknown wag to christen it the "Yaller Dawg," a name that stuck. One of the branches came to be known as the "North Dog," just as other local routes took on whimsical names—the "Cannon Ball," for the fast train that went directly from Clarksdale to Greenville, or the "Peavine," later celebrated in a blues by Charley Patton. At Moorhead, the eastbound and westbound trains crossed the north-south line four times each day. Here was the spot where the Southern crossed the Dog, the destination of the singer, and the subject of his lonely night song. And here, even in this earliest incarnation, the Delta blues was already singing of the rambling life, the trains and the crossroads, all themes that would loom large in its later history.

In most written accounts, this event is dated as taking place in 1903—in other words, around the time Handy moved to Mississippi. However, a close reading of Handy's autobiography shows that he does not specify the year of the Tutwiler encounter, and it is possible that it occurred at a later date. In any event, Handy continued to think back to this meeting during the following days and months, and he came to appreciate that the guitarist's music had been more than just an isolated performance, but represented nothing less than a regional style. The railway station singer was using what would later be called "blues form"—a repeating harmonic pattern, typically twelve bars in length (although the early blues singers were notorious for adding or subtracting a few beats here and there), with a stanza of three lines. In most blues, the first two lines are repeated, then followed by a third, rhyming line. The Tutwiler performer did without the rhyming line, and simply repeated

his single phrase ("Goin' where the Southern cross' the Dog") three times—
a simplification of the form that was probably more common in the days
before blues recordings. Handy now noticed similar songs in other settings,
and considered them as a primitive style of composition, one that had fallen
outside the purview of the mainstream music world.

Although these blues could be found outside of Mississippi—the early
roots of this music can be documented in all of the former slave states—
they seemed to flourish with a particular fervency in the Delta, perhaps
(Handy surmised) due to the singular concentration of black farmworkers
in the area. As a composer and arranger, his interest was piqued, but the
thought of incorporating this style of song into his own repertoire still gave
him pause. "At first folk melodies like these were kept in the back rooms
of my mind while the parlor was reserved for dressed-up music." He worried that the insistent repetition of the blues form, without modulation, or
development, or a contrasting middle section, might be beneath the dignity
of a commercial orchestra. And even if he did risk performing this music in
public, would people enjoy it? Or might they simply be offended, or bored,
or both? In the face of these concerns, Handy took the safest course: he put
the blues out of his mind, and most definitely kept it off his bandstand.

But a second moment of revelation, as important as the Tutwiler incident, soon jolted him back into awareness of the power of blues music.
While performing at a dance in Cleveland, Mississippi, audience members
requested that Handy and his men play some of their "native music." Handy
was unsure how to respond: his musicians were not minstrels, or improvis-
ers who could fake the sounds of the unschooled plantation entertainers.
He did the best he could, however, and offered up a traditional Southern
song, but one still played in a fairly sophisticated manner. The audience
was not satisfied, and now a second request came to the bandleader. Would
Handy object if a local band of black musicians played a few dance songs?
He agreed to the unscheduled break, and the professional performers in his
employ watched with amusement and barely disguised disdain as three local
musicians strolled into view, carrying an old, well-worn guitar, an equally
dilapidated bass, and a mandolin.

The music offered by these amateurs was much like the song at the Tutwiler train station. It had no clear beginning or end, and so little harmonic
and melodic variety that it could hardly be called a song. It was more like an
especially insistent field holler set to an equally unrelenting rhythm—a beat
that the players seconded with the *thump, thump, thump* of their stomping

feet—a "disturbing monotony," from Handy's perspective, not especially unpleasant, perhaps even haunting, but hardly worthy of presentation to a paying audience. According to all of the standards of composition, arrangement, and execution that Handy had so assiduously learned and assimilated, this rude entertainment was beneath contempt. He could hardly feel challenged by such competition, and wondered how long the audience would put up with this half-baked substitute for real dance music.

Yet Handy's triumphant sense of superiority was crushed after the completion of the song. "A rain of silver dollars began to fall around the outlandish, stomping feet. The dancers went wild. Dollars, quarters, halves—the shower grew heavier and continued so long I strained my neck to get a better look. There before the boys lay more money than my nine musicians were being paid for the entire engagement." In this moment, as Handy later recalled it, he "saw the beauty of primitive music." He understood that the same strong emotions he had felt in Tutwiler were not some aberration, not the haphazard response to the mood of a specific time and place, but stood as genuine testimony to the power of this strange, roughshod style of performance. In an instant, he saw that people would pay for these songs, audiences would flock to them. He would need to polish the rough edges to make them suitable for his orchestra, but only a little; he couldn't tamper with the music's essence. The blues, previously an obscure and often despised folk art, would now come to town as a hot property, a new form of commercial entertainment.

Within a day or two, Handy had written arrangements for several of the local plantation songs, and began featuring them in performances. He soon learned that the blues were popular with both black and white audiences. Although Handy was gratified by the enthusiastic audience response to this material, and the increased popularity of his orchestra, he also found, somewhat to his dismay, that he was now frequently invited to play in less respectable settings, especially in the red-light district "across the tracks" in Clarksdale. Yet here Handy furthered his blues education, learning boogie-woogie and other variants of Delta music, low-down styles found in no method book, taught in no conservatory.

Handy brought the blues with him to Memphis a few years later, when he started working Beale Street and elsewhere in the region, but his major breakthrough came in the unlikely setting of a local political battle. Handy's band was enlisted to help the 1909 mayoral campaign of candidate E. H. Crump, and—if we can believe Handy's account—he responded with a song that he later adapted for his "Memphis Blues." Here, as with his later "St. Louis Blues," Handy felt compelled to incorporate the twelve-bar blues form into a song which also had non-blues portions. Many of the earliest blues recordings follow a similar recipe, almost as if the undiluted blues were too raw, too overpowering to be consumed on its own. Yet even in this modified form, the music exerted its mesmerizing force. Handy tells us that "Mr. Crump" became so popular that he could not keep up with the public's demand for his band. He had to hire more musicians and create several bands—Handy later recalled that, at the peak of this local success, he had sixty-seven instrumentalists in his employ. In this pre-radio era, he managed to bring his song virtually everywhere in the city: dance halls, parks, on the rooftops and out on the street, on two separate excursion boats, in front of all types of audiences, black or white, high society or riffraff.

Again we need to hesitate before we take Handy's account at face value. We will give him the benefit of the doubt, accepting that he composed "Mr. Crump." But a case could be made that Memphis guitarist Frank Stokes was the originator—or that one of them borrowed the basics of the song from "Mama Don't Allow," which may have predated "Mr. Crump." Handy's story was further compromised when, many years later, E. H. Crump himself denied any knowledge of the tune. Handy accepted this retort without changing any of the essentials of his account—yet Crump's assertion at a minimum would seem to call into question Handy's claims for the immense popularity enjoyed by this piece.

The election of Crump to the mayor's office did not end interest in Handy's song, and he decided to adapt it for publication, albeit with new lyrics, as the "Memphis Blues." The song proved to be a tremendous hit, and was even credited with inspiring the famous dance team Vernon and Irene Castle, who used it in popularizing the fox-trot. Handy, however, enjoyed few of the financial rewards of this success, having sold away his rights to the song in exchange for a modest fee. But Handy's discovery of the blues, and his growing realization of its appeal, had churned his creative juices. In search of a respite from the noise and distraction of his four boisterous youngsters at home, Handy rented a room in the Beale Street district and set himself the task of writing a new hit song. He aimed to put all the low-down and exotic ingredients at his disposal into this composition. He peppered the score with minor thirds and minor sevenths, the so-called blue notes, and dared to open the verse with a dominant chord, a strange device at the time, but one which reinforced the blues quality of the music. Handy felt that most ragtime pieces sacrificed melody for the sake of syncopation, but he wanted a rich, seductive theme that would float over the rhythm. The melody he chose evoked the sound of a spiritual, and conveyed an ethereal otherworldliness that contrasted markedly with the licentious tone of the blues setting. But as a final twist, Handy added a contrasting section that employed a habanera rhythm. The dramatic arrival of this Cuban beat, akin to a tango, at an unexpected juncture in the song provided a powerful hook, and may well have been as important as the blues material itself in ensuring the popularity of the "St. Louis Blues," as Handy named his composition.

No blues song would ever become more famous than the "St. Louis Blues." "Well, they say life begins at forty," Handy later recalled. "I was forty the year 'St. Louis Blues' was composed, and ever since then my life has, in one sense at least, revolved around that composition." In time, Handy's "St. Louis Blues" would be adopted as a jazz and pop standard, embraced by a who's who of famous performers, in early years by Ethel Waters, Sophie Tucker, Bessie Smith, and Louis Armstrong, and in later years, by Nat King Cole, Stevie Wonder, and Dave Brubeck, among others. By one measure, only "Silent Night" was recorded more often during the first half of the twentieth century, and in time everything from a Hollywood movie to a major sports team would take its name from Handy's tune. The song achieved an even stranger destiny overseas: In Britain, Edward VIII requested it from Scottish bagpipers, and it was said to be a favorite of Queen Elizabeth II; Ethiopian soldiers used it as an anthem when defending their nation from Italian invaders in the 1930s; and under Nazi-occupied France, it led a subterranean life when renamed—to avoid prohibitions against American jazz—as "La Tristesse de Saint Louis."

The Delta may have inspired this music, but it couldn't hold on to it. And though W. C. Handy may not be the true father of the blues—we will leave it to others to dispute the fine points of that honor—he did inaugurate a time-honored blues tradition that would be emulated by almost every later Delta artist who achieved a degree of fame and fortune: he left the Delta region far behind almost as soon as he had a taste of success. Handy may not have been quite as defiant as John Lee Hooker, who proclaimed: "I know why the best blues artists come from Mississippi. Because it's the worst state. You have the blues all right if you're down in Mississippi." Yet Handy saw in New York a much more hospitable and profitable environment to pursue a blues career than either Memphis or Clarksdale. In 1918, he moved his publishing business to a desk in the Gaiety Building at 1547 Broadway, and took out an ad in *The Billboard* announcing the arrival of W. C. Handy, composer of "Memphis Blues" and "St. Louis Blues."

The next period in our story may be an important one in the development of the blues as American musical style, but it represents a long, dry spell for the traditional songs of the Delta region as a commercial form of music. Handy's arrival in New York helped set off a whirlwind of blues activity in that city, but the real country blues back in Clarksdale and its environs excited virtually no interest from the music industry. The so-called classic blues of the early 1920s were very much an urban creation, more at home in a Northeast theater or cabaret than on a plantation or in a humble juke joint. True, the musical riches of the Delta region were not exactly a secret. W. C. Handy was by no means the only composer who had heard this music. Nor were Charles Peabody and Howard Odum the only researchers who had called attention to its supple beauty. But when the blues came to New York, it took on a different tone, a sassier and more sophisticated attitude, a stylish veneer that made its Delta progenitor seem primitive and old-fashioned by comparison, an embarrassing country cousin with awkward manners and crude repartee, whom the city sophisticates preferred to keep out of sight and out of mind.

The success of Mamie Smith's "Crazy Blues," recorded on August 10, 1920, stands out as the turning point that established this new urban direction of bluesiness. Within a month of its release, Smith's OKeh recording of this Perry Bradford composition had already sold seventy-five thousand copies; but a count of disks shipped from the pressing plant, however impressive, hardly does justice to the sweeping cultural influence of Smith's innovation. A few months later, *Metronome* magazine pronounced its verdict: "One of the phonograph companies made over four million dollars on the Blues. Now every phonograph company has a colored girl recording. Blues are here to stay."

Yes, this was blues music, but as different from the rural Delta variety as the raw cotton fibers on the plantation were from the fine garments they made for New York emporiums. The songs revealed the craftsmanship, more than the blues roots, of professional tunesmiths, who wrote much of this material. The twelve-bar blues structure was more tightly defined, largely cleaned of the stray beats and uncertain harmonies of the untutored rural singer, and often set off with introductions or contrasting themes of more refined pedigree. And unlike the country blues singers, who typically accompanied themselves on guitar, the classic blues performers were vocalists first and foremost. They invariably relied on professional instrumentalists for support; and it was not uncommon for a jazz legend, a Louis Armstrong or Fletcher Henderson or Willie "the Lion" Smith, to grace their recordings. But perhaps the most striking difference between these two different shades of blues was an intangible one, psychological rather than musicological. Even at its most melancholy moments, the classic blues retained a confident, cheeky tone, belted to back row with brassy authority. Its pathos was not incompatible with a stately pride, like a tragedy presented on the amphitheater stage, whereas the Delta blues touched a deeper nerve, like a tragedy in your own household. With the classic blues, you always knew that it was, in the final analysis, a performance art. With the Delta singers, in contrast, the line between the private person and public entertainer was an undefended border, and the former always seems to infringe on the autonomy of the latter.

The women who sang the classic blues—and they were almost always women, providing a striking contrast to the male-dominated world of the Delta blues—were even more prettified than the songs. "I believe my audience wants to see me becomingly gowned," Mamie Smith commented in a rare surviving interview, striking the prevailing tone of the day, "and I have spared no expense or pains." Despite earning a reported hundred thousand dollars during the heyday of her career, Smith died virtually destitute, her income mostly consumed by the costly accoutrements and habits of her life as a blues diva. But the venues in which the classic blues flourished demanded a close attention to stagecraft, wardrobe, and presentation. Ma Rainey traveled with four trunks full of scenery, including special backdrops and lighting, in addition to a lavish assortment of fashion accessories, the plumes and sequins and headbands and jewelry—the last included a necklace of gold coins—that adorned her squat, generous figure on stage. But Rainey, like Smith, understood the expectations of her fans, who craved glamour as much as music. The performance spaces of the Delta, in contrast, could hardly have been humbler: a street corner or railway depot, a fish fry or open-air dance, a juke joint or even a jailhouse. But the classic blues inhabited statelier settings, cabarets or festive tent shows or downtown theaters. It lived—at least until the Great Depression arrived unceremoniously on the scene—at a higher pitch, in more fashionable surroundings, than its poor blues relations down on the farm.

But it would be wrong to view these trappings of success and refinement with suspicion, or question the "authenticity" of these big city blues. Ma

Rainey, born as Gertrude Pridgett on April 26, 1886, in Columbus, Georgia, had heard the country blues in her youth, and had been performing blues music for more than twenty years at the time of her recording debut. Often acknowledged as the mother of the blues, much like Handy is renowned as the patriarchal father figure, Rainey earned her reputation first throughout the South, the homeland of this music, long before she made her mark in the Northeast market. Although she was most at home on a vaudeville stage, with all its ersatz glamour, Rainey never let her music become as glittery as her attire. With a gravelly voice and narrow range, perhaps little more than an octave, Rainey knew that emotional fervor, and not vocal pyrotechnics, would be her calling card, and audiences were said to weep or laugh by turns in response to her performances.

A five-year stretch with the Paramount label produced close to one hundred sides, but Rainey's legacy may be best measured by the output of the next generation of blues singers, who learned from her example, and sometimes under her direct tutelage. Of these, Bessie Smith stands out first and foremost, and she too boasts a memorable nickname, "Empress of the Blues," a fitting appellation for a woman who for many listeners would come to define the sound of the classic blues. The story of Ma Rainey "kidnapping" the young Bessie Smith to bring her on the road is perhaps an exaggeration; but Rainey was no doubt a mentor and teacher, a surrogate mother of sorts, who helped Smith shape her own larger-than-life stage persona.

Smith was born in Chattanooga, Tennessee, probably on April 15, 1894, where she was raised in a dilapidated cabin frequently visited by illness and death. One sibling had already perished before she was born, and her father, preacher William Smith, passed away a short time later. Before her tenth birthday, her mother Laura and brother Bud had also died, leaving the eldest sister Viola in charge of a household of a half dozen youngsters. Smith learned the music of the streets long before she stood under the footlights, and her first performance took place on the corner of Thirteenth and Elm where she sang and danced, to the guitar accompaniment of her brother Andrew, in front of a local saloon. Smith worked the highways and byways of the South and eastern seaboard for a decade before her talents brought her to the attention of Columbia Records. The singer's 1923 recording of "Downhearted Blues," which sold 780,000 copies in its first six months of release, reveals the distinctive calling cards of Smith's art: her powerful voice, which required no amplification to fill a room, yet still retained an air of vulnerability; her broad vibrato and long, majestic phrases; above all, her deeply felt laments about "no-good men," moving performances that led the *Chicago Defender* to praise her as the "singer of blues that are really blue."

At a time when the record industry was just discovering the commercial potential of African-American music, Smith's success was a revelation, proof positive that black and blue could be transmuted into gold and greenbacks for the ambitious label executives, unwitting social engineers who proved mostly indifferent to distinctions of skin color provided the end result was a tidy profit. Before the end of the year, Columbia offered Smith a new contract which included an annual guarantee of $2,400—unprecedented at a time when an African-American musician might receive $10 or $15 for a recording. But soon, Smith would be making almost as much as this in a single week of performances, and by 1925 she had established herself as the most highly paid black performing artist of her day. She sang in the largest theaters—at least, the largest ones that would allow her on stage—or in capacious tents, much like a traveling circus or revival meeting. Sometimes Smith entertained under the footlights of a fashionable white theater, even in the South where she had developed a large following that crossed all color lines. Above all, she recorded prolifically, often in the company of the finest black musicians of her day—Louis Armstrong, Fletcher Henderson, James P. Johnson, and others—and during a period of roughly a decade, left behind over one hundred fifty performances that continue to define the classic blues style at it finest.

The story of Bessie Smith has little to do with the Mississippi Delta region—although it is important to our account as a sign of the growing popularity of blues music during the 1920s—until we reach its final chapter. Early in the morning on September 26, 1937, Smith and her driver Richard Morgan were in the heart of the Delta, on Highway 61, some seventy-five miles from Memphis, heading toward an engagement in Darling, Mississippi, when their automobile collided with a truck pulled over on the side of the road. Smith was severely injured, and she died in the ambulance while it headed toward Clarksdale's G. T. Thomas Hospital, the nearest medical facility open to black patients. She was forty-three years old at the time of her death.

This tragedy ended the life of the most celebrated blues singer of her day. But confusion over the circumstances of Smith's death initiated a controversy that would rage for more than a generation. A few weeks after the accident, talent scout John Hammond asserted in print that Smith had died because a white hospital in Memphis had denied her admission. The story was based on hearsay, and a few phone calls might have disproved the charges; yet the accusation continued to be repeated and accepted, told as a cautionary tale and a bitter critique of a society that held cheap the lives of even the most successful and honored of its black citizens. Chris Albertson's biography *Bessie*, first published in 1972, finally set the record straight, but as late as 1993 Alan Lomax was still offering up Hammond's flawed and inflammatory account in his book *The Land Where the Blues Began*. Still in print, and one of the most widely read works on the Delta blues, Lomax's moving and memorable survey was marred by more than a few factual errors, but none more unfortunate than this calumny. As we shall see repeatedly in the course of the pages that follow, the Delta has more than its fair share of real tragedies and abuses, and the impartial narrator has no need to invent more.

Bessie Smith left behind an impressive legacy, but her success in the mid-1920s did little to further the prospects of blues musicians back in the Delta. Indeed, during the entire quarter of a century that followed Charles Peabody's and W. C. Handy's separate encounters with the Delta blues, the musical riches available on almost any sizable plantation in Mississippi's rich cotton land were all but neglected by the world at large. A few books and articles were published that might alert a careful reader to the traditional blues of the Delta region, and the word-of-mouth accounts of travelers and those who had left the Delta must have spread widely, even into the offices of record company executives. But not until Tommy Johnson and Charley Patton made their first recordings toward the close of the 1920s would audiences have the chance to hear the best of the authentic Delta idiom on record.

And even these opportunities may not have arisen if a blind street musician from Wortham, Texas, had not shocked the music world into realizing that they could make money from the raw, unfiltered blues of rural America. Lemon Jefferson may have been blind from birth, on September 24, 1893, or perhaps he lost his sight as a youth. But his acute ears guided him unfailingly, both around his local community where he made his way through woods, over trails, or along complicated routes without assistance, and even more impressively among the strings and frets of his guitar, where

Jefferson displayed his extraordinary knack for performing blues, religious songs, and other folk material from an early age. According to most accounts, Sam Price, who worked as a salesman in a Dallas store, alerted Paramount Records about the talented Texas bluesman. Paramount invited Jefferson to Chicago to record, and his first blues releases were placed on the market in March 1926. Here was real country blues, unadorned and offered without apologies, Lemon's plaintive voice weaving and dancing in tandem with his free-flowing guitar lines, the music violating Tin Pan Alley conventions in pursuit of a more direct form of emotional expression. Just as Handy had learned in Clarksdale two decades before, Paramount executives discovered to their delight that the unvarnished, traditional blues could outsell its more sophisticated big city relations. Reliable measures are hard to come by, but Jefferson's more successful releases probably shipped in six-figure quantities. Paramount responded to this outpouring of interest in country blues with more recordings from Lemon, now the company's best-selling race artist, and began hunting for other, similar talent. But it was not alone: competing labels needed their own Blind Lemon Jefferson, and they too began looking to the Deep South, not just as a place to sell records (as they had always done), but also as a source of new recording artists. In many instances, the labels relied on the same retailers who had long been customers to act as informal talent scouts, counting on their familiarity with local markets that might be mystifying, or even dangerous, for New York or Chicago producers to explore on their own.

The success of Blind Lemon Jefferson's recording career spanned only four short years, before his death at age forty-six, probably from a heart attack, although other causes, from murder to a car accident, have also been suggested. The era of the rural blues singer seemed to be over, only a short while after it had begun. And if Jefferson's death had not signaled its end, the stock market Crash of 1929, eight weeks earlier, could easily have put it to rest on its own. But a few months before Jefferson's death, Paramount had discovered another recording artist, in the heart of the Mississippi Delta. Perhaps this new star couldn't reverse the economic decline; yet at a time when the whole nation seemed to have contracted a deep and protracted case of the blues, he soon made it clear that this old-style music still had a promising future ahead of it.

Charley Patton

chapter three

dockery's plantation

1. forty acres for a winchester rifle

The first sign were the letters—out-of-the-blue letters from complete strangers. Crazy, eccentric, some of them rambling on and on. They started showing up in the mailbox around the same time that the Freedom Riders arrived from up north, dicey days everywhere—things seemed on edge ever since Ike left office—but especially so in Mississippi, what with James Meredith riling up folks while trying to integrate Ole Miss and Medgar Evers getting shot.

But these letters came out of a time warp, from people who didn't seem to pay much attention to the news, good or bad, who were awfully worried about things that had happened a half century ago. No, these letters weren't from historians or elderly folks, or anybody like that who had earned a right to think about the old days. They were from record collectors and music fans, some of them pretty young, and most all of them living a damn long way from Dockery Farms.

Joe Dockery and his wife Keith had nothing against music, mind you. Their daughter Douglass possessed perfect pitch, and had studied music at school. She had even played piano for the Houston Ballet. And Joe and Keith, pillars of the community, liked to support public arts as best they could. But the music talked about in these letters was not the kind you wanted your daughter playing in recital halls . . . or even in the front parlor with the shades drawn down. It was the low-down blues, perhaps Mississippi's biggest export—and one that many in the early 1960s were glad to have sent away to the big cities up north. At first, Joe looked at the letters in incomprehension, but gradually it dawned on him that he was getting these letters *for a legitimate reason*. If he could believe what they told him, the blues had been born (or at least grew up to middlin' height) on his family's property.

Maybe those songs were okay down the way at Parchman prison, where Joe Dockery had served as a commissioner years back, and had even shown that researcher Lomax around—a visitor with peculiar ideas, who had been looking for just that sort of music. At least Lomax had the sense to know he'd find it in a hellhole like Parchman. But here on the family farm! Joe's daddy, Will Dockery (God bless his soul), would hardly have been pleased. Might as well have told him he was related to the town drunk. Old man Dockery looked askance at *all* music. He had even frowned on his son's interest in taking piano lessons. He would sometimes permit a black tenant on his plantation to play music in another town, if the occasion so warranted. But the farther away the better. Certainly no jukehouses had been allowed on the grounds of Dockery Farms. Let the other landowners allow those dens of iniquity on to their property. The late Will Dockery—who himself had abstained from smoking and drinking, and always dressed in an austere black suit—had aimed to uplift, not corrupt, his black workers, taking care of their needs, both earthly and eternal. Instead of jukehouses, he could boast of two churches (one Methodist, the other Baptist) and two elementary schools on his land, as well as a commissary, a sawmill, and a blacksmith's works. When he learned that town practitioners were overcharging his tenants, he hired a white physician to reside on the plantation and take care of all patients, whether black or white. He similarly established a non-profit burial society, and generously granted that anyone who had ever lived at Dockery's could also be laid to eternal rest in its cemetery. With good reason, a Mississippi newspaper had once lauded him as the Delta's greatest philanthropist. But, in his lifetime, no one ever praised old man Dockery as a patron of the musical arts. How odd that this is how posterity will best remember him!

The son eventually became reconciled to his family's role in the history of the Delta blues—but just barely. Joe Dockery would host, with patrician grace, researchers such as Robert Palmer, Gayle Wardlow, and Stephen Calt, answering their questions and putting his family property and tenants at their disposal. He showed Wardlow and Calt around the farm in his car, offering them a lecture on the plantation system, peppered with racial invective of the worst sort. "We got rid of our niggers—now they're your problem," was his most pithy characterization of his family farm's role in the social tumult of the times. Hosting his visitors to lunch afterwards at a restaurant in Cleveland, Dockery took exception to the "uppity" attitude of the black waiter, telling his guests in an undertone that he would have a talk with the local sheriff about him.

Passersby even today will see a sign that proclaims Dockery Farms to have been established by Will Dockery in 1895. But this description is far too genteel. Will Dockery didn't do any 'stablishin'. Rather, this Faulknerian character come-to-life wrested his land out of its wild existence, draining it, painstakingly preparing it for cultivation, sometimes clearing the cane— which might rise to a height of fifteen to twenty feet—with his own hands. Few thought land of this sort was worth much of anything. Dockery had seen one resident trade forty acres for a Winchester rifle. Another had given away a similar parcel for a cow. Owning soil in this swampy, overgrown hothouse was a burden, not a blessing. The land usually came to own you, and sometimes your family too, holding them captive for generations. But Dockery, a dour man of Scottish extraction, lived long enough to see his foresight and hard labors validated. At its peak, around four hundred tenant families lived at Dockery's. Some maps even showed the plantation as its own hamlet, and in point of fact it acted as a self-sufficient community, adopting quasi-governmental functions. Dockery's not only housed its own official post office but even printed its own currency, in the form of tokens and paper scrip, that were honored on the grounds and in nearby stores. Before he died, in 1936, Mr. Dockery had seen his estate's value rise to several hundred dollars an acre, making him that rarest of rarities: a Depression-era millionaire. Of course, by then, Dockery had moved to Memphis, where he enjoyed his landed property all the more when it remained at a considerable distance.

Yet for our purposes, the most important person here is not the virtuous and wealthy landowner residing in his city mansion, but a hard-drinking, loose-living, work-shirking field hand hanging out among the ramshackle cabins and broken-down boxcars that passed for living quarters on the northern end of the plantation. Charley Patton was nothing much to look at. He was frail in appearance, of small build, perhaps five foot seven inches if he pulled himself up to full stature. But he rarely did that: Patton walked with a limp, the result of a gunshot wound, which often caused him to move in a semi-hopping motion or by dragging his left foot behind him. A scar on the side of his forehead looked as if it had been cut with a knife or a bottle. If Patton opened his mouth, you were liable to notice the missing teeth.

Unless he were singing, that is. Then you forgot the man, and his limitations, and marveled at the voice, which seemed out of keeping with its owner's unprepossessing appearance. "Lord God, he could holler. He beat everybody hollerin'," recalled guitarist Johnnie Mack, who met Patton around 1930. Howlin' Wolf, who idolized Patton, boasted that his mentor had the voice of a lion. Booker Miller, another musician who associated with Patton, also gushed over the forceful baritone that cut through the noisiest surroundings: "He had a voice—he had a *voice*! You know what I heard a man tell him one time there in Ruleville, Mississippi? He told him, he said: 'You know, to listen at your records and then come to see you—I thought I'd see a man weighed 275 pounds! And you! You don't weigh 150!'" Patton politely pointed out that his interlocutor had overestimated—he only weighed 135 pounds. Sam Chatmon also testified to the power of Patton's vocal cords, but in less gracious words. "He just bring his voice out so *nasty*, he could hold it so long, it sound *nasty*." It is perhaps noteworthy that the only nickname Patton seemed to have attracted among his contemporaries was "Old Wide Mouth."

Maybe more than his singing prowess earned Patton the latter sobriquet. In speech, Patton pushed the envelope. He was proud and boastful, and often contentious. H. C. Speir, the talent scout responsible for Patton's first recordings, remembered him as "kinda forward" for a Southern black man of his day. Another associate claimed that an evening in Patton's presence could hardly transpire without the bluesman getting into a bad-tempered argument with someone. Whether black or white, no one escaped Patton's sharp tongue. Among his claims to fame, Patton ranks as the first African-American traditional musician to use his recordings to make unfavorable comments about specific white people from his own community—and if he dared to put this on record, he no doubt was willing to do the same, or worse, in more informal settings. Years later, when Son House was asked to recall some of Patton's witticisms, he refused, explaining that they were too offensive to repeat.

Casual acquaintances often surmised that Patton came from the North. His brashness and assertiveness seemed so out of character for a black man from Mississippi. Then again, Patton was light-skinned enough that he might pass for another race. Son House correctly assumed that Patton was partly Native American. Guitarist Hayes McMullen speculated that he must have been, at least, to some degree, of Mexican extraction. Ishmon Bracey suggested that Patton might have some white ancestry. A heavily retouched portrait of Patton, included as the frontispiece to Stephen Calt and Gayle Wardlow's biography of Patton, *King of the Delta Blues*, makes him look like a Mediterranean of Italian or Spanish extraction. Yet though these fine distinctions may be of interest to the contemporary biographer, in the Mississippi society in which Patton came of age, they amounted to little. For those he dealt with, day in and day out, Charley Patton was a black man, with all the heavy burdens and indignities that this entailed.

Patton was ostensibly the son of William Patton and Sara Garrett, probably born in April 1891 in the area between Bolton and Edwards, Mississippi, one of twelve children, seven of whom died in infancy. William Patton was well-to-do by Delta standards, eventually owning land, running a store, and managing his own sharecroppers. He was a big man, tipping the scales at some 350 pounds, who died shortly before his son began making recordings. He was of mixed Caucasian, African, and Native American ancestry, while Patton's mother also was partly of Indian extraction. The family unit was stable, and provided the youngsters with a strict upbringing with a heavy dose of religion.

Yet a plausible rumor has circulated that Patton's father was actually Henderson Chatmon, the patriarch of one of the most celebrated musical families in Mississippi and the grandson of a white planter and a black female slave. Henderson and his wife Eliza taught their children how to play a variety of string instruments, and several parlayed this early training into successful music careers. Various members of the Chatmon clan served as the core constituents in a number of well known ensembles, including the Mississippi Sheiks, the Mississippi Blacksnakes, and the Mississippi Mud Steppers. Bo Chatmon enjoyed a successful career as a solo artist, and recorded more than one hundred sides under the name Bo Carter. But Patton, if he were in fact a sibling, would stand out as the most famous of the Chatmon progeny. Henderson Chatmon had allegedly courted Patton's mother, and indeed a photo of his son Sam Chatmon bears a noticeable similarity to Patton's promotional photo used by his record company. Old man Chatmon, for his part, never acknowledged Patton as a son, and refused to respond to comments hinting at this connection. Perhaps he did not know for certain himself—his illegitimate children were said to be numbered in the dozens. And if Patton had any doubts as to his parentage, he kept them to himself. In the final analysis, whatever family or ethnic pride Patton possessed probably came less from any genealogical certainties, rather from his own tenacious sense of self-esteem and a quasi-instinctive assertiveness that may have rubbed some the wrong way, but contributed in no small part to his eventual success as a musician.

Historians of black music have often noted how the Creoles of New Orleans frequently resisted assimilation into black society, despite their partially African ancestry. Proud, quick to take offense, defensive of their prerogatives, often ambitious to rise in social status, they sought to distinguish themselves, as much as possible, from the black underclass of their day. Jelly Roll Morton stands out as the classic example—a man whose overweening pride and swagger contributed in no small part to his legendary status in the jazz world. "*All* my folks came directly from the shores of France," was Morton's own explanation of his "roots" to Alan Lomax. The Chatmons were cut from a similar cloth: when asked about juke joints and plantation frolics, they were likely to reply that they played mostly for white folk, since blacks could hardly afford *their* caliber of music.

Charley Patton—who often insisted that other plantation field workers call him "*Mister* Patton"—reminds us in some degree of these same attitudes. In his most famous song, "Pony Blues," Patton sings:

Brownskin woman is like somethin' fit to eat.
Oh, but a jet black woman, don't put your hand on me.

Today we may glibly see him as the quintessential representative of the black Delta underclass, as the conduit by which African performance styles were transformed in the Delta region, and became part of American popular culture. But Patton's actual relationship to his milieu and racial heritage is a much more complicated matter. David Evans even sees a calculated ambiguity in Patton's choice of the name China Lou for his daughter. She had no Chinese antecedents (although Chinese immigrants did reside in the Delta). Was this perhaps Patton's attempt to defy the inflexible racial stratification of Delta society? Could he be trying to find for her what he may well have desired for himself: a place outside the stark dichotomies of black and white?

Patton's assertiveness and flamboyance carried over to his performances, and among fellow musicians he was almost as well known for his guitar tricks and antics as for his blues playing. "Clowning" was Son House's dismissive description, and though other envious musicians might disdain such practices, they all took notice. Patton played the guitar behind his back, or between his legs, sometimes flipping it over, or snapping the strings, or tapping on it like a big drum. All the strutting and flaunting we associate with rock stars since Jimi Hendrix were already part of Patton's repertoire in the 1920s. He worked up the crowd with the shrewdness of a medicine show barker, taunting and teasing, and mouthing off an endless stream of lively banter. "That's the way he played," House explained with more than a little disdain: "he'd just say anything, the first thing he could think of . . . all that old kind of funny stuff." Modern listeners are often inclined to view the Delta blues as born in an atmosphere of high seriousness, dressed in black, amid tears and lamentations, but here we see a different aspect of this music, its informality and playfulness, its impatience with formalities and codes of decorum. Within the context of Delta society of that day, these antics were intoxicating for the sense of personal freedom they represented, rather than for the performance conventions they violated. Black music *took* liberties long before black people were *granted* them, and Patton was one of the first to grasp the opportunities as they came.

His assertiveness and fierce pride may have made Patton enemies. But they also proved valuable assets in securing him a rare chance to break free of the stultifying environment of Dockery's Plantation. Convinced of the superiority of his musical abilities, Patton decided to send a letter advertising his talents to H. C. Speir, proprietor of a music store in Jackson and part-time scout for nine different record labels, including Paramount, Victor, Gennett, and OKeh. Letter writing was not a simple matter for the bluesman. If Son House can be believed (which some have disputed), Patton could only spell one word: his first name; and even that he couldn't write down, but merely name the letters. Still, scribes could be found in any Delta community, capable of taking down dictation and drafting letters; and if Patton had trouble mastering pen and paper, he knew exactly what he wanted to communicate to the white storeowner in Jackson.

2. the broker and his talents

Henry Speir is a major protagonist in our story, but an unlikely advocate for black music in rural Mississippi. No altruistic ideals motivated his activities, yet he did more than any single individual to promote and preserve the music of the Delta region. He dressed like a banker, and thought much like one, too. For Speir, black music was a business, plain and simple. Even if he liked a singer's material, he refused to arrange for a record session unless he thought it would sell. And Speir's preeminent talent, in his own mind, was that he *knew* what the market wanted. At his Jackson store, he would sell between three hundred and six hundred records on a good Saturday, and almost 80 percent were by black musicians. And the percentage of black purchasers was even higher—he once boasted that they bought more records than white customers by a ratio of 50-to-1. Other white retailers in the South typically discouraged black clientele, but Speir appreciated the purchasing power of this underserved group of consumers. Once he sold several hundred copies of Blind Lemon Jefferson's "Black Snake Moan" in a single day. This marked a substantial payday: of the seventy-five cents Speir charged for a record, he kept thirty cents for himself.

Of course, Speir was not above cheap stunts to promote his wares: he even had a mechanical snake installed in his store, to try to further the record-buying frenzy. He never conducted fancy market research or even talked to his customers about their musical "tastes," whatever that might mean. Let others worry about making music according to a formula or, heaven forbid, for posterity; Speir got his feedback by watching the cash register. Even in his financial dealings with the record companies as a talent "broker" (the term he preferred, with its overtones of Wall Street), he focused on the here-and-now. While others—like Harry Charles, who scouted for labels in

Birmingham; or Ralph Peer, who discovered talent for Victor—would try to contract for royalties, Speir disdained such uncertain terms, demanding lump-sum payments for services rendered. And Speir was willing to work both sides of the talent business: in addition to collecting from the established labels, he would also make a test audition record for any musician who walked into his store and could pay five dollars per side. In fact, this was how Speir "discovered" the great Robert Johnson.

But the broker's practical mind-set made Speir attentive to details that a more altruistic man might have missed. He had fastidious ideas about the right tone for a guitar, the right setting for the microphone, the right shape of a room for recording, even how much shellac to put into a disk. He paid close attention to the instruments his musicians used for recordings, and if necessary provided them with something better. Whatever role he needed to play to ensure a successful record, he filled it with diligence and doggedness. If necessary, he would intercede with the local police to help a blues musician out of a difficult spot. He once put up a personal bond to get guitarist Tommy Johnson out of jail. "It was $150, and times was tight too!" he recalled years later. But even in these charitable moments, Speir remained a dollar-and-cents man at heart: when Johnson ran off, Speir tracked him down in Louisiana, and brought him back in handcuffs. If necessary, Speir would set up the session himself in Jackson or nearby. Most often, he worked with established labels that had their own set notions on how and where the music should be recorded. And Speir didn't let matters stop there. He would travel to these sessions, often at his own expense, to make sure things went smoothly. Didn't matter where: Atlanta, New Orleans, Dallas, Chicago, Memphis, even Grafton up in Wisconsin, the unlikely blues mecca where Paramount had its studio.

And wherever he traveled, Speir looked for talent . . . and usually found it. He never pursued laborious field trips, such as John and Alan Lomax made, driving around for months in a beat-up car looking for unknown performers of obscure songs. Speir didn't even care for the traditional folk tunes that got the Lomaxes excited—he always asked his performers to come up with new music of their own creation. And Speir rarely had the patience for a lengthy scouting trip; he typically combined his search for talent with more mundane activities. Yet the results testify to the wisdom of his methods. He found Ishmon Bracey singing for spare change on the street in Jackson. He encountered Isaiah Nettles at a train station in Rockport. He first heard

Blind Roosevelt Graves in a church. While in Louisville, Kentucky, purchasing rugs for his store, Speir scouted washboard players. During a single week in St. Louis, while visiting a major distributor, Speir discovered seven blues singers and a jug player. And, now and again, if a major trek were needed, he might consider it—*provided* it promised a big enough payoff at the end of the road. One time he traveled a hundred miles across the Mexican border in search of talent that might broaden the market and let him diversify (like any savvy broker) into a new field.

But his favorite source remained closer to home, in what he called the "Mississippi River Valley Area," stretching from St. Louis down to New Orleans and spreading out some seventy-five miles on either side of the river. He thought the local dialect and singing styles in this geography were the most suitable for successful records. In contrast, he was reluctant to record singers from Georgia and North Carolina for the same reason: their way of speaking and singing simply wouldn't go over with his customers. He was even less sure of himself with white singers—his biggest miss was the country music legend Jimmie Rodgers, who had actually walked into Speir's store to request an audition. After hearing his music, Speir sent him home, telling the future recording star to practice more and come back when he had some good songs.

We can perhaps find fault with Speir's cut-and-dried judgments, but the same posterity he disdained has validated the insights on the blues he gained, transaction by transaction, at his cash register. The list of artists he assisted reads like a who's who of the Delta blues, and includes Charley Patton, Robert Johnson, Son House, Skip James, Tommy Johnson, Willie Brown, and Ishmon Bracey. From the mid-1920s through the mid-1930s, his "ear" for talent defined the sound of a region, and created the musical legacy that remains the benchmark for traditional blues music even today.

Before Speir, the Delta tradition could hardly be said to exist on record. Freddie Spruell had recorded two songs for OKeh in late 1926—"Muddy Water Blues" and "Milk Cow Blues"—in a style that reflects the Delta idiom. Although Spruell hailed from Louisiana, he came from Lake Providence, right across the river from Mississippi, some fifty miles north of Vicksburg. Indeed, the artist was sometimes called "Mississippi" Freddie Spruell (or Papa Freddie Spruell), although he spent much of his adult life in Chicago, where he launched his record career. On "Milk Cow Blues," Spruell maintains a simple but insistent beat, crafting a primitive blues in the key of A.

As is often the case in these early blues, the countrified theme—Spruell is searching for his lost milk cow—is a flimsy cover for a more universal complaint.

Say my bed seem lonely, my pillow now it sure won't do.
Say my bed is lonely, my pillow, baby, it sure won't do.
I wake up for hours at midnight, I really have those milk cow blues.

Speir had no involvement in the Spruell session, but in the following decade almost every Delta blues artist of note relied upon his support in securing opportunities to record. Only seven months after "Milk Cow Blues," we encounter the debut session of William Harris, another stylist in a Delta tradition, who probably owed his big break to Speir. In fact, this may have been Speir's first involvement with a blues artist. As with so many events from this era, the facts are far from clear and open to dispute, and Harris continues to stand out as one of the more beguiling mystery figures of early blues.

When Gayle Wardlow played Harris's recordings to some of the older Mississippi musicians, they commented on the authenticity of the sound. "That's *pure* Delta there," judged Booker Miller. Moorhead resident and longtime blues listener Mandy Whigham's assessment was in the same vein: "His voice and his music all sound like the Delta to me—he *is* a Delta man." Both noted strong similarities between Harris's recordings and the performances of little known Delta guitarists that they had heard in their youth. In Harris's music, one hears echoes of the breakdowns and rags that figured so prominently on the plantations at the turn of the century. He must have played frequently for dancers; his fast songs carry a visceral drive, felt in the limbs rather than serving as mere fodder for the ears. His singing evokes comparisons with field hollers, but it is just as easy to imagine his penetrating vocals serving as an exhortation to dancers, cutting through the noise of a boisterous crowd.

Harris's "I'm Leavin' Town," recorded at his first session, in Birmingham, Alabama, in July 1927, offers us a tantalizing glimpse into the music that would have energized these informal entertainments. This song probably accompanied shimmy dancing, that African-American tradition as old as (or perhaps older than) the blues itself, but which became a nationwide craze only in 1922 after Gilda Gray brought it under the footlights in the

Ziegfeld Follies. In its most genteel form, the shimmy featured dancers shaking their shoulders; in less respectable settings, the undulations drifted southward. Harris likely inspired the latter sort with his songs. His music conveys a loose, uninhibited quality that no doubt responded to, and urged on, the licentious proceedings around him.

At times, however, the guitarist is unable to live up to his own ambitions. "Bullfrog Blues," another fast number for the shimmy, starts out at a metronome pace approaching 250 beats per minute, quite extraordinary for a Delta guitarist of this period. But after he begins singing, Harris can't maintain the tempo, and the beat awkwardly collapses into a more manageable 160 beats per minute. In general, Harris treats his guitar primarily as a rhythm instrument, and only makes the most tentative steps toward using the guitar lines as extensions of his vocals, a technique that would later become a trademark of the Delta sound.

In his liner notes to a 1991 release of Harris's recording, blues scholar Paul Oliver laments that "nothing is known about William Harris"—a sad starting point for future researchers. Some have even doubted Harris's Delta ties. The commonly given biography tells us that a William Harris, who perhaps is the musician on these recordings, was raised on a 4,000-acre plantation near Glendora, Mississippi, about twenty-five miles from Dockery's, which supported some three hundred sharecropping residents in the 1920s. Census documents and other public records offer little help: there are a number of individuals named William Harris who may have been the blues recording artist. Perhaps the most likely candidate is the nine-year-old Joe Willie Harris, son of Oscar Harris, whose name appears in the 1906 Educatable Children Census conducted in Tallahatchie County. This would imply that Harris was around thirty years old when he first recorded, a plausible assumption. But the youngster does not show up as a member of Oscar Harris's household in the 1910 census, perhaps suggesting some family tragedy or rupture, or an early start to a wandering life. Anecdotal accounts indicate that the musician William Harris traveled widely, entertaining with medicine shows and street corners, at jukehouses and house parties. Harris may have been discovered by Speir while playing at a church picnic—the talent scout's memory was far from perfect when recalling these early encounters, so we can only put halfhearted confidence in the details of this encounter. However, the church setting is a plausible one: the guitarist was reportedly a religious man, who avoided all strong drink.

Here, as in so many other instances when dealing with the early Delta blues, our history risks collapsing into a frail web of conjecture and anecdote. For my part, I prefer to remember Harris the way guitarist Hayes McMullen describes him at a house party on the Wildwood Plantation in the spring of 1927: the bluesman stood out as the center of attention, a dark and lanky figure smartly dressed in a suit and Stetson hat. In a jovial mood, full of jokes and raillery, Harris was playing the guitar and dancing with one of the women at the same time. Not long after this, he fades from our view, still a fairly young man and, one might well imagine, with many songs left to sing. Harris may have moved to New Orleans during the Depression, and died there. Or perhaps he journeyed to Chicago—a Willie Harris who recorded there in 1929 and 1930 is thought by some to be the same musician, but the vocal timbre and delivery on these later sides show enough differences to cast more than a reasonable doubt on this claim. In short, the trail here grows dark and the clues are scanty.

Years later, when he was tracked down by blues researcher Gayle Dean Wardlow, Speir had abandoned the music business to sell real estate, and William Harris was just a vague memory. Indeed, this pioneer in the preservation of the Delta blues had a hard time remembering many of the musicians he had helped, or the sessions he had attended. He had almost completely forgotten Robert Johnson, his most famous discovery, and could summon up only a dim recollection of the latter's audition. But he remembered the records that had sold the best at his store, and the guitarist who was responsible for many of them. "Ole Charley [Patton] was the best I ever seen," Speir told Wardlow. His guitar playing could not be matched, and from the moment Speir first heard Patton's voice, he knew that it was perfectly suited for recordings.

It had been an unusual audition, even by Speir's standards. Responding to Patton's letter, Speir had made the long journey to Dockery's plantation in the hopes of finding a blues singer suitable for recording. Success on this trip might result in a payday of several hundred dollars—but only if Patton were capable of performing at least four serviceable numbers in a recording studio. Nattily dressed in a blue suit, Speir must have shocked the foreman when he asked for one of the plantation's black residents. Few white men made such requests, and never for a good reason. The county sheriff or perhaps a state policeman would come by on occasion, but this always signaled some unfortunate event—a weekend party had gone out of control or an escapee from Parchman Farm (the nearby prison) might be hiding on the northern tip of the plantation. Even worse, however, were the labor agents—for a rival plantation or an industrial concern—who arrived with the aim of luring away residents with promises of better pay elsewhere.

Speir was familiar with these suspicions. Indeed, he had encountered many problems before in his "brokering" business. He had been run out of communities, been accused of serving as a labor agent, had even been harassed by police as a suspected drug dealer. At Dockery's this day, his calm and circumspect behavior assuaged the concerns of the overseers. But he now still needed to travel almost another fifteen miles to reach the far northern fringe of the plantation where Charley Patton resided. Speir passed shacks and various improvised shelters—barely habitable hovels most of them—each with its own subplot of land to cultivate. But Patton greeted his visitor with an air of self-importance that was oddly incongruous with this vista of poverty, toil, and oppression. He confidently announced to Speir that he was the equal of any other Delta bluesman. He was willing to prove it, but suggested that Speir provide some whiskey to initiate the proceedings. Speir had come without liquor (he did not make the same mistake again in his dealings with Patton), so the guitarist was forced to proceed with a "dry" audition.

Speir's standards, while clear-cut, were not especially exacting. He required a certain level of proficiency on the guitar, but had no expectations of dazzling virtuosity. Many of the blues guitarists only played in one or two keys. Some even struggled to tune their instrument properly. Singing styles could be gruff or sweet, no matter, and sometimes the words might be barely comprehensible. The records still sold well. Speir was less concerned with vocal range than with the range of a musician's material. He had seen many guitarists who made a positive first impression, but he soon discovered that they knew no more than one or two original songs. Many otherwise fine blues performers could play familiar tunes that had already been recorded, but few could put their own distinctive stamp on the music, crafting a blues sensibility that was distinctly their own. The plantations were full of musicians, but in Speir's experience, only a rare individual could put all the ingredients together: a reasonable level of skill on the instrument, expressive singing, and originality.

Patton delivered on all these expectations, and more. Above all, his songs captured a certain ineffable quality, a holistic union between guitar and voice, difficult to describe in words. His guitar lines seemed almost an extension of the words he sang. Sometimes his voice would fade out, and the guitar would complete the phrase, or comment back, almost as if Patton and his instrument were conducting an ethereal, melismatic dialogue. Speir had heard fine guitarists before, but Patton did something different. While other musicians, such as William Harris, battled and subdued the guitar, Patton seemed to coo and woo it. And just as his guitar notes emulated a voice, Patton's voice sometimes sounded like a seventh string. Most guitarists sing "above" the guitar notes, voicing chords in a lower register, and using them as a harmonic and rhythmic cushion for a melody in a higher range. Patton violated this convention; in fact, he almost seemed unaware of it. His voice moved in between the tones of his Stella: sliding, growling, declaiming. This was not singing a song; rather, it was *becoming* the song.

How much of this Speir heard or understood at the audition is debatable. But he comprehended enough to be excited by this talented performer hidden away on the outskirts of Dockery's farm. Before he left that day, the storeowner began planning his next steps. He hoped to make some sample recordings of his discovery, and use them to attract the interest of the race labels that, excited by the success of Blind Lemon Jefferson, were searching for more traditional blues talent.

3. the best of the twelve million

Thomas Edison *thought* he was inventing an office dictation machine.

In 1877, while working on a device to transcribe telegraphic messages through indentations on paper tape, Edison speculated that a similar instrument might be capable of preserving spoken words or messages. But Edison soon abandoned paper tape as the recording medium, instead envisioning a metal cylinder wrapped in foil as his "voice" in a tin can. A needle would etch the sound waves into the cylinder, preserving them for later playback. Once he completed the design, Edison handed a sketch to his mechanic John Kreusi, asking him to build a prototype. Kreusi was skeptical, betting his boss two dollars that the machine would never work.

But the mechanic set himself to the task, and within thirty hours returned with a small device. Edison immediately put the talking machine to the test.

Bending into the mouthpiece, he recited the nursery rhyme "Mary Had a Little Lamb." Turning the crank to start the playback, Edison was stunned and delighted to hear his own voice talking back at him.

The inventor quickly set up a public demonstration at the New York offices of *Scientific American*. On the scheduled date, he set up his little prototype on an office desk amid the gathered audience. The onlookers were amazed when the device inquired about their health, commented that it was doing well itself, asked the observers how they liked the machine, and bid them a cordial good evening.

No music was played on that fateful day. Indeed, Edison long misunderstood the ultimate impact of his breakthrough, which would transform the world of entertainment, while doing little to improve the efficiency of office tasks. When he established his recording company the following year, the inventor proudly named it the Edison *Speaking* Phonograph Company. A few months later, Edison suggested the potential uses of the invention in the pages of the *North American Review*. Although he included the reproduction of music on his list, it ranked behind letter writing, dictation, phonographic books, and the teaching of elocution. Eventually Edison gave pride of place to music in his ambitions for sound recordings—by 1899 the talking machine was being marketed as the Edison Concert Phonograph—but this was driven more by public demand and competitive pressures, rather than his own ambitions for the technology.

Although the blues may well be roughly same age as Edison's invention, the first recordings of blues music would not take place until more than three decades had passed. The first recording companies were reluctant to promote black music of any sort. The Victor label issued six sides by the Dinwiddie Colored Quartet, a male vocal group, as early as 1902, but this was a unique event, without precedent and, for many years, imitators. Mainstream America only gradually came to recognize the value of black music. At the time of Edison's invention, black secular music was most frequently presented to white audiences through the distorting mirror of the minstrel song, which both borrowed on the vitality of African-American performance styles while ridiculing and denigrating them. Black sacred music was the first authentic African-American music to gain respectability. Later ragtime managed to enter white households around the turn of the century, while jazz did the same after World War I, both "crossing over" into the mainstream of American culture long before blues music had been recorded.

Mamie Smith's recording of "Crazy Blues" on August 10, 1920, was a breakthrough event but, as we have seen, it did nothing to expose audiences to the traditional blues as played in the Delta region and elsewhere in the South. But not just the public's tastes were in flux, technologies were also changing. In 1925, when Mamie Smith entered Columbia's New York studios to make new recordings, she found that a microphone from Western Electric had replaced the primitive recording horns previously used. The sound quality of the new technology was noticeably superior to the acoustic recording equipment of the past. This breakthrough, combined with the expanding economy of the period, spurred a dramatic increase in the public's demand for recorded music. This in turn inspired record companies to explore niches and fringe styles of music that they had previously ignored. These combined circumstances contributed to a gratifying growth spurt in African-American music. From the mid-1920s onward, the depth and variety of relatively well recorded music allows us to gauge the evolution of black musical styles, assess performers, and pinpoint even subtle changes in techniques and tastes. In the world of the blues, we have left the Dark Age of myth and legend behind. We now know, with extraordinary exactitude, what was played and heard.

But another change in industry practices would prove to be even more important in our story: namely, the decision to bring the recording industry to the people, either through the efforts of talent scouts who sought out musicians in remote locations, or by means of portable recording devices which could be moved wherever performers might be found. "There are twelve million colored people in [the] US, and in that number there is hid a wonderful amount of musical ability," Harry Pace had announced as early as May 1921. Pace, an enterprising African-American businessman who had partnered with W. E. B. DuBois and W. C. Handy, was setting up his own recording company under the name Black Swan, to tap into this hidden reservoir of talent. "We propose to spare no expense in the search for and developing of the best singers and musicians among the twelve million." Unfortunately, Pace's ambitions far outran his abilities. He rarely ventured far beyond his New York environs in his search for talent, and his label declared bankruptcy in December 1923. But Pace's vision was the right one—the creative abilities of black Americans offered a potential gold mine to the record industry. Nonetheless, it would be left to others to realize Pace's dream.

Five companies dominated the market for race records in the late 1920s. Even a snapshot glimpse of their histories reveals the turbulent circumstances that marked the early days of the nation's music industry. Brunswick-Balke-Collender, founded in 1845 as a manufacturer of billiard and bowling equipment, entered the record industry in 1916 and acquired Vocalion in 1925. But the company was swallowed up in turn, selling out to Warner Bros. in 1930. The smaller Gennett label also resulted from ambitious diversification efforts: it was established in 1915 as a business unit of the Starr Piano Company of Richmond, Indiana. Like the managers at Brunswick, the executives running Starr presciently saw the rise of recorded music as both a threat to their base business and an opportunity to tap a new growth market. Paramount had a similar history, starting as part of the Wisconsin Chair Company, a furniture manufacturer which had begun selling phonographs in 1915 and entered the market for recordings three years later. In contrast, the Victor Talking Machine Company had started out as a technology company, and its executives could look with disdain at rivals whose expertise came from making bowling balls and rocking chairs. Since the turn of the century, Victor had seeded the market for recordings with its successful distribution of "Victrolas," and the company's work with Bell Laboratories in the mid-1920s resulted in the commercialization of electronic recordings and the revolutionary Orthophonic line of phonographs. But Victor also struggled to remain independent, and was merged into RCA in 1929. Finally, Columbia started as a distributor for Edison in the mid-Atlantic region, but began making its own records in 1901. Like Victor, Columbia understood the potential of electronic recordings and licensed a process from Western Electric in 1925. The company's position as a manufacturer and marketer of race records was incalculably strengthened by its acquisition of the OKeh label in October 1926—the smaller company had been unable to secure rights to the new recording technology and had been forced to capitulate. However, Columbia continued to operate OKeh separately for the remainder of the decade, although it took steps to prevent the two businesses from competing over the same artists.

Patents, mergers, takeovers, daring diversification moves, battles for market share, hardware companies moving into software: the story here is not altogether different from the overheated struggles between start-up ventures in the early days of personal computers and the Internet. But the most compelling part of the story lay encoded in between the grooves of the records themselves. Between them, these five companies—Brunswick, Gennett, Paramount, Victor, Columbia—were responsible for virtually all of the classic recordings of African-American musicians made during the period. Even a cursory list reveals the incalculable value of this legacy: the Louis Armstrong Hot Fives and Hot Sevens; sessions featuring Duke Ellington's Cotton Club band; the Charley Patton sides; the Blind Lemon Jefferson recordings; the music of Georgia Tom who, as Thomas A. Dorsey, would be lauded as the father of gospel music; Jelly Roll Morton's work with his Red Hot Peppers; the Apex Club band recordings with Earl Hines and Jimmy Noone; and so many others. Yet this golden age of black recorded music had little to do with enlightened views on racial equality, but was spurred rather by fierce competition and the intense economic and technological pressures outlined above.

These same factors no doubt motivated the labels' willingness to travel farther and farther in search of talent. Between 1927 and 1930, the major record companies launched no fewer than seventeen field trips to Atlanta in search of black recording artists. Eleven visits were paid to Memphis, eight to Dallas, seven to New Orleans. A group of pioneering talent scouts led this charge, and played decisive roles in shaping the practices of these labels—and through them the musical tastes of America. Ralph Peer, scouring the Southern states for talent for his employer Victor, changed the course of country music in August 1926 when he recorded the debut sides for both the Carter Family and Jimmie Rodgers at a makeshift studio in Bristol, Tennessee. Mayo Williams, who had helped build Paramount's successful blues line, took a position scouting for Vocalion in late 1927, and set about expanding that company's race record catalog. At almost the same time, Frank Walker, who had signed Bessie Smith earlier in the decade, brought Columbia's recording unit to Memphis and Dallas, where he recorded Blind Willie Johnson, Washington Phillips, Rube Lacy, and Lewis Black. Although New York and Chicago would continue to play the decisive roles in the commercialization of popular music in America, record companies could no longer afford to ignore the creative efforts of the rest of the nation.

While we can laud these early pioneers of field recording for their dis-
criminating judgments and savvy assessment of talent, the dross they
recorded far outweighed the memorable sides. Just as some professional
photographers take thousands of shots, clicking the shutter every few sec-
onds, in search of a few choice images, so did these talent scouts waste a
lot of shellac in their quest for the next hit act. Almost any musician with
enough persistence could get an audition with a major label, and many
found themselves in a recording studio with only the barest notion of what
to do once the session started. The range of styles and idioms recorded
during this period was extraordinary: jug bands, hillbilly groups, fire-and-
brimstone preachers, Cajun performers, Christian choirs, European polka
ensembles, vaudeville acts, Native American musicians, klezmer clarinetists,
mountain fiddlers; and the list goes on and on. Record companies seemed
to feel that their job was not to judge, but merely to record; let the marketplace decide what had commercial merit. From a sociological viewpoint,
this lax set of standards is a great blessing. A more stringent approach would
no doubt have limited recording opportunities to an elite group of artists,
and thus deprived us of this wonderful perspective of the musical melting
pot of the United States in the 1920s.

Oddly enough, the label with the least interest in setting up remote
recording sessions enjoyed the greatest success in recording traditional
blues. Paramount initiated no field trips during this period, yet maintained
an aggressive release schedule, which included over one hundred blues and
gospel recordings per year. Yet Paramount's very weakness may have been its
strength. Realizing that it lacked a local presence in the Southern cities, the
company was perhaps more willing to cultivate referrals from independent
parties such as Speir.

Speir had only one serious rival in the state, Ralph Lembo of Itta Bena,
another part-time talent scout who focused most of his energies on building his retail emporium. Lembo began his career inauspiciously, selling
dry goods from a wagon. He eventually opened a furniture store, entering
the music business as a profitable sideline. Lembo is best remembered for
arranging Delta bluesman Bukka White's debut session on Victor in 1930.
But he also had some notable "near misses": Lembo brought Blind Lemon
Jefferson to Mississippi, but failed in his attempt to set up a recording session with the legendary Texas bluesman. The trip turned into something of

a fiasco: few patrons were willing to pay the high prices charged to hear Jefferson play at Lembo's store and at a dance at the local high school. Lembo also made an unsuccessful bid to record Charley Patton—perhaps in tandem with Jefferson—but Patton balked at the opportunity, probably because of the storeowner's reputation for shady dealings. Lembo eventually gave up scouting for talent amid a maelstrom of accusations and recriminations. Musicians claimed Lembo failed to pay fairly, and Lembo had the same complaint about the record companies.

Speir had long been intrigued with the idea of making commercial recordings in Mississippi, and he eventually supervised a few sessions in Jackson and Hattiesburg in the 1930s. But it never proved practical to set up a permanent studio in the area. Speir's biggest opportunity—and what a windfall it would have been for blues fans!—was his failed attempt to purchase the foundering Paramount label in 1930 and move its Wisconsin recording studio to Jackson. Speir was short on capital: he had lost thirty thousand dollars in an oil-drilling venture the previous year, and his attempts to raise money through the local chamber of commerce met with indifference. This chance to establish a major label and full-scale recording facility in the middle of Mississippi during the glory days of the Delta blues must rank as one of the greatest missed opportunities in the history of American music.

Instead, musicians in the state needed to travel considerable distances to make commercial recordings. A letter from the OKeh label to Mississippi John Hurt, dated November 8, 1928, reflects this harsh reality: "If it is possible for you to make arrangements to get away from Avalon [Mississippi] for a week and come to New York for recordings, we will pay you $20.00 per accepted selection and all your expenses to New York and return for this work." Avalon to New York—a round trip of almost twenty-five hundred miles for the chance at making a record! Hurt agreed to the terms, successfully completed the session, then returned to his life as a common laborer in Avalon (where a blues researcher found him some thirty-five years later), but one wonders how many other musicians would have balked at the difficulties.

Hence, Charley Patton's "discovery" on the northern fringe of Dockery's plantation was just the first step in an arduous process of bringing his brand of Delta blues to the marketplace. Speir first needed to garner the interests of a record company, often through audition disks made on the simple recording machine he housed in his music store. Then a session needed to be arranged, a location determined, financial matters agreed upon, travel planned, a good guitar secured (if necessary)—a process taking weeks, perhaps months, before a commercial recording might be made. And then came the long wait until the records were released. *If* they were released: record companies had a habit of keeping music on the shelf for shorter or longer periods, and some of it never made its way into the marketplace.

Speir later recalled vaguely that Victor, the largest record company of the day, failed to be impressed by Patton's audition disks. But Paramount had great trust in Speir, and agreed to a session based on his recommendation. Arthur Laibly, a Paramount executive who had come out of the lumber industry—odd perhaps, until you remember that this record company had been started by a furniture manufacturer—sent Speir a train ticket for Patton's 750-mile trip from Jackson to Richmond, Indiana. Here a session was scheduled at the local facilities of Gennett Records for June 14, 1929.

4. hitch up my pony

Even seasoned blues musicians often found their first recording session intimidating. True, technology had improved tremendously in the five years preceding Patton's debut session: musicians now recorded using microphones rather than gathering around the primitive "horns," where they had once needed to exercise caution in avoiding loud sounds that might make the needle jump and mar the disk. But the newer microphone technology was still in its infancy, and even small changes in a musician's posture or position might ruin a take. Walter "Buddy Boy" Hawkins, who traveled with Patton from Jackson for the Richmond session, had wasted disk after disk at an earlier session, because he kept recoiling from the microphone while singing. Eventually Hawkins was forced to wear headphones which allowed him to hear instructions from the control booth: when he started to move, he was sharply reminded to stay still. This makeshift system worked, but Paramount still struggled to get four usable sides from an entire session. Mississippi John Hurt remembered years later the stringent requirements for his debut record date with OKeh. After the engineer had discovered the right position for the microphone, Hurt was admonished to make absolutely no head movements. His neck hurt for days afterward.

Other technology limitations hindered recordings in the late 1920s. Only a few minutes of music could fit on a 78rpm disk, and performers were alerted with a red warning light when time was running short. Sometimes novices froze when they saw the light and stopped playing immediately. In other instances, the performance finished in time, but a noticeable acceleration in tempo in the final chorus stood as lasting testimony to the jangled nerves of the musicians. Even under ideal circumstances, the sterility of the studio environment—with no dancers or an audience to inspire; only the hired personnel acutely watching the clock and dispassionately tending to details—tended to stifle the music's vitality.

Patton had other challenges to face at his debut session. Due to an extraordinary oversight, Gennett had established its recording studio close to railroad tracks. Sessions were often halted midstream because of the noise. Patton also decided to perform songs using three different guitar tunings on the session—either requiring multiple instruments or (more likely) a periodic break in the proceedings to retune. Finally, Patton needed to share studio time with Hawkins, who was making additional recordings for Paramount.

Given these constraints, we can only marvel at the fourteen sides Patton produced that day—something no traditional blues artist had ever done at a single session before. Yet the quality of the music is even more remarkable than the sheer amount of material recorded that day. Only a handful of events, such as Robert Johnson's San Antonio and Dallas sessions or Patton's later recording date with Son House, rival this momentous debut in importance to the history of the Delta blues. Paramount was put in the awkward position of having to release top-notch material on *both* sides of the 78 releases, violating the rule of thumb that good songs went on the A side, while second-tier material (sometimes of the most execrable quality) was relegated to the B side. Above all, the labels did not want to put two potential hits on a single disk. Nonetheless, "Pony Blues" from this session was paired up with "Banty Rooster Blues," "Shake It and Break It" served as the B side to "A Spoonful Blues," and "Tom Rushen Blues" adorned the flip side of "Pea Vine Blues." All of these would become blues classics, defining statements of the Delta idiom.

This abundance of riches posed other problems for Paramount executives. They must have worried about overwhelming their customers with too many Patton releases. As a result, the two-part "Prayer of Death" was issued under the name of "Elder J.J. Hadley," while "Screamin' and Hollerin' the Blues" and "Mississippi Bo Weavil" were released as the work of the "Masked Marvel." Paramount tried to generate publicity with a contest for fans to guess the real name of the latter performer—a charming gimmick, no doubt, but also testimony to the label's fear of saturating the market for this extraordinary new artist.

Decades after he died, Charley Patton's "Pony Blues" was still remembered vividly by those who had heard him perform. Interviewers seeking information on the bluesman invariably found this song mentioned in response to their questions about Patton; many even spontaneously repeated words from it. Later blues musicians and fans have largely shared this admiration. Patton's performance has been studied and emulated by several generations of guitarists, a number of whom have gone on to record their own versions of the piece. And with good reason! The sheer sweep and power of Patton's enduring classic is striking, and his originality and confident sense of self-expression were never on better display.

"Pony Blues" includes many of the elements that are most endearing—and maddening—about the country blues. The piece sounds deceptively simple, but many highly trained musicians would struggle to imitate Patton's rendition. Even the introduction, a lopsided five-beat bar, signals that this performer pays little heed to the nice symmetries of Western music, with its clear division into neat patterns, almost always with a steady and predictable number of beats to the bar and bars to the overall structure. And as if a five-beat intro were not quirky enough, Patton puts an odd hesitation into the opening beat—an idiosyncrasy that we hear elsewhere in his recordings. This violates another unwritten rule of Western music, which dictates that every piece begin immediately at the right tempo, usually counted off silently before the performance starts: typically a *sotto voce* "one-two-three-four" that sets the song in motion. Many traditional blues recordings sound as if no tempo has been counted off: the musicians simply "find" the beat collectively during the opening few bars. Patton records as a solo guitarist here, so he has no need of coordinating with other musicians. Yet here, as elsewhere, he tosses out a single odd beat, out of tempo, before settling into a steady groove. It almost sounds as if he uses this note to ground himself before heading out of the starting gate.

Of course, the eccentricities of this piece have hardly been exhausted with the introduction. Three separate melodies make up the "Pony Blues." The first is a sweet folksy tune that clearly establishes a major tonality for the piece.

Hitch up my pony, saddle up my black mare.
Hitch up my pony, saddle up my black mare.
I'm gonna find a rider, baby, in the world somewhere.

This section has been described as following a fourteen-bar structure. But the melody gravitates toward the standard twelve-bar blues with three sections of four bars each. The difference here is that Patton includes an extra bar (or half-bar) between the sections. These "pauses," endemic to traditional blues performances, also give trained musicians fits. But they do not interrupt the flow of the music: in Patton's hands, the pauses sound natural and essential to the piece, almost like a hesitation in a street basketball move, one that doesn't slow down the ball handler, merely makes for an easier (and more graceful) move to the hoop. But the second melody in "Pony Blues" is even trickier. Patton begins with a beautiful drooping phrase starting on a high tonic note: "Hello central, 'sa matter with your line?" In a typical blues, this phrase would take four bars and would then be repeated, or given Patton's "pauses" might last four and a half or even five bars. But Patton does something more peculiar here (even by the loose standards of country blues): he cuts off after only three bars, and drops his voice low for a repeat with a different melody (lasting five bars now!), a whispering growl that sharply accentuates the minor third. Jazz and blues musicians often stretch out phrases—even when playing in strict tempo, they like to convey the impression of phrasing behind the beat—but cutting a line short like this is quite rare. This surprising twist is all the more effective since the insistent flat third disrupts the folksy major mode feeling that has so far guided the piece. The third melody amplifies this technique, with the guitar pushing an acerbic, syncopated phrase that repeatedly echoes the minor third of the vocal. The closing lyrics are as provocative as the guitar lines. "I don't want to marry, just want to be your man."

Paramount liked these sexual innuendoes—they made for good business. Although modern-day fans of the early blues tend to focus on the appeal of its "authenticity" and "time-honored traditions," many of the record buyers who purchased these releases in the 1920s and the 1930s were no doubt attracted mainly by the "dirty parts." Patton's repertoire was chockful of bawdy songs, and much of it must have given even the Paramount executives pause. Son House later recalled Patton entertaining at Saturday night dances with verse after verse of lewd material, in songs he never recorded. Nonetheless, Patton obliged the prurient interests of his record label and its customers with an ample dose of suggestive tidbits. On the flip side of "Pony Blues," Patton's "Banty Rooster Blues" announces in the opening stanza: "I'm gonna buy me a banty, put him in my back door." The song refers to the belief, well known to Patton's listeners, that a rooster would crow at the sound of a stranger, thus alerting the singer that his woman's other lover might be approaching. This song probably served as backing for a slow drag, a contact dance of low repute that was popular in the Delta during the 1930s—"just dry screwin,'" in the words of one musician. Nor was intercourse the only illicit activity referred to in these early Patton sides. His "A Spoonful Blues" hinted at another taboo subject, cocaine addiction. He begins his performance with the spoken introduction: "I'm about to go to jail about this spoonful." "Tom Rushen Blues," named for Sheriff Tom Rushing, further reinforced Patton's persona as a man familiar with illegal activities of various sorts—an image he would reinforce with later songs such as "Revenue Man Blues" and "High Sheriff Blues."

The success of these recordings marked an important turning point in the history of the Delta blues. Today most music fans view the Delta the way wine connoisseurs see Bordeaux or the Napa Valley, waxing enthusiastically about some special quality in the land itself—viticulturists even give it a name, *terroir*, referring to the particularity of the soil and local ecological conditions—that produces the special flavor of the vintage. Blues fans are no different, seeing their favorite music as linked in some metaphysical way to what Alan Lomax has charmingly called "the land where the blues began." This music, so it seems, is grounded in the soil, a cash crop waiting to be harvested and sold. It is no exaggeration to say that the legend of the Delta *terroir* began with these extraordinary Patton sides. Hard as it may be to believe, the Delta region had not previously been seen by the music industry as an especially important center of blues activity. Blind Lemon Jefferson had hailed from south of Dallas, near Wortham; W. C. Handy came from Florence, Alabama; Ma Rainey was raised in Columbus, Georgia, and after her performing career, she retired and died there; Bessie Smith was born in Chattanooga, Tennessee, and enjoyed her greatest successes after moving to the Northeast (although she would die in the Delta, while on a tour). Yet today the Delta holds pride of place in histories of blues music, not only for the sheer number of outstanding players who came from the region, but due even more to the extraordinary intensity and emotional power of this music. Many contributed—and still contribute—to this mystical construct we call the Delta blues, but this inspired burst of creativity in the Gennett studio on June 14, 1929, was the decisive turning point, the moment when the Delta flexed its muscles and asserted its preeminent position in the blues world.

Almost fifteen years later, another Delta resident, Muddy Waters, would parlay a chance recording opportunity into a celebrated international career. Patton would never enjoy such acclaim—he spent almost his entire life within the confines of the Delta—but he did manage to better his life considerably by his new status as a recording artist. By today's standards, the $75 flat fee per side that Patton was likely paid for his recordings is an unpardonable crime, especially when we compare it to the millions of dollars of royalties earned by, say, the Robert Johnson estate. Yet to his neighbors on Dockery's plantation, the thousand dollars Patton brought home from a single day in Richmond would have seemed a stunning sum, an amount which they could hardly put aside after decades of sharecropping. Patton further enhanced his local fame, and probably increased his income, by selling copies of his recordings at Dockery's. He also had a card printed up with his photo on it, and space to write down the details of local performances, to serve as a handbill and flyer. Paramount was no doubt exaggerating when it first advertised Patton as "one of the best known singers and guitar players in the South," but within the more insular world of the Delta, he was now a celebrity of sorts, enjoying prerogatives—women, money, a certain degree of freedom—that few other African-Americans of his time and place could claim.

Patton's new liberties, however, are the biographer's lament. His movements become increasingly difficult to track during the months following his session in Richmond. Around this time, he was asked to leave Dockery's, after a dalliance with another man's wife. The summer of 1929 finds him in Merigold in Bolivar County, where he is said to have had affairs with at least three local women before moving on. Other accounts tell of him residing at the Anderson Plantation near Cleveland, at the Dakin Plantation near Skene, or at the Jeffries Plantation, across the Mississippi River from Helena. Other informants describe him playing on a sidewalk in Ruleville or at a dance near Doddsville, or residing in Pace, or even performing with a minstrel outfit in Memphis and elsewhere.

Perhaps he did all of these things, or maybe his rising status merely inspired gossip and speculation out of proportion to the true details of his comings and goings. In any event, H. C. Speir had some trouble finding his star performer—which he needed to do, since Paramount was soon clamoring for a follow-up recording session. When finally tracked down, at Jeffries, Patton was ready to make more records, and even suggested an accompanist, the string player Henry "Son" Sims, a childhood friend of modest talent, but with a knack for being in the right place at the right time. Sims made these memorable sides with Patton and never saw the guitarist again, returning instead to the quiet life of a plantation worker. But this obscure existence was interrupted, more than a decade later, by another brush with fame when Sims was "discovered" by Alan Lomax as part of the Fisk University and Library of Congress research into the music of Coahoma County. Again brought in front of a recording machine, the fiddler was featured on Lomax's classic Delta recordings of Muddy Waters.

The sides with Sims may not be Patton's best, but they do provide important insights into his playing. Early country blues artists are often accused of being unable to play "accurate" time. And as we have seen, Patton took great liberties with bar lines and metrics, adding and subtracting beats, and sometimes changing the length of his choruses during the course of a single song. Yet when he recorded with Sims, Patton knew how to rein in these ingrained habits, and adopt more symmetrical phrasing—thus allowing his accompanist to follow along more easily with the song. "Elder Greene Blues" and "Going to Move to Alabama" are obvious examples. They offer a very danceable beat, and reflect the more traditional approaches that predate the blues. But "Devil Sent the Rain Blues" is even more interesting: here Patton shows that he could play a straight twelve-bar blues, with even, symmetrical phrasing. Blind Lemon Jefferson had proven the same thing in his collaboration with pianist George Perkins: the free-flowing rhythms of Jefferson's eccentric solo guitar work were held in check, as he navigates through a conventional blues form.

Patton and Jefferson both understood, either consciously or instinctively, that they had to tighten up their rhythms if they didn't want to lose their accompanist. But here is something to ponder: when these two artists play "correctly," their music is less intense and compelling than when they break the rules. In this matter, we encounter one of the most salient (and over-looked) truths about the traditional blues: the supposed inadequacies of its most famous exponents were not limitations to be lamented, but rather inseparable from their brilliance. As such, they were no different than the avant-garde artists dazzling audiences in other genres in the 1920s—Joyce, Picasso, Eliot, and the like. Like these iconoclasts, the country blues players found that violating conventions and breaking rules enhanced the expressiveness of their work. The Delta blues players' lack of self-awareness as "experimental" artists, and the general (and mostly correct) perception of their work as traditional, clouds this fact, but does not change matters: they reached levels of artistry that a more conventional approach would never have achieved.

"High Water Everywhere," recorded and released in two parts, stands out as the highlight of Patton's second Paramount session. Patton again draws on contemporary topics, and perhaps autobiographical elements, in this account of the great Mississippi flood of 1927:

> *Looky here, the water dug out, Lordy something broke, rolled most*
> *everywhere.*
> *The water at Greenville and Leland, Lord, it done rose everywhere.*
> *I would go down to Rosedale, but they tell me there's water there.*

The Paramount execs clearly understood the commercial potential of this performance. They rushed the 78 to market, advertising it as Patton's "best piece," and boasting further that "you know that means it has to be mighty good because he has made some knockouts." For once the ad copy hype is justified. On part one, Patton casually juggles a foot-stomping ground tempo with a faster guitar-slapping counter-rhythm that spurs on his powerful six-string groove. Not until John Lee Hooker, another Delta player, arrived on the scene in the late 1940s would a solo guitarist be capable of creating such relentless *funkiness* on record, without the benefit of bass or drums. Yet Patton's vocals are as riveting as his playing. He stretches himself here, singing higher and harder than on any of the sides with Sims.

The roughness of Patton's voice has long been admired by blues fans, and the growl of his baritone has been held up as the sign of blues authenticity in the face of the sugary pop music of his day. The word "crooner" had recently entered the American vocabulary, descriptive of such mellifluous vocalists as Bing Crosby, Rudy Vallee, and Russ Columbo—all of whom began recording around the same time as Patton. But Patton is the anti-crooner here, keeping his listeners on edge with a bark that has more than a little bite in it. On the first part of "High Water Everywhere," he goes further: his voice is suffused with anger. Here Patton plays the role of the man in the maelstrom shouting out his blind defiance at the unyielding elements.

If ever America required songs of this sort, it was at this historical moment. Although the precise date of this session is not known, "High Water Everywhere" appears to have been recorded within a few weeks of the Crash of 1929. Yet if America needed blues music at the onset of the Great Depression, it could hardly afford it any more. Sales of recordings fell 40 percent in 1930 alone. Labels faltered, were shuttered or sold. Established musicians learned that their recording contracts would not be renewed, and younger artists found it impossible to secure a studio session. Patton's label Paramount faced an additional unexpected challenge when its biggest selling race artist, Blind Lemon Jefferson, died in December 1929.

The label's willingness to embark on one more Patton session in 1930 may well have been motivated by Paramount's pressing need to find a talent to replace Jefferson on its roster. It continued to advertise Patton's music in the *Chicago Defender* in early 1930, touting him as a "famous artist" who was "out of this world" and "too good to miss." But the execs hardly believed their own words. This May 1930 session in Grafton would be Patton's last recording date until 1934, when he would make one final studio appearance before his imminent death. Paramount itself was struggling for survival now. Just a few weeks before this session, in April 1930, Arthur Laibly had offered to sell the entire business to H. C. Speir for twenty-five thousand dollars. Now Laibly traveled personally to Lula, Mississippi, where Patton was residing, to engage him for a session, and enlist the guitarist's help in finding other artists to record.

In an odd twist of fate, Patton would not be the star of this event. Only four sides would be released under his name from the date—a surprising change given Patton's prolific output at his previous sessions. Instead, one of Patton's recent traveling companions and a sometime musical colleague would take center stage for several dramatic two-part performances. Blues fans rejoiced when a lost side from this session was recently discovered, in 2005—the disk had been zealously sought by collectors for decades, and it had been called the "Holy Grail" of the Delta blues. But, once again, this celebrated recording (of "Clarksdale Moan") did not feature Patton. Rather, these sides announced the recording debut of a failed preacher, convicted killer, and hard-drinking vagabond named Son House, recently released from the prison farm at Parchman.

Son House

chapter four

parchman prison

1. this old world is about to end

Son House was a man of sharp contradictions, of polar opposites that somehow co-existed in a single personality. Even at first meeting, these incongruous qualities made themselves felt. A forceful performer, who projected his powerful voice to the back rows, House was soft-spoken almost to an extreme whenever the music stopped. Listeners would need to lean in closely to pick up the almost whispered words. In such settings, even the most important declarations were murmured, mumbled, tossed off like unimportant asides. His head turning left and right, avoiding the direct gaze of any interlocutor, House spoke, it seemed, as if to himself, rehearsing a private speech for his personal edification.

A surviving film clip shows the bluesman, in this shambling manner, telling an awestruck audience that they must choose between the Devil and God, because the two *just don't get along*. But here we encounter another of

House's contradictions—because for him these two influences co-existed on intimate terms. He was, at one point, a preacher who denounced the blues. At another, he was a blues singer who ridiculed men of the cloth, as in the famous lyric to his "Preachin' the Blues":

> *Oh, I'm gonna get me a religion*
> *I'm gonna join the Baptist Church.*
> *Oh, I'm gonna get me a religion*
> *I'm gonna join the Baptist Church:*
> *I'm gonna be a Baptist preacher*
> *And I sure won't have to work.*

Yet for the most part, House brought both the spiritual and secular influences together. This very song, "Preachin' the Blues," recorded at the May 28, 1930, session in Grafton, must have scandalized many listeners by its evocation of blues singing as a homiletic activity.

This intermixing of the sacred and profane contributes, in no small part, to the hypnotic appeal of House's music. The listener senses that powerful forces are at work here, perhaps even at battle. House sings like a man possessed on "Preachin' the Blues," and the anguish of his performance is palpable. This recording transcends blues singing in any conventional sense, and reminds us rather of the Old Testament image of Jacob wrestling all night "till the breaking of day" with the angel of Jehovah. It's hard to fathom what expectations Paramount had of its new discovery, who broached a level of intensity unusual for popular singers of any style. At the time, recordings of sanctified preachers sold well in the same communities that purchased blues 78s, and the ministers often bellowed and shouted with more energy than the secular singers. Perhaps the label executives hoped that the combination of these diametrically opposed forces—the fervor of the converted and the salaciousness of the sinner—offered an opportunity for what record companies today quaintly call "crossover appeal." If so, they were sadly mistaken. Blues fans prize these Son House 78s highly, but a fair portion of their mystique comes from their exceptional rarity—which itself testifies to how poorly they sold. House will play an important role in our story, but his impact on Delta blues in the prewar years was felt primarily through his personal influence on other players rather than through the popularity of his recordings.

The call of religion came first in House's life. "I was more churchified," was how House put it, describing his youthful ardor. "Then that's mostly all I could see into." His world revolved around church, Sunday School, prayer and revival meetings. A half century later, he described in broken phrases, and with obvious fervor, a moment of conversion he had experienced in an alfalfa field during his twenties. "I was there in that alfalfa field and I got down, pray, on my knees in that alfalfa. Dew was falling. And man, I prayed and I prayed and I prayed . . . I hollered out. Found out then. I said: 'Yes, it is something to be got, too, 'cause I got it now!' Sure did." House was so moved by the experience, he immediately went to tell his cousin Robert what had happened. Then he walked two miles, and woke up his boss, a white man named T. F. Keaton. " 'Get up out of that bed and hear what I got to say.' He thought I was crazy!"

During House's childhood, music was just as pervasive as religion. Eddie "Son" House, Jr., was born on March 21, 1902, about two miles from Clarksdale, Mississippi. The nickname "Son" was used to distinguish him from his father, Eddie House, Sr., who played guitar and occasionally worked in a band with his brothers. An earlier birthdate of 1886 has sometimes been given—apparently by House himself. If the earlier date were true, as Dick Waterman has suggested may be the case, House would have been over one hundred years old at his death in 1988—but perhaps even harder to believe, he would not have begun playing guitar until he was in his forties! Phil Spiro recounted to me the mystery of the two conflicting birth certificates House possessed when rediscovered by blues fans in the 1960s, and Spiro's explanation of the discrepancy seems simple and elegant: namely, that the earlier document had been House's father's. Certainly House may have found the earlier date convenient at times, perhaps especially so when America entered World War I. When the draft was initiated on June 27, 1918, only men between the ages of twenty-one and thirty-one were initially conscripted. A birth certificate showing Eddie House's date of birth in 1886 would have exempted him—just barely—from military service at this time. It is worth noting that the Social Security Death Index supports the later date, March 21, 1902—even though House would have qualified for more Social Security benefits with an earlier arrival at retirement age.

House claimed that nine of his uncles played instruments, and that when they performed together they constituted a "whole outfit," including horns—an exceptional band by Delta standards where string players, either

solo or in small combos, were the norm. But though the youngster found
the guitar alluring, and felt an urge to emulate his father, he also had grave
reservations about embracing the musician's life. Just putting his hands on
a guitar, he thought, might be a sin. House's religious leanings made him
especially suspicious of the blues. "It always made me mad to see a man with
a guitar and singing these blues and things."

But House came to have another conversion experience, this time in
response to a bottleneck guitar. While in Mattson, a community near Clarksdale, one Saturday in 1927, House noticed a large group of people crowded
around two guitarists. He had heard many musicians over the years, but
this time something different struck him in the music, a vocal quality in the
strings, and a depth of expressiveness that he had not experienced before.

> Well, I stopped, because the people were all crowded around. This boy,
> Willie Wilson, had a thing on his finger like a small medicine bottle,
> and he was zinging it, you know. I said "Jesus, I like that!" And from
> there, I got the idea and said, "I believe I want to play one of them
> things."

Years later, when he was master of this same technique, House would
describe it in the simplest terms: "I could make [the guitar] say what I say."

House purchased an "old piece of a guitar" for a dollar and a half. The
back was broken and it only had five strings. Willie Wilson helped him
repair the back with tape and add a sixth string. But House still needed a
suitable bottle, which proved more difficult—he cut his fingers a couple of
times before he had his fixed like Wilson's. But from that point on, House
made fast progress, perhaps not toward any degree of virtuosity (which he
would never achieve), but rather in crafting an intense, personal style that
was suitable for public performance, and for supporting his extraordinary
voice, the most penetrating and haunting the Delta has ever produced. "It
commenced coming natural and natural to me," was House's own assessment of his early progress. A few weeks later, he showed Wilson how he
had copied one of his tunes, and was surprised when the more experienced
guitarist invited House to join him at a performance that Saturday night.
"I said, 'I ain't good enough for that.' He said, 'Oh, yes, you is. You just play
that. I'll back you up.'"

Other influences combined with Wilson's. House heard Rube Lacy around this time at Roy Flower's plantation in Mattson, and was very much taken with his bottleneck playing. House later related to Alan Lomax that he had also learned from an old Clarksdale guitarist named Lemon, so-called because he could play Blind Lemon Jefferson's music with reasonable accuracy. Lomax saw this as an important piece of evidence, viewing it as a partial explanation for the strong stylistic affinity between Jefferson and Delta players. Yet the popularity of Lemon's recordings in the Delta is well documented—H. C. Speir recalled selling several hundred in a single day at his Jackson store, and Jefferson even came to Mississippi to perform— thus the Texas bluesman required no intermediaries such as the Clarksdale Lemon in order to make his influence felt. The other musical role model for Son House from this period, James McCoy, never used the bottleneck, but he taught the aspiring guitarist two songs, "My Black Mama" and "Preachin' the Blues," both of which would serve as vehicles for tour de force record- ings by House.

House's reputation as a blues artist is beyond reproach, but even here the contradictions loom large. From one perspective, you could make a convincing case that Son House represents the single most important fig- ure linking together the various strands of the Delta tradition. He col- laborated with Charley Patton, mentored Robert Johnson, inspired Muddy Waters, guided Alan Lomax in his research during the 1940s, and helped spur the blues revival in the 1960s. "I thought Son House was the greatest guitarist in the world," Waters would later recall; and House returned the favor, pointing Lomax in the direction of the younger guitarist, and thus helping to arrange the "discovery" of one of the towering figures in the history of the blues. And by all accounts, House had the same hypnotizing effect on the young Robert Johnson, who would hang around the locales where House played, and on breaks would pick up the older musician's guitar, trying to imitate the sounds he had just heard.

Yet, for all this, Son House was merely a part-time performer, who could put aside the guitar for months or years with few regrets. Tractor operator, railroad porter, barbecue chef, cotton picker, cattle rancher, steelworker— over the years Son House always labored with his hands, but only rarely with them on a guitar. At one point, he put his music career on hold for over fifteen years. Here we encounter the great irony of House's artistry: he may have transformed the blues by his personal intervention, yet he was the most passive of individuals, letting events come to him, rather than seeking

out ways to make his name and exert his influence. His historical importance, albeit well deserved, seems almost a matter of happenstance—or (if
you prefer a more dramatic flourish) destiny.

As we have seen, House didn't begin playing guitar until his twenties, long
after most musicians of note have already become seasoned professionals.
More than a decade passed between his Paramount sides and his Library of
Congress recordings. Even at that stage, House showed a surprising indifference to his music. House told Lomax that he "about done quit" as a musician. "I'm gettin' to be an old man. . . . Got something else on my mind
now but the blues." Yet House was not yet forty years old, and the music he
recorded for Lomax demonstrated extraordinary vitality. But this was true
to form for House, whose records *always* happened because someone else
interceded—Charley Patton, Alan Lomax, Dick Waterman—and never on
his own initiative. Lomax, for his part, would describe the session in raptur-
ous prose: "Of all my times with the blues, this was the best one, better than
Leadbelly, better than Josh White, Son Terry and all the rest of them." Letters
on file at the Library of Congress show the repeated efforts Lomax made to
convince House to move to New York in the early 1940s—with promises of
engagements and possible fame. Perhaps House might have become as celebrated as Leadbelly while still in the prime of his career, but we will never
know because House failed to pursue these looming opportunities, chances
that almost any other musician would have immediately seized.

If one merely saw a notated transcription of House's guitar work, it
would be easy to dismiss as very simple stuff indeed, rudimentary chords
and figures. But hearing it is a far different matter. Even as an old man, he
attacked the strings with great intensity, almost like those flamboyant fla-
menco masters whose rapid hand flourishes serve as a crucial visual ingre-
dient of the performance. The music is not so much played as torn out
of the instrument, and House's slide technique adds a wailing, throbbing
quality, almost as if the guitar is begging for respite. His is one of the most
evocative and distinctive guitar sounds of modern times.

Yet House's vocal work is so powerful that he could have made his mark
on American music even without the benefit of a guitar. After House's rediscovery, Stephen Calt suggested, first to Dick Waterman and later to record
label owner Nick Perls, the idea of teaming the bluesman with Alan Wilson
(of Canned Heat fame) in a recording that would free House from the guitar and allow him to focus solely on his singing. Later, when House could

no longer play guitar, Perls decided to pursue a project of this sort, but by then Wilson was dead and House, he discovered, could no longer manage even the singing. But the idea was a powerful one, and the potential of Son House fronting a band of sympathetic musicians—whether coming from the worlds of rock, blues, jazz, or folk, no matter; all these approaches might have worked—fires the imagination. In the hypothetical American museum of recordings that might have been, where historians are free to speculate about lost Buddy Bolden cylinders and the missing "phonautograph" of Lincoln's voice, this one earns a place in the permanent collection.

House's impassioned singing was seemingly built for high dramatic effect. Some vocalists are praised for "telling a story" with their voices, but House is reading the riot act. Singing of the drought, in "Dry Spell Blues, part 2," he evokes a landscape less like the Delta, more like the imagery of the Book of Revelation:

> *It have been so dry, you can make a powderhouse out of the world.*
> *Well it has been so dry, you can make a powderhouse out of the world.*
> *Then all the moneymen, like a rattlesnake in his coil . . .*

> *It's a dry old spell, everywhere I been.*
> *It's a dry old spell, everywhere I been.*
> *I believe to my soul, this old world is about to end.*

Then again, the words themselves are almost irrelevant: whether talking of an old love, the weather, a milk cow, House always has the fire of an Old Testament patriarch warning of impending doom. In this instance, he draws on contemporary events for inspiration. The "dry old spell" refers to the drought of 1929, as cataclysmic in its own way as the great flood of 1927, affecting some parts of the country for up to a decade. When Stephen Calt asked House about "all the moneymen, like a rattlesnake in his coil," the singer replied that they were the rich men—"which, by implication, meant planters," Calt specifies, while "to be 'like a rattlesnake in his coil' meant to be a cheapskate (this from House)." The allusion, Calt adds, "had it been understood or circulated, would have enmeshed House in huge trouble." House explained that he eventually stopped singing this piece because audiences were disturbed by its lyrics.

Yet the Delta blues made its mark on American imagination through moments such as these—through a spirit that defied the commercial sensibility, the slickness that was coming to dominate the entertainment industry, reaching instead for a degree of personal expression both more intimate and psychologically turbulent, yet also more resonant of larger themes. Son House's work epitomized this aspect of the Delta idiom, and it was his burning ardor, more than any specific guitar technique or compositional acumen, that must have impressed the imaginations of Robert Johnson, Muddy Waters, and the others who were drawn to his music.

But all of this was almost lost to us. Shortly after he began performing professionally as a guitarist, and before he had made a single record, House was caught up in a violent incident at a Saturday night frolic in Lyon, Mississippi. As House later described it to Alan Wilson, one of the patrons became crazed and began shooting a gun. Son was wounded, and ended up shooting the man fatally. Despite his protestations that he was acting in self-defense, House was sentenced to fifteen years for manslaughter at the notorious Parchman prison farm.

Those trying to substantiate this story quickly run into problems. The only prisoner with the surname of House during this period, according to state records, was indeed an Ed House. But this inmate, who spent less than two years at Parchman, from September 16, 1930, until April 28, 1932, was incarcerated for bootlegging, not murder or manslaughter. The chronology here is also puzzling: if this convict is in fact the celebrated guitarist, it would imply that House made his recording about prison life, "Mississippi County Farm Blues," *before* serving time at Parchman—an odd, although not impossible, assumption. On the other hand, the charge of a lesser crime would make it much easier to understand how House secured his release after such a short time of imprisonment.

Yet a different version of the story emerges in the recently rediscovered recording of House's 1930 performance of "Mississippi County Farm Blues." On this 78 disk, the rarest of all blues recordings—it finally came to light in 2005 after decades of searching by blues collectors—House sings that he was imprisoned for murdering a woman.

> *They put me in jail, wouldn't let me be.*
> *They put me in jail, wouldn't let me be.*
> *Put me in jail, would not let me be.*
> *They said I killed Vera Lee.*

Stephen Calt relates his surprise when a similar lyric to the song resurfaced in a private tape made of House by Nick Perls shortly after the bluesman's rediscovery in 1964. In a hushed tone, almost as if he were speaking to himself, House sang about being arrested for the murder of Vera Lee. Calt recalls discussing this perplexing lyric with Alan Wilson, who had accepted (and published an account of) House's tamer version of the reasons for his arrest and incarceration. Wilson was taken aback, and simply said: "I have no explanation for it." Calt continues: "[House] told me he shot a man to death at a party in Long Island around 1953, but went free when a grand jury accepted his self-defense representations. . . . I would guess that this episode was probably the one House described to Wilson, and that his circa 1927 victim was one Vera Lee." The rediscovery of the 1930 recording, with the same reference to Vera Lee dated thirty-four years earlier—indeed, made only a short while after House's release from Parchman—raises troubling and unanswered questions about the circumstances that led to House's imprisonment.

2. six months ain't no sentence

Prisons are *not* supposed to play a role in the history of music. But in the topsy-turvy subculture of the Delta blues, everything is the opposite of what one expects. Here we find few names in bright lights. Indeed, there are no music careers by any reasonable definition of the term. And, hard as it may be to believe, fans would come to see failure as a token of success in this crazy, looking-glass world. Even today blues aficionados and researchers tend to prefer the musicians with the most troubled biographies, and prize the records that were the rarest, that sold in the fewest quantities, while scorning the blues artists who reached a larger audience. Let the fans of other musical genres seek out the lifestyles of the rich and famous; devotees of the Delta tradition, much like the Statue of Liberty, prefer instead to embrace the tired, the poor, and the wretched. No Juilliard graduate has yet made it to the Blues Hall of Fame—and none is likely to arrive anytime soon—but convicts and vagrants, drinkers and two-timers, are welcomed with open arms.

The early legends of the Delta blues tended to oblige their future admirers, although mostly by necessity not choice. They steered clear of the limelight, working as farmhands and manual laborers more than as guitarists and singers. Charley Patton's death certificate lists his occupation as "farmer." Willie Brown's death certificate describes him as a "tenant farmer." Robert Johnson's death certificate states: "He staid [sic] in the house with some of the negroes saying he wanted to pick cotton." Blues experts will talk glibly of Patton "performing" in Ruleville, Mississippi, or Johnson "performing" in Birdsong, Arkansas—but go to these places and see for yourself. The most recent census tabulates a population of forty souls for Birdsong, so imagine what type of exalted music "career" it supported back in the Great Depression. To be frank, we find none of the usual trappings of the musical performer's life in our inquiry into the early Delta blues. No careers, only a few odd dollars to be made from playing the guitar—maybe two or three dollars for a night at a juke joint, plus a few free drinks—certainly enough to live better than a sharecropper, but still modestly by the standards of modern entertainers. No concert halls, no music conservatories grace the landscape; instead, to the extent the music had a home, we find it on plantations and in prisons.

Parchman was both. Sprawling over twenty thousand acres of rich Delta farmland, Parchman put its convict population to work in a manner disturbingly reminiscent of antebellum slaveholders. Here repression was married to hypocrisy: for Parchman artfully doffed the *appearance* of compassion. No walls, no chain-link fences held its inmates in place. The front "gate" provided a merely symbolic restraint: free-standing, it stood unconnected to any other barrier. Visitors saw no cell blocks or stockades, only cheaply constructed wooden barracks. The prison superintendent lived in a picture-book Southern mansion, replete with spindles, gables, and a wraparound porch, the "master" in fact if not in official title. No guard towers marred the flat Delta landscape; much of the guarding was, in fact, entrusted to prisoners themselves—reliable, older convicts known as "trusties," many serving long sentences for murder and well equipped to intimidate and dominate the newer arrivals. Their role was precisely akin to the "slave drivers" of the old plantations: anxious to do "the master's bidding" in order to maintain their precarious privileges, they yet remained themselves in bondage to the system, serving as both victims and victimizers.

The trusties were often given the job of punishing infractions with "Black Annie"—Parchman's preferred tool for reforming the fallen angels in its care. But the superintendent could boast of no innovation here. This heavy leather strap, four inches in width, a quarter inch in thickness, and three feet in length, was merely another carryover from the days of slavery. More to the point, Parchman displayed a slower, steadier form of brutality in its very economic structure, a form of discipline perhaps less picturesque than "Black Annie" but even more savage in its long-term effects. For Parchman officials, prisoners were moneymakers rather than mere criminals, and profit maximization was the rule of the day. During its first half century, Parchman could boast that its convicts were the second greatest source of income for the state of Mississippi; only tax receipt generated more dollars. Indeed, Parchman invited emulation as the most cost-effective penal institution in all of twentieth century America—finally, one area of business acumen in which the Mississippi Delta led the rest of the nation!

Yet the prisoners also served as walking testimony to the hidden costs inherent in the system. "Everywhere we heard of men working till they dropped dead or burnt out with sunstroke," Alan Lomax wrote in recollection of his song-collecting visits to Parchman. " 'Knocking a Joe,' or self-mutilation, was one way out. The sight of a one-legged or one-armed man who had chopped off his own foot or hand with an ax or a hoe was a common one." The daily ordeal began at 4:30 a.m., when a steam whistle roused the convicts from their bunks. Marched at gunpoint and in close formation down to the fields, the prisoners began their arduous toil, which would continue until sunset. Convicts often worked in tremendous heat, their efforts measured against a daily quota. "I met one old-timer, respectfully nicknamed 'the River-Ruler' because he'd been leader of the number-one farm in the penitentiary for twenty years," Lomax related. "The River-Ruler's feet had turned into bags of pulpy bones from the long years of pounding the earth of the penitentiary fields. In the words of the song, he had run and walked 'till his feet got rollin', just like a wheel.'" Lunch was eaten in the fields, sometimes even moving to a shady spot was not possible, and the food was often laced with bugs and worms. Fights among prisoners were common, and rather than discourage them, the driver would sometimes take two combatants and let them slug it out, until one dropped.

But here music thrived, not as recreation or entertainment, rather as a tool for survival. When John and Alan Lomax embarked on their 16,000-mile road trip in 1933, aiming to discover and record the neglected folk music of the South, they soon learned that their most productive visits were to penitentiaries. They visited eleven in total, presenting their program to some twenty-five thousand African-American convicts. Chants, work songs, hollers, spirituals, blues, ballads: the musical creativity expended in these hellholes was both depressing and awe-inspiring. Yet Parchman, in the heart of the Delta, stood out amongst them all. True, the Lomaxes had found individual singers of great merit in other prisons: "Iron Head," an aging black prisoner at Central State Farm in Texas knew such a wealth of songs that Lomax lamented it would take "a volume of 500 pages" to transcribe the songs of this "black Homer"; Huddie Ledbetter, soon to be known to blues fans by his nickname "Leadbelly," dazzled his visitors at Angola State Farm in Louisiana, a setting in which very little music flourished given strict prison rules against singing while convicts worked. But here at Parchman, the sheer abundance of music was overwhelming. John Lomax lamented in a letter that it would require many months of field recordings to do justice to the music of the Parchman convicts. He was far too optimistic: in fact, it took more than a quarter of a century. John and Alan came back again and again, each time failing to exhaust the musical riches of this Delta prison farm.

We know about Mattie May Thomas solely from the recordings she made for Herbert Halpert during his two days of field recordings at Parchman in 1939. Singing unaccompanied in the women's sewing room, Thomas offered neither traditional songs nor artful compositions, but rather presented her interlocutor with a sung personal testimony that veers from the acrid to the heartbreaking with such vehemence that the listener is left reeling.

> *You keep on talkin' 'bout the dangerous blues.*
> *If I had me a pistol, I'd be dangerous too.*
> *Yeah, you may be a bully, then but I don't know.*
> *But I fix you so you won't give me no more trouble in the world I know . . .*
> *My kneebone hurt me and my ankles swell.*
> *Yes, I may get better, but I won't get well.*
> *There, Mattie had a baby and he got blue eyes.*
> *They must be the captain, he keep a hanging around.*
> *That must be the captain, keep a hangin' around.*
> *Keep on hangin' around . . .*
>
> *Six months ain't no sentence. Baby, nine years ain't no time.*
> *I got a buddy in the big house done from fourteen to twenty-nine . . .*

Ah, the jailhouse was my beginning and the penitentiary's near my end
And the electric chair is too big for me here.
I'm going' to tell you, baby, like the dago told the jew,
"If you don't like-ee me, there's things I don't like in you."

Even by the standards of blues lyrics—which have always shocked much of the public with their frankness and disdain for social niceties—these were unsettling words. But Thomas was clearly not one to adapt to the expectations of the society she lived in: at the time she sang this for Halpert, she was serving her third prison sentence. As far as we can tell, Thomas never recorded again.

Most of the musical careers glimpsed in the Parchman recordings are such as these. Extraordinary singers make their appearance on a few recordings, then disappear into obscurity. Only a small portion of this music has found its way onto commercial releases, documenting a few of the songs that permeated this doleful landmark of the Mississippi Delta. The Lomaxes heard women convicts singing with pathos at their machines in the sewing room; they recorded the rich call-and-response work songs of the gangs engaged in field work; they listened to reverent voices blending together in spirituals at an Easter morning religious service, singing out, "I'm troubled, Lord, I'm troubled; troubled about my soul." And the stories were often as moving as the songs. Almost always the prisoners recounted personal travails, injustices, and the eternal hope of pardon and freedom—which the influential white visitors, so it was believed, might be able to effect.

Yet even John Lomax, almost immune to surprise after years of song collecting in the strangest locales, must have been taken aback at his visit to Parchman in late May 1939. Here Lomax asked the prison authorities to help him identify convicts who might be worth recording during this follow-up visit to the prison. They proudly produced Vocalion recording artist Booker "Bukka" White, then under contract to Chicago record producer Lester Melrose, but in servitude to the state of Mississippi. Unlike almost every other convict Lomax had met, White showed little interest in making recordings for the esteemed visitor from the Library of Congress. White was accustomed to being paid—and paid well—for his music. He liked to boast about his earnings from his first Victor session in 1930; the figures he mentioned ranged from $240 to $400, and he didn't forget to mention the new guitar he was given for the date. Right before entering

Parchman, White had recorded "Shake 'Em on Down," a big seller that had been quickly imitated by a host of other blues players. A few months later Big Bill Broonzy had an even bigger hit covering the song, and before you knew it, half the blues artists in Chicago had a knock-off version . . . "Ride 'Em on Down" or "Break 'Em on Down" or "Truck 'Em on Down." Now White was expected to record for free? Feeling his vulnerable position as an inmate, White acquiesced, but limited his performances for the Library of Congress to two numbers, the old blues standard "Po' Boy" and a bitter song inspired by his second wife, Susie, entitled, "Sic 'Em Dogs On."

White was probably twenty-nine years old when he met the elder Lomax, who was more than twice his age—but it is hard to say which of the two had lived a more complete, wide-ranging life at the time. White had seen the world too, and in almost as grand a fashion. He had fought successfully as a prizefighter in Chicago, played semi-professional baseball for two seasons with the Birmingham Black Cats, worked as a roustabout and musician with the Silas Green traveling show, sold moonshine, played guitar at frolics and parties, and soaked up the Delta blues firsthand while living at his uncle's farm in Grenada—"as good a land as a bird ever flew over." But White's main role model was guitarist Charley Patton. Years later he would describe Patton as a "great man" and recall the excitement caused in Clarksdale by the release of a new Patton recording: White had to squeeze into the crowded room where an audience had formed around the phonograph.

As it turned out, White's travels put even the bohemian Patton's to shame. By the time he settled down for a spell at Camp Ten in Parchman Farm, White had gone "hoboing" (as he called it) to St. Louis, Baltimore, Cincinnati, Cleveland, even as far north as Buffalo.

> It was hoboing, sleeping on this railroad track—off from it, you know. . . . Wherever I seen a pear tree or an apple tree I could get to, I would go and fill my pocket up and get back on the freight train and start to playing that old guitar. That would get the other hoboes in a good mood, and pretty soon we'd make up some kind of meal together. Man' I'm telling you, I couldn't see no other way but to keep going.

If the hazy memory of his later years can be believed, White started traveling on his own when he was only nine years old. In truth, the inmate who faced down John Lomax at Parchman in May of 1939, reluctant to give away his music for free, was an accomplished and confident man of the world.

White had seen more than his share of personal tragedy, too, even before his incarceration. Married at sixteen, he was widowed before he was twenty. Years later he would recall his agony watching his young wife, Jessie Bea, die of a burst appendix in a Houston, Mississippi, hospital. And his music and travels had brought him face-to-face with the poorest strata of society during the toughest years of the Great Depression. White had picked cotton in the Delta and seen the poverty and dependency of the workers who supported the region's agricultural economy. His restless travels were no doubt driven, at least in part, by his desire to escape the confines of this harsh life.

Yet we shouldn't fall into the convenient trap of viewing White, and the other musicians who found their way into Parchman, as mere victims of an oppressive system. No doubt gross miscarriages of justice could and did take place. But many of the inmates were tough, sometimes ruthless characters, and the victims were often those unfortunates who crossed their paths at the wrong time. Stephen Calt recalls White boasting that he traveled the freight trains with a fake special agent badge, which he used to extort money or possessions from some of the other hoboes riding the rails—a claim that gives new meaning to his familiar refrain "Shake 'Em On Down." When asked about the shooting that led to his incarceration, White offered none of the expected excuses or denials. His response: "I just shot him where I wanted to shoot him."

Ralph Lembo, the sometime music scout and full-time storeowner in Itta Bena, arranged for White's recording debut with the Victor label in 1930. Only four sides were released from this 1930 Memphis session—another ten were apparently recorded but not issued—and the surviving performances make us lament the music we never got to hear. On "The New Frisco Train" and "The Panama Limited," White crafts the perfect "hoboing" guitar sound, emulating the rhythm and momentum of a freight train through his six strings. This must have been the music that White brought with him on the road during these years of constant rambling. One senses the same carefree spirit in his vocals, which move effortlessly from singing to breathless storytelling, or engage in banter with his partner Napoleon Hairston. At the same session, White patched together some impromptu religious numbers, filling in for the preacher who was supposed to record that same day, but had given in to the temptation to drink strong spirits the night before. "Miss Minnie" (probably Lizzie Douglas, better known as Memphis Minnie) was brought in to add some churchified responsorial singing on the sides.

These recordings did little for White's career. He remained in Memphis for a period after this session, trying to <u>earn a living as a musician</u>. In addition to his singing and guitar work, he also played some piano and could fill in on harmonica. But the economic rebound that had been expected since the stock market collapse the previous October never materialized, and the music industry suffered a worse decline than other sectors. White gave up on Memphis and returned to Mississippi, although he would try again four years later. In 1934 he came back, this time with his father, and attempted to interest the OKeh label in recording the two of them as a duet team. Once again, White made little headway and the pair had to return to Mississippi before they exhausted their meager savings. White would not record again until the 1937 session that produced "Shake 'Em On Down," and even this classic performance almost never took place. White had already been arrested for the shooting that would send him to Parchman, when he traveled to Chicago. According to Samuel Charters and Paul Oliver, White jumped bail in order to make this recording—although scholar David Evans suspects that producer Lester Melrose may have received permission from the authorities to conduct the session.

The success of "Shake 'Em On Down" earned White the status of a celebrity within Parchman. The inmates and guards pooled their money to buy him a guitar, and he was exempted from much of the heavy labor that oppressed his fellow convicts. White gave guitar lessons to the camp captain's son, and was asked to entertain on special occasions. When White performed for the governor of Mississippi, on the latter's visit to Parchman, he was surprised to learn that the politician already knew about him—apparently from Melrose's efforts to secure a pardon for his moneymaking musician. And one can easily imagine the pride of the Parchman officials when they were able to present Lomax with a professional recording artist during his 1939 visit. But even if White escaped the most degrading aspects of Parchman life, the experience fundamentally altered him. We can hear the change in his songs: the rollicking, carefree ethos of "The Panama Limited," of "Shake 'Em On Down," is replaced by a darker, more introspective mood in his later recordings. A sense of pathos enters his music for the first time, and White's songs are no longer light entertainments for frolics and parties, but take on a more overtly artistic dimension.

White's reluctance to record more material for the Library of Congress might have proven to be a disastrous mistake. He had now reached a new pinnacle in his music, one he would never surpass in the remaining decades of his career. What a loss to the blues if this music had never been documented! But White was determined to make commercial recordings again, not just archival disks for the Library of Congress. His release from Parchman later in 1939 finally gave him the opportunity to do so, which he quickly seized. After a brief reunion with his family in Chickasaw County, White hopped a freight train heading toward Chicago, where he hoped to enlist Lester Melrose's support in reigniting his music career.

Only two and a half years had passed since White had recorded "Shake 'Em On Down," but they had not been good years for acoustic blues. The Chicago scene had embraced more modern sounds; swing music was everywhere; the revitalization promised by the Chess brothers and a good electric pick-up were still just a dream for the future; and older blues players, hoping to hold on to their audience, relied on a popular mixture of dance tunes, hokum, and suggestive double entendre. Muddy Waters would later recall the resistance he encountered in Chicago, during the early 1940s, to the "sad, old-time blues." Club owners would "shake their head and say, 'Sorry, can't use you.'"

Perhaps White was aware of this: he first came to Melrose with material that emulated other successful blues recordings on the market. But the producer, either from inspiration or sheer irascibility, dismissed this music out of hand, and sent White to a nearby hotel, asking him to spend a couple days coming up with something fresh and original. The producer's admonition must have tapped some preexisting vein of musical creativity that White had nurtured while at Parchman. How else to explain the extraordinary material that White had on hand when he returned to Melrose two days later? The producer was astounded by the turnabout. White recalled the scene vividly years later: "I never had a man, black or white, kiss me dead on the mouth before; but that's what he done. He say, 'Lord man, you done 100 percent. I've been on this job thirty-five years and I never seen a man do what you done in two days.' He said, 'Just how the hell did you get it? Where did it come from?'"

Melrose quickly arranged for two recording sessions, held on March 7 and 8, 1940, at a little studio on Chicago's South Side. No concessions were made to modern tastes and trends in its planning and execution: White played a Gibson guitar borrowed from Big Bill Broonzy, and was accompanied solely by a washboard player, most likely Washboard Sam. Yet far from evoking an archaic old-timey aspect, White's 1940 Vocalion work captures a forward-looking spirit that might easily have inspired a whole new direction in blues composition, had its lessons been sufficiently appreciated. In truth, this music comes as close to art song as traditional blues has ever dared to go, but without losing any of the essential qualities of the Delta heritage. This was Delta blues at its best: a personal statement of deep emotional intensity but with larger, inescapable social overtones, rarely expressed so clearly or so well; and infused with a pulsating, grooving rhythm, an irresistible momentum that sweeps up the listener in its wake.

The "woke up this morning" clichés of traditional blues have no place in these songs. Instead, White attacks the justice system in his "District Attorney Blues," and does the same for the penal institution that housed him in "Parchman Farm Blues." His "High Fever Blues" and "When Can I Change My Clothes?" draw on other Parchman experiences in their bitter narratives, as does "Fixin' to Die Blues," inspired by a fellow prisoner and guitarist who went into a coma before expiring. Here the music throbs with a restless energy, completely at odds with the somber picture painted in White's bitter lyrics.

> *Look over yonder, on the burying ground.*
> *Yon stand ten thousand standin' to see them let me down . . .*
>
> *Mother, take my children back, before they let me down.*
> *And don't leave them standin' and cryin' on the graveyard ground.*

It's not clear what audience Melrose had in mind when he agreed to record these songs. Certainly they did little to assist White in his dreams of launching a successful performing career. With the exception of a brief notice in the *Amsterdam News* in July 1940—which dismissed them in a single sentence, not even calling them blues but rather folk music—the songs were virtually ignored in the black press, and their subject matter made them distinctly unsuitable for crossover appeal to white record buyers. White, for his part, would see his music career languish for most of the next quarter of a century. When his cousin B.B. King visited him in Memphis in the early 1950s, White helped as best he could in establishing his young relative in the local music scene. But the elder guitarist was getting by now working days in a tank factory, and living in a boardinghouse on Orleans Street. He played occasionally at Saturday night parties, or spent Sunday afternoons visiting and making music with another mostly forgotten old-timer, Frank Stokes. White even tried to adapt his guitar style to record with an R&B band. But nobody seemed to notice or care, and as King's career accelerated, White's continued to falter.

But the 1940 Vocalion sides attracted a subterranean following, in ways that White himself could hardly know about or, if he had known, believe. Bob Dylan would record White's "Fixin' to Die" on his debut album, at a time when it was unclear whether White himself was alive or dead. Another young guitarist, John Fahey—like Dylan born within a few months of the Vocalion sessions—would be so moved by this music that he and fellow Berkeley student ED Denson would try to find the bluesman, setting in motion White's return to recording and performing in the 1960s. Samuel Charters, who helped launch the blues revival with his writings from the late 1950s and 1960s, praised these recordings lavishly, both before and after White's reemergence, and devoted almost an entire chapter to them in his book *The Bluesmen*. Other writers—Peter Guralnick, Mark Humphrey, Simon Napier—would take up this theme, enshrining the 1940 Vocalion session as classics of the Delta tradition. In Humphrey's forceful words: "There is the weight of myth on these recordings."

3. can't tell my future, can't tell my past

Son House's post-Parchman career would parallel White's to an uncanny degree. Both would reemerge as celebrated figures in the 1960s, after years of hard manual labor—both of them unaware of the cult status their songs had acquired with a new generation of blues aficionados. But this important moment is still ahead of us in our story. Shortly after Parchman, House too had the opportunity to participate in a single commercial recording project, but only one. Yet like White's Vocalion sides, House's visit to the recording studio would rank as one of the defining milestones in the history of the Delta blues. The music industry paid little attention to it, of course, and no more offers came House's way at the time. But here too the recordings would eventually find their private audience, whose devotion made up for the indifference of the mass market. By then, however, House too would have disappeared—at least from the perspective of these fans, for whom these recordings seemed to have been made by phantoms, not flesh-and-blood men, who had briefly passed through, left a few songs for posterity, then went on to a silence and separation even more complete than any found on Parchman Farm.

According to most accounts, Son House was released from Parchman

sometime in late 1929 or early 1930. House claimed that this was largely
due to the intercession of his father—although it is likely that his family
had secured a letter from a boss or other prominent white man, otherwise
it is hard to imagine that the appeal of a solicitous parent would have much
impact on the authorities. In any event, the convict was brought to Clarksdale, where a magistrate set him free, but warned him never to set foot in
that town again. House promised that, if let go, he would cover as much territory as a red fox. True to his word, immediately upon his release he walked
the twelve miles to Jonestown, and from there got a ride to Lula, a flagstop
Delta hamlet of less than five hundred souls.

House pursued what few opportunities for musicmaking Lula allowed.
Playing at the train station, he parlayed this into a job performing at a local
café. Charley Patton, then living a few miles outside of Lula, in a shack on
a plantation, had heard House at the depot, and soon enlisted the fellow
guitarist in his projects and schemes. When Arthur Laibly came to Lula
toward the middle of 1930 to set up another recording session with Patton,
he asked the guitarist to secure additional talent for the Grafton trip. Patton
decided to bring two guitarists with him to Wisconsin—Son House and
Willie Brown—along with pianist and singer Louise Johnson, and a gospel
a cappella group known as the Delta Big Four.

Patton only recorded four songs on this visit to Grafton—a dramatic
drop-off in output considering the productivity of his previous sessions,
but understandable given the assemblage of talent and Paramount's exist-
ing backlog of unreleased Patton sides. The pairing of Patton and Brown,
however, was inspired, especially on "Moon Going Down," where the latter's
chording provides a cushion for Patton's syncopations and fills. Patton's
remaining contributions to the session came in the form of the suggestive
banter that he, along with House and Brown, provide during Louise Johnson's piano performances.

Johnson's role in the Grafton trip is remembered less for her music than
for the tawdry soap opera drama that was taking place behind the scenes.
This turn of events is unfortunate: the Delta has produced few first-rate
blues pianists—at least few that were ever documented on records—and
Johnson deserves recognition as one of the finest. When Alan Lomax interviewed pianist Thomas "Jay Bird" Jones in 1942, the latter boasted about
the talented keyboardists that performed in Clarksdale in earlier decades.
"Thirteen piano players was here," he recalled with odd precision, and reeled
off some of their names, largely forgotten figures with few or no recordings

to their credit. Jones's own music offers little of interest, and certainly noth-ing one could not have heard in many other cities. But Jay Bird frankly told his interviewer: "'Course I was the worst of all"—leaving us to wonder how much better these others might have been. Perhaps Johnson was one of the thirteen pianists referred to by Jay Bird: we know, for example, that she was apparently living on the King-Anderson Plantation, just outside of Clarksdale, in the 1930s.

As we have already seen, the renown of the Delta blues was built on the con-tributions of a series of pioneering guitarists. In the face of the great African-American piano traditions that flourished elsewhere in the country—such as Harlem stride, St. Louis ragtime, and Kansas City swing—it is tempting to assume that the Delta produced little that was original, merely rehashes of influences from elsewhere. But Louise Johnson dispels this myth. She had no doubt heard recordings of these other styles; but she probably had spent more time listening to the loosely structured guitar blues of the Delta. She incorporates some of the unique sensibility of this string music into her keyboard attack, and the result is both original and appealing. Her playing is supple and rhythmic, but with a winsome ebb and flow that frees it up from the ground beat. The music breathes and seethes, and Johnson sings with brassy assertiveness above the genial bounce and strut of the keyboard. If I were forced to speculate on the sources of the music, I would imagine a blues guitarist who woke up one morning to find eighty-eight strings had replaced the paltry six that had serviced before. This may be piano music, but it clearly comes to us from outside of the keyboard tradition.

Patton and Johnson had been having an affair around the time of the Paramount session, although the guitarist had also recently moved in with Bertha Lee Pate, who would remain his closest companion during the remaining years of his life. Johnson may, in fact, have been the woman Patton had sung about, the previous October, when he recorded his "Joe Kirby Blues"—here he had announced "the woman I love, Lordy, live in Robinsonville town." But on the drive to Wisconsin, Patton slapped John-son during an argument, and she climbed into the backseat next to House. In Grafton, Johnson spent the night in House's room at the boardinghouse where Paramount lodged its black visitors. House was concerned when Pat-ton pulled him aside the next morning, fearing that they would get into a conflict over the woman. But Patton showed—or at least pretended to show—a haughty indifference, telling House: "Listen fella, I didn't want her in the first place. Now you keep her." This dynamic inevitably colors how we

hear the apparently lighthearted chatter that the guitarists adopt as a foil to
Johnson's singing on "All Night Long Blues":

Patton [spoken]:	*Do it a long time, baby, for me!*
Johnson:	*I woke up this mornin', blues around my bed.*
	I woke up this mornin', blues around my bed,
Brown [spoken]:	*Do it a long time, Louise! Get 'em wild, get 'em wild!*
Johnson:	*I never had no good man, I mean, to ease my achin' head.*
House [spoken]:	*Lord, let's have a meetin' here now.*
Patton [spoken]:	*Ah, pshaw! . . .*
Johnson:	*Lord, I'm gon' get drunk an' I'm gon' walk these streets all night.*
Brown [spoken]:	*Come on, bad woman*
House [spoken]:	*Hey, hey!*
Johnson:	*Well, I'm gon' get drunk, I'm gonna walk these streets all night.*
	'Cause the man that I'm lovin', I swear he sho' don' treat me right
Patton [spoken]:	*Well, the law gonna git you, rider!*

Johnson could have hardly played or sung with more emotional intensity
than she did on that day in Grafton. Perhaps she always brought such fire
to performances—we lack other recordings to benchmark these against.
But it is hard not to hear Louise Johnson singing her own personal blues,
fired by the events of the previous twenty-four hours, in this memorable
recording.

The Paramount executives were clearly more fascinated that day with the
potential of Son House, who was allocated more studio time than any of
the other blues performers. Arthur Laibly urged House to record a version
of Blind Lemon Jefferson's "See That My Grave's Kept Clean"—in response,
House obliged with his "Mississippi County Farm Blues"—suggesting
that Paramount may have seen House as the replacement for the recently
deceased Lemon, whose tremendous sales had established the commercial
viability of traditional blues. Yet Son House would disappoint all these
hopes. His records sold poorly. Indeed, they hardly sold at all, as demonstrated by their extraordinary rarity. When Gayle Wardlow found a copy of
Son House's "Dry Spell Blues" in 1963, it was the only extant disk known

to collectors; and several decades later, after a lengthy career as a record hunter, it remained the only Son House 78 in Wardlow's renowned collection. "Clarksdale Moan" proved to be an even scarcer item—as witnessed by the seventy-five-year lag between the recording date and the discovery, by a fortunate blues collector, of the single known copy of the 78 featuring House's tribute to Jefferson.

But sales and artistry are, as we often must remember, two separate matters. House's reputation as a major blues artist was largely established that day in Grafton. His throbbing, spasmodic guitar sound is the stuff of legend. Did a guitarist ever do more with less? In the postwar period, John Lee Hooker would frustrate record producers with a similarly personal approach to the Delta blues, waxing endless groove songs, without clear beginnings or ends, and very little structure in between, but full of a pulsating, boogie-driven energy that exerts a quasi-hypnotic effect on its listeners. House shows equal disdain for the conventions of the recording studio. His three most celebrated works from this session—"Preachin' the Blues," "My Black Mama," and "Dry Spell Blues"—each refused to be contained on a single side of a 78, and required the unconventional expedient of release in two parts, filling up both sides of the disk. And even to describe these performances as "songs" is to exercise some poetic license. They are haunting, melismatic recitatives pushed and prodded along by House's jittery guitar work, which relies only on the simplest melodic and harmonic material for its building blocks. Yes, he sometimes deigns to hint at a subdominant or dominant chord, but in his hands, these are unnecessary frills: a simple tonic, laced with the intoxicating gin of his intense groove, is perfectly sufficient to drive the music onward in an exemplary fashion. Those seeking to uncover the roots of the blues in the epic works of the African griots will find support for their thesis in performances such as these, which defy all the pat expectations of Western pop music, and seem rather to be extracts from some personal *Iliad* or *Odyssey* which, with sufficient disk space and patience from the Paramount overseers, might easily have gone on and on into parts three and four and more.

Willie Brown, who recorded two celebrated performances at the same session, opens his "Future Blues" with the declaration: "Can't tell my future; and I can't tell my past." Certainly Brown did not intend this as a challenge to later biographers, but it might just as well have been one. No blues figure has generated so much debate on the basis of so few recordings, and the range of hypotheses offered on his behalf is truly impressive. Blues researchers have discovered many accounts of a Will or Willie Brown in the Delta, and have struggled to reconcile the incongruities in the descriptions of their physical appearance, and the specific biographical details that have come to light. Indeed, it is likely that several Delta musicians operated under that name. Brown is the fifth most common last name in the United States, and William is the fifth most common first name. As a result, many communities include one or two Willie Browns among their inhabitants—and the frequency is even higher among African-American populations. But researchers like to connect the dots and pull together disparate accounts into a single, unified biography. As a result, they may have overreached in their attempts to identify a single musician behind the many references to Willie Brown found in the annals of the Delta idiom. (We will encounter a similar challenge when we try to compile a coherent biography of Robert Johnson—a challenge compounded by the commonness of the name, as well as the many aliases adopted by the guitarist during his short life.)

In 1965, Gayle Wardlow tracked down a death certificate for a Willie Lee Brown, born in Mississippi on August 6, 1900, who died near Tunica, Mississippi, on December 30, 1952. He may be our best candidate for the guitarist who recorded for Paramount. House suggested that Brown died in Mississippi in the mid-1950s, and Willie Lee Brown's date of death is at least close enough in time to make a plausible connection with the blues musician. Wardlow supports his thesis with first-person accounts he tracked down from individuals in Tunica County who knew Brown, Patton, and House. Yet Wardlow is left to reconcile the death certificate with sources who told him Brown died in a Memphis hospital, as well as with a conflicting body of research gathered by David Evans.

Evans pursued an alternate line of inquiry, tracing a Willie Brown who was born sometime between 1890 and 1895, and was living on Jim Yeager's plantation near Drew around 1911. Evans clearly linked this Brown, who played guitar, to Charley Patton—in fact, by some accounts, he was said to be superior to Patton himself. In Evans's words, Brown "was generally considered to be the best all-around blues musician" in the Drew area. Yet the physical description of the Drew Willie Brown—said to be a large man, at least six feet in height—conflicts markedly with the firsthand testimony of Son House, who described his longtime musical companion as smaller than Patton (a man of modest stature, perhaps five feet seven inches). Moreover, the Willie Brown based in Drew was in his early twenties, according to Nathan "Dick" Bankston, when he met Patton around 1912—a fact impossible to reconcile with the death certificate and accounts gathered by Wardlow. We thus seem to be faced with two incompatible bodies of evidence, and are almost forced to conclude that Patton associated with two different Willie Browns, and that the Tunica County candidate (who fits Son House's description) is the man who recorded "Future Blues" and "M&O Blues" for Paramount in 1930.

But the true state of affairs may be even more confusing. In fact, more than two Willie Browns may have graced the Delta blues scene—or, at least, we should not rule out this possibility. In his "Crossroad Blues," Robert Johnson refers to his "friend-boy Willie Brown." Most have assumed that this was the same musician who played with House and Patton (and whose guitar playing had influenced Johnson's own). I share this assumption—but the evidence is far from conclusive. Both the Drew and Tunica Willie Browns were more than a decade older than Johnson, so it seems reasonable to question whether the younger guitarist would have addressed one of them in such terms. In fact, the relationship likely was reversed: the Willie Brown who recorded for Paramount reportedly viewed Johnson as a pesky boy who hung around the older musicians. We are perhaps safer assuming that the Willie Brown who recorded with Son House for Alan Lomax in 1941 is the same as the Paramount recording artist—most blues fans take this as a matter of course, and I tend to agree with them—but even this is far from certain. This musician's 1941 recording of "Make Me a Pallet on the Floor" reveals a far more flowing guitar accompaniment and a more poised vocal than the 1930 sides; but these stylistic differences can be plausibly explained as the natural evolution and refinement of the nervous musician who, a decade before, had been ushered into a studio in Grafton, Wisconsin, to record (probably for the first time) in front of two of his most respected peers.

Even more troubling, Lomax's documentation is far from straightforward. In the opening pages of *The Land Where the Blues Began*, Lomax tells of meeting a guitarist named William Brown in Memphis, who he describes as "tall, lanky, silky-muscled with a long, oval Sudanese face," and even Lomax is not sure whether this is the same person he recorded with Son House, although he is inclined to believe that he is. Yet, here again, the physical description is markedly different from Son House's own account of his musical sparring partner. And we have even less reason to link the Paramount recording artist to the exceptional blues singer and guitarist, also named William Brown, who recorded for the Library of Congress at

Sadie Beck's plantation in Arkansas in 1942. This musician sounds nothing like the Willie Brown who recorded for Paramount, and given his apparent age of twenty-seven when he recorded for the Library of Congress, he is too young to be either the musician traced by Evans or the one whose death certificate was found by Wardlow. But his blues are first rate—the dazzling "Mississippi Blues" he recorded for the Library of Congress is often emulated by blues and folk guitarists—and we would like to have more of his inspired music. There is some evidence that this musician, and not Son House's firend, is the William Brown encountered by Lomax in Memphis. For my part, I am inclined to accept three Willie Browns: the Memphis "William Brown" described by Lomax who recorded "Mississippi Blues"; the "tall Willie Brown" from the Drew area traced by Evans; and the short Willie Brown who associated with Son House, whose death certificate Wardlow has published. Certainly, the facts at our disposal are scanty, but it is hard to reconcile them with fewer than three separate individuals.

The patient blues investigator is thus blessed—or cursed?—with a full police lineup of suspects. Yet the disputes and uncertainties surrounding the name of Willie Brown hardly stop there. Some have tried to use his enigmatic story in order to solve another Delta blues mystery, drawing a connection between the Willie Brown recordings on Paramount with the work of the obscure musician known simply as Kid Bailey. How convenient this would be: if one Delta puzzle intersected another, at one of those beguiling crossroads so celebrated in the music, and thus helped us to put both mysteries at rest in a single stroke!

Kid Bailey's recorded legacy amounts to two elegant performances recorded at the Peabody Hotel in Memphis in 1929. "Way down in Mississippi, where I was bred and born, reason that will forever be my native home," Bailey begins his "Mississippi Bottom Blues." Unfortunately, this constitutes almost his full known biography. The field researchers who scoured the state during the 1960s and 1970s failed to find a single individual who could fill in the details of Kid Bailey's life with any certainty, although occasionally the name would summon up some dim recollection. Gayle Wardlow pursued Bailey's trail with the zeal of a *film noir* private investigator during this period, and he traced clues that placed the guitarist in various Mississippi communities—living at a plantation in Leland in the 1920s; accompanying Charley Patton in Skene; performing in Tutwiler; working alongside Tommy Johnson in Rankin County; playing mandolin at a juke joint in Moorhead in 1948 . . . or in Indianola, or Canton, and other locales. But the accounts never cohered, and the details were always sketchy—no one seemed to have been a close friend of the elusive guitarist—leading us to wonder whether another Kid (a common moniker for musicians) might be the one remembered, or whether the interviewees were simply being agreeable to the leading questions of their persistent interlocutor. Wardlow felt that Bailey might still be alive in the 1960s—and what a find that might have been!—yet the elusive bluesman proved devilishly hard to track, especially after the 1940s, when the trail grew cold. David Evans had no better luck with his efforts. "Several of my informants recognized the name of Kid Bailey," he noted, "but seemed reluctant to talk about him or simply knew little about him." In his *Big Road Blues* (1982), Evans speculated that Bailey may have been involved in some of the racial violence that afflicted the Drew area during the period under consideration, and notes that one of his informants referred to the bluesman as "Killer Bailey."

When Son House was asked about Kid Bailey, the name was meaningless to him. But when he heard Bailey's music on record, he announced with some assurance that he recognized the voice of his longtime friend and accompanist Willie Brown. Blues researchers hardly took this seriously. Brown's voice on the Paramount recordings of "Future Blues" and "M&O Blues" is gruff and raw, contrasting sharply with Bailey's honeyed delivery. Certainly there are instances of vocalists evolving from smoother to rougher timbres during the course of their career—in fact, Louis Armstrong was making a transition of this sort around the same time. But the change in this instance would have been a profound one: and all the more remarkable since only eight months separate the two sessions. The guitar styles on the Bailey and Brown recordings reveal a stronger basis for comparison: both opt for relaxed tempos, with the guitar accompaniment moving ahead with stately predictability, often repeating the same one- or two-bar patterns. In fact, the guitar work of both Brown and Bailey reminds me of the cautious approach musicians often take when accompanying another performer who they are afraid will lose the beat. The down beat is clearly marked, and the chord changes telegraphed with a clarity of intent that is far from standard on traditional blues recordings. This approach may be understandable for Brown, who earned his place in the history of the music primarily as an accompanist. But for Bailey—who, you will recall, seemed to have no close friends or lasting musical partners, at least among the many Delta players interviewed—this makes less sense. Yet if his recorded guitar part sounds like the careful work of a skilled accompanist . . . well, perhaps the guitarist on the Bailey session was an accompanist. Certainly one cannot dismiss out of hand the possibility that another guitarist (perhaps Brown himself) is featured on the Kid Bailey recordings, backing the singer. Another clue: Joe Callicott, who was present at the Peabody Hotel sessions, recalls seeing "two little guys" making the record which he later surmised was Bailey's 78—a description that, if true, would lend credence to the view that Willie Brown served as guitarist, and that further this was the short-statured Willie Brown who Son House knew, not the tall Willie Brown from Drew.

Although David Evans initially dismissed the idea that Bailey and Brown were the same person, he reversed course by the early 1990s. The Bailey performances, he determined, were too good to be by some forgotten nonentity who made no impact on the imagination of his peers. He now concluded that Brown had adopted an alias because he was already under contract with Paramount for the session that would take place eight months later. Evans explains that the rougher voice on the Paramount recordings may be due to the liquor that flowed freely at the session—a known irritant to the vocal cords. Wardlow, for his part, vehemently denies that Kid Bailey was a mere alias for Willie Brown. "I had three sources for Kid Bailey in Leland. Walter Vinson, of the Mississippi Sheiks, knew Kid Bailey," he emphasized during one of our conversations. "There were other sources who knew him. He was a real person."

Let us explore another possible solution to the Kid Bailey mystery, one that may help explain all the strange pieces of evidence that have confounded blues scholars. The puzzling gaps, lasting many years, in the firsthand accounts of Bailey collected by Wardlow are not unknown in the biographies of other Delta figures. But they are usually explained by incarceration, a move to a different part of the country, or a turn to the religious life—these being the three most common ways in which a blues career was interrupted. The view that Bailey may have been incarcerated fits with Evans's earlier suspicions (which he later dismissed) that Bailey had been involved in racial violence of some sort. Stephen Calt tells me that among the many leads on Bailey, one that he and Wardlow eventually discarded linked the blues singer to a homicide in St. Louis in the early 1950s. Calt recalls that, according to this account, "a police officer shot and killed someone subsequently identified, by this account, as Bailey, but there was a suggestion that the identity of the felon had been mixed up with Bailey. This somewhat screwy story got discarded somewhere along the line" in Wardlow and Calt's research. Recall that one of Evans's informants referred to the musician as "Killer Bailey"—something that Wardlow and Calt did not know at the time, otherwise they might have given this matter more consideration.

The supposition that Kid Bailey committed a serious crime might explain almost all the puzzling facts surrounding this mysterious musician. It would make clear the reasons for his lengthy disappearance from the music world, the long gaps during which no one remembered seeing him. It would account for the reluctance of others to talk about him. It would explain why no one stepped forward to claim Bailey as a close friend. It would also clear up enigmas like the nickname "Killer Bailey," or Skip James's peculiar response to Calt's questioning on the subject—who, when asked about Kid Bailey, answered haughtily: "I knew *of* Kid Bailey," and refused to say more.

4. my time ain't long

House's 1930 Paramount session brought together the finest Delta blues talent of its day, but the resulting 78s did little for the record company or for the careers of the musicians involved. Paramount lost its distribution channel into the Mississippi market—critical both to the supply *and* demand of these recordings—when its partner Artophone Corporation dropped out of the business. Even without this blow, record sales would have faltered in the face of the economic downturn, but the label took other steps during this period that would only accelerate the decline: cutting back on production runs, curtailing its advertising, delaying releases, and eventually firing Arthur Laibly, the guiding light behind the company's blues offerings. The final demise was not inevitable, and its farcical elements do not diminish its tragedy. Paramount eventually put a draftsman and engineer from its chair-manufacturing business in charge of the record label, and soon afterwards exited the business entirely. It sold its precious nickel masters for scrap and abandoned the Grafton facility, even leaving behind the recording machine, which eventually collapsed into the cellar when the rotting floorboards gave way.

Under a brighter economy and more favorable circumstances, so much more could have happened with these artists. Son House might have succeeded Blind Lemon Jefferson as a blues star; Louise Johnson and Willie Brown might have followed up on their exceptional debut recordings; Patton might have added to his already considerable legacy. Instead, they went their separate ways. We will not hear from House or Brown for over a decade after this unique Paramount session, and then almost by chance—which always played a role on the few occasions these musicians recorded—when Alan Lomax would find both guitarists while researching African-American music in the Delta for the Library of Congress. We know even less of the future career of Louise Johnson, merely some clues linking her to Helena and Clarksdale, and some of the smaller communities in between, and indications of a later move to Memphis. But no further recordings were made by this talented pianist.

Shortly after the Grafton session, Patton and Bertha Lee settled briefly in Robinsonville, some forty miles south of Memphis, a community known today for its nearby casinos, but then mostly for its cotton. Less apparent to the residents of Robinsonville, circa 1930, was the extraordinary assembly of blues talent in its midst, which also included Son House, Willie Brown, Louise Johnson, and a young Robert Johnson. We also hear of Howlin' Wolf coming here, perhaps during this same period, and playing with House and Brown. No major metropolis—not Memphis or Chicago or New York—would ever surpass this surprising concentration of traditional blues genius within a single city's limits. We know with certainty that Robert Johnson crossed paths with House and Brown, and many have speculated about a possible meeting between Patton and the future blues legend, a Delta equivalent of the older Mozart praising the younger Beethoven in Vienna in 1787 with the prophetic words: "Don't forget his name—you will hear it spoken often." Alas, our best source, Willie Moore, has done his best to dispel our starry-eyed illusions: Robert Johnson told Moore, the latter related years later, that the older Delta legend had made little impression on him. Or, in Moore's words, "Patton stomped both his feet and kept up too much-a noise for him." Yet we also hear of the young Robert Johnson performing "Pony Blues" and "Banty Rooster Blues" during this same period. Johnson would never record these songs, or any Patton composition for that matter, but attentive ears will hear hints in his music that seem to point back to the older bluesman.

Paramount continued to release new Patton 78s until 1932, but the fatal combination of spotty supply and paltry demand negated any positive impact they might have had on his career. Patton still insisted on the privileges of an artist, but few were willing to indulge his pretensions. Increasingly, his indiscretions met with hostility or outright violence. We hear of him being attacked at a house frolic in Itta Bena or Moorhead, circa 1930, by a jealous husband. Another account, from this same period, tells of him being shot in Sunflower. Perhaps these were just fanciful tales: many such circulated about Patton, recounting his imagined death by a gunshot or the blade of a jealous woman, even by a sudden bolt of lightning, a fitting end for a bluesman, that most godforsaken of occupations. In fact, heart disease would be the more prosaic cause of Patton's death in 1934. But the noticeable scar on his neck and the limp in his walk—the results, respectively, of a knife and a gun—served as lasting evidence of the troubles resulting from Patton's chosen profession and lifestyle.

By some accounts, his companion Bertha Lee administered the near-fatal cut that slit his throat. Certainly her relationship with Patton, despite its longevity, was marked by turbulence. Son House recalled a domestic squabble during which Lee held Patton pinned against the floor, while pummeling him with her fists. Yet Lee showed more loyalty to Patton than any of his other friends or lovers, leaving stable employment in Lula to travel with him to various Delta communities. Patton's commitment to her—or to any woman—is questionable. Patton family lore tells of the musician having eight wives, and at least six separate marriage records have come to light: four found at the Bolivar County Courthouse in Cleveland, Mississippi, and two at the Sunflower County Courthouse in Indianola. No divorce papers have been discovered, suggesting that the guitarist was cavalier about the legalistic details of his various vows and betrothals. But in the final months of his life, Patton's health was poor, and he may have come to appreciate the devotion of a nurse, even if he undervalued the fidelity of a lover. Patton's heart troubles may also have spurred Bertha Lee to develop her own singing talent, perhaps to give his voice a rest during performances.

Patton reconnected with Son House and Willie Brown in 1933, and the trio presented themselves for an audition with H. C. Speir as a gospel-singing group called the Locust Ridge Saints. Speir treated the matter as an elaborate joke, a put-on staged for his amusement by the blues guitarist; but it is unlikely that Patton would have gone to such trouble if he had not had serious aspirations for the group. Speir, for his part, made some test disks, but no commercial session ever resulted. Yet the audition was not without its impact: some blues music was recorded at the same time, which found its way to W. R. Calaway, a former Paramount employee who now served as sales manager for the American Record Company (ARC). Calaway must have been impressed by what he heard, or perhaps he admired Patton's Paramount recordings. Under normal circumstances, a record company would have provided a train ticket for a Delta musician to come to a recording session. But Calaway personally traveled to Mississippi, first to see Speir and secure Patton's address, then to Belzoni, where he needed to arrange the guitarist's release from jail.

For this final session, Patton and Bertha Lee made the long journey by train to New York toward the close of January 1934. Patton must have been in poor shape by then—he had only three more months to live—yet he still showed how productive he could be in a recording studio. Some twenty-nine songs were recorded over two days, although only twelve were ever released, with the remaining masters lost or destroyed. Much of this music revisits familiar ground: "Stone Pony Blues" stays close to the model set by Patton's most famous recording, while other performances evoke, with lesser or greater fidelity, songs he had recorded back at his first session in June 1929. But the tone is more subdued, at times lugubrious, the tempos more controlled, the rhythms less propulsive. It is hard to listen to this music without thinking about Patton's impending death. Patton himself seems to have it on his own mind, when he sings in "34 Blues":

> It may bring sorrow, Lord, and it may bring tear.
> Oh Lord, oh Lord, spare me to see a brand new year.

Or even more explicitly, he joins with Bertha Lee in singing a song called "Oh Death": "Lord, I know, Lord I know my time ain't long." Bertha Lee sang two numbers at the session that were released under her own name, "Yellow Bee" and "Mind Reader Blues," performances that reveal a genuine knack for blues phrasing and suggest that Patton saw her as a protégée of sorts. Patton sings about her in "Poor Me," recorded at the final session on February 1, revealing a forlorn tone that had rarely surfaced before in his lyrics about women:

> It's on me, it's poor me, you must take pity on poor me.
> I ain't got nobody take pity on poor me . . .

> Don't the moon look pretty, shining down through the tree?
> Oh, I can see Bertha Lee, Lord, but she can't see me.

Patton's death certificate indicates that his heart troubles worsened around the time of the trip to New York, and his sometimes labored vocals on these final recordings testify to challenges he must have faced in matching the energy of his earlier work. Back in Mississippi, he continued to perform, and persisted even when he had trouble breathing, which he attributed to bronchitis. In early April, Patton returned from a dance near Holly Ridge, hoarse and gasping for air. He remained in bed, and was visited twice by a local doctor, but his condition only worsened. Some consideration was given to bringing him to a hospital, but the spring rains made the roads impassable. In his final days, according to his niece Bessie Turner, he took to ruminating on the Book of Revelation and preaching to those who came to his bedside. He died on April 28, 1934—the death certificate noted a mitral valve disorder as the cause, a problem which might have been congenital, or perhaps the result of rheumatic fever or syphilis.

Patton was still a relatively young man when he died, probably forty-three years of age. His passing coincided with a period of relative obscurity for traditional blues, and an unprecedented economic downturn for the country as a whole. If he had survived, Patton's career would have inevitably experienced a major upswing. He (like Son House and Willie Brown) would perhaps have been recorded by the Library of Congress in the 1940s. His flamboyant performance style would have made him a natural star in the Chicago blues scene that would flourish after World War II. During the blues revival of the 1960s, he would have been fêted as a living legend, put on stage before thousands of fans. Instead, he spent most of his brief life on plantations, making music for others similarly situated.

Yet an important divide was crossed with Charley Patton. He was the first star of the Delta blues, his records traveling far and wide to locations he himself would never see. His music perhaps began as a folk art, but it ended up as an influential style of commercial music. And the timeless appeal of his songs derives from both sources: the rich traditions he drew upon, and the beguiling future of the blues as mass entertainment that his music promised. It is still something of a marvel that such songs—ostensibly about a pony, or a rooster, or a boll weevil and the like—could have such force in the modern industrial world. But they did, and still do. Yet it would be left to others—a Muddy Waters, a B.B. King, a John Lee Hooker—to enjoy the full fruits of success and stardom that could ripen on the old vines of this simple, rural music.

Tommy Johnson

hard time killin' floor

1. canned heat killing me

The Delta blues music that has survived from the 1920s and 1930s is precious, but the amount lost to us is incalculable. Mississippi's castoffs not only helped transform Memphis, St. Louis, and Chicago (and other cities) into hotbeds of blues activity, but the sheer number of talented players left behind, unrecorded and unrewarded, defies our best attempts to measure or document. "It's a *thousand* musicians down there," Honeyboy Edwards recounted to a blues researcher in the 1970s who attempted to probe this uncharted territory. David Evans found evidence of similar riches when he explored the blues tradition in the area surrounding Drew, Mississippi, during the 1960s and 1970s. In this small community of two thousand residents, but rich in blues history and lore, the musical exploits of dozens of great Delta musicians were recounted by those he interviewed, an unsurpassed concentration of blues talent somehow nurtured in an impoverished and sparsely populated area only a few miles in circumference. Alas, their greatness lived on mostly in memory, and even those who recalled their prowess are themselves now dead. But though the music itself may have been lost, the stories opened up intriguing possibilities.

Nathan Scott garnered admirers around Drew with his blues guitar and harmonica playing, and even more with his singing, during the 1920s, and sometimes played alongside his mentor Charley Patton. The basic facts of Scott's life remain a mystery to us, as is the sound of his music—unless he is the convict Nathaniel Scott recorded performing a spiritual and work song at Parchman prison in 1936. Or perhaps he is the Nathan Scott who recorded a test disk for Brunswick in Memphis in 1930. But since no known copies have survived, even proving this connection would not tell us much. We have perhaps too many leads here. The name Nathan Scott is a common one and more than a dozen candidates can be culled from census data.

We are even more interested in—and puzzled by—Henry Sloan. David Evans tells us that Sloan was a "major influence" on Charley Patton, and researcher Jim O'Neal has speculated that Sloan might have been the "lean, loose-jointed Negro" who played the blues for W. C. Handy at the Tutwiler train station circa 1903, the chance encounter that helped set off the history of the blues as a commercial style of music. According to census data, Sloan was born in January 1870, making him the oldest of any of the musicians discussed here, and he lived at Dockery's until 1918—less than thirty miles from Tutwiler! Is it possible that we have uncovered one of the original sources for the Delta blues style? Yet another school of thought dismisses Sloan entirely as an important figure. "I talked to people at Dockery's," Gayle Dean Wardlow advised me during one of our discussions, "and they told me that Sloan was just a chorder. He played what you would call pre-blues, just chords for dance music." Booker Miller, who knew and idolized Patton, and is among our most reliable sources of information about his music, told Wardlow that he had never heard of Henry Sloan. With such conflicting accounts, all second- or third-hand, and no recordings to cast additional light, we are unlikely to clear up this matter any time soon.

Or perhaps Ben Maree is our mysterious Tutwiler singer. Born around 1887, Maree would have been a teenager when Handy experienced his blues epiphany. Widely respected for his blues playing and showmanship, Maree is believed to be the originator of the song that became Patton's celebrated "Pony Blues." Maree was reportedly still alive in the late 1960s, but since he was never interviewed, we will never know much beyond these simple facts.

Tales of other musicians, equally interesting, only draw us outside the orbit of blues music proper, but we pause nonetheless to ponder (again) the music lost to us. For example, Roebuck Staples began learning guitar around Drew and Dockery's in the late 1920s, and might have developed into one of the greatest of the Delta blues guitarists. Instead, he turned his talents to sacred music, and after moving to Chicago formed the celebrated family band, the Staple Singers, which would gain renown as "God's great-est hit-makers." Late in life, he decided to feature his often neglected guitar and vocal work and earned a Grammy award for his solo recording *Father, Father*. But for every Roebuck Staples, there are dozens of others, not only lost to the blues, but to the music world in total. The switch from blues sing-ing to a religious calling was not unusual in this time and place—we are told of Willie Farris, O. M. McGee, Jim Holloway, and others from around Drew and Dockery's who made such a move—and their new path invariably led these individuals to leave behind the devil's music. To historians of the Delta blues, they are mostly names, and little more.

How can we hope to gauge the talents of these, and so many other Delta musicians, when our judgments are based solely on tenuous testimony and failing memories? Josie Bush was wife, or at least a longtime companion, to bluesman Willie Brown, and according to Evans, was "probably as good a musician as Brown when she married him." But since she too never recorded, we will never know with any certainty. Sometimes a musician's reputation survived, but even his true name was forgotten. The first field research-ers into the Delta heard tales of the musical prowess of "Hobo George" or "Bull Cow" or other such colorful monikers, names found in no census document or death certificate. Skip James recalled the dazzling work of an itinerant one-armed guitarist—who managed somehow to chord with the index and middle fingers of his left hand, while picking notes with the ring and little finger—whom he knew simply as "Chief" or "One-Armed Chief." The prison at Parchman housed hundreds of such enigmatic and tragic stories: individuals who show up briefly on a Library of Congress record-ing to dazzle us with their voices and then disappear, occasionally leaving behind a name, sometimes only a nickname, and frequently nothing at all beyond the poignant strains, resolute spirits held captive now merely on disk, no longer in the flesh.

Among the Drew musicians who recorded, Tommy Johnson stands out as the blues singer whose talent came closest to rivaling Patton's. Decades later, H. C. Speir would recall these two blues players, among the countless ones he had auditioned or championed, as his most distinctive finds, the singers who had developed the most original and appealing styles. In many ways, Johnson is the antithesis of Patton. If Patton excites us with his headlong passion, Johnson moves us with the logic and elegance of his guitar work. If Patton is the master of hot rhythms, Johnson is supreme at slow to medium tempos; his music unfolds with stately precision, his time is rock steady, largely immune to the acceleration of beat that is so common among Delta blues players as almost to serve as a defining characteristic of the style. On a piece like "Cool Drink of Water Blues," the song floats along at a drowsy 70 beats per minute, a tempo that would sound lugubrious in the hands of most other Delta players, but which Johnson guides with a masterful sensitivity to the ebb and flow of the melodic line. In contrast to Patton's astringent vocals, Johnson's singing is strong and clear, almost a pop crooner's voice. Not until Robert Johnson recorded, almost a decade later, would a Delta blues singer emerge with a voice so well suited for crossover appeal to a mainstream audience. But the lesser known Johnson has his own distinctive bag of tricks: his falsetto yodel is a country singer's dream, and the vibrato on his held notes is the kind that even today gets *American Idol* voters running to their phones. Above all, a sweet wistfulness—a rare quality in the Delta blues—infuses even his most tragic lyrics, almost as if this vocalist were intended to sing happier songs, lead a more uplifting life than the one destiny handed out to him. But though Tommy Johnson never enjoyed more than a small taste of stardom, his talent was far larger than his fame. With a less self-destructive personality, he almost certainly would have enjoyed a much larger success.

Tommy Johnson was born around 1896 on a plantation situated on the border of Hinds and Copiah counties, some twenty miles south of Jackson, Mississippi, near Terry. He was the sixth of the thirteen children of Idell and Mary Ella Johnson, who moved soon after Tommy's birth several miles south to the vicinity of Crystal Springs, the community to which the guitarist would invariably return throughout his life, and where he would eventually die and be buried. Music was both part of the heritage as well as the daily entertainment of the household. On his father's side, he could trace his relationship to the great jazz and blues guitarist Lonnie Johnson—

or so the family believed—while his mother came from a family of sixteen siblings, nearly all of them musicians. Johnson began learning guitar in his early teens, but much of his development must have taken place after he left home at age sixteen.

"That old lady stole him away after he learned how to play," was how LeDell Johnson described his younger brother's sudden departure from the homestead. "Just as soon as he learnt to play pretty good and make them notes that I showed him, well, that old lady, she got crazy about him then, and she stole him." Years later, no one could recall her name, or how much older she was—except that she was mature enough to pass as the mother of her young paramour. Johnson was gone for two years, most of it apparently spent halfway across the state, around Rolling Fork in the Delta region.

Johnson returned to Crystal Springs without his lady friend. None of his relationships lasted very long—"He had four wives and, I reckon, about as many concubines as King Solomon had," was LeDell's characterization. But a more enduring result of these rambling years was Johnson's newfound prowess as a blues guitarist. He told LeDell that he had taught himself how to play these songs, but when pressed for more details he offered a colorful story that has since become an established part of blues lore.

Shortly before midnight, Tommy Johnson had waited at a crossroads. A mysterious black man came up to him, took his guitar, tuned it, and returned it to him. After that, he was capable of playing anything he wanted. But the price was a terrible one: he had sold his soul to the devil in return.

We will encounter this identical story when we trace the enigmatic life of that other Johnson, Robert Johnson, whose career has become so closely associated with the crossroads tale that it has almost eclipsed the other facts of his biography. At that point, we will try to unravel those elements of fact and legend that have become shamelessly mixed in the telling and retelling. But even here we must dwell on the powerful effect such an admission must have had on its hearers at the time—especially to someone like LeDell Johnson, who took up preaching in 1924, and eventually gave up the blues because, in his words, he was "tired of living a devil's life." For most citizens of Crystal Springs, the devil was not an abstraction or metaphysical construct, and certainly not a myth, but a concrete force, malevolently active, leading people astray. A transaction of the sort described by Johnson would have horrified those who heard it. Perhaps a free-thinker—and maybe Tommy Johnson was one—might relate this story glibly, but his audience would hardly take it in such a casual manner. Yet the shock value may have been the very reason why a number of blues musicians reveled in such an infernal connection. Almost at the same time that Johnson was recording, blues singer Peetie Wheatstraw was promoting himself as "the Devil's Son-In-Law" or sometimes as the "High Sheriff from Hell." The notoriety enjoyed by Wheatstraw—and even more by Robert Johnson, given his tremendous posthumous fame and record sales—testifies to the attention generated by such claims. Just as satanic rockers would find their niche market a half century later, a group of early blues singers embraced the harshest attacks their critics leveled at them—deviltry, blasphemy, apostasy, call it what you will—and tried to turn them into marks, if not of distinction, at least of notoriety.

When Johnson returned to Crystal Springs, he already knew the basic elements of many songs he would later record, and even hinted that the devil had helped him compose them. But he must also have benefited from close contact with the many guitarists he encountered in the Delta, including Charley Patton. Johnson had the opportunity to renew his connection with Patton when he returned to the Delta with LeDell. Here they resided on the Tommy Sanders Plantation about eight miles from Dockery's, an area that was a hotbed of blues activity in these formative years before the first recordings of the Delta masters of the idiom. The Johnsons were part of a larger migration of families and individuals from Crystal Springs to the Drew area, drawn by the promise of ready employment picking cotton. The change in location must have also brought about a lessening in status: in Crystal Springs, Tommy Johnson stood out as one of the few guitarists who could play the blues, while in Drew, he was thrust among a legion of blues players, many of them considerably older and more experienced than him. In time, Johnson would be lauded as one of the finest exponents of blues in the region, but it is not clear how much recognition his music received at the time. In any event, Johnson remained in Drew for only around one year before responding again to the call of the open road.

These were unstable times for Johnson, and his whereabouts are hard to trace. He appears to have left Mississippi for two or three years. Much of this period may have been spent in Arkansas and Louisiana, but Johnson might have also traveled north. When he next showed up at Crystal Springs, he and his female companion had completely worn through the soles of their footwear—"didn't have nothing on but the top of their shoes," his brother recalls. But Johnson was by no means cured of his wanderlust. This stay, like all of his visits, was a temporary one. For the next two decades, he would periodically return to Crystal Springs, or to Jackson, or to the Delta, but rarely remain in any one place for more than a year, and sometimes only for a few weeks or months.

Johnson was especially attracted to Jackson, a city far larger than any in the Delta, with an active nightlife that offered ample opportunities for working musicians. At various points in the 1920s, the local blues scene was graced by the presence, for longer or shorter periods, of Charlie McCoy, Johnnie Temple, "One Leg" Sam Norwood, Slim Duckett, Ishmon Bracey, Rube Lacy, Walter Vinson, and Skip James, among others. Only a short distance separated Jackson from the heart of the Delta, but music in the state's capital city was no time-honored folk art. Rather, it was a serious profession, and musicians were expected to adapt to whatever performance style might be demanded by the occasion. Blues had its place, but so did waltzes and two-steps and rags, indeed virtually anything the patron cared to hear. When an unreleased test pressing of Johnson singing "I Want Someone to Love Me" was discovered by a Wisconsin antique dealer a few years ago, listeners were surprised to hear the Delta blues legend singing a sentimental waltz, his dreamy voice floating over a saccharine guitar accompaniment. But the competitive environment of Jackson demanded precisely this type of versatility. Johnson "got to be a pretty good musicianer," Rube Lacy later recalled. "Anything we played, Tommy got to the place he could play it too. . . . We played for dances together, so we had to learn it." This versatility is rarely hinted at in the blues recordings of the time—deliberately so, because the record companies prodded the artists to play original material, and not cover the popular and familiar songs that made up much of a working musician's repertoire.

In fact, when Johnson was auditioned by H. C. Speir, on a referral from Ishmon Bracey, the talent scout was especially concerned that his new discovery knew too few original songs to justify a recording session. Johnson, by Speir's assessment, had only two original songs ready for the studio, but he worked with the guitarist to ensure that Johnson would have at least four prepared—the minimum necessary to interest a record label. Speir then sent test acetates of Bracey and Johnson to Ralph Peer, who was almost single-handedly establishing the new sound of country music for the Victor label at this time, and who, Speir hoped, would also take an interest in these blues musicians. Peer did not respond at first—leading Speir to assume that he was unimpressed by the test disks—but then a telegram arrived from the producer announcing a recording session in Memphis at the beginning of February 1928.

Johnson would later complain to family members about the problems caused in Memphis by his lack of experience in recording. Takes may have been rejected because he tapped his foot too loudly (a pillow was subsequently placed under it); or he ended his performances too soon; or he didn't pronounce his words distinctly. Perhaps the ready availability of liquor at the session—oddly a practice more common during the Prohibition era than in later years—may have added to Johnson's difficulties. Yet the resulting releases show no signs of such hindrances. In fact, these performances sound remarkably relaxed and confident.

Both sides of the initial Victor release, "Cool Drink of Water Blues" and "Big Road Blues," rank as masterpieces of the Delta blues idiom. The former begins with a sweet vocal phrase that lazily climbs an octave, starting out as a bluesy slide and ending as a cowboy yodel. Here, from the opening bars, we know that we are in the presence of a great vocalist. Indeed, the whole song serves as a vocal showpiece, but Johnson never sounds like he is deliberately trying to dazzle. Rather, he tackles the labyrinthine twists and turns of his phrases with the easy mastery of those steamboat pilots who, Mark Twain tells us, came to be able to navigate the snags and blind reefs of the big river at night, just by their instinct for the rightness of the course. Johnson bends his blue notes in slow motion, and we palpably feel the tension and release.

In "Big Road Blues," Johnson tackles a much faster tempo—almost twice as fast as "Cool Drink of Water Blues"—and he sings louder and harder; yet he still shows tremendous restraint and patience here, allowing his voice to hang behind the beat set by the guitars. Almost any other Delta singer would use this song as a vehicle for blues *shoutin'*, one of the oldest tricks of the African-American vocalist, a fire-and-brimstone delivery which instills the urgency of the pulpit into a twelve-bar tune. But Johnson artfully modulates his volume and energy, creating crescendos and diminuendos, often both within a single phrase. A transcription of the lyrics, the kind found inside CD booklets, will tell you that Johnson opens the song with the verse:

Crying I ain't going down this big road by myself,
Why don't you hear me talking pretty mama.
Lord, ain't going down this big road by myself.
If I don't carry you, going to carry somebody else.

But the real bobbing and weaving of his delivery sounds more like:

Cry-HIGH-uh-ain't goin' down thi' BIG-ROAD BY myself.
Why DON-cha [pause] hear-me TALK-in' pretty mama
Laaaaawwd, ain goin' down thi' BIG-ROAD by myself
Iffahhhhh don' car' you guhn care somebody else.

And even this transliteration does not do justice to the precision of his delivery, which is not sloppy or drawling, but crystal clear, even the words elided or emphasized enhancing our understanding of the story behind the song. LeDell Johnson provides the details: "He was at a supper once, and his girlfriend wouldn't let him take her home. And he told her, well he'd get somebody else. He wasn't going down that big road by hisself." Yet the finished song transforms its original impetus into a lyrical celebration of the bluesman's rambling ways—a common enough theme in the Delta annals, but nowhere crafted more felicitously than in this anthem to the freedom of the open road.

The appeal of Johnson's vocals is all the more remarkable given that his speech was marred by a stutter and a pronounced lisp. The latter caused a noticeable hissing sound when Johnson spoke—Speir compared it to the sound of a snake—and the storeowner had doubts whether his new discovery would ever be able to make a suitable record. However, the mannerism disappeared on recordings. Johnson's singing conveys something of the majestic sweep of a field holler, with its flowing, melismatic rise and fall. Yet it tempers this traditional African-American style with the brash, declarative approach of the American popular song. In this regard, he reminds us of the two hit acts who had made their recording debuts six months before Johnson's session—the Carter family and Jimmie Rodgers (both, like Johnson, recording for Ralph Peer and the Victor label)—who found a winning recipe in transforming down-on-the-farm singing styles, replete with hoots and hollers, into commercial fare suitable for farmhands and city slickers alike.

Tommy Johnson never achieved the tremendous success of the Carter family or Jimmie Rodgers, but he earned a degree of local notoriety and his records sold well, especially in the region along the Mississippi from New Orleans to Wisconsin. Victor followed up the success of its initial release by issuing two more Johnson songs from the February session, "Maggie Campbell Blues" backed by "Bye-Bye Blues." Speir later recalled that one of Johnson's recordings may have sold as many as two hundred thousand copies. This seems highly unlikely—sales at that level would have ensured more widespread fame than Johnson ever enjoyed—but the music no doubt proved its commercial appeal. "People'd walk five or six or ten miles to hear him, if they heard he was gon' be in town," guitarist Houston Stackhouse concurs. "They'd say 'Tommy Johnson's in town! Got to go hear Tommy.' Yeah, he'd draw a crowd, man. . . . They'd block the streets." Johnson, for his part, received only thirty dollars per song from Victor, with no provision for future royalties. But the label made enough from these releases to prompt a follow-up recording session, again in Memphis, at the close of August 1928.

Here Johnson recorded one of his greatest, but also most troubling songs, "Canned Heat Blues." The canned heat in the title references a common name for Sterno, a branded cooking fuel sometimes used by alcoholics as a substitute for liquor. The advent of Prohibition drove many drinkers to imbibe these semi-legal alternatives, despite the potential risks. In March 1930, for example, U.S. newspapers began reporting on an apparent epidemic of neurological problems, popularly called "jake leg," marked by a pronounced weakening of the arms and legs, sometimes resulting in paralysis. The disorder was linked to the abuse of a patent medicine, an alcohol-based extract of Jamaica ginger. Between fifty thousand to one hundred thousand victims suffered the consequences. Southern blacks were disproportionately hit, and "jake leg" figures in a number of blues songs. "I drink so much jake, I feel it settlin' in my knees," Ishmon Bracey sang in his "Jake Liquor Blues," recorded at almost the same time Dr. Ephraim Goldfain diagnosed the first well-publicized case of "jake leg" in Oklahoma City. Other substitutes for liquor brought their own distinct side effects, such as blindness, sores, ulcers, nerve damage, and impotency. Johnson, for his part, took whatever he could find, whether it was beer, moonshine, canned heat, shoe polish, rubbing alcohol, or other equally dangerous concoctions.

Many blues artists have sung about intoxicants, but none so disturbingly as Johnson in his "Canned Heat Blues." The song confesses and denounces, sings of attraction and destruction, all at once—no different from the blues lyrics that deal with romantic attachments, only here the object of the singer's affection is not a person but a dangerous elixir. We confront the paradox of acknowledged addiction, in terms reminiscent of the Gospel verse about the spirit being willing but the body weak, all laid bare in Johnson's psalm of self-destruction. Yet if you listened to the music without paying attention to the words, you would be struck by the cheerfulness and warmth of the song—Johnson is perhaps singing about new prospects or a new love. But the words convey the dark night of the soul in the most stark manner. "I woked up, up this morning, / With canned heat on my mind," Johnson proclaims. The song concludes:

> Crying mama, mama, mama!
> Crying, canned heat killing me.
> Believe to my soul, Lord, it gonna kill me dead.

The end result is deeply chilling, a paean to an impersonal assassin. Few songs have captured the reality of addiction in more powerful terms.

This recording sold poorly on release, perhaps due to the subject matter or the limited promotional effort Victor put behind it. Johnson might have benefited more from Victor's legal actions, when it reportedly pursued litigation against the OKeh label alleging that the Mississippi Sheiks had violated the copyright of Johnson's "Big Road Blues" for their "Stop and Listen Blues." This popular ensemble, formed by members of the Chatmon family and their friend Walter Vinson, recorded extensively in the early 1930s, and enjoyed tremendous success with their hit song "Sitting on the Top of the World." In contrast to the anguished, personal tone found in many of the most famous Delta blues artists, the Sheiks offered a slicker, more commercial approach, and gained a wide audience with a repertoire that included dance numbers, cover versions of white country songs, original material laced with sexual double entendres, and traditional blues. Details of Victor's litigation are sketchy and perhaps exaggerated, and the incident is by its very nature unusual—early blues musicians invariably borrowed material from their peers, so defining the "original material" in their work can be a challenging, often chimerical pursuit. And few recording artists had their pockets picked more often than the Sheiks themselves, whose "Sitting on Top of the World" inspired countless knock-offs. Nonetheless, Johnson would have potentially been included in any settlement as the official composer of "Big Road Blues," but he had signed away his rights (or, at least, so he believed) in exchange for a trifling sum. In any event, this would have marked Johnson's final dealings with the label. Though Victor continued to record in Memphis, Johnson was not invited to any further sessions.

However, Johnson would have one last chance to record, this time under the auspices of the Paramount label. Charley Patton had just finished his second successful session for Paramount, and the label enlisted H. C. Speir's assistance in finding additional talent for its budding line of race records. The death in December 1929 of Blind Lemon Jefferson, Paramount's biggest selling blues act, may have also motivated this quest for promising new talent to fill the gap in the catalog. In early 1930, Speir dispatched a group of performers to Paramount's Grafton, Wisconsin, facility, which included Tommy Johnson, Ishmon Bracey, and two musicians who performed under the name of the New Orleans Nehi Boys: pianist Charley Taylor and clarinetist Kid Ernest. The musicians took almost a week to make their recordings, most of it spent waiting for their turn in the studio, as Paramount brought in a number of acts in assembly-line fashion. The music eventually recorded by the Delta players also has a manufactured quality about it. The pairing of Johnson with the Nehi Boys sounds forced, an unresolved tension capsizing this planned mixture of blues and traditional jazz. Johnson's feature numbers, although more compelling, resurrect much of the same material he had recorded, in superior versions, for the Victor label. "Alcohol and Jake Blues" reminds us of "Canned Heat Blues," just as "Ridin' Horse" returns to the familiar territory of his "Maggie Campbell Blues." These songs were paired on the same Paramount 78, and sold so poorly that no copies surfaced until a single disk was found, some sixty years after the recording session. "I Wonder to Myself" breaks new ground, offering us a rare glimpse into Johnson playing a rag-type tune, but the unfortunate inclusion of kazoo on the performance gives it the flavor of an oh-so-cute novelty number.

In its desperation to find a replacement for the deceased Blind Lemon Jefferson on its roster, Paramount had now attracted a tremendous cadre of talent—almost a monopoly on the leading Delta blues players of the day—including Charley Patton, Son House, Tommy Johnson, Willie Brown, Geeshie Wiley, and Ishmon Bracey, among others. But the economy had entered a precipitous downturn at the very moment when the label seemed poised to do the most. In such circumstances, Johnson was just another casualty, one of many musicians who found that their status and renown as recording artists had vanished almost as quickly as they had come.

Yet the reality is that Tommy Johnson was not yet thirty-five years old, and his career had mostly run its course. On the surface, little would change. His life would continue to coast along without stable anchors. His residences always proved temporary. His relationships with women were just as fickle. Johnson led, to all appearances, the same wandering existence, free of entanglements, that he celebrated in his songs. Bracey recalls traveling with Johnson in medicine shows during the Depression, entertaining audiences throughout the Delta and southern Mississippi. During this same period, Johnson moved south to Tylertown, then across the Louisiana border to Angie, and finally back to Jackson in 1937. He played parties, dances, wherever he might pick up two or three dollars, seldom more, from his talents. Yet even Tommy Johnson must have felt the occasional pull toward a more permanent mode of life, as witnessed by his attempt to establish a café in Jackson (which failed because Johnson drank up most of the profits), or his occasional return to farming activities. Especially as he entered his forties, the makeshift quality of home and hearth, calling and career, may well have given him pause. Certainly Johnson's music, particularly a song like "Canned Heat Blues," tells us that he was prone to self-reflection, and did not spare himself in his critiques.

Troubling accounts from Johnson's final years support this view of a man wrestling with his own demons; although in this case no devil at the crossroads, but rather spirits of a more tangible, liquid sort were the antagonists that haunted him most. Ishmon Bracey recalled an encounter on the streets of Jackson, where he tried to convince his friend to stop drinking. Johnson broke into tears, and vowed to give up alcohol. He even talked of joining the church and becoming a preacher. But he never carried through with such aspirations, which proved as temporary as all his previous plans. LeDell Johnson tells of his brother going to the hospital for treatment, and then immediately after release starting to drink again, in violation of the doctor's orders. And as his health deteriorated, Johnson's playing and singing suffered as well, which must have been a blow both to his self-esteem as well as to his ability to earn a livelihood.

At the very end, he may have even had a premonition of his death. On

Halloween day in 1956, Johnson was leaving Jackson to play at a party for his niece in Crystal Springs, when he told his brother LeDell: "I'm going a long way this time I go, and I ain't coming back." LeDell puzzled over the remark, which didn't seem to make sense. Johnson arrived at the party, and played well into the night. Although he usually ended his performances by singing his trademark "Big Road Blues," in this instance he chose to close with a church song. Shortly after he finished playing, and the guests had left, Johnson toppled over from the couch where he was resting. His niece heard a scuffling and groaning sound, and rushed to her uncle's side. But before anything could be done, Johnson was dead, the apparent victim of a heart attack.

2. let the buzzards eat me whole

Facts are scarce, and the stories often confusing or incomplete. But even based on our scanty knowledge, we can only stand in awe of the unparalleled aggregation of blues talent situated in the Delta region during these years. The few records that have come down to us testify to this fact, even before we begin speculating on the lost music of a Henry Sloan or Ben Maree. Yet our satisfaction in enjoying the music that has survived is haunted by the realization of how arbitrary its preservation has been, in the face of so much lost. If this history teaches anything, it underscores how large a role chance played in this entire process. Under slightly different circumstances, the music of a Son House, a Willie Brown, even a Robert Johnson might have been totally lost to us. And other artists, equally great, might have dazzled us, had they been given the opportunity to do so. One inevitably wonders what additional blues classics we would have gained had H. C. Speir been successful in his attempt to purchase the Paramount Record Company in 1930 and relocate its operations to Mississippi, or if other record labels had been more active in seeking out talent in the region. The historian of the Delta blues is not entirely different from those archeologists who try to re-create a lost society on the basis of a few potsherds, bones, and broken tools. We seek to measure the whole, but we only know the smallest part.

Even when recordings survive, they sometimes merely reinforce our sense of what we have missed. Geeshie Wiley left behind only six recorded performances, but on the strength of these she has attracted a growing number of devoted admirers who laud her as one of the finest traditional blues artists.

Had she recorded more, she would almost certainly have achieved a measure of fame, if not during her lifetime, at least posthumously, her name mentioned alongside Bessie Smith's and Ma Rainey's in the blues pantheon. As it stands, her total recorded output can be heard in less than twenty minutes, and what is known of her life recounted even more quickly.

Ishmon Bracey met Wiley in Jackson in the late 1920s, and said that she originally hailed from Natchez. She resided for several months on John Hart Street in Jackson, and was romantically involved with guitarist Charlie McCoy. Robert Wilkins reported seeing her in the eastern part of the state around 1930. The Jackson location suggests that she was discovered by H. C. Speir, who may have arranged for her recording with Paramount in 1930 and 1931. Herbert Wiley, a musician residing in Oxford, Mississippi, has provided me with a few more details. He relates that Geeshie Wiley was his cousin on his father's side, and that the family came from South Carolina, where they owned a 1,500-acre farm. His father told him that Geeshie died around 1938 or 1939. He believes that she might be buried in Oxford where a family burial plot exists, but has been unable to confirm this. Yet Mack McCormick tells me that he visited Wiley's home, and met with members of her immediate family while doing fieldwork in Oklahoma. These bits and pieces of information are inconclusive and contradictory, and it will be left to future researchers to unravel this story of one of the unsung greats of the blues idiom.

Had she lived longer and enjoyed more success, Wiley might have set in motion a new type of Delta blues, more nuanced, a chiaroscuro music in which subtle shades of light and dark play on the surface, and the emotional intensity is no longer declamatory, as with a Son House or Charley Patton, but wistful and poetic. Listen to how she shapes the opening guitar phrases—even the very first note with its lazy, arcing sureness—on her "Skinny Leg Blues," or her work accompanying Elvie Thomas on "Motherless Child Blues," and you know that you are in safe hands. Her performances build with a calm confidence, never rushed or striving for effect, but with an ineffable rightness. She is adept at setting down a rock-solid dance rhythm, as on "Over to My House" and "Pick Poor Robin Clean," but perhaps even more impressive when creating musical effects largely unknown to the prewar blues, as with "Motherless Child." The latter is that greatest of rarities: a true blues lullaby. The song follows an unusual sixteen-bar blues structure that states the opening line of each stanza thrice, rather than the more typical two times. Here Elvie Thomas, floating over Wiley's accompaniment, confesses:

> *Oh, daughter, daughter, please don't be like me,*
> *Oh daughter, daughter, please don't be like me,*
> *Oh daughter, daughter, please don't be like me,*
> *To fall in love with every man you see.*

But Wiley's masterpiece is her "Last Kind Words Blues," a dolorous art song that evokes the spirit of the blues while departing markedly from its harmonies and structure. Images of great violence are juxtaposed with the tender expressions of love, showing that Wiley could be just as surprising in her lyrics as in her guitar work.

> *The last kind word I heard my daddy say,*
> *Lord, the last kind word I heard my daddy say,*
> *If I die, if I die in the German War,*
> *I want you to send my body, send it to my mother, Lord.*
> *If I get killed, if I get killed, please don't bury my soul,*
> *I say just leave me out, let the buzzards eat me whole . . .*

Wiley's recording of this song was featured prominently by Terry Zwigoff—a musician and collector of rare 78s, in addition to a filmmaker—in his documentary on artist Robert Crumb. Many who saw the film were struck by the emotional power of the song, and it is sobering to think that this placement in a low-budget indie film gave more exposure to Wiley's music than all the records she sold during (or after) her lifetime.

Wiley's situation is not atypical. Many blues musicians from this period are mostly forgotten today, not due to lack of talent, but simply because they did not record enough music to fill even a single compact disk. Kid Bailey's reputation, as we have seen, rests on two elegantly recorded blues, and a biography so sparse in detail that some doubt any artist of that name ever existed other than as a pseudonym. The Vocalion/Brunswick team who recorded the mysterious Bailey in Memphis a few days before the stock market Crash in 1929 undertook a number of sessions at the Peabody Hotel in that city around this same time—sessions that almost seem deliberately arranged to tantalize us with glimpses into promising talents who flash briefly into perspective, and then disappear, sometimes forever, from our view. Garfield Akers's reputation, for example, rests on only four recordings, yet he regaled the Peabody Hotel visitors with a hot, pulsating guitar sound on "Dough Roller Blues" and "Cottonfield Blues." Here chord fragments ricochet like bullets off the fretboard, serving as bits of harmonic shrapnel underscoring Akers's piercing vocal attack, a long lingering wail that contrasts pleasingly with the rapid-fire pulsations of his guitar. Joe Callicott, who accompanied Akers on record and continued to perform with him at suppers and frolics into the 1940s, notes that Akers had more songs available to record but producer J. Mayo Williams needed to move on to other musicians. Callicott tells us that Aker's guitar style was unique to the area surrounding Hernando, where the two musicians met and collaborated. But Callicott's own playing, resonant of an older ballad-singing tradition, does not bear out this influence. Callicott, for his part, was given permission by Williams to record two—and only two!—songs, "Fare Thee Well Blues" and "Traveling Mama Blues." We are fortunate that Callicott lived almost long enough to see his seventieth birthday, and was thus recorded again, and at a greater length, in the late 1960s. The same cannot be said for Mattie Delaney, who also recorded two songs at the Peabody Hotel before being dispatched into obscurity. Her pungent vocals convey an almost painful urgency, and bring a special intensity to "Tallahatchie River Blues," one of the best of the many Mississippi flood songs.

The Louisiana side of the Delta also served as birthplace or home to many talented blues musicians, but their life stories have been even more difficult to piece together. Blind Joe Reynolds had been discovered by H. C. Speir during a visit to a lumber camp near Lake Providence, Louisiana, in 1930, and the artist was dispatched to Grafton, Wisconsin, where he recorded four memorable sides for Paramount. No more was heard about Reynolds for almost forty years, until Gayle Wardlow followed the trail of clues back to the area around Monroe, Louisiana. In 1968, Wardlow found Reynolds's surviving family members here, but the guitarist had died only a short while before, unaware of the resurgent interest in prewar blues players that might have reignited his performing career. Wardlow learned that Reynolds's real name was Joe Sheppard, and the intrepid blues detective pulled together a fascinating mini-biography marked by crimes, incarcerations, loose living, and more than a little musicmaking. Wardlow also played the sleuth in identifying the mysterious King Solomon Hill, whose eerie falsetto-and-slide-guitar style was recorded by Paramount in 1932. Although most people had accepted that Hill was a pseudonym for Big Joe Williams, Wardlow convincingly identified the musician as Joe Holmes, a native Mississippian relocated to Sibley, Louisiana, where he died in 1949.

With other musicians, we have perhaps a dozen or fewer recorded performances, each roughly three minutes long, allowing us to gauge the musical talents of Freddie Spruell, Arthur Petties, Isaiah Nettles, Jim Thompkins, and Willie "Poor Boy" Lofton, among others. Yet here, too, the material is sometimes too scanty to make more than the most preliminary assessment of a musician's talent. Otto Virgial evokes a throbbing, hypnotic rhythm, in his few recorded performances, which scarcely establishes its sway over us before the song is over. Some see this jittery style as merely a sign of nervous energy, but if Virgial could sustain this momentum for nine or ten minutes, he might have an audience in a frenzy. We can safely assume that he is the Otto Vergial, age twelve, listed in the 1920 Lowndes County, Mississippi, Census, which would make him around twenty-seven when he recorded on Halloween 1935—still a young man, who could have easily survived for many more decades. As it stands, we are intrigued by his early—and brief— burst of creativity, and left waiting in vain for more.

We have four blues sides made by the mysterious Mississippi Bracey at the King Edward Hotel in Jackson, Mississippi, in December 1930, and we have good reason to believe that he is the same Caldwell Bracey who recorded four religious songs, accompanied by his wife, during that same session. But beyond that, we know almost nothing. Some have speculated that the King Edward Hotel recording artist is, in fact, Ishmon Bracey or perhaps a close relative, but Gayle Wardlow confirms that he asked Ishmon point-blank about the bluesman who shared his surname. Ishmon Bracey was aware of the musician, but claimed no kinship, although he did not rule out some distant connection. Unless more information comes to life about Caldwell Bracey, we will be left merely to admire his recordings, and wonder about his origins.

A few Mississippi musicians managed to record extensively, even into the Depression years. Bo Carter left behind over one hundred sides—which include both recordings under his own name, as well as with the Mississippi Sheiks—almost all of them waxed after the stock market crashed. As a member of the celebrated Chatmon family—he was born Armenter Chatmon, circa 1893 in Bolton, Mississippi—Bo may have been a half brother to Charley Patton. But despite this connection, and although the family moved to the Delta in 1928, his music is a world apart in tone and technique from Patton's. With its slick passing chords and dexterous execution, Carter's music displays a degree of sophistication rarely found among country blues players. His recordings sold well during the 1930s, yet they never curried much favor with later fans of early blues, for whom slickness is not a virtue, and popularity in the marketplace as much a cause for suspicion as celebration. Carter is best known today for his double entendres songs—"Banana in Your Fruit Basket" or "My Pencil Won't Write No More"—which once titillated record buyers, but have less impact today, when *single* entendre, of the most explicit sort, is the calling card of the music industry. Although he survived until the beginnings of the blues revival, Bo Carter did not benefit from the career turnarounds experienced by Son House, Skip James, and others. When researcher Paul Oliver tracked Carter down in 1960, he found the down-and-out bluesman living in an "unfurnished slum" in Memphis. Four years later, Carter died penniless at the age of seventy-one.

At the opposite extreme, we encounter Big Joe Williams, who also recorded prolifically, but without ever flagging in his allegiance to the most primitive stylistic elements of the country blues. And just as zealously as Williams stuck to the traditions of this music, he also retained the wandering, intemperate blues life until he was an old man—a walking, singing anachronism that brought the flavor of Depression-era Mississippi with him wherever he traveled. And travel he did, throughout Mississippi, into the rest of the South and the Midwest, finally covering the entire United States and heading overseas, seldom carrying little more than his guitar and his larger-than-life personality. Someday a novelist or filmmaker will create something marvelous and moving from this man's life story. Mike Bloomfield wrote a small book, *Me and Big Joe*, which focuses on a few wild days traveling with the bluesman, and it reads like a Kerouac-inspired tribute to life on the open road. But Bloomfield could hardly keep up with Big Joe for a short trip—so how can we do justice to his tumultuous career in a few paragraphs?

He was born Joe Lee Williams, the son of John Williams and Cora Lee—the first of her sixteen children—probably on October 16, 1903, although a nineteenth-century birthdate has sometimes been given for the guitarist. Williams did not hail from the Delta, coming instead from Crawford near the eastern border of Mississippi, some fifteen miles from Alabama. But Williams played extensively in the Delta during his formative years, and soaked up the guitar sounds of the region. The songs of Charley Patton,

Robert Johnson, and other Delta pioneers formed the lasting foundation of his repertoire during his long career, but he added to these many of his own that have become staples of the traditional blues repertoire, most notably the widely covered "Baby, Please Don't Go."

Williams's song is the classic lament of the lover who fears his woman will leave town; but Williams was the one who seldom stayed long in any locale. For a time he worked as a musician with the Rabbit Foot Minstrels, and was a habitué of levee camps, barrelhouses, brothels, and wherever else a blues singer could eke out a few dollars from his music. Unlike most other blues musicians, who maintained other jobs from time to time, Williams earned his living almost exclusively from his guitar. "He wanted to work *no* way," was "Honeyboy" Edwards's description of his former traveling companion, whom he anointed as "the laziest man you ever saw. . . . I don't think he'd work in a baker's shop if you gave him a cake every time the pan came out." But in his pursuit of opportunities to perform or record his music, Williams was relentless, and at times it almost seemed as if the guitarist possessed a sixth sense guiding him to any concert promoter or record producer who might be in need of a blues artist.

Williams's travels started sometime around 1918, when a stepfather sent him packing—an event he memorialized in his "Stepfather Blues":

> I have a mean stepfather, he done drove me away.
> When I was a little boy, Lord, my stepfather didn't allow me around.

"Lord, I'm a little boy, I'm crying all night long," Williams sang poignantly when he performed this song at the first recording session under his name in 1935. The music from this session, the first of two undertaken by Williams for the Bluebird label during that year, is exceptionally raw and invigorating. Williams relies on the simplest harmonic support, and the listener searches in vain for the clearly distinguished tonic, dominant, and subdominant structures that supposedly define the blues form. For Williams, a single, jangly chord, with only the most modest variations—more a sound than a proper harmony—serves for virtually all his needs. But what Williams lacks in subtlety, he makes up for with intensity, and his meager chord is played with the vehemence of Wagner introducing his Valkyries. Williams's guitar is equally frugal in its melodic contributions: when not providing harmonic support on these early sides, it flings out isolated notes that act less as fills than as rhythmic interjections to whip the song into shape. Given the paucity of his technical resources, Williams's "Providence Help the Poor People" is hardly a song by any definition, more a soapbox exhortation spurred on by periodic jabs from Williams's guitar. But it is overwhelming in its intensity. Other sides from this Chicago session, such as "Highway 49 Blues" and "Somebody's Been Borrowing That Stuff," would be re-recorded by Williams in more refined versions later in his career. But he would never surpass the unbridled passion of these debut versions.

In 1937, Williams returned to the studio, joined this time by guitarist Robert Lee McCoy, and harmonica wizard John Lee "Sonny Boy" Williamson—who is sometimes referred to by blues fans as Sonny Boy Williamson #1, or "the first," in the manner of royalty, to distinguish him from Aleck "Rice" Miller, who also adopted (some would say usurped) the name. Williamson was a sympathetic accompanist to Big Joe, his voice-like sounds on the harmonica providing a melodic counterfoil to Williams's craggy voice. Their successful collaboration anticipates the later incomparable combination of Muddy Waters and Little Walter, and reveals the fundamental affinity between the Delta guitar style and this humble instrument, sometimes referred to as the "Mississippi saxophone." Their 1947 recordings for Columbia, undertaken less than a year before Sonny Boy Williamson's death from stabbing at the age of thirty-four, the apparent victim of a robbery, rank among their finest moments in the studio. On "Stack of Dollars," Williamson shadows Williams's vocal, phrase by phrase, before launching into his solo with a glorious arching high note that soars majestically over the proceedings for half a chorus, then swooping down in hot and dirty jabs with a minor third—an attack that draws Williams's voice, now hoarse and breaking, back into the fray. Traditional blues had few fans at this time, when the musical style struck many as old-fashioned, but bracing performances such as this classic pairing were anything but quaint antiquarian exercises, and announced to anyone who cared to listen that down home music still had a powerful kick to it.

Despite his reputation as a die-hard traditionalist, Big Joe Williams retained a curiosity for novelty and experimentation. He came to prefer a quirky, homemade nine-string guitar as his instrument of choice. But Williams hardly had need of the extra three strings, given the starkness of his approach, and his playing changed little for their addition. He was one of the first traditional bluesmen to use amplification—like the extra strings on his guitar, this was perhaps driven less by musical considerations than by a need to give a boost to his instrument to match the power of his voice. But the changes in Big Joe's arsenal were less noteworthy than the constants, and his playing seemed immune to the passing fads and fashions of the music industry. Even so, his performances sometimes revealed surprising facets: a recording of "She Left Me a Mule," made for the Trumpet label in Jackson during the fall of 1951, sounds like full-fledged rock and roll. Only the lyrics, which describe the death of a mule—a disaster for a sharecropper, but of no concern to a sock hopper—show a mismatch with the new sound that would soon dominate America's airwaves.

Williams never really settled down. For a time, he called St. Louis his home, and later Chicago. But his "residence" in the latter city was often little more than the basement of a record store, and even this home base was frequently abandoned when Big Joe felt the call of the open road. Yet while other traditional blues players languished, Williams always managed to find a recording contract; unlike most of the other musicians dealt with in these pages, Williams never experienced a gap in his discography of more than a few years' duration. By the time of his death in 1982, he had recorded dozens of LPs, and had seen his music released on almost as many labels. Sometimes these merely covered the same musical ground he had traveled in the past, but they never lacked for passion and authenticity.

Despite the prodigious output of Bo Carter or Big Joe Williams, we need to recall that these are rare exceptions. Few Mississippi blues artists could interest a label in recording their works during the 1930s. Prospects were so bleak, many even gave up trying. We blame the record labels for their lack of insight in not preserving more of this music during the decade, but perhaps we should bless them for the riches they preserved, given the circumstances under which they operated. "We only know how good you are by your sales figures," was J. Mayo Williams's candid assessment of the gold standard for blues music—an attitude that perhaps explains his unwillingness to record more material by talented yet commercially unproven artists such as Bailey, Akers, Delaney, and others. Yet the sad truth is that the Great Depression, not the fickleness of the record producers, served as the overwhelming, insurmountable force that signaled the end of the boom in traditional blues recordings of the late 1920s. No record producer, however sympathetic or perceptive, could have stemmed this tide. Still, the Delta music itself had not spent its life force, far from it. When the collapse came, the music remained in a state of creative ferment, and seemed on the verge of a veritable golden age. The greatest generation of Delta blues musicians were in the prime of their lives and playing at the peak of their abilities. But

Son House, Willie Brown, Geeshie Wiley, Kid Bailey, and many others had the misfortune to make their debut recordings within a few months of the 1929 Crash, and their careers, which under other circumstances might have built momentum, fell as precipitously as the blue chips on Wall Street.

In fact, demand for 78s dropped even more sharply than the stock market during the period. Between 1927 and 1932, record sales in the country fell from 104 million to 6 million units—a collapse of 94 percent from peak to trough, compared with the 89 percent decline in the Dow. But even this staggering measure understates the impact on the demand for recorded blues, since the share of race records in the market fell from around 5 percent to 1 percent during this same period. The whole U.S. market for race records, which amounted to several million copies per year in the late 1920s, eventually bottomed out at an annual rate of less than 100,000 units in the early 1930s. This was not a declining market so much as a disappearing one. For not only did the economic collapse sharply curtail demand for music, the rise of the radio industry put a lower cost alternative into millions of American households, just as the emergence of talking movies represented one more competitor for the few dollars now spent on entertainment by the average American family. And, as a final blow, the end of Prohibition in 1933 gave a tremendous boost to nightclubs and bars as purveyors of live music, and these superior alternatives to the inferior sound of the phonograph further crowded out the market for recordings.

As fast as the record companies cut back the supply of blues records, demand fell even more sharply, requiring further retrenchment. In 1927, Columbia pressed 11,000 copies of each new blues and gospel release, but this was reduced to 5,000 by the end of 1929, and to 2,000 by May 1930. By the close of 1930, the company manufactured only 1,000 copies of their new releases. By the fall of 1932, this already paltry figure had fallen further, to between 350 and 400 copies—and even these failed to sell out. Columbia still had all these releases in their catalog two years later, suggesting that total demand in the United States for many race artists amounted to a little more than a dozen or so copies per month! The implication—as hard as it is to believe—is that a blues musician could reach a larger audience by playing in an obscure juke joint in the Delta than by recording for a major national label.

In this unpromising environment, a young man walked into H. C. Speir's store on North Farish Street in Jackson one day in early 1931, boasting of his musical talents and asking for an audition to make a record. Nehemiah

James, known then to some of his Jackson friends as "Skippy," had earned his way in the world in many diverse undertakings: bootlegging, pimping, gambling, logging, working in levee camps, sharecropping, or, as a last resort, even picking cotton as a day laborer. But now James had set his sights on the musician's life, and hoped that his skills as a guitarist, or perhaps as a pianist—he had developed a quirky, personal style on both instruments— would provide him with an escape from menial pursuits. Yet times were tough, and Speir was often difficult to impress even in a more forgiving marketplace. On the day James auditioned, his companion Johnnie Temple, a musician of considerable talent who would establish himself as a successful recording artist with Decca in the late 1930s, was peremptorily dismissed by the talent scout. When James's turn came, another musician in his place might have tried to dazzle Speir with a jaunty commercial number, a fast dance piece or some flashy guitar work. Instead, James began plucking the doleful introduction to one of the slowest songs in his repertoire, his moody blues ballad "Devil Got My Woman."

Opening instrumental passages of this sort were unusual enough in the Delta blues, where most players just jumped into the first chorus, but James drew out his introduction with the stately reserve of a curator unfolding some rare papyrus, willing to display its mystical symbols, but only at the proper moment. Finally, James's voice entered, sounding high and eerie above the guitar strings: "I'd rather be the devil than to be that woman's man." Speir was by now familiar with the peculiarities of the blues music played up and down the Delta, with its odd language of torment and elusive redemption, so out of character with the pop songs found anywhere else in the world. But even by these standards, the music of this auditioning guitarist must have stood out as especially melancholy and haunted.

I laid down last night, tried to take my rest.
My mind got to ramblin', like wild geese from the west, from the west . . .

The storeowner quickly sensed that he had discovered a musician of rare talent—James later boasted that he passed the audition by the time he finished his second verse. Almost immediately, Speir contacted his closest ally in the recording industry, Arthur Laibly at Paramount, and together they arranged for a session in Grafton, Wisconsin, for the artist whom the talent broker rechristened, either in ignorance or as one more snap decision in a career of such moves, as "Skip" James.

3. can't find no heaven

Time and time again, as we pursue the history of the music, we are struck
not just by the power of the blues, but by its malleability. Only the crudest
of musical tools were available to the Delta pioneers: a simple six-string
instrument; a paltry assortment of harmonies, even fewer than the monks
had at their disposal in the fourteenth century; a compositional structure
based on repetition, with no scope for modulations or countermelodies or
sophisticated thematic development; and, added to all this, the complete
absence of formal training, where even the basics—tuning the guitar properly, or just owning a decent instrument—could hardly be taken for granted.
Yet despite these limitations, the blues pioneers charted musical territories
never navigated—no, not even dreamed of—by the symphonists. Like
painters whose magical palettes conveyed hitherto unknown shades of the
spectrum, these humble musicians of a despised race and class offered their
contemporaries a vivid world of new tone colors, vibrant with a clash and
clang, a howl and wail, that seemed precisely the soundscape demanded by
the modern American scene, with its surface social cacophony and deeper
anomie, its stark contrasts and newfound zeal for self-reflection.

The lyrics of the blues songs only accentuated this piquant, modern
mind-set. Psychology was the discipline of the day, a science of introspec-
tion most suitable for this nation on the cusp of adulthood: Harvard professor William James had published his grand two-volume study, *The
Principles of Psychology* (1890), almost at the same time that the Delta was
creating its own psychological primers in twelve-bar form, and it is hard to
say which of the two probed more deeply. Certainly the Delta blues, with
its novel language of fall and redemption rewritten in secular terms, with
its transformation of sociological ills into the personal dimension of individual hopes and longings, was new ground not only for popular music
but for the American sensibility. As such, the blues, this idiom of an outcast
minority, somehow would become—at first falteringly, then with greater
and greater confidence—the catalyst that would help reconfigure the musical self-identity of the whole.

We can trace the steps by which the blues tested its powers. First we find the
folk musicians, their names largely unknown to us, who initially employed
the distinctive aural legacy of their African forebears in reconfiguring the
language of Western song. Then came the entertainers, such as the Delta's
Charley Patton, or Blind Lemon Jefferson in Texas, who demonstrated the

commercial appeal of traditional blues music, its potential to reach beyond the plantations and street corners of its origins, and enter into parlors and dance halls, its ability to compete in the marketplace with other professional styles of performance, and capture its share of the American audience. For many folk arts, this alone would have been a great achievement. But Son House, the failed preacher who brought his fire-and-brimstone to the pulpit of the blues, showed that this music could journey beyond the limitations of popular song, tapping into powerful currents of soul-weariness and transcendence that no tunesmith had hitherto broached. Given these precedents, the stage was set for that unique poet and visionary who would take the next step, and channel the energies and potentialities of the blues into true art song, holding on to the vitality that had engaged the listeners of Patton and Jefferson, but refining this rough ore into a more subtle and delicate form of musical expression.

Skip James was this poet. Both his unusual temperament and his native abilities prepared him admirably to fill this role. Like the visionaries of many traditional cultures, James claimed that his songs came to him in dreams. And the exquisite peculiarity of his music, its haunting, unworldly ambience, might well convince a listener that these blues dirges arrived from no conventional source. Peter Guralnick has described how fans speculated that only a rare, custom-built guitar could produce such "hollow, doomy tones." Others sought for a musical explanation, hypothesizing on some unique meeting of Western and Eastern modalities, which allowed James to put his original stamp on the music.

The truth was less esoteric. James built his distinctive sound from a series of individual choices, each one setting him apart from his peers. He preferred an alternative scheme for tuning his guitar—open E minor tuning, an unusual but not unknown approach in which the six strings are set to E–B–E–G–B–E. He adopted a technique for plucking the strings with his nails, rather than the fleshy part of his fingertips, which imparted a tart, incisive quality to his music. And he employed his middle finger in plucking, in addition to the thumb and index finger, in contrast to many other traditional blues guitarists who relied almost entirely on the latter two digits. Yet, above all, James's voice established the singularity of his vision, his range much wider than one heard in traditional blues, his eerie falsetto soaring above the spare guitar notes. If ever the blues had its own siren song, alluring and hypnotic, it was here with Skip James, the most distinctive vocalist the idiom has yet produced. His mournful, epicene wail, with its distinctive

timbres, evoking an incongruous mixture of feminine and masculine qualities, had little in common with the rough-and-tumble delivery so typical of
James's contemporaries.

"Skip was a born musician, a natural born musician," Johnny Temple
would declare. Yet James, more than any of his peers, disdained using his
talents to entertain, and was inclined to look down upon, if not actually
despise, his audience. For a time he took on music students, but had equal
scorn for his pupils, whom he denounced as thickheaded—James claimed
he was happy when they stopped their lessons, because he didn't really care
to show them anything worth knowing. In his own musical education, he
remained equally apathetic. Unlike Robert Johnson or Charley Patton,
James rarely studied blues recordings, and was hardly more receptive to the
guitarists he met in person. In the world of the blues, famous for its musical
borrowing and lending on easy terms, James was the odd man out: he didn't
want to share what he did, and hardly deigned to imitate what others played.
Nor was making money from his music a strong motivator for James—he
earned far more from bootlegging. "You can't put a price on a song," was his
rejoinder to those who calculated the value of their talents in dollars and
cents. Convinced of his own genius, James sought above all to create a body
of work that would stand head and shoulders above the efforts of his rivals.
And this attitude, an overweening pride coupled with his marked talent,
led him to construct a new sound for the blues, not just a form of personal
expression for the man, but an important step forward for the music.

Born as Nehemiah Curtis James on June 21, 1902, the youngster grew
up on the Woodbine Plantation a mile and a half outside of Bentonia, a
small community located sixteen miles south of Yazoo City on the road to
Jackson. James was an only child, whose mother, Phyllis James, worked in
the household of the plantation owner, earning him some added status in a
community of farm laborers. But Skip was more in the mold of his father,
Edward James, a bootlegger and guitarist who left the area around 1907.
James had only the vaguest childhood recollections of his father, and could
not remember hearing him play guitar. But he felt that his own musical talents had been inherited from his father, and he admired—and would come
to emulate—the elder James's ability to raise himself above the lot of the
common worker, give himself a high school education, and earn a degree of
independence in a hostile world.

Skip James was raised primarily by his maternal grandparents, but moved
with his mother to Sidon in the Delta when he was twelve years old. Here

Phyllis James met up again with the boy's father, but the family reunion proved to be short-lived. "He gave me a few lashes with his belt, and then mother and him had a tie-up about that," James later recalled. "I didn't see him after that." Years later, when James had just made his Paramount recordings, he would encounter his father again, and find that the wayward husband had become Reverend E. D. James, a Baptist preacher who operated a seminary in Texas.

The younger James would eventually find himself drawn to the religious life as well, and in his thirties he considered a career in the ministry. But no sudden conversion or moment of revelation would spur this transformation. Rather, the various life changes of Skip James all followed a consistent pattern, each new vocation drawing inspiration from his unwavering desire for a sense of independence and superiority, a craving for intensity of experience, and a commitment to self-expression and earnest admonishment. Years later, James's biographer Stephen Calt would find that it was almost impossible to conduct a conventional interview with the bluesman—it was far more productive simply to sit back and let the man discourse. Both the pulpit and the guitar offered a channel for James's predilections, and the move from one to another was a natural one for him—and common enough among Delta residents, despite the popular prejudice that saw the two paths as sharply opposed.

In his youth, Skip James showed few signs of sanctification, or any higher calling. He ran away from home in his early teens, and traveled to Florida and Georgia, returning even more willful and independent. He carried a switchblade and a gun, and prided himself on knowing how to handle both, much as he bragged of his growing skill on the guitar and piano. In his own words, he was a "mean bastard." Yet James also had access to opportunities enjoyed by few of his peers. He attended high school at a time when half of the black population of Mississippi was illiterate. He owned a pony, a gift from his grandmother. And he was never sent into the fields to pick cotton, at a time when this was all but inescapable for a young black man seeking employment.

Despite his tough demeanor, James learned how sheltered his upbringing had been when he joined a road construction camp near the Delta community of Ruleville around 1919. The violence and obscenity of his colleagues dismayed him. Decades later, this subject was the only one he tended to avoid in his discussions with Calt. He felt that it would be best for younger people not to know about the low and base ways of such characters. Given

James's candor in discussing other matters—he frankly admitted to shooting, perhaps fatally, a mule driver after a heated argument around this same time—his reticence in this regard is striking. James stayed only briefly with the road construction group, before leaving to work as a dynamite blaster in the area around Drew and Doddsville.

This region was a hotbed of blues activity, circa 1920, and James's confidence in his musical skills developed apace during this period. Soon he was earning spare money on Saturdays, playing in front of country stores in Delta communities, and began composing his own music. He continued to work as a laborer—moving from sawmill to lumber camp to levee camp—but James eventually learned that he could make easier money from less exhausting activities, not just music, but also hustling, card-sharking, and bootlegging. He returned to Bentonia in 1924, ostensibly to work on a plantation, but the profits from selling corn whiskey were the real attraction that kept James on the farm. Bootlegging could bring in sixty or seventy dollars per week, far more than a sharecropper—or even a successful musician—might hope to earn. When he organized house frolics, James would draw an audience with his music, but made more money from the liquor he sold.

Around this time, he married Oscella Robinson, the daughter of a clergyman, an educated young woman from a respectable family. The pair moved to Texas, where James worked in Whistling Joe's Kazoo Band, but his wife soon deserted the guitarist in favor of a World War I veteran who captured her affections. James was distraught, wavered between thoughts of suicide and plans for violent revenge, but ultimately returned to Bentonia, while his ex-wife and her lover remained in Texas. James would not marry again for twenty years, and always remained distrustful of women. But his brief marriage and its attendant heartbreak left its lasting mark in the somber strains of his song, "Devil Got My Woman," which would so impress H. C. Speir at James's audition in Jackson.

Later in life, James avoided discussions of the musicians who had influenced him and the ways in which he had developed his distinctive style. He preferred to convey the impression that his music sprang from his own unfathomable sources of inspiration. "I don't pattern after anyone or either copycat," he told Bruce Jackson shortly after his rediscovery by blues fans in 1964. "It's just Skip's music. . . . I don't sing other people's voice. I can't." To another fan, he bragged: "Skip taught hisself. . . . I'm a self-made man. Everything you hear me sing, it's my own arrangement, my personal experience. That is it up till this day." Yet James clearly benefited from the musical ferment of Mississippi during the mid-1920s, and his own playing grew in maturity as he listened, learned, and borrowed techniques from the other blues players he encountered. Henry Stuckey, who sometimes accompanied James on guitar, showed him the open E minor tuning—which James called "cross-tuning"—a trademark of his compositional and playing style. Stuckey had picked it up while a soldier in France from some black soldiers he believed were from the Bahamas, and when he returned to the States he shared it with other guitarists he met. James's aspirations as a pianist—he had studied the instrument briefly as a youngster—had been fueled during his time as a sawmill worker, when he learned enough from pianist Will Crabtree to sit in at the keyboard during the latter's breaks. But his encounter with Little Brother Montgomery in 1927 gave further impetus to these ambitions. He boasted to Montgomery: "If you stay where you are, I'm gonna catch up to you."

Montgomery, who hailed from Kentwood, Louisiana, located across Lake Pontchartrain from New Orleans, would later become a fixture on the Chicago blues scene, but even in the 1920s he had crafted a rough-hewn piano sound of impressive lineage. Blues, boogie, ragtime, jazz, gospel, whatever he could pick up in a barrelhouse, a lumber camp, a dance hall, even a church: all this became another musical color in the kaleidoscopic keyboard work of this well-traveled pianist. His signature piece, "Vicksburg Blues," was likely to appeal to Skip James, since here Montgomery had accomplished the rare feat of evoking much of the loose, unfettered sound of the Delta blues guitar in a piano piece. Where others would pound out four or eight beats to the bar, Montgomery let the rhythm flow at its own organic pace. James's own mature music would follow a similar muse—his piano full of sudden silences, alternating with declamatory outbursts of chords. Not until Thelonious Monk arrived on the jazz scene after World War II would a pianist do more with rests and hesitations, and listening to James's keyboard music, one is reminded of Monk's supposed admonition that it is not the notes you play, rather the ones you leave out, that are the most important.

In 1927, James was approached by a scout working for the OKeh label, and offered a chance to record. The session, although scheduled, never took place, yet the reasons for its cancellation remain unclear. James was certainly unhappy with the money offered. Unlike most of his peers, James haggled over terms, and almost walked away from his dramatic comeback in the 1960s due to his reservations about contracts. The fifteen or twenty dollars per side offered by OKeh in 1927 were less than he could make bootlegging on a weekend. But James may also have felt that he was not yet ready as a musician to make recordings at this time. He was somewhat candid about his limitations as a pianist, as his comment to Montgomery about "catching up" indicates, but he may also have had doubts about his guitar work. Further, Henry Stuckey recalled, when interviewed in 1965, an illness may have prevented James from making the session. James, for his part, confirms that he was hospitalized for the influenza around this time. Whatever its cause, this missed opportunity is much to be lamented. Had James started his recording career in 1927—some two years before Charley Patton's first visit to the studio—he might have had the chance to complete several sessions before the economic collapse forced the labels to cut back sharply, and often curtail completely, their release schedules.

Whatever doubts James may have had about his skills in 1927, he had risen above them by the close of the decade. He set up as a music teacher in Jackson, and dispensed lessons on guitar, piano, and even violin. But not just raw beginners, even musicians of genuine merit were now falling into James's orbit, drawn by his artistic vision and musicianship; perhaps also by his imperious personality. Johnnie Temple, a later staple on the Chicago blues scene, became a protégé of sorts, helping James with his music school and learning his songs. Ishmon Bracey, who saw James perform around this time, marveled that his fingers moved like lightning on the fretboard. The degree of James's fame at this period was perhaps modest—recall that he had to solicit Speir's attention, despite James's frequent activity in the Jackson area where the talent broker worked and lived—but he nonetheless came to fear that other musicians were trying to steal his ideas. He developed a series of feints and ploys to discourage these pilferers, adopting new arrangements of his pieces, accelerating the tempo, taking whatever steps necessary to protect his trade secrets. But these hardly stopped the borrowings. Jack Owens, a Bentonia native like James, learned enough from James to inspire later talk of a "Bentonia tradition," which possibly encompassed local blues musicians who never recorded, such as Rich Griffith and the Stuckey brothers, Henry and Shuke. Temple and others would later record James's songs, and sell more copies than James had himself. But the most inspired student of James's oeuvre would be Robert Johnson—who may have learned these songs on record, or perhaps through Temple, when their paths crossed in 1931. As we shall see in the next chapter, Johnson would turn to James's music for inspiration in his darkest (and arguably his most creative) moments.

James was almost thirty years old before he made his first recordings. But sometimes the most distinctive stylists are the musicians who do not record until the first flush of youth has passed. The prodigy captivates our imagination, but the annals of African-American music are full of examples of late starters, who give us all the benefit of their extra years of maturing: Duke Ellington waited until he was twenty-four to make a record; Robert Johnson didn't enter a studio until the age of twenty-five; Lester Young participated on his first session at twenty-seven; Chuck Berry did the same at age thirty; and Leadbelly was a middle-aged man, forty-five years old, before he made a recording. Skip James, for his part, was more than ready to embark on this new stage of his career when he arrived in Grafton in February 1931 for his studio debut. Before dropping James off at the hotel where he would rest before his afternoon session, Arthur Laibly of Paramount asked him how many songs he was prepared to record. The bluesman haughtily replied: "As many as you want." Nor did he disappoint when the session began. Eighteen different songs would eventually be released from this Wisconsin visit, featuring James on both guitar and piano. And if James can be believed, he recorded twenty-six sides for Paramount before the proceedings drew to a close.

Given James's reputation as a singer of foreboding, angst-ridden songs, it is somewhat surprising that his composition "I'm So Glad" would earn him the most money of any of his efforts for Paramount. Thirty-five years after James recorded this song, the rock group Cream would feature their own fiery version of it on their December 1966 album *Fresh Cream*. Eric Clapton, the twenty-one-year-old guitarist who had already earned a reputation for his virtuosity on the fretboard, would do more than any other musician to introduce younger fans to traditional blues songs. And unlike many other rockers who appropriate the work of aging blues artists, Clapton freely gave composer credits to James—who, ironically, may have borrowed the song from an older pop tune known as "So Tired" or "I'm Tired." As a result, the young rock star's choice of James's uncharacteristic ode to joy, which Cream reconfigured into a driving, euphoric jam song, would earn the bluesman somewhere between six thousand and ten thousand dollars at a time when he was financially strapped. James's 1931 version, in contrast, has an aura of feverish unreality about it, celebrating a joy that seems as unsustainable as the song's accelerating tempo, which crests at close to 270 beats per minute. The lyrics and form are simple to an extreme, the force of the songs coming from repetition and the sheer vehemence of the refrain:

I'm so glad, and I am glad.
I am glad, I am glad.

James sings like a man possessed, but the bliss he celebrates has the uneasy tone of a bipolar up cycle that will soon come crashing down into the depths of despair.

The Paramount executives, for their part, preferred the darker side of James's musical personality. The label released ten other James performances before issuing "I'm So Glad" in the fall of 1931, backed by "Special Rider Blues." Arthur Laibly was more drawn to the song James had written about the economic collapse that was devastating the country—and would cost Laibly his own job a few months later. The blues idiom by its very nature was well suited for "testifyin'" to the devastation wrought by acts of God, or even the lesser tribulations wrought by man himself. And just as Charley Patton had found inspiration in the flood and boll weevil, and Son House had cursed the drought in his "Dry Spell Blues," Skip James created a blues masterpiece from the ravages of the Great Depression in his "Hard Time Killin' Floor Blues."

Hard time here and everywhere you go.
Times is harder than ever been before.

This bleak song might easily have served as the anthem for the new decade. At a time when many believed that prosperity was "just around the corner"—as President Hoover would confidently announce the following year—James proclaims that "these hard times can last us so very long." James's imagery is powerful: his struggle to get off the "killin' floor," with its evocation of the slaughterhouse; his descriptions of people who "can't find heaven" as they drift from door to door, seeking work or shelter. He departs from the standard blues structure, but retains its emotional quality in the compactness and repetition of his eight-bar form. With each stanza, a lyric of four bars is followed by a wordless vocal, a cross between a whimper and a moan, of equal duration.

Paramount selected this performance as its first release from James's session. Laibly perhaps felt that the topical nature of the song would appeal to record buyers. If so, he was sadly mistaken. The record sold poorly, even when measured by the diminished expectations of the period. True, the market was receptive to songs about the economy, but preferred more upbeat lyrics. Rudy Vallee scored a hit in 1931 with his "Life Is Just a Bowl of Cherries," and other titles from the year include "We Can Live on Love" and "There's No Depression in Love." People looked to music for escape, not a reminder of their malaise. "Hard Time Killin' Floor" would eventually be acknowledged as one of James's most powerful works, but not until three decades had passed after its debut.

The label responded by issuing two of James's piano pieces—"22-20 Blues," backed by "If You Haven't Any Hay Get On Down the Road." Both are important milestones in the evolution of American piano music. Aaron Copland had performed the premier of his landmark "Piano Variations" only a few weeks before James recorded these pieces, and the development of the serious composer's eleven-bar theme and the bluesman's twelve- and sixteen-bar excursions show a similar desire to purge the keyboard of the romanticism inherited from the Old World, to craft a harder-edged, more trenchant style, streamlined for the modern sensibility. "If You Haven't Any Hay Get On Down the Road" is rarely mentioned when James's music is discussed, and Paramount felt it deserved B side status; but it contains the most flowing piano work James ever recorded, the interaction between the vocal and instrumental parts perfectly realized. "22-20 Blues" features an even sparser accompaniment, with James's stomping foot almost as prominent as the piano notes. And though the music is rough and unforgiving, the lyrics are even more so:

> If I send for my baby and she don't come,
> All the doctors in Wisconsin, they won't help her none.

Like many blues songs, this one is about a woman, but James murmurs words of affection here solely to his firearm. He brags about the superiority of his 22-20, and disses the guns of all rivals. As for his woman, he threatens to take his weapon and "cut her half in two."

The irony here is that there is no 22-20 gun. James claims that the song was written at the session, with only three minutes preparation, in response to Laibly's request for a number like Roosevelt Sykes's "44 Blues." Calt sees this as unlikely: Sykes's song was neither current nor a big seller, and hence it would never occur to a commercial record producer to emulate it. James probably arrived at the studio wanting to record a cover version of "44 Blues," but was discouraged by Laibly, who asked him to come up with something original instead. Certainly the slapdash quality of the song is evident—the caliber of the gun changes during the course of the performance—but the rawness of the music is also one of its virtues. James defies the predictable, riff-based grooves that define so much of blues piano from the period, and instead offers us a fresh perspective on the keyboard, unsettling and unfamiliar, but also full of life force. Few later musicians followed up on this musical vision, but I suspect that even today a pianist could construct a new, devastating style by building on the implications of James's 1931 work. Of course, the lesson was not entirely lost on the guitarists: Robert Johnson built his own tough-love primer, "32-20 Blues," from James's model, and gun songs, of various calibers, would long remain in the arsenal of blues musicians.

The Paramount executives must have held great hopes for James, given their willingness to record so much material, and their determination in issuing nine 78s under his name, during a period when the label's activities were being sharply retrenched. Yet Paramount was hardly in a position to promote the career of any musician at this point. H. C. Speir later recalled trying to order four hundred Skip James records for his Jackson store, only to learn that the company didn't have enough copies in inventory, and would not press additional ones. Yet, even after Arthur Laibly was fired, in the spring or summer of 1931, the company continued to back its new discovery, and a Paramount representative—probably Laibly's successor Henry Stephany—traveled to Bentonia to discuss a follow-up session with James. James signed a contract, and even began planning to record with his frequent duet partner of the period, his teenage cousin Willie Mae Polk. But Polk's mother—James's Aunt Martha—vetoed the plan, and the session never materialized.

As it turned out, James would not make another record until he was an old man. Yet he owns his share of responsibility for this lengthy hiatus in his musical career. H. C. Speir told Gayle Wardlow of an aborted session in Memphis, when James refused to sing blues material because he "got religion," and instead only wanted to perform gospel music. The date of this incident is unclear. Calt places it in late 1931 or early 1932, while Wardlow believes it may have occurred in conjunction with the 1935 sessions Speir conducted in Jackson, and suggests that the cities became confused in the talent scout's mind. In any event, James was a changed man when this opportunity came his way.

James's reunion with his father, the Reverend E. D. James, in late 1931 signaled the beginning of a new phase of his life, and a retreat from the world of bootlegging and blues playing. His subsequent decision to participate in his father's ministry in Plano, Texas, completed the rupture with his previous fast-and-loose ways. Blues fans are inclined to lament these religious conversions, so common among the Delta players—perhaps not surprisingly, given how much the lyrics reflect tormented soul-searching—as unfortunate moratoriums in the careers of many prized performers. Yet many a Delta bluesman benefited from the salutary influence of religion, not counting on the compensations in the afterlife (which this book makes no pretense at measuring), but even in their immediate circumstances. James, like Son House and so many others, relied on religious fervor to counter, to some degree, cravings for alcohol and other sundry vices that might otherwise have led to an early grave. It is perhaps no coincidence that the Delta musicians who embraced the religious life tended to live longer than those, such as Robert Johnson, Tommy Johnson, and Charley Patton (to name only the most prominent), who remained firmly committed to the blues lifestyle, with all its attendant risk factors. James's conversion was less a matter of born again—in fact, he had no sudden experience of spiritual rebirth—as "dry again," and his occasional lapses were driven more by the desire for hard liquor than by any of the world's many other temptations.

James never became a full minister. He had many of the requisite skills: self-confidence, intelligence, a flair for self-expression, as well as a dose of worldly ambition, which is not without its place even in the pulpit. But he lacked the theatricality and larger-than-life personality that had assisted his father's ministerial career. Indeed, James failed as a preacher for the same reason his blues records failed to sell well during the Great Depression: he was perhaps too deep, too introspective, too likely to remind his audience of all the problems they wanted to escape, too hard-edged to offer an easy path for transcendence. Skip James was, after all, the bluesman who sang, in his composition about these "hard times," and insisted that the people "driftin' from door to door / Can't find no heaven, I don't care where they go." This attitude hardly made for a successful song, and was bound to fall flat as the subject for a homily.

Yet James found a way to apply his distinctive talents to his new circumstances. He played music in the church, sang in the choir, and eventually became lead singer and pianist for the Dallas Jubilee Quartet, booked by the church's deacons throughout the region, and as far north as Kansas City. James also earned money as a piano tuner and technician. But he never found a means of self-expression in religious music that would approach the pathos and intensity of his blues. Around this same time, another former blues performer, Thomas Dorsey—who had recorded bawdy secular music under the name "Georgia Tom"—exerted enormous influence on the sacred singing of the day. Dorsey is credited as the father of gospel music, and left behind a tremendous legacy, some several hundred songs testifying to his new calling. James was a more inspired blues musician than Dorsey, and one of the most original composers in the history of African-American music; yet he had virtually no lasting impact as a performer or writer of religious music.

In fact, James would hardly find a real calling, religious or secular, until he was rediscovered as a blues singer in the 1960s. He drove a tractor, or worked in the mine industry, or farmed a piece of land, or cut timber, or ran a delivery truck, or sold whiskey from his home still. Sometimes he even played the blues again, earning a few dollars, seldom more. He moved frequently, reuniting with his father for a time in Alabama, returning to his native Bentonia, or trying to reignite his music career in Tennessee. His greatest source of stability during this period was his second wife, Mabel James, whom he met while working in Birmingham in the early 1940s.

But unbeknownst to James, a small but devoted cult following was emerging amongst blues fans, who greatly prized his 1931 work for Paramount. In 1935, his "If You Haven't Any Hay" was reissued by the Champion label, and over the next several years, several other blues artists, most notably Robert Johnson, borrowed heavily from James in crafting their own recordings. In 1944, John Steiner and Hugh Davis reissued James's "Little Cow and Calf Is Gonna Die Blues" on their specialist label Fine Jazz Documents—a milestone that some credit as initiating the then novel practice of re-releasing old country blues recordings for the benefit primarily of white record collectors. Each of these steps individually had little impact on James's reputation at the time; but cumulatively they set the stage for an even more intense interest in his music during the 1950s and early 1960s—a time when Skip James captivated devoted blues listeners as a quasi-mythical figure from the past who, as far as they could tell, had disappeared from the face of the earth, leaving behind a handful of exquisitely anguished songs.

Robert Johnson

chapter six

hellhound on my trail

1. biography of a phantom

For seventy years now, devotees have followed the elusive trail of Robert Johnson. At times the pursuit has taken on the aura of a vision quest, a chimerical attempt to come to grips with a figure more legendary than real. In this version, Robert Johnson emerges as a larger-than-life folk hero, but one who happened to leave behind a stack of 78s before being apotheosized alongside Pecos Bill, John Henry, and Paul Bunyan as a colorful piece of Americana. At other moments, the chase has adopted the hard-boiled edge of a detective story, with clues painstakingly gathered, evidence scrutinized and debated, witnesses tracked down and forced to testify. At the climactic moment, a real murder mystery is presented in this version of the story, with an enigmatic culprit—the supposed killer of Robert Johnson—identified, but known only to a single ardent researcher-detective, who has taken a vow of secrecy, unwilling to unravel the tangled threads of his tale until the final chapter, yet to be written.

But there is yet another perspective on the biography of Robert Johnson, one that takes on the aura of a religious parable: it is the story of a young man who sells his soul to the devil in exchange for an unparalleled ability to play the blues guitar. He enjoys stunning success as a result, at least as a performer, but his soul is beset by an irrepressible melancholy that permeates his music.

This edifying version of Johnson's story has two contradictory endings: in one, the haunted man wails in misery as he is dragged off to the underworld, like the final scene of *Don Giovanni* come to life in Depression-era Mississippi. The second ending, more suitable for the made-for-TV movie, depicts the stricken bluesman experiencing a deathbed conversion, a renunciation of dark ways, and a moment of final peace before departing the scene.

So many angles, on so short a life. And with so few hard facts to get in the way of whatever lesson one wants to extract, almost anything can be sought and found in the tale of Robert Johnson. Biographers should always be so blessed! But they have added a further layer of intrigue to the tale, replicating in their own endeavors the mysterious and enigmatic qualities they have attempted to elucidate in their subject. Indeed, the story of investigating Robert Johnson has proven to be as topsy-turvy, as surprising, as the man himself, and just as problematic. Some have imagined a mysterious man standing at a crossroads, cutting a midnight deal with the devil. Others have taken the more prosaic approach of searching through old census documents and death certificates, pounding on doors, tracking down bits and pieces of information about men named Johnson. But all the efforts converge on the same end point, an individual now validated as real in the recovered photographs and first-person accounts: a lanky black man of medium build; sharp features set in a lean, Modigliani face, right eye focused ahead, left eye cast aside in an amblyopic side gaze; sociable—especially with women—but restless, rarely remaining in any community for very long; pictured invariably with his guitar, as worn and scratched as the man is young and vital, suggesting a music that has also been on long and intense journeys.

Many have contributed to our knowledge of the historical Robert Johnson. And, whatever their methods, the various researchers have shown remarkable persistence, ultimately reclaiming Robert Johnson's biography from the murky bits of legend and lore that threatened to transform the bluesman's story into a tall tale and little more. There is still much we do not know about Robert Johnson, much we will never learn, but more than ever before, we can look upon him as a living, breathing person. We always had the music. Now we can claim to know, at least in some degree, the musician.

The pursuit began, oddly enough, a few weeks after Johnson's death. Impresario John Hammond was the first of many to seek the deceased Delta guitarist: his goal was to present Johnson at his December 23, 1938, "From Spirituals to Swing" concert at Carnegie Hall. But Johnson had died on August 16. Hammond was told that the blues singer "had been killed by his girl friend," and he was forced to settle instead on Big Bill Broonzy for the historic concert. Of course, the story about the girlfriend proved unsubstantiated—initiating what would prove to be a time-honored tradition in Johnson research, in which untruths and wild speculations loom large in the various published accounts.

Three months after the Carnegie Hall concert, on March 26, 1939, Alan Lomax wrote to Harold Spivacke, his boss at the Library of Congress, expressing great curiosity in learning more about this extraordinary blues musician. He mentions his plan to enlist the help of his father, the pioneering folk song collector John Lomax—then seventy-one years old, but still actively involved in fieldwork—in undertaking research about Johnson. "Father has written me several encouraging notes about his work lately. . . . I am writing him this afternoon to persuade him to investigate one Robert Johnson of Robinsville [sic], Mississippi, on whom Hammond and I are going to do an album soon." As far as we know, nothing came of this decision to probe the life and times of the late Robert Johnson. If only the elder Lomax had managed to devote some time and energy to the project, the Delta's most mysterious musician might be, in some appreciable measure, less of a cipher to us today!

As it stands, when Samuel Charters embarked on his research twenty years after Hammond and Lomax, the situation was little better. "Almost nothing is known of his life," Charters explains in his pioneering book *The Country Blues* (1959), and the author devotes a scant five pages to his chapter on Johnson. Paul Oliver offered readers even less in his *Blues Fell This Morning*, published the following year, merely noting in passing that Johnson was "a singer who walked hand-in-hand with the devil in life," and stating (again incorrectly) that the guitarist had died at age twenty-three, poisoned by a jealous lover. But by the time Oliver published his *Conversations with the Blues* in 1965, he had gathered more information, drawing on recollections by Robert Lockwood and Sunnyland Slim. Charters also was on the Johnson trail: in his *The Bluesmen*, from 1967, he managed to add more details, drawing largely on an interview he had conducted with blues guitarist Henry Townsend in 1962, and Julius Lester's 1965 interview with Son House. Charters followed with a small book on Johnson in 1973, mostly filled with lead sheets of the bluesman's songs but also including a lengthy essay. These scattered publications may have offered few hard facts, but they did provide greater perspective on Johnson, whom Townsend praised extravagantly, setting the tone for Johnson's growing reputation as *the* preeminent exponent of the Delta tradition. "I mean he was amazing. I was a little bit older than him, but I didn't think anybody had any seniority over me on the guitar, but this guy made me look little."

Yet the Robert Johnson of this period was little more than a wisp of the imagination. The music was now widely available, thanks to high-profile reissues on Columbia, but even this largesse tended to add to the confusion. Fans couldn't even agree on what the songs were about. The lyrics were often impenetrable, and aficionados labored over transcriptions with the zeal of Egyptologists deciphering the Pyramid Texts. And even when listeners managed to determine what words Johnson was singing, the problem remained to decipher what they actually meant. Researcher Stephen Calt went so far as to compile and publish an invaluable guide to "The Idioms of Robert Johnson"—clarifying for the unenlightened the meaning of such enigmatic phrases as "I'll do the Breakaway on your liver" and "I woke up this mornin', my biscuit roller was gone."

Fans were equally unsure what their hero looked like. In 1971, *Living Blues* magazine commissioned the artist Otis Rathel, who had worked for the Chicago Police Department for fourteen years creating drawings of criminals from the descriptions of their victims, to make a sketch of Johnson based on the input of surviving musicians who had known the guitarist. Rathel had a stellar track record—his efforts had resulted in many arrests, perhaps most notably in the notorious case of mass murderer Richard Speck, who was apprehended after Rathel's uncannily accurate drawing had helped identify the suspect. For whatever reason, Rathel's recreation of Robert Johnson proved less inspired; indeed, the person depicted looks more like a space alien than a blues legend. (In all fairness, the artist was hardly to blame—his informants hadn't seen Johnson in over thirty-five years.) The magazine also secured a second drawing, made by an art student, Joe Lavender, from a description by Johnny Shines—a quasi-Cubist interpretation, with Johnson's lips threatening to float off the side of his head. But in the absence of better images, the *Living Blues* representations at least filled the gap, and the magazine quickly moved to copyright both drawings.

Little wonder that folklorist Mack McCormick, who began researching a biography of Johnson around this time, decided to call his proposed magnum opus *Biography of a Phantom*. As it turned out, McCormick's book was the real phantom. Blues fans eagerly awaited its arrival, but it never appeared. Nonetheless, the advances made by this single researcher were substantial. He found at least half a dozen women who had had relationships—of two or three weeks' duration—with the guitarist. He uncovered photographs of the guitarist, the first to come to light. And not only did McCormick track down eyewitnesses to Johnson's alleged murder, he even claimed to have identified the culprit, who supposedly broke down and confessed under the interrogation of the surprised blues scholar. Alas, McCormick's treasure trove may not have led to a full-scale biography, but it provided rich material for other researchers. Peter Guralnick interviewed McCormick in 1976, and relied heavily on this source for his seminal book *Searching for Robert Johnson*.

But many others were also searching for Robert. Gayle Dean Wardlow had been among the first of the modern researchers documenting the early history of the Delta blues, literally going door-to-door in black neighborhoods during the 1960s, seeking recordings and information on missing musicians. He even took a job as an exterminator in a black neighborhood with the hope that it would gain him entrée into households where these treasures might be uncovered. Wardlow successfully tracked down several individuals who had known Johnson, most notably H. C. Speir, the talent scout whose intervention led to Johnson's first recording session. Perhaps Wardlow's most important contribution was his 1968 discovery of Johnson's death certificate, "after a three year search through four states." Stephen Calt, Wardlow's sometime collaborator, was another dedicated Johnson scholar, conducting interviews in the 1960s and 1970s with individuals who had known the guitarist, such as Son House, Johnny Shines, and David "Honeyboy" Edwards. Stephen LaVere, another researcher on the trail of Robert Johnson, brought to light substantial new information, some of it included in his accompanying essay to the influential 1990 release *Robert Johnson: The Complete Recordings*. Previously, many of the specifics of Johnson's early music education had eluded us, but LaVere tracked down the widow of Ike Zinermon, an important mentor to the guitarist, and also gained additional insights from others who had known the future Delta blues legend.

LaVere located Johnson's half sister Carrie Thompson in 1973, who proved to be an important source of information. Mack McCormick had already visited Thompson, but LaVere came away with far more than an interview: he secured rights to the artist's work in exchange for an agreement to pay Thompson (representing the guitarist's heirs) 50 percent of all royalties collected. LaVere later mounted a successful effort to prove that Johnson's music had not fallen into the public domain, and generated income "in the neighborhood of seven figures," according to a knowledgeable source, for Johnson's estate.

But these steps, far from resolving matters, merely initiated another chapter in the Johnson story. As much an American institution as the blues, litigation ensued. Mr. Claude Johnson appeared on the scene, producing a birth certificate stating that he was the son of an "R. L. Johnson." Claude's mother, Vergie Smith Cain, provided details under oath of her liaison with the now famous blues guitarist, specifics which one of her childhood friends corroborated. Almost ten years of legal maneuvering—including two trips to the Mississippi Supreme Court as well as two to the U.S. Supreme Court—elapsed before the matter was resolved in favor of Claude, who was established as sole heir. He used his sizable inheritance to move into a lavish pink brick home on a large estate. The Court gave great credence to the argument that no evidence could be produced that a different R. L. Johnson had fathered the boy. Blues discographers were less impressed with the coherence of the mother's story—and asked how she could have heard Robert Johnson play "Terraplane Blues" in 1931, when the Terraplane automobile (for which the song was named) had not been manufactured, marketed, or even had its brand trademarked at the time. But even if some of the evidence seemed puzzling or contradictory, Claude Johnson's claim of descent from the famous bluesman struck many experts as plausible, perhaps likely. And the investigation, now by a court of law, into the life and times of Robert

Johnson—sixty-two years after his death—brought some new information to light, and added one more strange chapter to this unfolding tale.

By this time, of course, the search for Robert Johnson had taken on a life of its own, as old-timers latched on to the legendary figure to validate the authenticity of their own blues. One brazen musician claimed to have been playing a second guitar on a Johnson recording, aiming to convince the credulous that if they but listened carefully enough, they could pick out his six strings in the background. Another elderly Chicago blues player kept a European researcher on tenterhooks for years, hinting that he knew the location of a choice photograph of Robert Johnson. Despite the long buildup, he never produced the goods. The very persistence of the researchers, their fervent hope to learn more about the enigmatic artist, merely increased the likelihood of mistakes and deceptions. Note, for example, that Muddy Waters mentioned in his 1941 interview with Alan Lomax that he knew of Johnson, but had never seen him perform. As time passed, Waters changed his story, asserting that he had seen someone who looked like Johnson play the blues. But by 1970, in response to the incessant questioning, Waters was now claiming to have witnessed Johnson performing on a few occasions.

Of course, this multiplying of dubious sources is well known to Johnson researchers. Not one, but *three* possible burial sites for Johnson have come to light—an unexpected boon given how many African-Americans of the era lay forgotten in unmarked graves. Even cemeteries, it seems, were vying for a few rays of the limelight shining on the Delta legend. Ministers, anxious for a piece of the action, graciously overlooked the claim that the most famous resident of their burial ground had made a deal with Satan, forgiving all. "Legend says this man sold his soul to the Devil," Reverend James Ratliff mused in his sermon to commemorate the laying of a grave marker for Robert Johnson at Mount Zion Church in 1991. "Now, I don't know what Robert Johnson told the Lord. *You* don't know what Robert Johnson told the Lord. We *all* have come short of the glory of God."

Forget about the bluesman . . . someone should write a book about the mystery and intrigue of the people who have followed in Johnson's wake. In 2006, a collector offered for sale a Gibson L1 guitar that looks like the one Johnson is playing in a famous photograph—and who knows, perhaps it is the same instrument. The asking price: a cool $6 million. The following year, a photo of a man resembling Robert Johnson, found at a swap meet, was listed on eBay—and who knows, perhaps it is the famous musician. The required starting bid: a modest $795,000. A film clip from Depression-era Mississippi recently came to light, and the camera lingers for a moment on a guitarist. Could it be—please don't disappoint me!—the great Robert Johnson? Perhaps during the Middle Ages, a similar obsessive passion was focused on collecting the relics of saints and pieces of the "true Cross." But has any figure from modern music history inspired such goings-on?

Of course, this state of affairs inevitably leads to backlash. At eighty years old, Johnson's stepson Robert Lockwood, Jr.—who passed away a few weeks before the eBay photo went on auction—could only look with bemusement at the growing body of anecdotes and reminiscences gathering around his now long dead stepfather. "You hear people talk about they played with Robert. They lyin' . . . hah! He definitely did want nobody to fake what he played—didn't want nobody watching him play. . . . Johnny [Shines] said that he played some with Robert, but I just can't understand how he did. I know he knew Robert—but, see, Robert was a loner—Robert didn't want nobody around him. He wouldn't sit and face another guitar player and let him see what he was doin'." Scholars have followed suit in recent years, approaching the accumulated evidence with newfound skepticism and scrutiny. Writers such as Elijah Wald, Barry Lee Pearson, Bill McCulloch, and others have preferred to showcase this new, "purified" Robert Johnson, stripped of the mythical and dubious, presented in what these hard-nosed researchers see as starkly realistic terms.

For all this, what do we know with certainty about Robert Johnson? We have accumulated a rich amount of information from hearsay, anecdotes, conjectures, but often our sense of the chronology and relative importance of the events recounted is hazy and imprecise. Despite the tremendous amount of research outlined above, we can assign only a few specific dates and places, milestones marking key events, his birth, his death, his recording sessions, and little else. Our story begins on May 8, 1911, when Johnson was born in Hazelhurst, Mississippi, the eleventh child of Julia Major Dodds. But even this often cited "fact"—attributed to Johnson's half sister Carrie Harris Thompson, who recalled it as the date always given by her mother as Robert's birthday—is subject to dispute. Looking at the contradictory ages found in a handful of surviving documents—school records, marriage licenses, death certificate—one could just as easily assign a birthdate as early as 1907 or as late as 1912. However, Thompson's date at least explains an otherwise puzzling gap in the 1910 census, which fails to include Robert in the list of Julia's children, and thus casts doubt on various attempts to add several years onto the bluesman's life.

Of course, there were valid reasons why Robert Johnson might have been around, yet still left off the 1910 census form. Unlike his ten older siblings, Johnson had been born illegitimate. The rest were the lawful off-spring of Julia's marriage to Charles Dodds in 1889. This was a tumultuous time in southern Mississippi. At least three black men had been lynched in Hazelhurst that year. Charles Dodds may have been a successful crafts-man, farmer, and a landowner, but this did not exempt him from the risk of personal injury and violence at the hands of fellow citizens. A dispute with local white landowners, the Marchetti brothers, forced Dodds to flee to Memphis sometime around 1909, where he changed his name to Spen-cer. In the absence of her husband, Julia took up briefly with a man named Noah Johnson, who would become Robert Johnson's father. While Robert was still an infant, Julia set out in search of better opportunities, with the boy and her baby daughter Carrie in tow. For the next few years they lived in migrant labor camps in Mississippi, finally rejoining Charles "Spencer" in Memphis, where he was now residing with his mistress Serena and her two sons, as well as with some of Julia's children. Here was a combination rife with the likelihood of friction and animosity: wife and legitimate children; the wife's offspring from another liaison; mistress and her children; and the patriarchal Charles presiding over the full clan. Yet we are told that the vari-ous parties co-existed peacefully, although Julia eventually departed to find a life of her own elsewhere.

What was Robert Johnson's attitude to home and hearth? The evidence indicates that his family ties were weak at best. Of course, his songs them-selves might suggest as much, with their talk of "ramblin' on my mind" and "I got to keep movin'." But we also have Johnson's own changeable attitude to his family name. Before his tenth birthday, he rejoined his mother in the Delta, where she was living with a new husband, Dusty Willis, and it appears that boy was known as "Little Robert" Dusty during this period. However, he adopted the Spencer name during his mid-teens—at least he seems to have used the name Robert Spencer while a student at the Indian Creek School in Commerce, Mississippi. At some point he took on the name John-son, perhaps in response to learning about his biological father. But even in his adult years, he would adopt pseudonyms. He might be known as Robert Moore in one community, but twenty miles away would answer to the name of Robert Spencer. In fact, researchers have linked him to no fewer than *eight* last names! On occasion, his first name would also change, although Robert tended to be the most consistent part of his identity. Some have suggested that this puzzling assortment of aliases helped Johnson elude legal or other enemies, but the constant alterations of name also reinforce an image of rootlessness and anomie, impressions that are inseparable from the blues he sang.

Various accounts suggest that Johnson showed an early knack for music, revealed in his singing and playing on the harmonica and Jew's harp. Before he owned a guitar, Johnson also learned how to play music on a variant of the diddley bow, the humble, makeshift string instrument constructed from objects at hand. In its simplest form, the diddley bow relies on a single string—usually a broom wire or cotton baling wire—stretched between two nails attached to the side of a house. A portable diddley bow can be constructed with a wooden bridge—anything from a broom handle to a pool cue will suffice—attached to a hollow object, such as a cigar box, that serves as a resonator. A bottle or other object is wedged under the wire to create the proper tension, and the string is plucked while the pitch is modulated by running a metal or glass object on it. In the hands of a skilled musician, this primitive instrument is capable of great expressiveness, rendering a haunting blues or an intricate melody—the late Lonnie Pitchford delighted audiences by playing "the Star Spangled Banner" on his diddley bow. Wink Clark, who attended church and Sunday School with Johnson, recalled him making a three-string instrument in this fashion, before finally scraping together enough money to purchase an old guitar.

In his late teen years, Johnson fell under the influence of Son House, much as Muddy Waters would do a decade later. Some writers describe House as Johnson's "mentor," but such a label gives too much credit to the older bluesman. As he made clear in several interviews, House barely tolerated Johnson, who came to his attention when he noticed "a little boy standing around" at the Saturday night balls where blues were played. Johnson's mother and stepfather objected to their youngster's late night haunts, but he would wait until they had gone to bed, then climb out the window and make his way to the music. Johnson sat in rapt attention watching House and Willie Brown perform, and sometimes during the break he would pick up one of the guitars and try to play it himself. As House tells the story:

> Such another racket you never heard. It'd make the people mad, you know. They'd come out and say, "Why don't y'all go in there and get that guitar away from that boy! He's running people crazy with it." I'd come back in and I'd scold him about it. "Don't do that Robert. You drive the people nuts. You can't play nothing."

Such is the "mentoring" that Robert Johnson received at the hands of his idol, Son House. If House were flattered by his role in the development of the Delta's most famous bluesman, he did a good job of hiding it. Dick Waterman recalls House's barely disguised irritation when he met John Hammond (by now an executive with the Columbia label) in 1965 to discuss a comeback recording, only to find the producer more interested in talking about Robert Johnson than in the legendary artist sitting in front of him. After the meeting, Waterman and House repaired to a local bar, where Waterman offered a toast to "John Hammond . . . for bringing you to Columbia Records." House lifted his double bourbon, and responded: "Here's to Robert Johnson . . . for being dead."

Perhaps a less ambitious musician would have been discouraged by the reproaches coming from House and others, might even have put down the guitar forever. But Johnson responded with greater tenacity, apparently as much inspired by House's disdain as others would have been by words of encouragement. House remembers the young guitarist leaving the Delta around this time—for Arkansas, as he recalled it, although the preponderance of evidence indicates that Johnson returned to his birthplace in Hazelhurst, Mississippi, perhaps with the intention of reuniting with his real father. The length of Johnson's departure is also subject to dispute: House claims six months; other sources would point to a longer period, perhaps one or two years. But the end result was startling, if we give House credence. The conventional story is neat and pat, cinematic in scope—the classic "musician-comes-of-age" scene. When House and Willie Brown next saw "Little Robert," the pair were playing in Banks, Mississippi, a small community five miles east of Robinsonville. The younger musician enters the room confidently, a guitar swinging from his shoulders. Johnson ignores the derisive comments of the other musicians, and begins playing the blues. But here is no rank amateur, rather a polished professional, who handles the guitar with such speed, facility, and ease that the others are left dumbfounded.

2. me and the devil blues

At this point in the story, the Devil typically enters our drama, stage left.

Ah, if we could only skip this interlude, what hand-wringing and consternation we might save ourselves. To many blues scholars, this part of the Johnson biography is an acute embarrassment, the most shameful calling card of our trade. But it is—oh woe!—the best known chapter in the saga of the Delta blues. When I meet people with only the most remote understanding of the music, this is the one "fact" they are sure to have heard. "Robert Johnson? Isn't he the guy who made a deal with the devil?"

The story makes for great drama: a Faustian bargain in which the aspiring guitarist sells his soul in exchange for a preternatural ability to play blues. No wonder it has been written up in countless books and articles and has even supplied the plot for a Hollywood movie. And the story won't be forgotten anytime soon, if only because it makes for good business, too. A writer for *Esquire* captured the mood perfectly when he entitled his article on the reissue of Johnson's music "Satan, Now on CD." Packaged in this manner, Robert Johnson becomes the Marilyn Manson or Ozzy Osbourne of his day. Who can deny that a tabloid angle like this sells loads of CDs to folks otherwise little concerned with the niceties of prewar acoustic blues? And it sells more than just music. The state of Mississippi incorporates it into its tourism literature, growing the local economy tangibly, all at Lucifer's (and perhaps Johnson's) expense.

We don't have the guitarist's firsthand account of the transaction (and we will discuss below whether he really had a firsthand account), but the closest version we may hope to find derives from the story of another Delta bluesman named Johnson. In this instance, the guitarist is Tommy Johnson, and the narrator is his brother, Reverend LeDell Johnson.

> Now if Tom was living, he'd tell you. He said the reason he knowed so much, said he sold hisself to the devil. I asked him how. He said, "If you want to learn how to play anything you want to play and learn how to

make songs yourself, you take your guitar and you go to where a road crosses that way, where a crossroad is. Get there, be sure to get there just a little 'fore twelve o'clock that night so you'll know you'll be there. You have your guitar and be playing a piece sitting there by yourself. You have to go by yourself and be sitting there playing a piece. A big black man will walk up there and take your guitar, and he'll tune it. And then he'll play a piece and hand it back to you. That's the way I learned to play anything I want." And he could.

David Evans, the blues scholar who tracked down LeDell Johnson and collected this anecdote, has gone on record that he did not solicit this sordid tale from LeDell Johnson—it was offered spontaneously, without prompting. Evans, for his part, prefers to explore more concrete sources for Tommy Johnson's knowledge of the blues, his learnings from Charley Patton, Nathan "Dick" Bankston, and the many great blues players in the vicinity of Drew, Mississippi. The Robert Johnson tale has been similarly deconstructed— especially by recent researchers, for whom demystifying the overly romanticized aspects of blues lore has become a major theme in their scholarship.

Elijah Wald, in his recent book on Johnson, *Escaping the Delta*, treats the crossroads story as, at best, a bad joke, at worst, a blot on blues scholarship. He wants music writers to "get over the cliché," and even proposes a moratorium on discussions of the subject, which "tell us less about the realities of Johnson's music, than about the leanings of his later, urban white listeners." Barry Lee Pearson and Bill McCulloch, in their *Robert Johnson: Lost and Found*, are so upset at the story that they talk of "'Hellhound' conspirators" guilty of foisting "romantic distortions" onto the Johnson story.

Yet Robert Johnson himself must be part of this cadre, since his own songs are the primary source, predating any critic's or scholar's theories, promoting this image of the bluesman as a devil-haunted man. Even without the benefit of any biographical facts, record listeners might construct a story similar to the one LeDell Johnson related about his brother simply on the basis of Robert Johnson recordings such as "Hellhound on My Trail," "Me and the Devil Blues," "Crossroad Blues," and "Preachin' Blues (Up Jumped the Devil)." Pearson and McCulloch dismiss this possibility in a casual aside. "It is always possible, of course, that some of Johnson's life experiences did filter into his lyrics," the authors admit in passing. But their final conclusion is firm and unequivocal: "There is no verifiable link between Robert Johnson and the devil. The historical evidence is tainted by hearsay, dubious research, compromised methodology, and questionable reporting."

Yet we would be wrong to dismiss the "crossroads" story as a mere embarrassment of blues history, something to be swept under the carpet, dismissed in a few derisive sentences and then put aside. The story is an important part of the Johnson biography, and must be dealt with accordingly. In particular, we must ask ourselves to what degree Johnson himself is responsible for the account. Was he the originator of the tale? And, if so, did he believe it himself, either literally or symbolically? Or was it attached to him by others—during his lifetime or afterward—either to denigrate the bluesman, or perhaps to add to his mystique? And, in any case, what did it mean for his contemporaries? And what does it tell us about the man and his music? In short, we probably should be grateful for this admittedly lurid tale, in that it gives the opportunity to probe into matters especially relevant to the culture and communities that produced the Delta blues.

Among blues experts who have taken a serious interest in this matter, the most common response is to explain the crossroads tale as a carryover of African belief systems. As such, the roots of this story go well beyond the confines of the Delta region. When I explored the musical traditions of Brazil during the 1990s, one of the locals told me how he would sometimes see offerings left at crossroads, because these locations are considered to hold spiritual significance for the adherents of Candomblé, a religion that derives substantially from Yoruban belief systems from West Africa. The trickster-god Exu dwells at the crossroads, which represents the meeting point between the realms of the human and the divine. We encounter the same elements in the Santeria religion of Cuba, where the trickster-god is known as Eleggua, or among the Vodou adherents of Haiti, where he is called Legba. In the United States, Harry Middleton Hyatt found similar beliefs when he conducted extensive fieldwork among African-American communities in the South during the late 1930s. His research eventually published in a weighty five-volume, 4,766-page collection, included numerous accounts of musicians (and other individuals) going to the crossroads to secure supernatural skills.

Placed in the context of these belief systems, the Robert Johnson story does not seem to be a mere tall tale told by white blues fans to bamboozle the credulous, or even to sell records to the masses, but rather a modern

American echoing of a timeless African story. And though I have no dis-
agreement with this interpretation, I am still left unsatisfied. For it offers a
sociological answer to what remains a biographical question. We can study
the traditional stories of individuals making "deals with the devil" at great
length, without it bringing us one whit closer to understanding why this
account was attached to this specific individual, Robert Johnson.

In my conversations with Mack McCormick, who has studied the life of
Robert Johnson over the course of a half century, we explored this matter
at length. My initial instinct was—much like Pearson and McCulloch—
to dismiss this story as a fanciful add-on to the Johnson legacy, as one of
those dubious anecdotes music fans tell about their favorite recording artist, designed to titillate, not elucidate. As such, dwelling on the story was
likely—or so I feared—to prevent me from seeing the "real" Robert Johnson. But McCormick cautioned me against such hasty judgments. "My gut
feeling is that Johnson spread the story himself," McCormick commented.
"It's a good story. It catches people's attention. To some degree, Johnson
created his own legend—not just this one, but several other legends too."
McCormick continued:

> When I went to New Orleans in the late 1940s to visit some record
> collectors, they told me that same story. You need to remember that
> almost nothing had been published on Robert Johnson at that time. A
> little bit had been written around the time of the "Spirituals to Swing
> Concert," and a couple of record reviews had appeared, but they were
> full of mistakes. Yet these record collectors had heard about Robert
> Johnson selling his soul to the devil. I subsequently heard the same
> story within the black community. The fact that the same story cir-
> culated among these two groups—groups that had very little contact
> with each other—impressed me. It suggests that the story had deep
> roots, probably linking back to Johnson himself.

For his 1992 documentary *The Search for Robert Johnson*, director Chris
Hunt tracked down many individuals who had known Johnson, and two of
them confirmed that Johnson himself had spread this story. "I done heard.
I asked him," a former girlfriend known as Queen Elizabeth tells the interviewer. Willie Mae Powell, who was romantically involved with Johnson
during a several month period in the mid-1930s, asserts vehemently that

her cousin, the well known guitarist David "Honeyboy" Edwards, heard it directly from Johnson's lips. Edwards, for his part, has not denied this, but merely says ambiguously, in his autobiography *The World Don't Owe Me Nothing*, "It may be Robert could have sold himself to the Devil." But in his interview with Alan Lomax from the latter's 1942 fieldwork in Coahoma County, on file in the Library of Congress, Edwards is less equivocal, offering his opinion that Johnson died unredeemed and unsaved, caught up in the "Devil's business." In the face of this evidence, it is hard to accept the accusation that the overheated imaginations of blues writers—the so-called Hellhound Conspirators—bear primary responsibility for the linkage between Robert Johnson and the devil. And there is even less evidence to support Pearson and McCulloch's claim that the Faustian story of Johnson's deal with the devil was initiated in the 1960s. This story, in all its lurid details, sprang up decades before, and in all probability came from the musician himself.

If Johnson was the source of this account, the obvious next question is why he would spread such a story. The tremendous amount of publicity accorded to this tale over the years may partly provide an answer. It's an attention-grabbing claim, one that might make a name for a musician struggling for visibility during the height of the Great Depression. When Skip James's "Devil Got My Woman" was released by Paramount in 1931, H. C. Speir promoted the release with posters depicting a cartoon image of James replete with tail, horns, and pitchfork. The "devil angle" made for good marketing, and Speir wanted to capitalize on the opportunity. Only a few years before Johnson made his first records, bluesman Peetie Wheatstraw successfully promoted himself as "the Devil's Son-in-Law" and "the High Sheriff from Hell." This outlandish story proved so popular that Wheatstraw's biographer, Paul Garon, would find people still talking about it decades after the musician's death. When he asked informants about Wheatstraw, it would typically be the first thing they would mention. "Yeah, the Devil's Son-in-Law." Over and above the sheer boldness of the claim— bound to capture notoriety—Garon sees other reasons why this moniker would attract interest in the black community. "These designations gave Peetie a sense of power, opposition, and resistance and it gave his listeners a figure of great majesty with whom they could identify. . . . The Devil, as a sign of evil, couldn't help but conjure up a sympathetic feeling among those listeners who felt that as African Americans in a white world, they needed an *agent of opposition* to carry on through their lives."

Certainly a substantial component of the black community was horrified and outraged by any activities linked, explicitly or implicitly, with the devil. Yet this pious group of consumers was unlikely to purchase blues recordings under any circumstances—hence, for Robert Johnson and others, there was little financial downside to spreading these tales. Indeed, almost every aspect of the crossroads story shows the marks of its time and place; and even if we lacked the testimony of McCormick, Edwards, Powell, and others, we would hardly think to associate such an account with the attitudes of white music fans from the 1960s. If we wanted to "date" these perspectives, we would almost certainly trace them instead to African-American communities in the South during the first half of the century. In the 1940s, B.B. King found that many Delta churches would cancel the performance of his gospel-singing group when they learned that the vocalists relied on guitar accompaniment—the six-string instrument had been so tainted by its association with the blues that many ministers could not bear seeing it inside the House of God. John Lee Hooker's father, Reverend William Hooker, refused to let the youngster bring his guitar inside the house, so fearful was he of spiritual contamination. Many families were torn asunder by this conflict. When Henry Sims arrived with his friend Charley Patton at his sister's house in Memphis with test pressings from their recent recording session, she refused even to listen to them, firmly convinced of their evil nature. When Howlin' Wolf, late in life, met his mother by chance during a road tour in Mississippi, she denounced him and threw the money he gave her on the ground, unwilling to benefit from the wages of sin.

The career of Reverend Robert Wilkins provides a telling case study in how these conflicts could profoundly impact a musician's craft and livelihood. Wilkins, born in Hernando, Mississippi, in 1896, was active on the thriving Beale Street scene in Memphis during the 1920s. In 1928, Victor brought him into a recording studio, and he later made 78s for Brunswick and Vocalion. His performances reveal a sure-fingered guitarist with a reedy voice, rich in vibrato, in the same tradition as Furry Lewis, Frank Stokes, and Joe Callicott. Wilkins's blues recount the timeless themes of the music, loneliness and departures and the musician's rambling ways, poignant subjects which recur in the lyrics to his songs from this period, such as "Rolling Stone," "Fallin' Down Blues," "Get Away Blues," and "That's No Way to Get Along." Perhaps these pervasive feelings of despair and disillusionment helped spark Wilkins's religious conversion, or it may merely have come about, as he claimed, from his dismay at the violence he saw at house parties and juke joints. In time, Wilkins became a minister in the Church of God in Christ, a calling he felt was incompatible with the music he had previously performed.

Yet Wilkins refused to give up the guitar, and instead crafted a personal style of gospel music that drew heavily on his blues techniques. He participated in the blues revival of the 1960s, but relying now on these new *sanctified* blues which, he hoped, would bring listeners to God. The celebrated rock musicians who performed as the Rolling Stones may not have been converted, but they were listening, and decided to cover Wilkins's "Prodigal Son" (a remaking of his "That's No Way to Get Along") on their 1968 release *Beggar's Banquet*. Wilkins may well have been dismayed to see his song rub shoulders with "Sympathy for the Devil" on the same disk. Nor did he have the consolation of lavish royalties to lessen the pain, since he had lost the copyright to the song.

Ishmon Bracey, born at the turn of the century in Byram, Mississippi, stands out as another major bluesman who turned away from the music of his youth after a religious conversion. On a Saturday morning during the winter of 1927–28, H. C. Speir discovered Bracey entertaining passersby on Mill Street, and was struck by the guitarist's rendition of his blues "Shaggy Hound." Under Speir's supervision, Bracey made a test disk of the song, which the talent broker renamed "Saturday Blues"—Saturday is not mentioned in the lyrics, but Speir thought the name would sell better!—and used it to convince Victor to record the Bracey at the same February 1928 session in Memphis that also marked Tommy Johnson's recording debut.

In fact, Bracey would travel and share studio time with Johnson at every one of his sessions. Speir's judgment was perhaps odd, but astute: the rechristened "Saturday Blues" sold six thousand copies on first release, an impressive figure in a day when initial pressings were around twelve hundred records. And just as Speir cavalierly changed the song's title, the record company altered the singer's appellation, perhaps simply due to carelessness—listing Bracey's first name as "Ishman" on these sides, a misspelling that is still often found today in books and articles dealing with this underrated figure from the golden age of the Delta blues. Victor agreed to a follow-up session in late summer, and a few months later Paramount also recorded Bracey. The latter sides remain collector items—during a long career hunting for blues 78s in various Mississippi neighborhoods, Gayle Wardlow never encountered a single Bracey Paramount release, and some of Bracey's recorded music from this period may be lost to us permanently.

Bracey's mournful voice carried tremendous expressive force, but its rawness must have put off many potential record buyers. The melancholy wail of "Trouble Hearted Blues" is a howling at the full moon, a lament almost too blue for a casual listener to bear. "Leaving Town Blues," "Woman, Woman Blues," and "Brown Mama Blues" are more subdued, but even here the anguish of Bracey's vocalizing is palpable, highlighted further by his supple, note-bending guitar accompaniment. Bracey is strongest at these slow-to-medium tempo blues, where his time is rock steady, and the guitar lines flow with the sad, stately momentum of a funeral procession. If we can believe Bracey, Louis Armstrong once offered the Delta bluesman a job in his band. If so, it must have been the guitarist's sure rhythmic sense that appealed to Armstrong. Nonetheless, Bracey's temperament was more suited to the blues idiom than to New Orleans jazz, as some of the surviving Paramount sides make clear. Here, in the company of the New Orleans Nehi Boys, the distinctive emotional flavor of Bracey's musical personality is all but lost in the midst of a traditional jazz setting.

Wardlow "rediscovered" the former bluesman in 1963, but by then he had become Reverend Bracey, and looked with disdain on the music of his youth. Bracey resisted Wardlow's attempts to get him to play the blues, except for a short interlude when the minister was sure his wife was not listening. "He had terrible guilt about the blues and the blues life," Wardlow recalls. "He was almost paranoid about it." But, like Wilkins, Bracey tried to resurrect his musical career as a performer of sacred music. "He told me 'If you get me five hundred dollars, I'll record a gospel album,'" Wardlow continues. "We put together a few songs, and sent it to [Richard] Spottswood at the Piedmont label. But he already had Reverend Robert Wilkins, and didn't need another blues musician to record religious music." And unlike Wilkins, Bracey cleansed his sacred performances of blues licks, perhaps making them less offensive to his congregation, but further limiting their commercial appeal. Bracey thus remained on the sidelines during the blues revival of the 1960s. He died in Jackson, Mississippi, on February 12, 1970, never having made his peace with the music that will remain his lasting claim to fame.

Yet some musicians saw the blues and scripture as complementary forces. When Rube Lacy, the blues singer turned minister, was asked by researchers about the relationship between his two apparently incompatible callings, he artfully interpolated the Gospel of John into his response: "The blues are true and the Truth shall set you free." Lacy even gave a sermon to his congregation to that effect. Lacy's reputation as a blues singer derives almost entirely from a single Paramount release, his "Mississippi Jail House Groan," backed by "Ham Hound Crave," recorded in Chicago in March 1928. Lacy's wordless vocalizing on the former, somewhat reminiscent of Blind Willie Johnson's classic "Dark Was the Night—Cold Was the Ground," is haunting and effective. In its marketing, Paramount praised the piece for its "weird moaning and groaning," yet the performance retains a certain spiritual quality not incompatible with Lacy's later pastoral vocation. It could serve as a suitable homiletic commentary on the Gospel verse: "I was in prison, and you came unto me." But one wonders what Lacy's congregation would have made of the bawdy lines from "Ham Hound Crave," such as "Mama, got a hambone, I wonder can I get it boiled / 'Cause these Chicago women are about to let my hambone spoil."

We do not know to what degree Robert Johnson's conscience wrestled with the conflicts between his life as a blues musician and the religious values of his day, but we can hardly doubt that he relished the attention generated by tales of dealings with the devil. And though a midnight encounter at a crossroads may have never happened, some other biographical incident might have spurred Johnson to publicize these accounts. His brief marriage to Virginia Travis perhaps served as just such a turning point. Johnson was seventeen years old at the time, and his marriage signaled the last (perhaps the only) serious attempt he made to settle down into a more conventional life. The newlyweds resided with Johnson's half sister Bessie and her husband Granville Hines, a preacher—both of whom encouraged him to give up the blues, which they saw as low and evil. Johnson turned to farmwork, relegating music to an occasional activity to supplement his income. But when Virginia became pregnant, she returned to her family to have the child, and Robert took the opportunity to travel as a working guitarist, picking up spare coins and dollars wherever he could find them.

When he came to visit his wife, he learned that she had died in childbirth. Here, amidst Travis's friends and relatives, Johnson found himself the focal point of accusations and condemnations. He had been gone, playing blues as an itinerant musician, while his wife died trying to give birth to his baby. Some may have said openly, and many must have felt, that his decision to give preference to his evil calling as a blues musician had contributed to this tragedy, which was perhaps an act of divine retribution. Johnson, for his part, never tried to settle down again, and to some extent he became the devil-hounded persona that matched his already besmirched reputation.

This story is far less colorful than the account of a midnight transaction with the devil in exchange for an unparalleled ability to play the guitar. But both tales have the same end point: before his twentieth birthday Johnson had embraced the musician's life with a vengeance, had started on his ramblin' ways, and had adopted an attitude that was, at best, devil-may-care and, at worst, hell-bent on self-destruction.

3. travel on, poor bob

Whatever help the Devil may have given to Johnson's musical development was supplemented by more practical lessons, drawn from the guitarist's assiduous study of records by other blues players. Tracing the various sources of inspiration for Johnson's body of work can be a challenging task—often the music and words to any given song show similarities with several earlier blues recordings. But the overall effect is clear: Johnson's vision of the blues is more indebted to the phonograph than to the plantation, more a reflection of commercial tastes than the continuation of a folkloric tradition. No cause for lament here: Johnson's posthumous success, his tremendous influence and appeal, came from his ability to transform the blues into marketable popular music. "He came out with such compelling themes," Keith Richards, of the Rolling Stones, has enthused. "They were actual songs as well as just being blues."

The methodical care that Johnson put into constructing these songs has sometimes been hard for blues aficionados to accept—it defies their belief in the freewheeling inspiration that must have given birth to music of such vivid immediacy. "I can't tell you how disappointed I was when I first heard the alternate takes of Robert Johnson," Phil Spiro has explained, describing for me a sentiment that must have been shared by many blues fans at the time. "The guitar parts that I thought had been spontaneous and improvised, and couldn't possibly be duplicated—well, he did the same thing on the alternate take. What a letdown!" Mack McCormick emphasized the same point, insisting that he would not have released the alternate takes had he been in charge of reissuing Johnson's music. "[Johnson] simply showed that if you asked him to do it again, he could do it again." Despite these understandable laments, the formulaic quality of the alternate takes provides us with an important insight into the discipline with which Johnson developed his craft. This meticulous care reflects no deficiency on his part. In truth, it stands as a necessary part of his legacy. Robert Johnson, more than anyone, transformed the Delta blues from a folk art to a commercial force, and this would hardly have been possible had he entered the recording studio trusting solely to the inspiration of the moment. In this regard, Johnson is more akin to a Brill Building songwriter or a pop record producer, relying on his craftsmanship in finding the precise recipe that makes for an enduring hit, than to a jazz musician striving to play something different on every take.

A full study of the influences that may have shaped Johnson's music would make a good dissertation topic for a Ph.D. in bluesology, but even a cursory examination makes clear that, although the mentoring of Son House and Willie Brown may have played an important role in Johnson's development, their influence was outweighed by the recordings of musicians from outside the Delta region. The 78s of Kokomo Arnold, a skilled slide guitarist and singer from Georgia, clearly fascinated the younger musician. Arnold's "Milk Cow Blues" anticipates Johnson's later "Milkcow's Calf Blues," just as a generation later the young Elvis Presley drew on the same song for an early regional hit. The flip side of the Arnold's 78 featured "Old Original Kokomo Blues," the most likely source of inspiration for Johnson's "Sweet Home Chicago," just as Arnold's "Sagefield Woman Blues" looks forward to "Dust My Broom." Tennessee-born Peetie Wheatstraw, who as we have seen promoted himself as "the Devil's Son-in-Law," may have influenced both Johnson's singing and his attempt to gain notoriety with talk of satanic affiliations. We hear, for example, Johnson emulate Wheatstraw's trademark "ooh well" aside, and transform the latter's "King of Spades" into his "Little Queen of Spades." Elsewhere we can detect the influence of Leroy Carr, Lonnie Johnson, and other successful recording artists of the era. Even when traditional blues masters were near at hand, we cannot always assume

that the future guitar legend heard them in person. Johnson may have witnessed Skip James in the flesh, or learned his music through Johnny Temple
when their paths crossed in 1931; yet given these other instances, it seems
just as likely that he studied James's recordings. Johnson's "32-20 Blues"
reveals an obvious debt to James's "22-20 Blues," while "Hellhound on My
Trail" and "Come On in My Kitchen" reflect the influence of James's "Devil
Got My Woman." The irony here is that James was among the least commercially successful (at the time) of the musicians Johnson emulated, yet
the songs the younger musician drew from this source of inspiration are
among his most famous.

Johnson also benefited from the private tutelage of Ike Zinermon during
this important period in his musical development. Zinermon, who hailed
from Grady, Alabama, claimed that he had learned guitar while practicing
in a graveyard at midnight, sitting on top of tombstones. Perhaps Johnson's
own account of a midnight encounter at the crossroads was a response to, or
an outgrowth of, this odd tale; or a transaction with the dark side may even
have been Johnson's colorful way of describing his late night guitar education at the hands of this devilish older musician. Johnson had remarried by
this time—to Callie Craft, whom he wed at the Copiah County Courthouse
in May 1931 and would desert a short while later—but he was often away
after sunset with his new mentor, an adept guitarist who frequented the
juke joints and worker camps in the area. Yet Johnson could have just as
easily learned the crossroads story, as well as some blues-playing tips, from
Tommy Johnson around this same time. Tommy Johnson returned periodically to nearby Crystal Springs, some ten miles from Hazelhurst, and
had (as we have seen) recounted to his brother a colorful tale about selling his soul at midnight virtually identical to the one later associated with
Robert Johnson. Johnny Shines's recollections about Robert Johnson are
interesting in this regard. When asked about the other guitarists his former
traveling partner admired, he remarked: "As far as musicians that he liked,
he only mentioned the Johnsons, Lonnie Johnson and some other Johnson
who was a good guitarist at that time." Could Tommy Johnson be the "other
Johnson" referred to here?

When Johnson returned to Robinsonville, he was no longer the "Little
Robert" scorned by Son House and Willie Brown some time before. "I gave
him a little instruction," House would boast about this second encounter,
but in truth there must have been little he could teach Johnson at this point

about guitar technique. Johnson only remained in the area a few weeks—he had probably come to visit his mother. The next time House heard Johnson would be on the latter's successful recording of "Terraplane Blues," which earned the older guitarist's begrudging respect. Soon afterward, House learned that Robert Johnson was dead. Yet the brief intersection in these two careers would be seen as an important interlude in the biographies of both musicians, the celebrated personal connection by which the Delta blues tradition was passed on to the youngster who would become its most famous exponent.

Biographers will probably never be able to trace with much precision the movements of this peripatetic musician during the remaining years of his life. Johnson's travels revolved around familiar landmarks—Helena, Arkansas, might serve as a convenient base for Johnson (and other musicians of the day); family ties in Robinsonville might draw him back from time to time. But these were more resting places than homes. The rambling figure depicted in his songs was no romantic invention on Johnson's part, but an accurate reflection of the wandering life he now led. Johnny Shines, who joined Johnson on some of his travels, recounts a dizzying list of destinations and stopping points: Arkansas, Missouri, Tennessee, Michigan, Illinois, New York, New Jersey, even Canada. But Shines was only an occasional companion, and even when he was with Johnson on the road, he sometimes found that his fellow guitarist had slipped away on his own private itinerary. Despite these tales of lengthy road trips, Johnson did not neglect the area in and around the Delta and greater Mississippi, and, if the various accounts can be believed, the legendary musician brought his blues music personally to the communities of Clarksdale, Coahoma, Drew, Friars Point, Greenville, Gunnison, Hollandale, Inverness, Itta Bena, Jonestown, Leland, Lula, Midnight, Moorhead, Rosedale, Shaw, Tunica, Tutwiler, and Yazoo City, among other locales.

Yet the bluesman's constant traveling is perhaps the least of our obstacles in following the trail of Robert Johnson. The many false identities the guitarist adopted seem almost a defiant challenge to those who later hoped to track his movements—perhaps necessary to elude real or imagined enemies at the time, but now a daunting complication for the historian or biographer. Johnny Shines knew him only as Robert Johnson. Gayle Wardlow found that many of his informants knew Johnson as Robert Sax or Robert Saxton. Johnny Temple met him in Jackson, where he was known simply as "R.L." Mack McCormick's research indicated that the guitarist might be called Robert Spencer in one community, but in a nearby town go under the name of Robert Moore or Robert James or Robert Barstow. At other times, Johnson would call himself Robert Dusty. Sometimes even the first name Robert might change, although it tended to be the most consistent part of his identity. This multiplicity of names raises as many unanswered questions. Are the researchers themselves guilty of overheated imaginations, finding traces of the legendary guitarist in every community they visited? Did Johnson have dangerous adversaries—an angry husband? a jealous lover? or some other de facto hellhound on his trail?—that required such varied aliases? Or was it merely a psychological quirk that led him to disguise his identity, perhaps a carryover from a childhood that dealt him like an unlucky card, passed from father to father, family to family, with no stable foundation of kin and clan?

Yet even if he had kept to a single name, the track would still be hard to follow. "Do you know how many Robert Johnsons there are?" Mack McCormick asked me, when I probed into his many field trips in search of the "real" Robert Johnson. I didn't hazard a guess. "One out of every ten thousand black males in Mississippi at that time was named Robert Johnson." A number of them were blues musicians—David Evans, for example, interviewed a Delta bluesman named Robert Johnson who was not our celebrated figure, and one suspects that there were many other guitarists who went by this common name. The sleuth on the trail of *the* Robert Johnson might find that he has merely picked up the scent of *a* Robert Johnson. McCormick, for his part, continues to question many of the supposed certainties of Johnson biographical research, and now doubts some of the information he supplied to Peter Guralnick—material which provided much of the substance of Guralnick's *Searching for Robert Johnson*, a coherent biography of the blues legend that remains a major source for other researchers.

Even during his lifetime, Johnson was elusive, difficult for family and friends to track. Guitarist Robert Lockwood recounts a revealing tale about hearing that Johnson was playing in a community in Arkansas. Lockwood immediately took off on the trail of the man whom he looked upon as a stepfather and mentor—only to find when he arrived that the story had been based on Lockwood's own appearance in the same town a short time before. "I realized that the man done come and looked at me playing and got me going back down there looking for myself!" How much more likely we are today to lose the trace and find that we have followed the wrong man. And though it may be hard to invalidate any one piece of evidence, it is almost certain that many of the stories that have come down to us about Robert Johnson have no origin in the activities of the man who made the classic recordings of the Delta blues.

Johnson was, in fact, only four years older than his "stepson." He took up with Lockwood's mother sometime in the early 1930s, and would rely on her household as a home base whenever he was in Helena. "Robert was like a father to me, or a big brother," Lockwood recalls, "and he accepted me like a baby brother or a son. He was real open with me, and he had me playin' inside of six months." Perhaps the whole blues world today traces its musical roots back to Robert Johnson, but Lockwood is the only undisputed disciple to learn his craft directly at the hands of the master. Johnson even helped the youngster make his own guitar, using parts from an old Victrola, a cheese box, and assorted pieces of wood to construct this primitive instrument.

Lockwood's mastery of the guitar serves as eloquent testimony to Johnson's tutelage. Although he never matched the intensity of his teacher, Lockwood would come to rank among the most technically accomplished blues guitarists of his generation, equally at home navigating through complicated bebop changes as in playing low-down juke joint fare. Lockwood made his name as an exponent of the Delta tradition, but he never felt constrained by its stylistic conventions. He introduced the sound of the electric guitar to many listeners in the Delta—and claimed to be the first to broadcast it over the local radio airwaves. He also adopted the practice of playing single-note lead lines, a jazzier approach at odds with the ways of traditional blues guitarists. Lockwood stood out as well for his interest in different instrumental textures, and asserted that his advice was responsible for B.B. King moving from a small combo to a larger band playing written charts. Lockwood further understood the importance of mass media and, along with Aleck Miller (Sonny Boy Williamson II), helped launch the influential *King Biscuit Time* broadcasts from Helena, Arkansas, in late 1941—a programming success story that would be widely emulated throughout the South. In the light of these developments, one wonders whether Lockwood's forward-looking approach to his craft hints at the scope of musical developments Robert Johnson might have pursued had he lived longer.

The association with Lockwood and his mother formed the most stable family relationship Johnson would ever enjoy, but it is unlikely that it was a monogamous one. Researchers have followed Johnson's trail as much through his girlfriends as by his music. His approach to these women was straightforward and pragmatic to a surprising extent. He would often pick out one of the homeliest women in a community, sensing that here he would have the best likelihood of success and the least chance of incurring the wrath of another man. His proposition was never crude or vulgar, but direct: could he come back home with her? Johnson knew, of course, the tactical value of a romantic gesture, but these came not from his conversation, or even gallant actions, but rather through his songs, which were the decisive tools in his techniques of seduction. The man himself was shy, according to these women; but the songs were bold, especially in the manner he presented them. Johnson developed the habit of identifying a specific woman in the audience, and directing his songs at her—a method that, for all its merits in romantic conquests, contributed to Johnson's untimely death at the hands of a jealous husband. Many of Johnson's songs were written with specific women in mind—the gentler or more sultry songs in his repertoire, such as "Come On in My Kitchen" or "Kindhearted Woman Blues" or "Love in Vain"—or, at least, the women he serenaded preferred to believe that they were the inspiration behind his music.

I sometimes wonder whether Johnson's subtle use of his songs in the art of seduction did not contribute, in an indirect way, to the tremendous posthumous success of his music. No traditional blues singer has ever sold more recordings, or appealed to a broader slice of the public than Robert Johnson, and the very songs he used to captivate his female admirers are among those that have been the most popular with the general public. Could it be that the cooing and wooing, the emotional expressiveness of his vocals, ranging from whispered asides to orgasmic hollers, bewitch us, much as they did the ladies he solicited through his songs? Certainly his predecessors in the Delta blues tradition—a Son House, a Charley Patton, a Willie Brown—sound rough and foreboding by comparison. Audiences may have been transfixed by the fire-and-brimstone of House's "Dry Spell Blues," with its proclamation: "I believe to my soul, this old world is about to end." They may have been amused by Patton's "Banty Rooster Blues" or his "Pony Blues." But modern consumers of music seek a more personal, intimate connection to the songs they cherish. For them, Robert Johnson provided this connection. Never before had a Delta blues singer been so beguiling.

Johnson's music was thus tempered and tested in the school of romance long before it was held up to scrutiny in the dim light of a recording studio. Yet commercial recordings were the obvious goal for an artist like Johnson, who had learned so much from the 78s of other blues artists, who had worked so relentlessly to surpass the competing guitarists of his time and place. Johnson would not have been content to neglect his craft for years at a stretch, as Son House did, merely recording when, and if, the opportunity came knocking on his door. Johnson would not have been satisfied keeping his songs on the plantation, or presenting himself as a humble exponent of a folkloric tradition linked inextricably to the Delta soil. His aspirations ran much higher. Even in his teens, he had boasted that he would someday go to New York and make records. Now in his mid-twenties, secure in his mastery of the music, the time had arrived for him to make his mark on the world.

For a Delta blues musician who hoped to become a recording artist, an obvious path beckoned, indeed almost the only available path—the same one already followed by Charley Patton, Tommy Johnson, Skip James, and so many others. Accordingly, Robert Johnson strolled into H. C. Speir's emporium one day in 1936, and announced his intention of becoming a recording star. The timing could not have been worse. Speir had soured on his recent relationship with the ARC label, having recorded over one hundred masters at sessions in Jackson and Hattiesburg, only to find most of them unissued, and his promised payment never arriving. But Speir agreed to make a test acetate. Impressed with Johnson's skills at this audition, Speir passed on the name of his new find to Ernie Oertle, who covered the Southern region for ARC. Speir soon forgot about the whole matter: when tracked down by Gayle Wardlow in 1964, the former talent scout failed to recall Johnson until Wardlow played him a recording of "Kindhearted Woman Blues." Johnson's falsetto high notes stirred only the faintest memories—Speir's most famous discovery, the intercession which changed the course of American music, hardly registering on his imagination!

But Oertle followed up on Speir's lead. He sought out Johnson and personally accompanied the guitarist to San Antonio in late November 1936, where ARC's recording director Art Satherley and A&R representative Don Law were conducting sessions at the Gunter Hotel. These two British expats were unlikely advocates for the emerging styles of American popular music. Law had started in the music industry as a bookkeeper, while Satherley began by grading the timber that went into the construction of phonographs. But both became important forces in the recording of country and blues music in their adopted homeland. Indeed, both Law and Satherley have been inducted into the Country Music Hall of Fame—an honor accorded to fewer than one hundred individuals—and one suspects that it will be a long time before another non-musician from Britain joins them on its roster.

Don Law has long been considered our best source of information on these sessions, yet his condescending attitude to Johnson has tarnished the value of his testimony. The otherwise unexplained interruption of two days during Johnson's San Antonio recordings perhaps substantiates Law's claim that the guitarist had a run-in with the police. But the drama and the color of Law's account suggests that his tale was embellished in the telling. Years later, he described being interrupted at dinner, summoned to the city jail, and finding Johnson beaten and with his guitar smashed by the police. Law secures Johnson's release, returns him to the boardinghouse, and gives him forty-five cents for breakfast the next day. Yet before the night is done, Johnson calls Law again demanding another nickel, so he can afford a fifty-cent streetwalker. Law refers to the musician as "boy," and comes across much like the old plantation owner spinning yarns about his irresponsible slaves. A true incident probably undergirds this fanciful account, but its exact proportions elude us today.

Posterity has judged Johnson not by Law's testimony, but rather by the more substantial evidence of the music recorded during this Texas sojourn. Listeners are immediately struck by the versatility and variety of these songs. Johnson has an almost endless number of guitar tricks at his disposal: churning boogie rhythms, dancing triplets, syncopated turnarounds, masterful slide phrases, ingenious counterpoint lines, fidgety vamps, tasty instrumental breaks and interludes, dramatic changes in tone and texture. His vocals are, if anything, even more wide-ranging. Johnson's phrasing moves effortlessly from rough to sweet, from whispered aside to full-throated holler, and when words alone are insufficient for him, he hums or hoots or yodels or offers a moody, wordless vocal, more an expression of feeling than a proper melody. At the same time, he artfully plays with the contrast between his singing and his guitar playing. With many earlier Delta blues players, one senses that the guitar is an extension of the voice—often a phrase would start with one and be finished by the other. But with Johnson, the delineation is far more sharply drawn: he sets his guitar and his voice a range of challenging, often divergent tasks, and only on rare occasions do they double up on their journey.

The earliest Delta blues tradition had been as much about creating *sounds* as it was about playing *notes*. The same had once been true of the jazz world, too. In 1923, King Oliver could construct a whole solo just using several notes, relying on his rich tonal palette to give texture and vitality to these simple phrases. But Louis Armstrong came along and played such an endless variety of notes and complicated phrases that the simpler, heartfelt solos of King Oliver were seen by many—wrongly, in my opinion—as outmoded and primitive. One encounters a similar transformation in the history of the blues when the baton passes from Son House to Robert Johnson. If you transcribed House's music on a piece of sheet music, the notes on the page would never do justice to the sound, to House's mastery with the bottleneck or his hell-raising voice, and you might be tempted to dismiss the artistry involved in its creation. But you would never make this mistake with Robert Johnson's music. Whether transcribed, played by another guitarist, or transferred to another instrument, the inventiveness and versatility are unmistakable. True, something may have been lost in this shift from an African focus on sound to a Western preoccupation with notes. But, as with Armstrong, even more was gained. Above all, a folk music found the tools it needed to enter into the mainstream of modern music.

Johnson's "Terraplane Blues" was the only song that sold well at the time, helped no doubt by the suggestive double entendres of which record companies and blues fans never seem to tire—in this instance, the workings of an automobile (the Terraplane of the title) coyly standing in for the mechanics of coition. (The same is true of Johnson's "Phonograph Blues," with its evocative uses for the Victrola never foreseen by Thomas Edison: "We played it on the sofa, we played it 'side the wall.") But many of the other songs eventually demonstrated their hit potential. "I Believe I'll Dust My Broom" would later transform the career of Elmore James, selling so well that James would record it over and over again, and even named his band the Broomdusters. "Sweet Home Chicago" has gradually become entrenched in the popular imagination as an important part of musical Americana—helped along by Junior Parker's successful recording in 1959, and later versions by Fleetwood Mac, Foghat, and the Blues Brothers—so much so that it now threatens to displace Sinatra's "My Kind of Town" as

During his archeological work in the Delta region in 1901 and 1902 (depicted here), scholar Charles Peabody documented some of the earliest examples of Delta blues. (FROM CHARLES PEABODY, *EXPLORATION OF MOUNDS, COAHOMA COUNTY, MISSISSIPPI, JUNE 1904*)

Parchman was a cross between a prison and a plantation, and served as home, for shorter or longer periods, for many great Delta blues performers. This photo, circa 1916, shows inmates in front of the superintendent's home. (MISSISSIPPI DEPARTMENT OF ARCHIVES AND RECORDS)

A famous blues lyric mentions where "the Southern cross the Dog." It refers to the Yellow Dog passenger train, shown here at Clarksdale in 1909. (PHOTO COURTESY OF GAYLE DEAN WARDLOW)

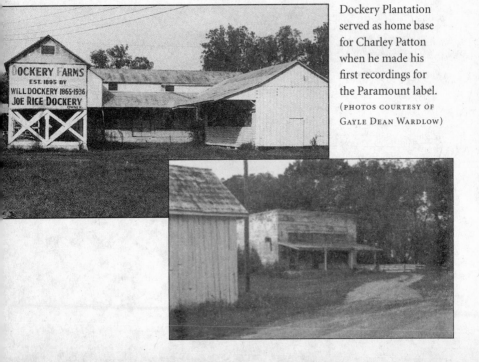

Dockery Plantation served as home base for Charley Patton when he made his first recordings for the Paramount label. (PHOTOS COURTESY OF GAYLE DEAN WARDLOW)

DOCKERY FARMS
EST. 1895 BY
WILL DOCKERY 1865-1936
JOE RICE DOCKERY
OWNER

Many blues musicians also found work in medicine shows—one of the few forums that allowed them to perform in front of large audiences in the South. (PHOTO COURTESY OF GAYLE DEAN WARDLOW)

H.C. Speir's store in Jackson, Mississippi (pictured here in 1929), was a magnet for blues musicians, such as Robert Johnson and Skip James, who came here to audition for record labels. (PHOTO COURTESY OF GAYLE DEAN WARDLOW)

Tommy Johnson ranks among the most influential Mississippi musicians from the 1920s and 1930s. But only one photo of him—from a 1929 record company catalog—is known to exist. (PHOTO COURTESY OF GAYLE DEAN WARDLOW)

The Paramount label promoted Charley Patton as the successor to Blind Lemon Jefferson, whose recordings had proven the commercial viability of traditional blues music. (IMAGE COURTESY OF GAYLE DEAN WARDLOW)

Advertising images for traditional blues recordings often played on stereotypes of dissipation and disreputable behavior. (IMAGES COURTESY OF A. PAUL PEDERSEN)

Delta workers, shown in this 1938 photo, would often work from dawn until dusk for only one dollar per day. (PHOTO BY DOROTHEA LANGE, COURTESY OF THE LIBRARY OF CONGRESS)

The Hopson Plantation, depicted in this 1940 photo, would help spur the great migration of workers out of the Delta when it introduced the mechanical cotton picker a few years later. (PHOTO BY MARION POST WOLCOTT, COURTESY OF THE LIBRARY OF CONGRESS)

On Saturdays during the Great Depression, store owners in Clarksdale, Mississippi (shown in this 1939 photo), would send trucks out into the surrounding rural areas to bring farm workers to their stores. (PHOTO BY MARION POST WOLCOTT, COURTESY OF THE LIBRARY OF CONGRESS)

W.C. Handy brought the blues into the world of popular music, most notably in his composition "St. Louis Blues," after being inspired by an unknown Delta guitarist at a railway station. (PHOTO BY CARL VAN VECHTEN, COURTESY OF THE LIBRARY OF CONGRESS)

John and Alan Lomax found the prisoners at Parchman Farm Penitentiary (shown here in 1959) to be an almost inexhaustible source of blues, work songs, and other traditional styles of African-American music. (PHOTO BY ALAN LOMAX, COURTESY OF THE ALAN LOMAX ARCHIVE)

Fred McDowell, a star of the blues revival movement in the 1960s, is shown here with his wife and guitar on the porch of their home in Como, Mississippi.

Alan Lomax, shown listening to a playback during his 1959 Southern U.S. field trip, played a major role in recording and documenting the music of the Delta region. (PHOTO BY SHIRLEY COLLINS, COURTESY OF THE ALAN LOMAX ARCHIVE)

John Hurt and Skip James both enjoyed a tremendous uplift in their careers during mid-1960s, but neither would survive the decade. Here they are shown at Newport in 1964. (PHOTO BY DICK WATERMAN)

Skip James entertains the audience at Newport in 1964, in a celebrated performance. (PHOTO BY DICK WATERMAN)

Two great American institutions: Son House and the Liberty Bell, from a Philadelphia visit in 1965. (PHOTO BY DICK WATERMAN)

Booker White disappeared from the blues scene until two intrepid fans tracked him down in 1963. This photo shows him performing at Newport in 1965. (PHOTO BY DICK WATERMAN)

Muddy Waters and James Cotton were both Mississippi natives who also helped shape the sound of Chicago blues. Here they are pictured in New York City in 1965. (PHOTO BY DICK WATERMAN)

These three blues legends—Son House, Skip James, and John Hurt—all reemerged on the music scene in the mid-1960s after decades of obscurity. This photo was taken at Newport in 1965. (PHOTO BY DICK WATERMAN)

Robert Lockwood learned guitar from his stepfather, the legendary Robert Johnson. Lockwood's experimentation with jazz techniques and electric music perhaps gives us an indication of the direction Johnson himself might have taken, had he lived longer. (PHOTO BY DICK WATERMAN)

Howlin' Wolf energizes the audience at Newport, 1966. (PHOTO BY DICK WATERMAN)

The first Ann Arbor Blues Festival in 1969 was a signal event in bringing blues music to the attention of a larger audience. Here B.B. King entertains the audience with his soulful guitar stylings. (PHOTO BY DICK WATERMAN)

Ike Turner and John Lee Hooker, both raised in Clarksdale, Mississippi, took different musical paths—Turner embraced rock and roll and R&B, while Hooker stayed true to his blues roots. They are shown here in Los Angeles in 1998. (PHOTO BY DICK WATERMAN)

the anthem for the Windy City. The influence of this body of music has, in fact, expanded with each passing decade, and Johnson the blues musician has almost become eclipsed by Johnson the hit songwriter, whose compositions, almost all of them unknown to the general public a quarter century after Johnson's death, are today rendered with devotion by rockers, lounge acts, garage bands, and karaoke machines. Even if these imitators often fall short of the intensity of the original, their reverence at the feet of the master stands as fitting homage to the man who brought the Delta sound into the wider orbits of global pop music.

On the final day of his San Antonio sessions, Johnson recorded two of his best dance numbers, "They're Red Hot" and "Last Fair Deal Gone Down." Both of these songs, evoking the pitches of street vendors, look backward to the world of medicine shows and itinerant merchants in their lyrics (at least the surface meaning—again, double entendres may beckon), but even more markedly anticipate the future evolution of jump tunes and rhythm-and-blues. The tempo accelerates markedly in "Last Fair Deal Gone Down": the intro starts at a slow, stately pace; the pulse increases by half during the first chorus, and picks up further steam as the song progresses, eventually hopping along at more than 200 beats per minute. The quickening pace may perhaps be seen as a defect on Johnson's part, but it may equally be due to Johnson's long experience that acceleration during a song can energize the dancers. Or perhaps he simply rushed in order to finish the song before the primitive "disk space" of 1930s recording technology hit its limits. "They're Red Hot" adheres more closely to a strict tempo, and shows again the versatility of Johnson's vocalizing: it almost sounds as if the singer is creating several separate personas on this one song, each with a distinctive timbre, evoking a dialogue between them. Johnson growls and shouts and even offers some muttered comic hokum reminiscent of Fats Waller. This is the most lighthearted interlude in all of Johnson's oeuvre, opening up a different perspective on this supposedly devil-haunted soul.

Yet at the close of the San Antonio sessions, the darker, more apocalyptic side of Johnson's work emerges. On "Cross Road Blues," "Preaching Blues (Up Jumped the Devil)," and his final song "If I Had Possession Over Judgment Day," Johnson evokes the themes of damnation and redemption, darkness and light, in searing, intense performances that have struck many as autobiographies in acetate, glimpses into the musician's inner life, and all its attendant turmoils. Here the blues is "like consumption killing me by degrees," and Johnson describes falling down on his knees by the crossroads, praying, "have mercy, save poor Bob, if you please." The guitarist again uses his own name in "Preaching Blues (Up Jumped the Devil)," where he sings: "Travel on, poor Bob, just can't turn you around." Blues fans have been accused of overly romanticizing these songs, drawing too heavily on them in their perspectives on the man who sang them. Yet Johnson himself, with these personal references in the lyrics, seems to intend that these songs should be heard as revelations of his own private demons.

The same unsettling themes would emerge—in fact, would be even more prominent—when Johnson returned to the studio the following year in Dallas, to make what would prove to be his final recordings. This should have been a happy time for the guitarist. In the months following the San Antonio sessions, Johnson must have enjoyed a taste of the kind of fame commercial recordings bestow upon a musician. "Terraplane Blues" was issued in March 1937, with "Kindhearted Woman Blues" on the flip side, and was a modest hit, appearing on Delta jukeboxes and gaining notoriety for the man who sang it. Years later, blues researchers would use this song to help establish the places where Johnson traveled. It was so well known that it would spur recollections from those who otherwise might have forgotten the itinerant guitarist. ARC followed up by releasing more Johnson 78s in April and May, and arranging for additional recordings to be made in Dallas in June.

These follow-up sessions took place in a makeshift recording studio housed in the offices of Brunswick Records, two blocks east of the Dallas City Hall. Here Johnson started the proceedings with the same anguished tone that he had adopted at the close of the San Antonio sessions. In "Stones in My Passway," he returns to the themes of physical and mental malaise, treachery and danger, and again addresses himself by his Christian name: "My enemies have betrayed me, have overtaken poor Bob at last." The song revisits the musical landscape of "Terraplane Blues," but the salacious hints of the earlier piece are replaced by a jeremiad in blues form, a modern equivalent of the Psalms offered up by David in his moments of deepest despair. Here, and elsewhere in the songs from the Dallas sessions, Johnson touches briefly on the classic blues subjects of love and longing, but rarely for long and usually with a heavy dose of cynicism or coarseness. The brief "Honeymoon Blues," with its promises of eternal devotion, is the only true love song from these sessions, but the sentiments sound perfunctory in comparison with the piece Johnson recorded next, his poignant "Love in Vain," with its disillusionment and dolorous pronouncement of the impotency of human affections. Others have sung of romantic failure, but one senses here a deeper strain, a lament of the failure of romance—in totality, both in abstraction and its most concrete manifestations. It is hard to accept that a successful, young musician in his mid-twenties would write a song of this sort, a pronouncement of such total resignation and despair. But throughout the works he recorded in Dallas, Johnson constantly overturns our expectations, violating almost all of the sacred conventions of popular music.

Nowhere is this clearer than in "Hellhound on My Trail." This remains one of Johnson's best known and most admired performances—many would say it is his greatest—yet (in comparison with his other works) few other musicians have dared to record it. Haunting and haunted, it steps on perilous ground where popular songs rarely go, trespassing on the rightful domain of the confessional or counselor's couch. "No matter how many times I have listened to it," Peter Guralnick has written, "it still seems to come out of a void, it seems impossible to imagine a recording engineer saying, 'Could we have another take of that one, Bob?' . . . When the song was concluded, one might have expected the singer to be enveloped in a swirling mist." Johnson's singing, usually so controlled, sounds strained, his voice ready to crack or run off pitch. If this were the last performance of the day, this might make sense, but "Hellhound" was the first song he recorded on his final day in the studio on that Sunday in Dallas. The next song he records, "Little Queen of Spades," returns to the casual, carefree delivery we associate with Johnson the traveling musician. It is hard to believe that the same person is singing these two songs, so different is the tone and timbre.

For "Hellhound," Johnson turned to that master of the mournful minor-key blues, Skip James, relying on James's trademark open minor tuning and drawing inspiration from his "Devil Got My Woman." As we have seen, Johnson typically borrowed from the most popular blues records; hence James is an odd choice as a role model. Yet if the Bentonia guitarist sold poorly, he was the most ambitious of Johnson's predecessors, the one who had the highest aspirations for the blues as a form of poetic expression. James aimed to create something akin to art song, rising above the conventions of popular entertainment. So we should not be surprised that when Johnson breaks out of the confines of the blues idiom, reaching for the highest effects and the most profound level of expression, he should look to the composer of "Hard Time Killin' Floor" and "Devil Got My Woman."

"Hellhound on My Trail" deals with the familiar blues theme of the rambling musician, but now the trip takes on darker tones, the traveler is *pursued*. The listener is left to ponder whether the hellhound of the title is real or metaphorical, but the sense of being chased and hunted is powerfully evoked, as in those nightmares that leave you struggling to outrun some vaguely understood but deeply felt danger. Later that same day, Johnson returned to this troubling theme in "Me and the Devil Blues," and here the demoniac aspect is addressed with even greater directness, no longer presented in hints and asides, but stated explicitly. Johnson sings: "Hello Satan, I believe it's time to go. Me and the Devil was walkin' side by side."

The record company, for its part, must have seen a good marketing angle here: "Hellhound on My Trail" was the first recording released from the session, and the final 78 releases of Johnson's output included his "Me and the Devil Blues" and "Preaching Blues (Up Jumped the Devil)." For better or worse, Johnson's reputation as a devil-haunted man was now firmly established.

4. three forks

Johnny Shines recalls meeting up with Johnson in Red Water, Texas, after the Dallas sessions and working around the state for much of the year, moving to the south as the weather drew colder. Perhaps Shines has confused these final recordings with the earlier San Antonio sessions, which took place in November 1936, and would have been a more likely preamble for a winter tour of the border area. Although the precise chronology of the trips made by the two is lost to us, the amount of time they spent together was substantial, establishing Shines as our single best source of information on Johnson's years as a traveling musician. In particular, Shines's testimony allows us to calibrate the troubled singer of "Hellhound on My Trail" against the man himself.

Shines's whole later career would be led under Johnson's shadow—unfairly so, since this fine blues shouter never was a Johnson imitator. His earliest influence had been Howlin' Wolf, and Shines even earned the nickname "Little Wolf." In time, he developed his own distinctive blues voice, but popular recognition always seemed to elude him. In 1946, Shines recorded for Columbia, but the music remained unreleased for a quarter of a century. Later, when he was making his best recordings for the Chess and J.O.B. labels in the 1950s, Shines was never able to keep a regular working band, and was forced to devote his day hours to exhausting construction work. By the close of the decade, he was so disgusted with the music industry that he pawned his last guitar and tore up the ticket. But the reissue of Johnson's work in the 1960s, and the tremendous exposure given to it, and to other traditional blues artists, created new opportunities for Shines at this late date in his career. Even so, Shines's extroverted, high-energy style was unlikely to appeal to the fans who wanted him to play mournful traditional blues in the style of Robert Johnson. At his death in 1992, the obituaries memorialized him less for his own artistry than for his sporadic travels with this legendary figure during the 1930s.

The Robert Johnson described by Shines bears little resemblance to the mythical figure standing at the crossroads of blues lore. No signs of anguish or psychological turmoil could be detected in the guitarist's day-to-day behavior. And though many have seen Johnson's recordings as evidence that he had premonitions of an early death, his traveling companion saw no indications of such gloomy preoccupations. Yet Johnson was a quirky person, and the eccentricities noted by Shines support McCormick's view that Johnson led a compartmentalized life, with different personas coming to the fore depending on the setting, while much of his inner life remained zealously guarded. Arriving in a new community, Johnson exuded a rare degree of charisma, and Shines marveled at how quickly he could gather a crowd around him, how intensely people were drawn to him—not just the women, who responded to the overt sexuality of his music, but even the men, who may have resented his presence yet still found themselves attracted by his aura of power. Yet in other settings, Johnson came across as solitary and aloof, leaving Shines to wonder how much he really understood his friend. Johnson must have deliberately avoided self-disclosure in his casual conversation, since years later Shines could not recall a single comment he ever made about his home, his parents, his upbringing, his many half brothers and half sisters—only an occasional reference to his stepfather. At times, Johnson would disappear, without saying good-bye or giving any indication why he was leaving or where he was going. In following Johnson's trail years later, McCormick frequently encountered similar descriptions of unexpected departures; and he eventually came to feel that this telling detail served as confirmation that a mysterious guitarist named Robert—the last name varied, as we have seen—in any given account was actually the famous bluesman, so characteristic were these unexplained absences, this urgent need to keep on moving. Shines made particular note of Johnson's restlessness. "See, Robert was a guy, you could wake him up anytime and he was ready to *go.* . . . You say, 'Robert, I hear a train, let's catch it.' He wouldn't exchange no words with you; he's just ready to go. . . . It didn't make him no difference, just so he was going. He just wanted to go."

Although Johnson showed no premonitions of death, at least as far as Shines could tell, he did reveal the judgment lapses that may have led to his early demise. Alcohol certainly contributed to this problem, but was not its underlying cause. "He wasn't able to take care of himself when he started drinking," Shines explains. Then adds: "As a matter of fact, he wasn't man enough to take care of himself when he wasn't drinking." Johnson would get into a fight with a larger man, or with a group of men, even though "he couldn't punch hisself out of a wet paper sack." Sometimes Shines would step in to defend his companion, only to take a beating himself. Above all, Johnson tempted fate through his forwardness with other men's wives and girlfriends, which sometimes led to unpleasant confrontations or required a hasty departure by the duo, guitars in hand.

"He loved whiskey and he was crazy about his women," David "Honey-boy" Edwards substantiates. "That's two things he was crazy about. And that was his downfall." Edwards hooked up with Johnson a short while before the latter's death, and is our best source of information on the circumstances of the final chapter in the bluesman's biography. Yet though we rely on Edwards, the inconsistencies in his various statements are troubling. In later years, he would explain how he occasionally accompanied Johnson to perform at a jukehouse outside of Greenwood—at a location known as Three Forks, found at the intersection of Highway 82 with Highway 49—where the fatal events unfolded. But an earlier account, typically ignored by researchers, presents a different story. In an interview conducted by Pete Welding in July 1967, Edwards claimed that Three Forks was the name of the cemetery where Johnson was buried, and that Johnson was poisoned at a country dance, not a jukehouse. Mack McCormick, for his part, tells me that he canvassed the area extensively, and that it is difficult to substantiate the existence at that time of either a cemetery or a jukehouse under that name.

But there is little dispute about the motivation for the alleged murder. "Now this guy that Robert was working for, he had a wife," Edwards explains. "A nice-made woman, nice-looking, brownskin. . . . And she had a sister lived out in Greenwood, near where Robert was rooming at, and every Monday she had to go see her sister. And would lay up with him all day. She kept doing that every Monday. The man thought, 'You go see your sister every Monday.' And someone, his friends, whispered, 'She layin' back there with Robert.' Robert should have left her alone—he would have lived longer." The jealous husband made no show of his suspicions, and continued to befriend Johnson; but this would be the guitarist's last indiscretion.

On Saturday, August 13, 1938, Edwards arrived at the jukehouse shortly before midnight to find Johnson sitting in a corner, with his guitar under his arm, too sick to perform. Patrons urged him to keep on playing; told him to drink some whiskey and he would feel better. Johnson tried once or twice to play something on the guitar, but soon abandoned the effort. Edwards believed that the vengeful husband had someone give Johnson poisoned whiskey. Johnson was placed on a bed in the back of the house, and before dawn was brought back to his room in Greenwood. Sonny Boy Williamson II, who visited Johnson shortly before his death, told Shines that the guitarist was crawling on the floor like a dog, howling in agony—in the eyes of the credulous, a sign that the devil had come to take his due. Edwards's account is more circumspect, but no less tragic: when he visited Johnson on Tuesday, the guitarist was unable to talk, heaving and bleeding at the mouth. Later that day, he died.

Researchers have attempted to fill in more details of the circumstances surrounding the death of the Delta's most famous bluesman. Johnson's death certificate, found by Gayle Wardlow in 1968, opens as many questions as it answers. A note on the back of the certificate, summarizes the findings of the LeFlore County Registrar, Cornelia J. Jordan:

> I talked with the white man on whose place this negro died and I also talked with a negro woman on the place. The plantation owner said this negro man, seemingly about 26 years old, came from Tunica two or three weeks before he died to play a banjo at a negro dance given there on the plantation. He staid [sic] in the house with some of the

negroes saying he wanted to pick cotton. The white man did not have
a doctor for this negro as he had not worked for him. He was buried
in a homemade coffin furnished by the county. The plantation owner
said it was his opinion that the negro died of syphilis.

Almost every fact here runs in the face of our knowledge of Johnson
and the details provided by Edwards and others. The banjo, the plantation,
Johnson's apparent desire to pick cotton, the attributed cause of death, the
length of Johnson's stay in the area—not only do they fail to add to our
store of information, they actually run counter to what we think we know.
The reliability of the death certificate is further compromised by the fact
that the person listed as the source of the information—"Jim Moore"—is a
name that Mack McCormick insists is an alias. He believes that one of Johnson's brothers-in-law adopted this false name for reasons that are far from
clear—except, perhaps, to McCormick, who now suspects that facts on the
document may have been deliberately falsified. Yet another source, Rosie
Eskridge, who claimed that her husband dug the grave for Robert Johnson,
has confirmed that a Jim Moore lived on the Luther Wade Plantation. But
this does not necessarily disprove McCormick's assertion—the name Jim
Moore is common enough, and the Wade Plantation resident may not have
been the source listed on the death certificate. Eskridge's testimony has also
led to an alternative account, in which Johnson dies on the Wade Plantation,
after being carried there from Greenwood, or perhaps from the jukehouse.
Problems with chronology and coherence, as well as McCormick's unpublished research, cast considerable doubt on Eskridge's story. The fact that
she gave her testimony more than sixty years after the event does not add to
our confidence in her account.

McCormick has offered us a few tantalizing details of his quest for Johnson's supposed killer. His inquiries pointed him to a specific individual. But
when he arrived at the man's home, the suspect came out of the door with a
shotgun. Eventually the man's hostility subsided and he invited McCormick
in to talk. At first he offered a detailed alibi for the long-distant day in 1938,
but as the conversation progressed, he broke down and admitted to the
murder. He never realized, he said, that killing this itinerant musician would
be the cause of such long-lasting troubles for him. McCormick dutifully
provided the information to the LeFlore County sheriff, who disdained the
idea of pursuing a lead on an incident after more than thirty years had

elapsed. McCormick, for his part, has refused to publicize the name of the person who confessed to Johnson's murder.

But even without a conviction in a court of law, or more substantial testimony from McCormick, the evidence that Johnson was murdered is compelling. Except for the dubious suggestion of syphilis on the back of the death certificate—a document which seems riddled with, at best errors, at worst intentional deceptions—all indications point to foul play. Johnson had no history of poor health, no reason why he would suddenly take ill in the midst of a performance. He was young and at the peak of his powers, and the onset of his affliction surprisingly sudden. A motive of revenge is easy to substantiate. Moreover, those who knew Johnson during his life believed that he was murdered. Even blues fans who never met Johnson heard rumors of his murder, at a time when virtually nothing had been published about the man or his music.

The only substantial reviews of Johnson's music during his lifetime had appeared in *The New Masses*, an influential voice for left-wing politics and commentary during the Great Depression. The first piece, from March 2, 1937, is attributed to Henry Johnson, which we now know was a pseudonym for John Hammond—Hammond's FBI files indicate that this was the "party name" he used as a political activist. The article lauds Johnson as the greatest African-American blues singer of recent years, comparing him favorably to Leadbelly. A follow-up discussion of Johnson's music, from the June 8 issue of the same periodical, is specifically attributed to Hammond. Hammond's involvement with *The New Masses* would soon catch the attention of J. Edgar Hoover and the FBI. In a letter to Agent E. J. Connelley, dated July 3, 1941, Hoover specifically mentions Hammond's relation to *The New Masses* and his musical interests in a directive to conduct an appropriate investigation "to determine whether this person should be considered for custodial detention" in the event of a "national emergency." Around this time, the FBI put considerable energy into investigating Alan Lomax, another great advocate of African-American music—an interest that suggests that, at least to some authorities in positions of power, the blues was not mere idle entertainment but a potential lightning rod for sentiments of protest or even open revolt.

As events turned out, the political implications of the traditional blues would remain latent, rarely becoming overt or direct, just as Hammond's role in politics would be modest, although his impact in the world of music would be profound. Indeed, had Johnson lived only a few years longer, it is likely that Hammond would have helped transform him into a commercial artist of wide renown, perhaps even stardom. Toward the end of 1938, Hammond began planning a concert at Carnegie Hall to raise money for *The New Masses*; the performance, which he called "From Spirituals to Swing," would present a mini-history of African-American music. Hammond hoped to feature Robert Johnson at this historic event, but soon learned that Johnson had died the previous summer. The promoter enlisted Big Bill Broonzy in Johnson's stead. Yet Hammond remained intent on sharing Johnson's music with the assembled audience in America's most honored concert hall. At the event, held on December 23, Hammond praised Johnson lavishly from the stage, and played two phonograph records—"Walking Blues" and "Preaching Blues (Up Jumped the Devil)"—for the attentive listeners. Here, if only through the medium of recordings, Hammond used his considerable influence at this historic event to advocate a position of preeminence for the late Delta bluesman.

The legend of Robert Johnson was no doubt born that winter day in Carnegie Hall. Decades would elapse before the meaningful details of a biography would emerge. But in the very absence of information, fanciful accounts were inevitably embellished, unimpeded by facts. Yet even with our much deeper knowledge today, the figure of Robert Johnson still carries with it the aura of myth. To a certain extent, the facts cannot compete with the larger-than-life persona that Johnson himself helped to craft. He imparted to the blues a lasting mark, the imprint of his tumultuous life, that would ensure that these songs would always retain an anguished, otherworldly element, an intangible quality that resists our best efforts to codify, define, and explain. And though the prevailing trend is to try to demystify and debunk—to bring Johnson back into the realm of everyday people, not much different than you or me—this effort is almost certainly bound to fail. Johnson *was* different; his life and music fell outside the mainstream; almost everything we know about him makes this abundantly clear. Just as the Delta blues retains its dark and impenetrable shades, no matter how much light we try to put on it, so does its greatest exponent.

We may never be able to fully explain Robert Johnson's dark night of the soul, but even less should we try to explain it away, or refuse to admit its hypnotic power. Johnson may have set in motion new grand schemes for popular music, recrafting the blues as a commercial form of expression, but a core element of his music and persona remained hidden from view, not available for public consumption. And just as Johnson went by different names in various communities, so his music presents different faces to the world, shifting meanings and identities, some easily accessed and understood, others holding on to an element of mystery we are unlikely ever to penetrate.

Muddy Waters

i'm a rolling stone

1. gonna pack my suitcase and make my getaway

Robert Johnson did *not* take the stage of Carnegie Hall on December 23, 1938, to regale the assembled audience with his blues. But what happened that night was perhaps even more remarkable. The gathered crowd sat attentively while John Hammond played 78 recordings of the late bluesman, and the rich symbolism of this moment should not be lost on us. Other musicians had graced the stage of Carnegie Hall, but who had received the rare distinction of having a chic audience assemble in such august surroundings to listen to a *recorded* performance? For the first time, the Delta blues was treated as almost a museum piece, as an important legacy from the past worthy of preservation and veneration. The fact that Johnson was dead—Hammond described, with characteristic hyperbole, how the guitarist had died at the "precise moment" he received the invitation to perform at Carnegie Hall—only magnified the special mood of awe and reverence that marked this extraordinary interlude. If for just a few minutes, the blues transcended all the limitations of its marginalized existence, and became more than just another out-of-fashion style of commercial music, more than just the lowbrow artistic expression of a segregated and repressed minority.

The blues revival would not gain momentum in the United States for another two decades. But we can date the first stirrings of the spirit of that revival to Hammond's daring move. Elijah Wald has suggested that John Hammond was the "only man on earth," circa 1938, to hold such an exalted opinion of Johnson and his Delta blues music. But as fate would have it, Hammond was the man on stage that night, the evening's impresario and holder of the bully pulpit. And, as his long career testifies, Hammond possessed the rare gift of imparting his personal enthusiasms to the rest of America. He did it with his passion for Johnson, just as he did it for Billie Holiday, Count Basie, Bob Dylan, Aretha Franklin, Stevie Ray Vaughan, Bruce Springsteen, and so many others during a career of some five decades. Hammond's tastes were impeccable, and his timing consistently a few steps ahead of the crowd. For all his faults, he retained a childlike zeal for promoting the underappreciated artist who deserved a better hearing, a trait that is both endearing and deserving of emulation today. Since his death, no one has filled this role on such a grand stage in the world of popular music. We deserve a new John Hammond, but fumble along with the likes of Dr. Dre and Simon Cowell.

But if a blues revival were in the making, it would inevitably attract the interest of that other keeper of the musical zeitgeist of midcentury America, Alan Lomax. Lomax was even more relentless in promoting out-of-favor music than Hammond, and even less constrained by commercial considerations. On his pioneering field recording trips, conducted initially as an assistant to his father John Lomax and later under his own direction, he would cover the widest possible range, both geographically and stylistically. For a time, it seemed that Alan Lomax was everywhere, tracking down obscure blues singers and hoary old balladeers, hooting hillbillies and lonesome cowboys, uncovering the neglected musical traditions of levee camps and prisons, celebrating fiddlers and fifers, square dance callers and shapenote singers, finally taking his act overseas to England, Spain, and Italy, looking for new settings where he might find a neglected musical tradition in need of nurturing and care. Along the way, he made recordings and films, produced radio and television shows, wrote books, compiled anthologies, conducted oral histories, even sang and played the guitar. His presence looms large over any attempt to come to grips with vernacular American music of the last century.

Lomax was not without his detractors. J. Edgar Hoover and the FBI were the most vehement of these adversaries. They remained suspicious of his far left leanings, and investigated him sporadically over a period of forty years. Of course, they had done the same for Hammond—whom they contemplated arresting if changes in the political situation justified, or allowed, such forceful measures against Communist Party members and fellow travelers. But Lomax received even greater scrutiny over a far longer period of time. As late as 1979, the Bureau was considering allegations, on the flimsiest of grounds, that Lomax had impersonated an FBI agent. During the course of their several investigations, federal agents interviewed Lomax's colleagues and acquaintances, kept note of his drinking habits, his credit record, his personal hygiene and mannerisms, tracked down his college grades, his pattern of traffic violations, whatever they could find. The investigators uncovered little evidence of criminal activity, but they compensated for it in their reports with vague criticisms of his appearance and demeanor. One informant stated that "Lomax was a very peculiar individual, that he seemed to be very absent-minded and that he paid practically no attention to his personal appearance." One can only laugh at the assessment, provided by this same anonymous individual, that Lomax's eccentricities and poor grooming habits came from associating too closely with the "hillbillies" who taught him folk tunes. No charges were ever filed against either Lomax or Hammond, but not for lack of zeal on the Bureau's part.

Yet Lomax was hardly better received in music circles. Critics carped that Lomax and his father exploited their role as advocates for the Texas bluesman Huddie Ledbetter, better known as Leadbelly, whose performing career they worked to further after the singer's release from prison. Some sensed a tone of condescension in the Lomaxes' relationship to their "find"—Lomax Senior had the singer serve as his driver, and asked him to pass the hat after he finished singing at their joint engagements. Moreover, the Lomaxes' contract with Leadbelly gave them a whopping two thirds of all his earnings, and prevented him from being represented by any other party for a five-year term. The benefits the pair enjoyed from this relationship were substantial: Alan Lomax's travels to Europe in the 1950s were largely made possible by the financial success of Leadbelly's song "Goodnight, Irene." Nor was this an isolated incident. Even today, a visitor to the Web site of BMI, the organization that collects license fees for some 300,000 songwriters, composers, and publishers, can conduct a quick search to see the long list of songs for which Alan Lomax apparently claimed composer credit—including "Amazing Grace," "Buffalo Gals," "John Henry," "Stagger Lee," and some eight hundred other titles. True, Lomax was not alone in this practice: many performers have recorded traditional material with their own name listed as composer. Yet Lomax's position with the Library of Congress, and his self-appointed role as custodian of America's music traditions, should have led him to aspire to a higher standard of ethics in such matters.

Alan Lomax's fieldwork in the Delta region in 1941 and 1942 would also lead to controversy, although not until more than sixty years had elapsed. In their book *Lost Delta Found* (2005), Robert Gordon and Bruce Nemerov charge Lomax with taking undue credit for the results of the Delta research project, and claim that he unfairly downplayed the contributions of his collaborators from Fisk University. Sketching out a tale of "name-calling, hostility, deception," in Gordon's words, the editors suggest that Lomax lost—or, even worse, may have deliberately hidden or appropriated—the research materials compiled by his colleagues John W. Work, Lewis Wade Jones, and Samuel Adams, Jr. Gordon and Nemerov also take exception to Lomax's own account of his Delta fieldwork, published in 1993 as *The Land Where the Blues Began*, complaining that it is full of "historical inaccuracies," and in particular conflates two separate trips into the Delta into the story of a single visit. These charges achieved such prominence at the time of the publication of *Lost Delta Found* that they spilled over into the mainstream press, and were covered prominently by the *New York Times* and other newspapers and periodicals. A sixty-year-old squabble among researchers would hardly have such visibility, except for the fact that Lomax was white, and his Fisk collaborators were black. Hence a charge of racism was the real "story" latched onto by the press—a reproach all the more striking since it was made against a man whose career was largely built around the advocacy of African-American music.

Gordon and Nemerov have done us a great service in tracking down the scholarship of Work, Jones, and Adams, and presenting it in book form. Yet their accusations against Lomax are less praiseworthy. Gordon certainly must be disingenuous when he describes his surprise upon learning about "the other guy," namely, John Work III, who participated in the Delta research. In point of fact, Work's participation was never kept secret—not by Lomax, during the 1940s or at any other point, nor by anyone else. Even a casual fan who has read the liner notes to the commercial recordings of the Library of Congress material can see it in plain print: I count a dozen citations in the notes to my 1999 Rounder compact disk *Mississippi: The Blues Lineage*, released at a time when Work's contributions had supposedly been "erased" by his more prominent colleague. And the three Fisk collaborators are the very first names mentioned by Lomax in the opening sentence of his acknowledgments to *The Land Where the Blues Began*. Of course, Work's reputation does not rely on Lomax's citations alone: his 1940 book *American Negro Songs and Spirituals* has long remained in print, and should be on the shelf of every serious scholar of black musical traditions. Given this, one finds it hard to believe any knowledgeable blues scholar would see Work as some unknown person whose identity has to be uncovered by research and sleuthing.

Did Lomax work to hide the contributions of these scholars? Roger Abrahams, a noted scholar of African-American culture, has indicated that Lomax was very open in talking about his Fisk collaboration. Lomax even opened up his files, showing Abrahams the Fisk documents, and offering to share them. Don Fleming has further pointed out that the supposedly "lost manuscript" that Nemerov and Gordon found was a mimeographed copy—in other words, Lomax kept a copy of the research, not the original. Surviving correspondence in the Library of Congress shows that Lomax sometimes served as an advocate who promoted Work's efforts. Certainly Alan Lomax had his faults, and a critical survey of his career would uncover more than a few blemishes and oversights. But the Delta project—which is now viewed by some as the classic example of his bad faith as a scholar—does not deserve this reproach. And the implication that Lomax was a racist, perhaps the most lasting impact of *Lost Delta Found*, is especially unfortunate and unwarranted.

Lomax may have already had the idea of a field trip to the Delta in mind when he visited Fisk University in late April 1941 to participate in the festivities surrounding the institution's seventy-fifth anniversary. Even as a teenager, when he served as an assistant to his father on field recordings made at Parchman, Lomax had witnessed firsthand the musical riches of the region. The potential benefits of a more extensive follow-up project must have long

been obvious to him, and according to his account (although viewed skep-
tically by Nemerov and Gordon) he was the initiator of discussions about
a collaborative project between the Library of Congress, where Lomax
worked, and Fisk University. John Work had previously been struggling to
garner institutional support for his own fieldwork in Mississippi, but Work
wanted to focus on the Natchez area, well outside the Delta region. In April
1940, a devastating fire in Natchez had claimed two hundred victims. Work
hoped to make a visit to the area the following spring, on the anniversary
of the fire, and document any songs memorializing the event and its victims. Work's proposal failed to attract support, and following Lomax's visit,
which took place after the first anniversary of the fire had already come
and gone, the Fisk scholar seemed more interested in focusing his attention on Tennessee fiddlers and singers. Lomax, for his part, was rebuffed
in his efforts to secure the active participation of Fisk sociologist Charles S.
Johnson, but accepted Johnson's research assistant Lewis Jones and graduate student Samuel Adams as members of the team. The upshot of all this
was that Lomax emerged as the key leader of the project, supplying equipment, expertise, funding, and above all the vision of tracing the roots of the
blues in the Delta region.

Lomax was convinced that the blues idiom had originated in the Delta
region sometime around 1900. Unraveling the roots of this storied music—
which he saw as a "creative deployment of African style in an American
setting, the operation of African temperament in new surroundings"—
fascinated him, perhaps more than any issue he had addressed during his
long and active career. Its hold on his imagination can be measured by the
striking fact that he continued to obsess on the topic for another fifty years,
and was almost eighty years old when he finally completed his book on the
Delta, a work that would prove to be his last major publication, and the
most in-depth study he would ever write on any style of music.

The team's efforts were commensurate with the richness of the subject
matter at hand. Although Lomax was first and foremost a song collector, the
Coahoma County project encompassed much more. Attempts at a rigorous,
sociological methodology, no doubt fostered by the influence of Charles
Johnson, who had used statistical techniques in studying African-American
culture in the past, complemented Lomax's impressionistic approach. A
four-page questionnaire was completed by a hundred families—including
Muddy Waters's—and a wide range of cultural practices documented. The

study encompassed folk tales, customs, religious beliefs, plantation poverty, midwifery, a whole panoply of social activities and attitudes, far beyond anything Lomax had tackled in the past. Yet the makeup of the team was as remarkable as its methodologies: mixing white and black researchers together on a project of this scope had never been attempted previously in the Deep South. And though such diversity might give the team access to people and information closed to a more homogenous group, the close collaboration of the Library of Congress and Fisk University was likely to meet with suspicion, and perhaps overt hostility, in the Delta region itself. The United States' entry into World War II also threatened to stop the project, and Lomax considered terminating the research in the aftermath of Pearl Harbor. In short, the Delta project represented one of the most ambitious scholarly projects of its day.

Yet, on some levels, the project was a failure. The team's efforts were expected to result in a book, jointly edited and published by Fisk University and the Library of Congress. But this never happened. And the charges of Nemerov and Gordon have further tainted the reputation of this historic enterprise. Nonetheless, the music itself, the tremendous recorded legacy of the 1941 and 1942 field trips, is beyond reproach. Lomax documented some of the finest blues ever to come out of the Delta. Here is our last chance to hear Son House as a young man—he would not record again for over two decades. Here is our final encounter with the enigmatic and brilliant Willie Brown. Here is our introduction to David "Honeyboy" Edwards, never recorded by the commercial labels in his youth, but destined to become one of the most lauded elder statesmen of the traditional blues music. And here is our first glimpse of the great Muddy Waters—playing guitar in a humble sharecropper's shack—whose talent would raise him to a level of stardom no previous Delta musician had enjoyed.

In the late 1930s, John Hammond had told Lomax about Robert Johnson, and communicated his enthusiasm to the young song collector. Lomax had concluded that Johnson ranked alongside Blind Lemon Jefferson as the finest traditional blues singer ever recorded by commercial record companies. During his Mississippi fieldwork, he tried to follow Johnson's trail, and even describes an encounter with Johnson's mother in his book. His reference to her as Mary Johnson—in fact, the bluesman's mother was named Julia—casts some doubt over this entire account, yet the details of it ring true. Mary Johnson laments her son's attraction to the blue's life, indicates that "whippin' never did him no good," talks about his wandering ways, and describes his death from poisoning. These match closely details later gathered on Johnson from other sources.

Yet if Robert Johnson was no longer alive, and thus unable to regale the Library of Congress representative with his songs, Lomax managed to track down and record many of the musicians who had played alongside Johnson. Lomax found Son House living on a plantation a few miles away from Johnson's mother, and surprised the tractor driver with his interest in talking about the blues. "I'm used to plowin' so many acres a week and saying Yessuh and Nossuh to the boss on the plantation, but for sitting down and talking about my music with some man from college like you, I just never thought about it happenin' to me." House would also oblige Lomax by bringing the researcher to Robert Johnson's mother, introducing him to other musicians, and putting on an impromptu performance, which Lomax would later recall as one of the highlights of his career.

> I don't know where Son took me. Down dusty roads, along a railroad track, into the back of an aging country grocery store that smelt of licorice and dill pickles and snuff. There was a jug there that gurgled, and it was so hot that Son House and his buddies stripped to the waist as they played. Of all of my times with the blues this was the best one, better than Leadbelly, better than Josh White, Son Terry, and all the rest of them.

House's voice is at top form on his Library of Congress recordings, strong and authoritative, and it provides the compelling centerpiece of these performances. His vocal line sometimes drops far below the register of his guitar accompaniment, rumbling under the chords like a ground tremor pulsating through the music; or he hums along in counterpoint, or pulls back to let his bottleneck continue or respond to a phrase, the instrument now emulating the singer. On "Pony Blues" and "The Jinx Blues," House vividly recreates classic performances he had learned from Charley Patton, and they sound just as fresh and immediate here in the midst of World War II as they had in the 1920s; but he also draws on his own experiences for inspiration on his "County Farm Blues," which describes in ironic terms House's impressions of Parchman Farm. "Down south, when you do anything that's wrong," House bellowed, "They'll sure put you down on the county farm."

Put you down under a man they call Captain Jack.
Put you under a man called Captain Jack.
Put you under a man they call Captain Jack.
He'll sure write his name up and down your back.

One didn't need to know how to read or write to understand this "message" from the Captain, whose writing utensil of choice was a four-foot-long strap, a quarter of an inch thick, with holes punctured at its extremity to give more crack to its whip.

The sound quality on the Library of Congress recordings is less than ideal, especially when House is accompanied by mandolin and harmonica. The textures of the individual instruments are mostly lost in a churning cauldron of blues sound. As if this were not distracting enough, a passing train from the nearby railway line adds its own unanticipated contribution to the informal session at the country store. Yet House projects himself magnificently over all the other sonorities, man-made or mechanical, perhaps most notably on "Walking Blues," where we hear the bold, declamatory style that had already influenced Robert Johnson and would continue to inspire Muddy Waters.

We might have been blessed with more music from this gathering, except for the unplanned arrival of the plantation bossman who, Lomax tells us, put a damper on the activities. Lomax was even called into the county sheriff's office—an official who was alarmed at reports that the visitor from Washington, D.C., had shaken hands with a black man, and who became even more exasperated when Lomax, in an unguarded moment, referred to his musical discovery as "*Mister* Son House." Such a term of respect for a black man was, in itself, a cause of suspicion in the Delta region of the period, and Lomax narrowly missed being held in jail while his credentials were checked by the authorities.

After Lomax's encounter with House, the great Delta blues singer would disappear from the music world for more than twenty years, and even then his rediscovery and reappearance in a recording studio was very much a matter of chance. Yet Lomax understood the commercial potential of Son House from the start, and hatched plans to bring him north and make him into a star much as he and his father had done with Leadbelly during the mid-1930s. Unpublished correspondence on file in the Library of Congress shows Lomax repeatedly trying to convince House to make this decisive move. In a letter to House dated Christamas Eve, 1941, Lomax writes: "Would you be interested in coming to New York and playing with a group of singers who are friends of mine and very nice people? They would be able to keep you while you were in New York and could pay you something for performances with them. They plan to make recordings so that you would be paid your share and also could probably provide you with chances to make recordings on your own."

No response from House can be found in the files, but another letter from Lomax, dated January 28, 1942, presses the matter again. "These are friends of mine and very dependable. They need somebody who can make his own songs and play a good guitar, and who is experienced in Negro music. . . . Unless you have some strong reason against it, I would suggest that you consider the matter seriously." Perhaps House was concerned about who would pay for his travel fare to New York, so Lomax wrote again in February, stating that his friends would lend the money for transportation. Blues fans can only dream what the impact might have been of Son House making a high-profile debut on the New York scene circa 1942. He was at the peak of his musical powers, and with the right backing from Lomax and his contacts, he would almost certainly have achieved tremendous celebrity, perhaps stardom. As it stands, the correspondence depicts one more dead end in a frustrating career marked by false starts and unfulfilled potential.

Much of Lomax's efforts in 1941 and 1942 focused on the musical activities in and around Clarksdale, the largest city in Coahoma County, whose population of 12,000 accounted for almost one quarter of the county's residents. Here, in a schoolhouse room with a thunderstorm brewing outside, Lomax recorded David "Honeyboy" Edwards, whom he had heard earlier regaling a crowd of listeners outside a storefront. The country's entry into war was the major topic of the day, and inspired Edwards's lyrics:

> Well lemme tell you now, now,
> What Uncle Sam will do to you
> He will take you out of jitterbuggin'
> Put you right in a khaki suit.

"Uncle Sam ain't no woman, but he sure can take your man," Edwards sang, in a humorous twist on the classic blues theme of jealous lovers. Lomax later played the song for a recruiting officer from the U.S. Navy, who demanded to know the name of the subversive who performed it and expressed his intention of having the song officially suppressed.

In contrast to the stentorian approach of Son House, Edwards showed a lighter touch in his blues. His music breathes, dancing along in a lithesome manner conveying a sense of relaxation, but without losing the rhythmic drive so essential to the Delta sound. His voice contributes immeasurably to this effect. The nickname "Honeyboy," the singer tells us, derived from a family term of endearment, but one could easily believe that it referred to the bluesman's silky singing style. His fame in the blues world is due mostly to his association with Robert Johnson; and though this connection no doubt helped sustain his long career, spanning more than seventy-five years, it does not do justice to the distinctive virtues of Edwards's music. In a region where rawness is sometimes celebrated as a musical performance's greatest virtue, Edwards showed that a more mellifluous style also had its place. And, despite the invariable comparisons to Johnson, the upbeat spirit of his music is a world away from the darker moods so prominent in that bluesman's legacy.

Edwards was born on June 28, 1915, in Shaw, Mississippi, at the western tip of Sunflower County. He learned guitar from his father, Henry Edwards, who played songs like "Joe Turner Blues," "Stagger Lee," and "John Henry." At age nine, Edwards started working in the fields, but before his fifteenth birthday he was performing at country dances. In the fall of 1927, the Edwards family moved to the Wildwood Plantation near Greenwood, and the arrival of a wind-up phonograph in the household a short time later exposed the youngster to the music of Blind Lemon Jefferson, whose recordings made a big impression on him. But an aspiring blues player did not require a record player in this part of the Delta in order to get access to the leading exponents of the music, and over the next few years Edwards encountered firsthand Charley Patton, Tommy Johnson, Howlin' Wolf, Aleck "Rice" Miller (the "second" Sonny Boy Williamson), Tommy McClennan, Robert Petway, Rube Lacy, and Kokomo Arnold.

At the end of 1932, Edwards met Big Joe Williams and spent most of the next year on the road with him. In 1935, at age nineteen, he traveled to Memphis, where he marveled over the blues riches of that city—here he heard Sleepy John Estes, Memphis Minnie, Memphis Slim, Roosevelt Sykes, Frank Stokes, and many others—and played with the Memphis Jug Band. Edwards may have only been twenty-two years old when he met Robert

Johnson, but with all these experiences under his belt, he was already a polished professional entertainer. He certainly learned from the older guitarist
(Johnson was twenty-six at the time), but this brief association probably did
little to change his own distinctive approach to the blues.

Edwards credits Big Joe Williams with instructing him in the ways and
means of the blues musician's life on the road, and like his mentor, Edwards
tried to avoid the demands of a day job and earn his living through song.
Sometimes this was not possible, and Edwards would pick cotton, or work
in an iron yard or on the railroad. But for most of the 1940s and 1950s,
Edwards continued to perform, and even managed to record, although
without much success. His recording of "Drop Down Mama" for the Chess
label was not released for twenty-seven years (due, Edwards believes, to the
interference of Muddy Waters, who thought that the song was too close
to his own style), and Edwards made no more headway in his attempts to
interest Sun Records in Memphis. By the 1960s, Edwards had all but given
up on the musician's life, and took regular work in construction jobs, or
operating forklifts and other equipment. But Robert Johnson's later fame
would serve to thrust Edwards into the limelight, and the recording career
that had eluded him as a young man took off in earnest once he had passed
his fiftieth birthday. His performances, featured on recordings for more
than a half dozen labels, showed that his music had aged little, evoking the
same carefree spirit that captivated Alan Lomax in 1942.

If the Delta research project had only brought us these musical riches
from Son House and Honeyboy Edwards, we would value its contribution to American music. But an even more dramatic moment came early
in the fieldwork on a Sunday afternoon, the last day of August 1941, when
Lomax and Work visited a ramshackle cabin on Stovall Plantation. Here
the researchers encountered McKinley Morganfield, who had been living
on this 4,500-acre farm for as long as he could remember. Lomax always
liked musicians with colorful nicknames, and McKinley was known in these
parts as "Muddy Water"—sometime later a sly record label executive, or
perhaps just a printer's error would make a plural out of the last name, the
murky flow symbolically broadened into a confluence of many streams. In
this closed society, Morganfield had worked his way up the few rungs open
to him, rising from picking cotton and pulling corn to operating a tractor.
But his modest renown in these parts owed more to his bootlegging and
guitar playing.

Waters was cautious with his visitors. He feared that they might be revenuers who had learned that he was selling whiskey. But when Lomax produced his Martin guitar and plucked a few notes, Waters became more curious than suspicious. Waters had never heard of the Library of Congress, so the name made little impression on him. However, the ponderous recording equipment and accessories that filled most of Lomax's backseat and trunk caught his attention. Soon his visitors were setting up the machinery in Waters's front room with wires running from the window to the porch, and out to the car where the automobile's battery kept the whole contraption running.

Waters was a mannish boy some two years older than Lomax, and had already been playing guitar for more than a decade when this unexpected recording session came literally to his doorstep. Born on April 4, 1913, the son of Ollie Morganfield and Berta Grant, Waters heard the blues firsthand at home from his father, who could "sing, blow a jug, play a guitar, beat a washboard," in the words of Robert Morganfield, Muddy's half brother. But an encounter with Son House, when Waters was in his early teens, proved decisive in his musical development. Four decades later, he would still recall vividly the impression made on him by the older Delta master: "Son House played this place for about four weeks in a row, and I was there every night, closer to him than I am to your microphone. You couldn't get me out of that corner, listening to him, what he's doing." The youngster had already learned the rudiments of the bottleneck technique from a friend, but Waters now realized how little he really knew. "When I heard Son House, I should have broke my bottleneck because this other cat hadn't learned me nothing." At seventeen, Waters got his first guitar, a used Stella, which he purchased for $2.50. When he made a half dollar from his first performance, and then got a raise to $2.50, he knew he was on the right track. Soon Waters had saved enough to purchase a new instrument from Sears, Roebuck in Chicago, and was establishing a local reputation for his music in the Clarksdale area.

We often hear of those fateful moments in which a great creative talent is discovered, but rarely can we eavesdrop on the actual process unfolding, minute-by-minute. What we would give to be able to follow Brian Epstein, on November 9, 1961, as he visits the Cavern Club to hear the Liverpool lads who had recently started performing as the Beatles. Or listen in as Elvis auditions for Sun Records at Scotty Moore's house on the Fourth of July, 1954. Or watch sixteen-year-old Richard Rodgers playing the piano at

the home of a new acquaintance, Larry Hart, and leaving that day in rap-
tures, proclaiming, "I have found a lyricist! I have found a lyricist!" These
moments are the stuff of legend, but—alas!—merely that. No documentation exists beyond the vivid memories of the participants, which become
more faded or embellished, usually both, with the passage of time. But with
Muddy Waters, the recordings made on that August afternoon offer us a
unique glimpse into a process that was both discovery and self-discovery.
Waters himself has remarked how hearing his own music played back that
day radically changed his conception of himself, gave him an unprecedented
sense of confidence as an artist and performer, and perhaps even an awareness of how he might reach others through his playing. Listening to the
Library of Congress recording, we can pick up on that same powerful vibe,
and we feel that we are experiencing not just a historical audition, a soon-
to-be-famous musician getting his "break," but something even more magical, an instance of self-realization that is unique in the annals of American
recorded music.

The song was simply entitled "Country Blues" by Lomax, but Muddy later
recorded it as "I Feel Like Going Home." When the latter version was released
in 1948, the first pressing sold out within a day, but here on Stovall Plantation, the song served merely as entertainment at fish fries and dances.

It gets late on in the evening
I feel like blowing my horn
I woke up this morning
And find my little baby gone . . .

At the close of the song, we hear Lomax's footsteps as he walks over to the
musician and begins an interview, typical of those the researcher undertook
in conjunction with his field recordings. When did Muddy write that blues?
Where was he sitting? What was he thinking about? In the time-honored
manner of blues singers, Waters connects the song to thinking about a
woman who had mistreated him. He tells about his admiration for Son
House, describes how he uses the bottleneck on his little finger, and provides other details of the experiences and attitudes that contributed to his
music. Then he plays another song.

On the Library of Congress recordings, the next performance is listed
as "I Be's Troubled," but Waters would also transform this piece into a

later hit recording, his landmark "I Can't Be Satisfied." And if his previous country blues had looked back to Son House and Robert Johnson, this passionate performance anticipates the future of the blues, with its sassier, more independent attitudes, its celebration of raw appetite, not softened by metaphor or coy allusions as in so many earlier blues songs, but presented with unprecedented starkness. Even Muddy's own later move to Chicago is hinted at in its opening phrases.

Well, if I feel tomorrow like I feel today,
I'm gonna pack my suitcase
And make my getaway . . .

This is no lament over bein' mistreated, but something far more carnal in its origins. "I *never* been satisfied," Water proclaims, his bottleneck drawing out wavering moans from the guitar behind his vocal. It is no coincidence that the Rolling Stones drew inspiration from this song for their biggest hit "(I Can't Get No) Satisfaction." The same sexual bravado, the boldness, the in-your-face posturing that Muddy would bring to Chicago would later be imbibed by rock and roll in its infancy. When Keith Richards ran into his childhood pal Mick Jagger on a train in 1961—another one of those legendary encounters discussed above—he was struck forcibly by the Muddy Waters album in his friend's possession, and they spent most of the rest of that day listening to it in silent rapture. When the Beatles first came to the United States, the mop-top bandmates told interviewers about their admiration for Muddy Waters, and were amazed when an interviewer asked, "Where is that?" A major American musical icon was mistaken for some *spot on the map*! But if the mainstream journalists didn't recognize the name, they would become all too aware of the bad attitude it represented, as a whole generation was soon demanding satisfaction on a wider and wider range of fronts.

Waters received twenty dollars in exchange for permission to allow the release of these two songs by the Library of Congress on a commercial recording. They were issued in January 1943 as part of a six-album package. The money was appreciated by the artist—Waters was earning twenty-two and a half cents per hour driving a tractor at the time—and hearing his own music on record must have been even more gratifying to the guitarist. But above all, Waters's ambitions were fired by this sense of himself as a recording artist. If Waters had been dissatisfied with the stultifying life on the plantation before Lomax's visit, his desire to break away was now even more pressing. He remained at Stovall Plantation through the spring planting season, and then on a Friday afternoon in May, the now *former* farmer caught the 4:00 p.m. train out of Clarksdale on his way to Chicago.

2. bound for the promised land

A few months after Muddy Waters left Clarksdale, almost one thousand cars descended on the small community. Their destination was not the train station or anywhere downtown, for that matter, but the Hopson Plantation just outside the city, on Highway 49. The automobile tires left tracks and ruts over a wide parcel of land set up as an improvised parking lot, as almost three thousand people hiked to the field that proprietor Howell Hopson called C-3, some forty-two acres devoted to the cultivation of cotton.

Visitors had been making their way to Hopson's plantation for quite some time, often appearing uninvited at the door, or even heading directly to the fields in secrecy. Sometimes Howell would find them, stealthy and unannounced, wandering over his fields, and on occasion the intruders even got lost in the surrounding wooded areas. Almost every day, they came. They arrived as individuals, or in families or groups, or in whole delegations. Finally, in desperation, he opened up his plantation on this Monday in the fall of 1944 for a public showing, and was amazed at the onslaught. One would think that the county fair had moved to Hopson's farm!

The people came to witness a demonstration of the new technological wonder of the day, a mechanical cotton-picker. The Hopson family had been working with the International Harvester Company since 1927, offering up their land as a test site for the next generation of farm equipment. By 1944, the company had finally perfected a production-ready machine capable of doing the work of fifty people. The visitors who crowded around field C-3 looked in rapt admiration at eight shiny red machines, each one housing a row of rotating spindles—they looked like devouring mouths turned sideways, ready to gnaw away at the plants. The spindles stripped the cotton, which was then whisked through a tube by a vacuum and deposited in a big wire basket on top of the unit.

The Delta had witnessed such demonstrations before—John Rust had caused a sensation with the public trial of his picker in Leland in 1936—but the earliest machines had not proven themselves ready for mass production and widespread use. Howell Hopson achieved a breakthrough in 1944, stunning the agricultural community with his boast that, for the first time, he had produced his entire cotton crop without hand labor, employing machinery from planting through harvesting. At this one and only "open house" in the fall, he demonstrated that his eight machines could clear the forty-two acres of C-3, producing some sixty-two bales of cotton, all in a single day. But even more compelling than the awe-inspiring sight of these cotton-eating monsters were the numbers in Hopson's ledgers. His meticulous bookkeeping showed that the cost of hand-picking a bale of cotton was $39.41, while the machine-picked cotton brought this down to $5.26, representing a whopping savings of over 85 percent.

Yet the sociological implications of this innovation would prove to be far more profound than any economic or agricultural impact. For decades, the white Mississippi ruling class had worked to hinder black migration away from their plantations. Visiting labor agents had long been actively discouraged, both by the legal authorities and by private landowners, who harassed, threatened, and sometimes physically assaulted these advocates for better jobs and living conditions in the North. For many years, the Delta had prided itself as a preferred destination for African-Americans from nearby areas, with its promise of ready work for even the most unskilled laborer. Mississippian Peg Leg Williams became known as the "king of the labor agents" for attracting blacks from the South Atlantic states *into* Mississippi around the turn of the century. These new arrivals would sometimes only stay briefly, then continue onward to Memphis or Chicago or some other urban area. Still, the influx tended to compensate for the departures during the early years of the twentieth century.

Now this would all change. And, once again, the realities of the marketplace drove the process. The price of cotton mostly rose during this period of growth in the Delta workforce, but hit its all-time inflation-adjusted peak in 1919. The bust of 1920 gave the Delta a taste of a Depression-style collapse a full decade before it was felt elsewhere, and the region would never fully recover its allure as a center of opportunity for black workers. Robert S. Abbot, the publisher of the *Chicago Defender*, the leading black newspaper of the day, gave further impetus to the migration by promoting sweeping,

Bible-inspired slogans and songs that told of "The Flight Out of Egypt" or "Bound for the Promised Land" or "Going into Canaan." Even more powerful inducements came from the black Chicagoans who returned to the South on family visits, typically around Fourth of July or Christmas, with their fancy wardrobes and fine automobiles. They served as walking, talking advertisements for the better life up north that no sheriff or plantation owner could counter.

The introduction of the mechanical cotton-picker, at first a novelty but ultimately a necessity for the Delta planters, represented the tipping point, the innovation that made black migration not just an option but for many a necessity. Previously, the black Delta worker had traveled to Chicago in search of opportunities, but now mere survival demanded the move. One by one the plantations in the South terminated their sharecropper agreements, shut down their commissaries, and sometimes forcibly evicted black residents. A few paternalistic landowners, such as the Stovalls, allowed their former sharecroppers to remain in their cabins, but others would bulldoze the shacks to make room for more cotton. Most plantation owners waited until they had a fleet of cotton-picking machines ready to go, then made a sudden announcement that, from now on, only day laborers, for hourly hire, would be employed, for running the machines and for chopping, the only parts of the process still done by hand.

As the workforce moved north, the blues traveled with it. Music writers have seldom given sufficient attention to the impact of these patterns of migration and their attendant economic influences on the evolution of regional performance styles. But how else can we understand the puzzling anomalies in the history of American music, peculiarities that no amount of map-gazing will explain? Why did most of the defining performances of New Orleans jazz—by Louis Armstrong, Jelly Roll Morton, King Oliver, and so many others—take place in Chicago? Why did what we call "Chicago jazz" find its greatest fruition in New York? Why did the Latin music sound developed by Cubans in Havana exert most influence as a style played by Puerto Ricans in New York? Why was the "West Coast" jazz sound made by people born far away from the Pacific Coast? Music writers often treat these as anomalies or humorous peculiarities, but they are the quite predictable results of broader social trends. Each of these supposedly "artistic" developments was driven primarily by the flows of people and money. In short, the Delta blues could hardly have remained in the Delta for long, and if it had, many of the finest players the region has produced would never have been known by us.

And just as labor agents came from Chicago and elsewhere to attract workers and talent, so did music company executives. In 1939, Bluebird scout Lester Melrose drove to Mississippi in search of promising musicians, and encountered such hostility that he had to abandon his car and run in fear of his life. He determined never to return. Yet before he departed, he left money to cover blues singer Tommy McClennan's travel expenses to Chicago. McClennan had been born on a plantation outside of Yazoo City in 1908, but the family later moved to Greenwood, a hotbed of blues activity in the 1920s and 1930s. Like many of his generation, McClennan eventually decided to settle permanently in Chicago. "I left my babe in Mississippi, / Pickin' cottton down on her knee," he sings in his "Cotton Patch Blues." "She said, 'Babe, you get to Chicago all right, / Please write me a letter, if you please.'"

David "Honeyboy" Edwards, who is our best source of information on McClennan, describes his friend in memorable terms:

> Tommy was dark and had big eyes like a frog. He was real little, about four foot and ten, just touched me right along about the shoulder. Tommy didn't weigh a bit over 115 pounds. There wasn't no hat would fit Tommy's head. His hats would be coming down around his ears. He was a funny guy. He'd pull his hat off and comb his hair down and look in the mirror and talk to it, saying "Good! Now you got all night to rise!"

But McClennan's voice was out of proportion to his diminutive stature. "Tommy had a big mouth!" Edwards continues. "He could holler loud. You'd think it was a big man playing when you heard him." Many great blues shouters have hailed from the Delta region, but none was better than McClennan at spicing his bellowing vocals with hoots and whispers, spoken asides, scat phrases and wordless growls. A casual listener might mistakenly conclude that there are two vocalists on some of his sides, one singing and the other providing an ongoing spoken commentary. But McClennan juggles both roles effortlessly, his vocals moving hither and thither with a dazzling stream of consciousness that sometimes looks back to field hollers and a moment later anticipates the modern-day rapper. The blues may have produced better singers than Tommy McClennan, and certainly more polished ones, but it has yet to find a vocalist less inhibited by the cold sterility of the recording studio.

With his racially loaded lyrics to "Bottle It Up and Go," recorded at his debut session for Bluebird in November 1939, McClennan shocked listeners then—and even more now. The guitarist got into an argument with Big Bill Broonzy, present at the studio, who tried to prevail on McClennan to change the words to his song.

> *The nigger and the white man playing seven up;*
> *Nigger beat the white man, was scared to pick it up.*
> *He had to bottle it up and go.*

"In Chicago and New York, they don't use that word," Broonzy later wrote. "But that was Tommy's first time in the North." McClennan got angry, and declared, "Hell, no. I'll never change my song." After the session, Broonzy went with McClennan to a party in Chicago where many blues musicians were present, and tried again to deter him from singing these lyrics. But McClennan remained stubborn about the words to his song, and trouble ensued. "I had to put Tommy out the window and me and him ran about five miles," Broonzy explains. McClennan, for his part, reflected pensively that they had indeed been forced to "bottle it up and go."

As such anecdotes reflect, the Delta blues did not always translate well into more sophisticated environments. Indeed, before Muddy Waters's arrival in Chicago, the Delta sound had enjoyed few successes in America's second largest city. Robert Johnson's "Sweet Home Chicago" is now held up as an anthem of the community's central place in the history of the blues, but Johnson never made much headway in this city, as far as we can tell. Nor did many of his peers. This indifference was typical of the prewar years, when Chicago had not yet discovered its affection for Mississippi blues singers. During the late 1930s and early 1940s, swing music dominated the Chicago nightlife, drawing both black and white audiences to clubs and dance floors with its hot rhythms and larger-than-life stars.

By almost any measure, McClennan was doomed to failure in this setting. His unprepossessing figure, his sandpapery voice, his simple guitar stylings, his controversial song lyrics—all these were ill-suited to urban audiences circa 1940. Yet Melrose and Bluebird persisted in trying to build McClennan into a star. In the months following his debut recording, he participated in several more sessions for Bluebird, and the spontaneity and uninhibited vocals of this music would earn him a secure posthumous reputation, even if they did little for his fortunes at the time. We almost completely lose track of McClennan after America's entry into World War II. A striking photo taken by Broonzy on the South Side of Chicago, around 1953, shows the diminutive musician in esteemed blues company, sharing the pavement with Little Walter, Aleck "Rice" Miller, and Elmore James. But his career at this point had been eclipsed by all of these peers.

David "Honeyboy" Edwards recalls a tragic encounter with McClennan, a decade later, at a junkyard at 22nd and Frederick, in a run-down area known as "the Jungle," frequented by winos and homeless people. Here McClennan lived in a truck trailer converted into a makeshift shelter, his wife gone and his music mostly a faded memory from the past. Edwards brought him back to his own home, and even took McClennan to gigs, where he showed he still possessed a powerful voice, although he was no longer able to play much on the guitar. Yet McClennan's chronic alcoholism made any comeback a moot point. He would start drinking wine soon after he rose in the morning, and would continue throughout the day—until Edwards balked at his friend's constant demands for alcohol, and both determined that McClennan should return to the Jungle. Our last glimpse of McClennan is a haunting one. Michael Bloomfield describes accompanying Big Joe Williams on a visit to Cook County Hospital in the early 1960s, where Tommy McClennan was dying of tuberculosis. He could no longer talk, and his already slender frame was completely emaciated by alcoholism and illness. "He was just a skeleton," Bloomfield recalled, "but his eyes were like hot coals burning at you."

McClennan's friend Robert Petway also made the move from Greenwood, Mississippi, to Chicago, but we know little about him beyond the music he recorded at two sessions for Bluebird in March 1941 and February 1942. Yet his "Catfish Blues" ranks as one of the greatest performances of Delta blues, often emulated by other musicians. The song is deceptively simple, the harmonic structure little more than a single throbbing chord, the guitar offering none of the melodic embellishments, licks, or bass lines that add variety to other traditional blues performances. The pulse is insistent and unrelenting, and though you could notate it in 4/4 or 2/4, to the ear it sounds like the basic unit is a single beat, repeated over and over, more akin to the rhythm of a work crew with their hammers or drills than to any musical composition. But the melody is artfully constructed, dancing over two full octaves, the interval leaps coyly following the lyrics, descending when Petway describes the hooks dropping to catch the catfish, who symbolizes the singer himself:

> Well if I were a catfish, mama,
> I said swimming deep down in the big blue sea,
> All these gals now, sweet mama,
> Setting out, setting out hooks for me.

The song may be biographical. Honeyboy Edwards tells us that Petway had already been married two or three times before he moved to Chicago. His tastes ran to sanctified church women, and these encounters inspired him to bring his guitar into the house of worship, where he would play religious music, at least for a spell. But neither the marriages nor the conversions lasted long, and Petway would soon be back performing the blues, drinking whiskey, and playing cards.

Edwards later heard that Petway was living on the North Side, but he never saw him in Chicago, and we know little beyond this about his activities after he recorded for Bluebird. The Social Security Death Index includes a Robert Petway who was born on October 18, 1907, and was living in Chicago when he died in May 1978. However, this birthdate does not match either of the two Robert Petways listed in the 1920 Leflore County Census, aged eighteen and twenty-six at the time, and apparently related, given their location in adjacent households. Although Petway may have survived until the late 1970s, our knowledge of his music ends with his few 78s from 1941 and 1942.

Around the time of McClennan and Petway's first recordings, Robert Nighthawk also made the move to Chicago, and he too struggled in establishing himself in these new surroundings. Yet Nighthawk had already participated in several recording sessions, and had developed a degree of fame in the blues world. "He was popular all over Mississippi," later recalled Muddy Waters, who had known Nighthawk in Clarksdale. "He left and came north in the 30s. The next thing I heard he had a record out and on the market." Nighthawk had been born as Robert Lee McCollum in Helena, Arkansas, on November 30, 1909. He had learned the rudiments of blues guitar from his cousin Houston Stackhouse in 1931, and over the next several years he roamed widely, and honed his craft. He changed his name to Robert Lee McCoy around the time he arrived in St. Louis in 1935—both moves made, perhaps, to avoid prosecution for his involvement in a shooting in Louisiana. He thrived on the St. Louis scene, and his popular recording of "Prowling Nighthawk" likely prompted his final name change to Robert Nighthawk. At the end of the decade, he decided to move to Chicago.

Robert Nighthawk was far better suited for success on the Chicago scene than either McClennan or Petway. Nighthawk's single-note guitar style was imbued with a distinctly modern, urban flavor, and his singing voice possessed a fullness and warmth that would allow him to tackle ballads or swing tunes as well as country blues. His recording of "Friars Point Blues," made in Chicago on June 5, 1940, is a strong, confident performance, and demonstrates his growing skill with the slide, a technique that would become a trademark of his later work. Yet Nighthawk failed to establish himself in Chicago, and the next year found him back in Helena. He would not make another recording under his own name for eight years.

Not until Muddy Waters had paved the way—and also helped his old friend secure a record deal—would Nighthawk experience a brief resurgence in his career. During the late 1940s and early 1950s, Nighthawk would ride the wave of popularity for Chicago blues and record career-defining performances of "Black Angel Blues," "Annie Lee Blues," "Crying Won't Help You," and "The Moon Is Rising." But by the end of 1952 he was again without a record label. Nighthawk soon resumed his peripatetic ways, and we hear of him playing in St. Louis or Mexico, or back in Mississippi or Arkansas. Over a decade transpired without a single record made; but Nighthawk resurfaced in Chicago for his 1964 *Live on Maxwell Street* recording. The circumstances of the session—which took place literally outside on the pavement, not inside a club or studio but at a noisy open-air market—bespoke the fallen state of this once promising master of the slide guitar. Yet the down-and-out setting could not obscure the abilities of this still potent musician, and the recording would eventually earn a W. C. Handy Award as the outstanding vintage blues recording of the year—but not until 1980, long after Nighthawk's death. At the time of his passing in 1967, not a single LP had been released under his name.

Muddy Waters arrived in Chicago a few months after Nighthawk departed, and seemed destined to become one more Delta casualty, ignored or dismissed by the cosmopolitan big city audience. Waters had already failed when he attempted to establish himself in St. Louis in 1940. He had given up after a couple of months: "It was unpleasant . . . just too tough," he later explained. "I was playing the old blues, and it wouldn't go there. So I went back to Mississippi." Now, in Chicago, he encountered the same hostility to his "sad, old-time blues." Swing music continued its hold on the city; the nascent sounds of bebop were in the air; and young black singers from Muddy's generation, rising stars like Nat King Cole and Billy Eckstine, were crafting a sophisticated style of popular music that appealed to both African-American and white audiences. When Waters approached club owners and told them he played the blues, they would shake their heads dismissively and show him the door.

Waters took a job at a paper factory, clocking in an eight-hour shift each day, and a less determined person might have abandoned any serious musical aspirations amidst the comparative prosperity of his new situation. If he worked overtime, Waters could bring in over a hundred dollars in a week— more than ten times what a typical black worker earned in the Delta. But Waters's mind was set on a music career, and he never stayed long at any of his Chicago day jobs. He performed mostly on weekends, at house parties, where he might earn five dollars, good side money but little more. His uncle bought him an electric guitar, and Waters struggled to adapt to the new instrument, which amplified every little finger slip, calling attention to mistakes that would escape notice on an acoustic guitar. In time, this acquisition would prove to be a major step forward in the history of Chicago blues, a harbinger of the electrified sound of that music. But a more immediate boost came to Waters's musical career when, after his grandmother died in 1946, he used her life insurance payout to purchase a rust-colored Chevy. His automobile made Waters a welcome addition to blues bands, who found his skills as a chauffeur almost as welcome as his guitar work. Soon Waters was gigging regularly with John Lee "Sonny Boy" Williamson, and gaining greater notoriety on the local music scene.

Waters parlayed his growing reputation into two opportunities to record in 1946, but neither helped to advance his career. His recording of "Mean Red Spider" for the obscure 20th Century label received so little attention that even Muddy was unaware that it had been released. When researcher Jim O'Neal showed a copy to him in the 1970s, the guitarist marveled:

"I thought that record was drownded in the river." It didn't help that the record was listed under the name James Carter, who does not appear on the track, and that Waters's guitar is almost lost behind the clarinet, saxophone, and piano. But Waters got no better results from the tracks he recorded as a leader for Columbia in September. These were not released until almost a quarter of a century had elapsed. Waters's efforts accompanying pianist Jimmy Clark from the same session were issued at the time, but he was not credited on the label, which simply described the band as "blues singer with piano, string bass, drums and guitar." Waters was no longer a young man—he would celebrate his thirty-fourth birthday the following April—and the only recordings out under his name were still the Library of Congress performances done back on Stovall Plantation.

But just as had happened with Lomax, the opportunity, when it arrived, came looking for him, showing up literally at his doorstep. Various accounts differ on the details, but they all agree that a tall tale was contrived to get Waters off work in order to participate at a recording session. In the most commonly told version of the story, a strange call came in at work telling Waters's boss at Westerngrade Venetian Blinds Company that his delivery truck driver needed to come home immediately because his mother was seriously ill. When Waters heard the news, he may well have been baffled—his mother was long dead. But he hurried home only to find, in place of his mother, the tall, imposing frame of pianist Sunnyland Slim, who was waiting impatiently for him. Slim was another Mississippian, born Albert Luandrew in Vance in 1907, trying to make a name on the Chicago music scene. Unlike Waters, he had left the region early in life, not just to play the blues but to escape an abusive stepmother—the only alternative, in his mind, was to shoot her. He had worked jukehouses and movie theaters, made a name on Beale Street in Memphis, backed Ma Rainey, met Robert Johnson in Helena, and along the way had developed a sixth sense for tracking down gigs. The opportunity he had caught wind of today was a big one. Leonard Chess, a new record producer on the scene, wanted them in the studio to record for the Aristocrat label. And unlike Waters's previous sessions, this one would hit paydirt. Slim would soon become a mainstay of Chicago nightlife, and Waters would embark on a partnership with the Chess brothers that would last almost thirty years, and transform the sound of postwar blues.

3. gonna be a son of a gun

Like Muddy Waters, the Chess brothers were outsiders trying to establish themselves in Chicago. They had come from Motele in Poland, their parents part of the wave of Jewish immigration to the United States in the early decades of the century. And just as Waters had found that he could, advance his career better under a new moniker, rather than his birth name of McKinley Morganfield, Leonard and Philip Chess took on these new, Americanized identities in place of Lejzor and Fiszel Czyz. Their father, Jasef Czyz—soon to become Joseph Chess—had been the first to arrive in Chicago, and had sent for the rest of his family in 1928. The adaptation to their new surroundings was difficult. The boys continued to speak Yiddish at home, while trying to master English at school. Philip, age seven, was so unsure of his vocabulary that, when he tried to buy a Valentine's Day card for one of his classmates, he ended up getting a hot dog instead!

The path by which the Chess brothers became entertainment industry moguls is both strange yet entirely logical. Joseph Chess sold old bottles at his Wabash Junk Shop—it too was later renamed, quite elegantly, as "Chess and Sons"—and one of his customers was a member of Al Capone's organization, who used the bottles for bootlegging activities. From selling empty bottles to vending ones already full of liquor was a natural and profitable step, and Leonard accordingly decided to operate a liquor store servicing mostly African-American customers, first on South State Street and later on 47th Street. Liquor and music are natural companions, and Chess dabbled in the combination almost from the start, hooking up a jukebox in his first liquor store, and eventually opening a nightclub called the Macomba Lounge. Selling recorded music to supplement the live performances was an equally obvious extension—and this was the decisive move that spurred their involvement with Aristocrat and the later Chess label. These strategic "chess moves" continued in the future, with the brothers investing in radio stations as a new pillar in their music industry portfolio. At the time of his death from a heart attack in 1969, Leonard Chess was looking to make inroads into television. The whole beautiful game, starting from the empty bottles in the junkshop, would make for an engaging case study at Harvard Business School, each step building on the previous one, but cumulatively serving to expand a humble family business into a mini-empire.

But the Waters success story—a key turning point in this tale of rags-to-riches—almost got derailed from the start. Leonard Chess had his doubts about Waters's singing style, and was especially reluctant to anchor the recordings on his guitar sound. Today, we are so familiar with the guitar serving as the foundation of the rhythm section in popular genres of music—not just blues, but also rock, country, soul, and everything in between—that we can hardly understand such reservations. But in the mid-1940s, the piano dominated rhythm sections, establishing the harmonic foundation for almost every style of popular music, providing a cushion for the rest of the band and largely determining the texture of the accompaniment. In this context, the guitar was often viewed as merely optional, an incidental add-on, or even just a novelty to differentiate the sound of a particular band. Advancements in amplifying the guitar in the 1930s and 1940s had started to change all this, but the process took place in fits and starts. At Waters's debut session with Sunnyland Slim, the piano overshadows the guitar from the opening bars, and though this is Waters's session, it is not yet Waters's *sound* that fills the grooves.

The records sold well enough, however, to justify a follow-up visit to the studio. Yet the return of the same group, further augmented by saxophonist Alex Atkins, did not bode well. On the first two numbers recorded, Waters's guitar work is again obscured by the sound of the other instruments. However, the novelty of Waters's bottleneck playing had intrigued Leonard Chess and his business partner Evelyn Aron during rehearsals, and now they agreed that he could record two sides with just bass accompaniment. Waters chose songs he had performed for Lomax and Work, "I Can't Be Satisfied" and "I Feel Like Going Home"—but with one radical twist: these compositions from his Delta days would now be played on the electric guitar. Many listeners at the time must have agreed with the reviewer for *Billboard* magazine, who couldn't accept the rawness of this music, preferring to see it as some terrible mistake. "Poor recording distorts vocal and steel guitar backing," was the journal's curt dismissal. Ah, welcome to the brave new world of hard-edged urban music, Mr. Reviewer, where songs *sound bad on purpose*, where the goal is to affront, not soothe, your eardrums. This lesson would not be lost on Keith Richards and Mick Jagger. (Though not for some time yet—they were, respectively, four and five years old at the time.) The response was more immediate from the legions of Chicago record buyers who ensured that this first pressing would sell out within twenty-four hours of release. Some stores limited customers to a single copy, so great was the onrush of demand. Other retailers raised the price from the standard seventy-nine cents to more than a dollar. Perhaps *Billboard*'s reviewer could not understand the appeal, but that same periodical's ranking of "Most-Played Jukebox Race Records" showed the new Muddy Waters release rising to number 11.

Leonard Chess had been skeptical when he first heard Waters's electrified Delta style, but the sales figures made a believer out of him. Perhaps he attributed this success to the migration of black workers from the South who were nostalgic for the unpolished sound of their "down-home" music. In any event, the next session found Waters, accompanied only by bass, performing two more songs addressing the same subject of homesickness that had inspired "I Feel Like Going Home." "You know I'm going down south, child, this weather gets too cold," Waters sings on his "Down South Blues." He dwells on the same theme in his "Train Fare Home":

> *If I could get lucky and win my train fare home*
> *I believe I'll go back down in Clarksdale, little girl that's where I belong.*

Neither Muddy, nor many of his listeners, would ever move back to Clarksdale; but such sentiments must have appealed to a growing urban population, black or white, uprooted from the traditional ways of their youth.

If these performances had been simple exercises in nostalgia, Waters would have never exerted such tremendous influence on American—and global—music over the coming decades. His songs looked to the future, even if they pretended to dwell on the past. The new sound that Waters was crafting—Whitmanesque songs of himself, full of attitude, celebrating his life force and increasingly his libido—represented a sharp rupture with the plantation society that had nurtured the blues in its earliest forms. The singer, and much of his audience, would always bear the stamp of the South, but they could not go back, they had changed too much, and this only added to the bittersweet bluesiness of the songs about back home. When Waters next hit the charts with his 1950 recording of "Louisiana Blues"—which hit number 10 on *Billboard*'s R&B rankings the following January—he sang movingly about "going down in New Orleans" to "get me a mojo hand." But no mention is made of staying in Louisiana. Waters's songs now were less about returning to some idyllic home than about rambling in search of new adventures. We also hear this same theme in two of his most memorable recordings from the start of the new decade, Waters's powerful cover of Robert Johnson's "Walking Blues" and his classic statement "Rollin' Stone." Above all, these songs celebrate the new mobility and self-assertiveness of African-American culture.

No blues singer—indeed, no popular singer of any style—had ever sung about himself with such vehemence, with such a glow of self-satisfaction, as Muddy Waters. In his very first Chess side, Waters touched on a favorite theme that he would repeatedly address in later recordings: the extraordinary events surrounding his birth. His song lyrics are forever quoting auspicious sources—a Gypsy woman or even the doctors in attendance—who herald, like biblical prophets, the momentous results of this nativity. The stars were in alignment; he was born, we are told, "On the seventh hour, on the seventh day, on the seventh month." A specific prediction is always made about the young Muddy Waters. In "Mannish Boy," we are told that he will be "the greatest man alive." In "I'm Your Hoochee Coochee Man," the Gypsy woman proclaims that "he's gonna be a son of a gun." In other songs, we are indulged with equally memorable prognostications: that the youngster is "born for good luck" or is bound to be a "rollin' stone." Sometimes the tributes to himself are passing interludes in his songs, but often they take center stage in the title, as in his 1951 recording "They Call Me Muddy Waters." But when Waters put himself in the title of his song, it is usually to celebrate . . . no, not his blues singing or slide guitar work . . . rather his prowess in bed. And if clueless record buyers didn't understand the significance of a "hoochee coochee man," celebrated in Waters's 1954 release, the artist obliged them later that year with song titles requiring no graduate degree in hermeneutics for their interpretation, recordings such as "I'm Ready" or "I'm a Natural Born Lover."

Of course, blues recordings had *always* dealt with sexuality, but rarely so openly or with such willfulness. The record companies that promoted this music in the 1920s and 1930s were complacent, or perhaps even supportive, if the lyrics reflected negative stereotypes of black culture, such as alcoholism, shiftlessness, or promiscuity. But Charley Patton or Blind Lemon Jefferson could hardly have convinced Paramount to let them sing "I'm a Natural Born Lover." Nor should we underestimate the sociological importance of such apparently personal and quirky statements, which increasingly set the tone for Chicago blues in the postwar years. As Gunnar Myrdal showed in his survey of the attitudes of Southern whites in the final days of desegregation, no aspect of racial equality was more worrisome to the white ruling class than the assertion of black sexuality and the resulting potential for miscegenation. By comparison, concerns about black voting rights ranked fourth in his survey, while anxieties about blacks demanding good jobs placed sixth. The bedroom, not the boardroom or voting booth, was the locus of white fear, albeit mostly unspoken in popular culture—until now. Waters sensed that the time was ripe for challenging these attitudes head-on, and the exhilaration felt by his audience at his assertiveness, at the Delta blues singer repeating like a mantra "I'm a man, I'm a full grown man" in his "Mannish Boy," was less a vicarious enjoyment of some tawdry encounter than an awestruck sense that social restraints were toppling down.

But if Waters had the right message for the time, its effectiveness would hardly have been so great if he had not also translated it into a powerful musical idiom. With the addition of harmonica player Little Walter, pianist Otis Spann, and drummer Elga Edmonds at his recording sessions from the early 1950s, Muddy Waters would earn bragging rights as leader of the greatest blues band in the world. The combination of Walter and Waters was especially fortuitous, even if never predicted by a Gypsy woman or a team of seven doctors at the seventh hour. The blending of the harmonica and slide guitar is a time-honored blues sound, and no one would ever do it better than this pair. Sometimes they would shadow each other's steps with uncanny ease, vibrato matching vibrato, bent note matching bent note; their very breaths and heartbeats, it seemed, now moving in tandem. Hear the two on "All Night Long" from December 1951 and marvel at one of the great sounds of blues history, the magnetic attraction of two instrumental tones wrapping themselves together with tremendous life force, creating the groove that drives the entire performance. Yet at other times the duo would diverge sharply, each creating a separate cacophony, an outburst of blues bravado that follows its own wild impulse; yet even when seemingly most at odds, the two sounds would suddenly coalesce magically into a greater whole, the divergent pitches and rhythms and timbres merging together in a wonderful sound-dance beyond anyone's capability to dissect or emulate.

Born as Marion Jacobs, some thirty miles from the Mississippi River in

Marksville, Louisiana, on May Day, 1930, the future harmonica wizard Little Walter grew up in a musical vortex where Cajun music, blues, marches, jazz, and other vernacular styles mixed and matched. He acquired a harmonica at age eight, and the first local player who influenced him was a white man who played hillbilly music and yodeled. But Walter may have learned more from the Blind Lemon Jefferson recordings he listened to as a child, and his skill in playing along may have set the stage for his later intuitive ability to match Muddy Waters's guitar with such ease. Walter's teen years found him performing on the streets in New Orleans, Shreveport, Helena, Memphis, St. Louis, and elsewhere, soaking up a universe of sound and refracting it through the vent holes of his thirty-five cent instrument. By the time he arrived in Chicago around V-E Day, 1945, Little Walter may have been only fifteen years old, but he had already earned the respect of David "Honeyboy" Edwards, Robert Lockwood, and Sunnyland Slim, and was ready for the larger stage offered by his new surroundings.

If the Delta sound was to morph into the urban blues, it needed to put on bulk, and Waters's band grew in response to the challenge. The addition of drummer Elga Edmonds and pianist Otis Spann may not have had the electrifying effect of Little Walter's contributions, but they beefed up the sound of Waters's working band and helped establish the emerging Chicago style of blues. Waters now often preferred to have a second guitar in the band, relying on fellow Mississippi transplant Jimmy Rogers to augment his ensemble and help drive the rhythms. This lineup—two guitars, harmonica, piano, bass, and drums—had little precedent in the Delta heritage, but would come to define its own tradition in urban America. The grooves would now become more insistent, the beat steadier, the instrumental textures thicker, but, above all, the whole sound grew louder and more penetrating.

In truth, Waters had no need for a conventional rhythm section. His guitar sound, for all its technical limitations—often his strongest blues licks were little more than the repetition of a single note—possessed tremendous vitality and he could drive a performance single-handedly. Yet Waters was often insecure about his guitar playing, and as his fame advanced his confidence as an instrumentalist seemed to lessen. In a freewheeling interview from the late 1960s, Don DeMichael asked him whether white guitarists could play the blues, and Waters lamented that "many can play the blues better than me . . . I'm just telling the truth about it. White boy can run a ring around me playing the blues." However, Waters was quick to add: "They'll never be able to sing them as well as me." Perhaps Waters felt that the expansion of his band gave him a surer instrumental foundation for his performances. In any event, many later blues bands would emulate this same instrumentation.

Spann's piano work would anchor Waters's band for much of the next two decades. His versatility and sensitivity to the music made him an ideal sparring mate. Unlike many other blues pianists, whose eight-to-the-bar poundings possess all the subtlety of a Chicago L-train, Spann could tinkle lightly, groove softly, or kick into high gear, as the occasion warranted. He could slide into a quasi-Latin feel on "She's Into Something," keep the band cooking even at a slow 60 beats per minute on "She's Nineteen Years Old," or blend seamlessly into the churning cauldron of noise that underpins "I've Got My Mojo Working." If need be, Spann could also serve as master of ceremonies for the band, or even sing a blues number himself, as he did to close Waters's celebrated performance at Newport in 1960, a success which generated offers from record label executives, who were now interested in featuring the longtime sideman as a leader on his own dates.

Willie Dixon, who sometimes accompanied Waters on bass, may have exerted an even greater impact on the band's success, but his contribution came more from his songwriting than his instrumental skills. He had arrived in Chicago in 1936, playing a one-string tin-can bass and looking to make a name for himself as a boxer. Dixon won a Golden Gloves title the following year, but his greatest talent would prove to be his uncanny knack for capturing the idioms and rhythms of African-American vernacular speech and translating them into catchy blues lyrics. Like Waters and Spann, Dixon was a Mississippi native, born in Vicksburg in 1915, who helped shape the sound of the emerging urban blues style. Any listing of the defining songs of Chicago blues would inevitably draw on his impressive catalog of compositions. He helped shape Muddy Waters's image as the testosterone king of the blues with compositions such as "I'm Your Hoochee Coochee Man," "I Just Want to Make Love to You," and "I'm Ready." He propelled Howlin' Wolf's success with "Little Red Rooster," "Wang Dang Doodle," "Evil," and "Back Door Man." His "I Can't Quit You Baby" earned a hit record for Otis Rush, while "My Babe" and "Mellow Down Easy" did the same for Little Walter. And in time, Dixon's blues hits became rock anthems, as white musicians with British accents—the Rolling Stones, Led Zeppelin, Eric Clapton, and others—took these same songs and demonstrated their timeless appeal for later generations of record buyers.

By the mid-1950s, the Chicago blues scene was reshaping the sound of popular music, and Muddy Waters was the king of the new movement. The band personnel might change—with Francis Clay replacing Elga Edmonds; Junior Wells or James Cotton filling the shoes of Little Walter; Muddy even stole guitarist Hubert Sumlin, the cornerstone of Howlin' Wolf's band, for a spell—but through it all Waters always seemed to be fronting the hottest blues band in town. Backed by his high-energy ensemble, and spouting off the sassy, in-your-face lyrics, Waters was emerging as a counterculture force during the Eisenhower years, one whose influence spread far beyond the confines of the Windy City. His first impact was felt in black communities, but his music soon spread beyond the traditional racial confines of blues music. A jukebox operator boasted to *Billboard* magazine that he could resell his used Muddy Waters records to the growing number of white teenagers who were drawn to the raw new sound. But Waters really shook things up with his visit to England in the fall of 1958, sharing the lineup with string quartets at the Leeds Festival, and sending the audience into shock with his loud and raucous performance. The agents who had booked Waters on the tour had thought they were getting a folk singer in the vein of Big Bill Broonzy, but soon learned that they were promoting the amplified sound of urban blues, Chicago style. The next day, the newspaper headline read: "Screaming Guitar and Howling Piano." But if the British hoity-toity did not appreciate the hoochee coochee man, the youngsters were listening, and the sound of British music would never be the same.

Eric Burdon saw Muddy Waters during this tour and the experience played a role in the formation of his later band the Animals. Eric Clapton studied Waters's recordings, and felt that a major breakthrough in his guitar playing came when he could imitate part of the bluesman's "Honey Bee." British bands would spring up with names drawn from Muddy's songs, such as the Mojos, the Mannish Boys (with a young David Bowie), and, of course, the Rolling Stones. Yet Waters himself was unaware of this seismic shift in British music and tended to think he had made a mistake in bringing his electric guitar to England. Before leaving, he promised a reporter that he would come back next time playing "soft guitar" and "old blues." And he did just that. But when Waters returned in 1963, performing traditional songs on an acoustic guitar, he found, to his amazement, that he was constantly asked why he had left his Telecaster back home.

4. got my mojo workin'

Even back in Chicago, Waters had barely gauged the scope and degree of influence he was exerting on the next generation of musicians. When Waters saw up-and-coming blues rockers Paul Butterfield, Elvin Bishop, and Nick Gravenites stroll into Smitty's Corner one night, he sized them up immediately—and decided that they must be IRS agents after him for back taxes. That evening, he hid out in the office in between sets. Yet he could not miss the coming wave of rock, which eventually respected no hiding place. Waters had paid attention when his own label signed Bo Diddley. Waters even built his "Mannish Boy" off of the rocker's "I'm a Man," and enjoyed one of the biggest hits of his career. But when Chuck Berry, who had admired and learned from Waters, started outselling him, Waters may well have felt more pressured than flattered by the success of his musical progeny.

In truth, Waters hardly knew which way to turn when, in his late forties, he tried to adapt his sound to the new realities of the marketplace. On the one hand, he saw other blues artists, such as Howlin' Wolf and Buddy Guy, moving onto his home turf, challenging his preeminence as the king of urban blues. Waters knew he had to assert himself in the face of these rivals, but he was also tempted to court the favor of the younger rock audience. Record buyers less than half his age were driving the music ahead into uncharted areas, and they were increasingly setting the tone for the whole entertainment industry. His music seemed to appeal to them in some telekinetic way that Waters himself could barely fathom. Could he afford to ignore this trend? Yet, at the same time, Waters saw the first stirrings of the folk and blues revival, and this prompted him to return to his own Delta roots, and promote himself as the exponent of this time-honored tradition. He had seen the benefits of this "return to the roots" firsthand in England, and now back in Chicago he hosted British blues researcher Paul Oliver, who stayed in Muddy's house and constantly peppered him with questions about the old days and traditional styles of playing.

In response to the pull and tug of these possible paths, Waters decided to

pursue *all* of them. His work in the late 1950s and early 1960s is a tremendous hodge-podge, not without its moments of greatness, but sometimes
dispiriting in its lack of overall vision and direction. Waters could appeal to
younger audiences, and he proved it with his landmark 1960 performance
at Newport, where he electrifies the crowd with "I've Got My Mojo Working." Standing, clapping, many starting to dance, the audience responds
with such frenzy that Waters is forced to perform an immediate reprise of
the song. Four decades later, when comedian Mike Myers wanted to celebrate sixties-era grooviness and the loosening of sexual mores in his Austin Powers movies, he caught on to the "mojo" celebrated by Waters as the
totem and symbol of the whole shebang. The term, of disputed etymology,
originally referred to a voodoo charm, but Waters brought it into the popular discourse as part of his powerful on-stage sexual persona. As a result,
the "mojo" took life as some sort of metaphysical Viagra, a kick in the pants
for those plugged into the right cosmic vibrations. Performing the song at
Newport, Waters shook his hips suggestively, leaving no doubt about where
his mojo worked its *baddest* magic. Here Waters showed that he could light
up the sixties generation while staying true to his own musical identity. But
when he followed up in January 1962 with a lame effort like "Muddy Waters
Twist," his hips might still be shakin', but the lack of conviction in the contrived material was apparent to his longtime fans, and probably even to the
wide-eyed teenagers who were the target audience for the record.

By the following year, Waters had forgotten the twist and returned to
the studio in his new identity as *Muddy Waters Folk Singer*, featured in the
Chess album of the same name. The blues revival was now in full swing, and
Leonard Chess suggested that Waters go back to Mississippi and find some
older musician who could play with him on the record. Waters surprised
everyone by bringing Buddy Guy into the studio instead. Guy was another
gritty, urban blues performer, who may not have possessed authentic Delta
credentials, but fit in admirably at this back-to-the-plantation session. But
though the performances were credible, they were hardly likely to make
anyone forget the powerful music Waters had recorded for Lomax when
the guitarist really was immersed in an acoustic, vernacular style. Even more
to the point, Chess lacked a consistent vision for the label's longtime blues
star—and was just as ready to package him with electric organ or saxes or
a chorus of singers. Other Delta blues artists were having successes during this period—Howlin' Wolf or the rediscovered Son House—by proudly

demonstrating their unique and distinctive sound, which time and changing trends could not erode. But Muddy Waters relied too heavily on the advice of his record company, and as the Chess brothers lost touch with the music scene, their most loyal artist suffered accordingly.

When the Rolling Stones visited the United States in June 1964, the band made sure that their itinerary included a visit to the Chess studio, where they hoped to record. Yet Leonard Chess barely spoke two words to these oddball rockers, who struck him as simply bizarre. He had similarly underestimated the Beatles when they hit the scene, and now he showed that, even when the "next new thing" literally came to his doorstep—indeed, walked right through the portal at 2120 South Michigan—he had no sense of what the moment represented. Keith Richards would later tell a fanciful story about finding Muddy Waters wearing coveralls and painting the ceiling, apparently because his records weren't selling well and he needed to earn some extra cash. The story itself is highly doubtful, but its scornful tone clearly reflects the bad vibes the British rockers picked up from the Chicago record execs. Nonetheless, the Chess family would soon comprehend the sheer marketing power of the Rolling Stones, and try to capture a piece of the action. By 1968, the label was asking Waters to sing the Stones' "Let's Spend the Night Together" on the ill-fated *Electric Mud* LP. Critics savagely attacked this crass attempt to make money by repackaging Waters as a psychedelic rock icon, and though the initial shipments were impressive—reaching close to a hundred thousand copies in the first few weeks after release—returns also proved to be sizable. Eventually Waters joined in the criticism, blaming his record company and disparaging the blues credentials of his sidemen.

Waters's biggest competition came neither from upstart rockers or new blues acts in town, but rather from his own recorded legacy, which threatened to overshadow any attempt to redefine his sound or audience. Chess was actively repackaging Waters's old material, and though *The Best of Muddy Waters* compilation was already on the market, they jumped in with compilations *Real Folk Blues* in 1966 and *More Real Folk Blues* in 1967. The bluesman's Library of Congress material was also reissued and further muddied the waters for those trying to find the true Muddy Waters. Yet the heritage represented by these past landmarks would remain the best guidepost, not just for fans, but even for Waters himself. From the mid-sixties onward, Waters's strongest performances came about when he stayed true to his own personal history, working in the style and setting that had brought him his greatest early successes. Recordings such as "My Dog Can't Bark" and "I Got a Rich Man's Woman" from 1965 are powerful blues statements, plain and simple. They jump on no bandwagon, make no pretensions to crossover appeal, and succeed on that basis. Now in his fifties, Waters showed he could still be a vital presence on the contemporary blues scene—but only by being true to himself.

By the same circuitous path, Waters eventually found the right attitude to take toward the new rock generation. They were his *progeny*, not his peers. "The blues had a baby and they named the baby rock and roll," he would aptly sing, a sentiment that summed up not just a musical genealogy but his own personal opinion. In the wake of *Electric Mud*, Waters came out with *Fathers and Sons*, building on this theme of lineage and descent. Instead of the makeshift studio band of the former release, Waters relies here on the help of Paul Butterfield and Michael Bloomfield, younger players who respected and understood his music. When he heard the title Chess had selected for the release, Waters was delighted. "That's a very good title, 'cause I am the daddy, and all these kids are my sons." And just as the former project had been met with hostility from the critics, *Fathers and Sons* was widely praised.

Waters's band was working steadily, sometimes earning thirty-five hundred dollars for an hour's performance. But the applause and paydays could not hide the turmoil that surrounded Waters at the close of the sixties. Waters's record company was sold in a sudden surprising move, the Chess brothers taking $6.5 million in cash and twenty thousand shares of GRT, the new owner. GRT stood for General Recording Tape, and its move into African-American music was a puzzling diversification for a Silicon Valley company that had previously been relegated to manufacturing tape cartridges for Chess and other labels. The new owners showed remarkable ignorance of the mystique and personal touch that had made Chess great: GRT eventually shut down the headquarters and moved Chicago's greatest independent label to New York, where it became just one more second-tier player struggling in the marketplace. When GRT resold the label in 1975, the company received only $3 million, less than half of what it had paid for the business—it had taken the new owners only six years to destroy most of the value of what they had acquired. Leonard Chess would have been dismayed, but he was no longer around, having died of a sudden heart attack a few months after the sale. A distraught Waters may not have foreseen all of the calamities set off by this unexpected death, but he knew that a vital part of his own career had also passed away. When he heard the news, the guitarist phoned in a spontaneous tribute to a radio station, lamenting the end of a collaboration that spanned more than two decades. "I think if he was livin', he would say what I'm sayin' now: he made me, and I made him."

Chess was not the only casualty of the era. Otis Spann, Muddy's longest musical associate, left the band, and died in April 1970. And Waters's own health was not good. His blood pressure had long been sending warning signals, and Waters grew especially alarmed when a nosebleed persisted for a week, and then blood started coming out of his eyes. In response, Waters took his doctor's advice, and swore off whiskey—but he began drinking champagne in prodigious amounts. And then, only eleven days after Chess's heart attack, Waters almost died himself, in a car accident, when his Chevy station wagon slammed into a Pontiac while the band was returning from a gig. Driver John Warren died in the collision, as did both occupants of the Pontiac. Suffering from multiple fractures, Waters remained hospitalized for three months; when he was released in January 1970, he was walking with a cane, his hands still suffered from swelling and numbness, and a prominent scar above his left eye signaled to his audiences the mortal blow the guitarist had just barely dodged.

In the final leg of his career, Waters relied increasingly on his reputation with rock stars and fans to secure gigs or sell records. At times, Waters himself was sometimes only vaguely aware of the reputation of these newfound admirers: when Bob Dylan sat in with the band at the Bottom Line, the bluesman introduced him to the audience as John Dylan. At "The Last Waltz," the celebrated final concert of The Band, Waters mistook Joni Mitchell (who came up to introduce herself) for a female fan, and slyly propositioned her, not realizing that she was one of the performers on the bill. But even when Muddy was unsure of his bearings, he willingly played along. The new owners of Chess arranged for him to record with a group of British admirers for his 1971 *The London Muddy Waters Sessions*, and the session might have produced a strong album—if the label had not decided to over-dub horn parts in one more failed attempt to adapt the Delta legend's sound according to the flavor of the month.

Waters had spent three decades of his life in the paternalistic environment of the Southern plantation, and the Chess label filled much the same role in his life for an almost identical length of time. The business had been run like a family, musicians coming and going like so many relations, money meted out for their car payments or medical bills, rather than by the strict schedule of a payroll department. Waters was not one to interfere or ask hard questions. After Leonard Chess's death, he obligingly signed away many of his publishing rights in exchange for a check representing six months worth of royalties. Of course, the transaction was accompanied by reassuring talk that he was being "protected" and "looked after." Nonetheless, a personal, family-type relationship had always been what Waters had found most reassuring, and when he signed with his new agent Scott Cameron in the early 1970s, he again readily agreed to paternalistic terms that, in authentic plantation style, extended beyond the two parties' lifespans through to their descendants. Yet Cameron fought vigilantly for Waters's interests, getting him better gigs, and providing a much needed source of stability in the period following Leonard Chess's death.

Waters needed a similarly sympathetic advocate in the recording studio, and finally found one in the unlikely guise of a long-haired, albino guitarist, less than half his age, whose records were selling twice as well. Johnny Winter had enjoyed a meteoric ascent since 1968, when *Rolling Stone* magazine featured him in an article on the Texas music scene, setting off a bidding war between record companies (eventually won by Columbia) for the services of the blues rock sensation. Winter had met Waters when the two shared a bill at an Austin club, and they later worked together on the Chicago television show *Soundstage* in the mid-1970s. When Waters's relationship with Chess ended in 1975, his own services came up for grabs, and he gravitated toward Winter's Blue Sky label, affiliated with Columbia, and began collaborating with the young rocker on what many people saw as a comeback recording. True, Waters had never gone anywhere, but after the car accident, the decline of the Chess label, and the mixed reactions to his several attempts to reach a crossover audience, his reputation in the industry was based more on his history than his perceived sales potential.

Any doubts about Waters were resolved by his electrifying performance on *Hard Again*, recorded in October 1976 under Winter's guidance, and with the rock star's active participation, both as a member of the band and inside the control booth. Winter is credited as producer, but his great achievement here is achieving a sound that seems so natural and *un*produced. "We recorded most of the songs in just one take," Winter later recalled. "We were having fun, and it came through in the recording." After so many attempts at "packaging" Waters, at "updating" his music and "jiving" his fans, *Hard Again* refreshes with its no-nonsense blues in the style that Waters had made his own. Much of the material here, and on Waters's follow-up projects with Winter, revisits familiar ground; but even when he returns to old songs like "Mannish Boy" and "I Can't Be Satisfied," Waters offers versions that can withstand comparison to the classic performances. "I was unhappy with the last Chess recordings," Winter adds, "and wanted to show Muddy to be as great as I knew he was." The release would earn a Grammy award, and Winter and Waters followed up with three more projects—*I'm Ready* (1978), *Muddy "Mississippi" Waters Live* (1979), and *King Bee* (1981)—perhaps none of them as spectacular as *Hard Again*, but each one valuable additions to Waters's legacy.

These would be Waters's final major musical statements. In 1981, Waters found out that he had lung cancer. Part of his lung was removed, and he underwent radiation treatment. The following spring, he learned that the cancer had gone into remission, and he began preparing for a new tour. But the cancer came back in July, and though the doctors thought another surgery might help, they doubted whether Waters was strong enough to undergo an operation. Waters refused chemotherapy and spent his final months at home, finally succumbing on April 30, 1983, the official cause of death listed as carcinoma of the lungs and cardiorespiratory arrest.

Waters, who had often sung about the singular events surrounding his birth, may well have found some symbolic meaning in the auspicious circumstances of his final rites. An overflow of mourners, many of them idle onlookers with no connection to the singer, threatened to turn the funeral into a media event. Muddy had asked that his red Telecaster be buried with him, but the casket hardly had enough room to accommodate it, and the neck of the instrument broke off when the lid was shut. Then, at the burial, a loud sound was heard almost simultaneously with the pallbearers setting down the casket. A crack had appeared in a large floral arrangement made in the image of a red guitar, almost in silent mockery of the indignities suffered by Waters's prized instrument. Some of the women in attendance let out a scream. "I'm skeptical about the supernatural," commented Mike Kappus, one of the pallbearers, "but this was amazing." Most of the luminaries of the blues world had shown up for the funeral—B.B. King, Buddy Guy,

Memphis Slim, Willie Dixon, Junior Wells, Johnny Winter, James Cotton—and some of them jammed at an informal wake held at Buddy Guy's Checkerboard Lounge. But Waters, who never liked to be upstaged, would have been happy to know that his influence, musical and perhaps otherworldly, served as the chief topic of conversation, and that without playing a note he somehow had managed to dominate one last all-star blues event.

John Lee Hooker

chapter eight

hooker's boogie

1. been jumpin' ever since that day

The great blues players always retain an element of mystery. Again and again we encounter the enigmatic gap in the biography, the vague "ramblin' years," the sudden departures on the last train out of town, the arrival in a strange city under a new name. The whisper of illicit activities, the cash-and-carry sidelines, the action out back or upstairs or down in the alleyway. And, of course, the beguiling story songs that—who can doubt it?—come straight out of the pages of a troubled life, sketching a few enticing details, before the book snaps shut abruptly, so many questions still unanswered.

The music of the Delta tradition is always accompanied by this thick fog, it seems. It forever promises more than it delivers, and we live as much for the promise as for the genuine goods on hand. No wonder the researchers who have pursued its elusive leads end up acting like so many detectives on the trail of a wily culprit. But here the suspect always remains at large, at least a step ahead of the pursuer, never 'fessing up, never offering all the revealing answers. Yes, we have learned much about the history of the music over the last half century, but what we have ascertained pales beside what we still want to know. Ever since W. C. Handy encountered that nameless, "lean, loose-jointed" guitarist playing the blues with a knife at the Tutwiler train station circa 1903, his face marked with the "sadness of the ages," the music has repeatedly come to us in the guise of many such enigmatic figures, masters without a pedigree, travelers with no official visa, no clear starting point and no certain destination.

John Lee Hooker artfully retained the bluesman's mystique into the new millennium. One of the last surviving Delta bluesmen who honed their craft during the pre-Depression era, he lived long enough to be celebrated by the ravenous electronic media. In his final years, Hooker was fêted on *The Tonight Show* and *The Late Show with David Letterman*; he hobnobbed with the president of the United States and was immortalized on the Hollywood Walk of Fame; he was honored at a Madison Square Garden tribute, and collaborated with everyone from Miles Davis to the Rolling Stones. But for all the scrutiny, for all the interviews, he remained a cipher, an unknowable element that even round-the-clock coverage couldn't penetrate.

Try to figure it out. When was he born? John Lee Hooker would tell you straight up that he arrived on the scene on August 22, 1917, just outside of Clarksdale. But that's when he wasn't claiming 1920 . . . or 1915 or 1923 or some other birthdate. Of course, you could go to the county courthouse to get the date of record. But the building burnt down in 1927. Siblings? Hooker had nine . . . or was it twelve? Depends on who you ask. And marriages? Well, Hooker admitted to three of them. Except when he confessed to four. Children? Let's not even ask! Sure, it's hard to forget a marriage, even a bad one, or a sibling, for that matter; but in the world of John Lee Hooker, all facts were subjective, all truths provisional. Only the beat goes on.

Of course, you could turn to his letters, or his journals, or his private papers. Sorry, but John Lee Hooker could hardly read or write. You could study the photographs of him from his early days. Sorry again, not a single image from the first thirty years of his life has been discovered. You could probe the surviving interviews and first-person accounts of other old-time blues players from the Clarksdale area to learn what they could tell you about the young John Lee Hooker. Another dead end: John Lee Hooker is all but invisible in these accounts, almost as if he grew up in a Clarksdale from some parallel universe, far from the Delta region of Mississippi. Or, you could find out what Hooker's family members had to say; but their surviving accounts merely relate how the young guitarist "just vanished out of the world" one day, with little to say for himself before the fact, and next to nothing to communicate after the event.

Finally, you could go to his earliest recordings. But here Hooker's deceptiveness gets positively wicked. He sometimes recorded under the name of John Lee Cooker or John Lee Booker or just John Lee—easy aliases to penetrate—but he mixed these up with trickier pseudonyms, "Delta John" or "Texas Slim" or "Birmingham Sam" or "The Boogie Man" or "Little Pork Chops." So many sessions, so many labels, so little information: with John Lee Hooker, even the hard facts of discography take on a suggestive, hypothetical quality.

Yet the biggest mystery of all resides in between the grooves of these records, in the music itself. Even the guitarist, at his most truthful moment, could never describe how he had acquired his extraordinary beat, how Hooker got his groove, the pulse that separates his sound from the work of all his peers. Hooker calls it a "boogie," but it bears as much relation to the standard boogie-woogie beat and its various derivatives as a laser does to a kerosene lamp. Hooker's beat is like a solution to a quasi-Newtonian puzzler: How to pack the maximum amount of forward momentum into the fewest number of notes. The sound mesmerized record buyers in the 1940s and 1950s, captivated them as something hip and modern, but paradoxically, it also sounded primal, older than the hills. "What he picked up has got to come from one generation further back from anyone else," Keith Richards has speculated. "John Lee plays the blues like I heard 'em when I first started to play," B.B. King relates. Trying to pin down its essence, Hooker's biographer Charles Shaar Murray describes this sound as "older than the earliest country blues records."

"I'm the first person that really got the boogie goin'," Hooker liked to boast, but when asked to elaborate, he always stumbled for words. "It's just there. I can't explain it. And it just comes out." The audience grooved on it, and so did Hooker. "I get carried away, too. 'Cause I feel it just as much as they do."

But the boogie is not entirely a mystery, because Hooker knows exactly where he learned it—from his stepfather, Will Moore. Musing on his huge hit "Boogie Chillen," which introduced his "boogie" to the mass market, Hooker admits that "I got that from my stepdad. That was his tune. That was his beat." In interview after interview, Hooker always credited Moore for all the key elements of his style. Moore's approach was "identical like me, identical," Hooker insisted to interviewer Pete Welding. "He taught me what he knowed, and I loved what he knowed, and I dug what he knowed, so I just went that way." But even this clear acknowledgment of an original source leaves us empty-handed. For we know almost nothing about Will Moore, except from what Hooker tells us, and the only indication of what the stepfather's guitar sounded like comes from Hooker's own records.

A sharecropper who originally hailed from Shreveport, Louisiana, Will Moore stands out as another one of those grand mysteries of early Delta blues. Hooker began learning guitar from him around 1930. He tells us that Moore played alongside Charley Patton and Blind Lemon Jefferson— in fact, he remembered both men visiting his stepdad at home, seeking him out because he was such a great guitar player. The latter represents quite a claim, since Lemon spent little time in Mississippi, and was already quite a celebrity when Ralph Lembo brought him to Itta Bena in 1927. Lembo even paraded the visiting guitarist through town on a wagon, like a visiting dignitary, and charged the unheard-of amount of seventy-five cents to hear Jefferson perform at a local dance. We are perhaps right to be skeptical before linking Moore to Jefferson or even to Patton—and Hooker himself, as we have seen, is a less than reliable informant. Even more striking is the absence of Moore's name in the leading source documents about Delta blues from this period. Researchers scoured the region for information about the great flowering of blues music that took place in and around Clarksdale in the 1920s and 1930s, and this important figure eluded their grasp. Both David Evans and Gayle Wardlow, the two most persistent on-the-ground researchers in the Delta, confirmed to me that they had not encountered any reference to Hooker's stepfather during their extensive fieldwork. Alan Lomax's major study on the Delta blues makes no mention of Moore, and one seeks in vain in other likely sources for substantiating information. Hooker almost certainly exaggerated Moore's local reputation. Yet one is also left to marvel at the blues riches of this small community, where talents of the caliber of Moore and Hooker hardly warrant a mention by the other players on the scene.

If we are left to puzzle over Willie Moore's musical career, we can have little doubt about the decisive role he played in John Lee Hooker's life. Hooker's father, Reverend William Hooker, objected to sinful secular music, and when an itinerant bluesman courting one of his daughters gave John Lee a guitar, the youngster was allowed to keep it only on the condition that he never brought it inside the house. After his mother, the former Minnie Ramsey, moved in with Willie Moore, all of her children decided to remain with Reverend Hooker—except for John Lee. For him, the choice was not just between two parents, but a decision about the irreconcilable values represented by the dueling father figures: Reverend Hooker, with his righteous path of the Lord, or Willie Moore, the man who played the blues. In his youth, John Lee Hooker earned admiration for his strong, sure singing in church. He was only nine or ten, but even then his vocal abilities caught everyone's attention. "I was a great gospel singer," he later boasted. "Everybody around in the county looked up to me and said, 'Oh, that kid is somethin' else, he can sing better than anybody I ever seen.'" A commitment to Reverend Hooker and the church would not have meant a renunciation of music, merely channeling it down this sanctified path. But Hooker decided instead on Willie Moore and the blues.

Yet Hooker's later blues recordings, with their exhortations and long spoken passages in overheated prose, often sound like they come straight from the pulpit. He expostulates on the life-changing essence of the "boogie" in language that could just as easily describe a born again experience at a revival meeting. When Bernard Besman brought Hooker into the studio for a landmark session in November 1948, the guitarist spread the good news with the conviction of a true believer who had just discovered a new creed:

> [spoken]:   *I sat around, you know.*
> *After awhile I started jumpin'.*
> *Boy I was jumpin'.*
> [shouting]:   *Then I started jumpin'.*
> [singing]:   *I been jumpin' ever since that day.*

This was Hooker's Pauline moment, rockin' and shakin' to the beat of a guitar and a stomping foot. And his proselytizing was not without its impact. "Boogie Chillen," recorded that same November day, climbed with startling ease to number 1 on *Billboard*'s R&B charts. Some have claimed that it eventually sold a million copies—an extraordinary figure for any record, let

alone one featuring a hitherto unknown black guitarist, performing unaccompanied, on a tiny independent label. The song has almost no melody.
Even less harmony. In fact, it is hard to call it a song. It's more like a bit of
jive stream of consciousness in 4/4 time. But the boogie was there . . . and
it proved irresistible.

2. deep blues

"I know why the best blues artists come from Mississippi," Hooker told an
interviewer from *Melody Maker* in 1964. "Because it's the worst state. You
have the blues all right if you're down in Mississippi."

John Lee Hooker had no affection for his home state, but only gradually
came to understand that his music would provide a pathway for escape.
Although Hooker spent much of his childhood on the Fewell Plantation
near Vance, and his father had enjoyed some success as a sharecropper,
working and living on a hundred-acre plot, this type of life held no appeal
for the youngster. In a moment straight out of a Muddy Waters song, he
long remembered a dramatic childhood encounter with a Gypsy woman
who promised that he would be famous all over the world and achieve great
riches. His friends taunted him for the prediction, and though Hooker
wanted to believe it, he wondered how it could ever come true.

He visited Clarksdale frequently, and even lived for a time on Issaquena
Street. But his musicmaking gained him few admirers in this community
teeming with blues guitarists. When asked, late in life, about his favorite
places to perform during this period of life, Hooker mentioned no jukehouse, no social gatherings, not even a street corner or train depot; instead,
he told of playing on his front porch or going out by himself in the woods.
In the midst of the Delta region that put blues on the map, Hooker honed
his craft in isolation. When asked about jamming with friends, he couldn't
recall any. Nor did his brothers or sisters share his passion for music; more
likely, they viewed it with suspicion or contempt.

Hooker, like many of his generation, abandoned the Delta for better prospects in the North. But we would be wrong to assume that he
departed primarily to advance his musical career. True, Hooker came to
describe his coming-of-age in such decisive terms. "I know, living in Mississippi, I wouldn't get nowhere. People kept telling me that—the older

people. . . . They say, 'Kid you gotta leave here. You so good. You gotta go north. You can make it.' I didn't know whether they was right or wrong." Yet Hooker's obscurity in his hometown hardly supports this tale of a talent that had grown too large for Clarksdale. His music career had barely started at the time he made his decision to leave, and the young John Lee Hooker had far from exhausted the opportunities to perform and develop that were immediately available to him on his native soil.

His first move was a cautious one, a journey of less than one hundred miles to Memphis. Even with no money, he could travel that far, and safely get back home if no better prospects emerged. Hooker quickly found his niche in Memphis's entertainment industry, circa 1933, even on famous Beale Street. Alas, it was merely as an usher in a theater. His guitar playing and singing were—again!—pursued in isolation, usually in his room at his aunt Emma Lou's boardinghouse, where he resided. Overhyped accounts tell how young John Lee Hooker hung out with B.B. King in Memphis during this period. But since King, eight years old at the time, would not come to Memphis until more than a decade had elapsed, this must be discarded as one more dubious incident in a biography full, as we have seen, of faulty factoids. Hooker, for his part, didn't have time to wait for B.B. King to reach manhood: his mother and stepfather came and brought him back to Mississippi after a few weeks.

Yet it would prove impossible to keep John Lee Hooker down on the farm after this brief but intoxicating taste of city life. Only days later he ran off again to Memphis—avoiding his aunt this time, better to hide his tracks. He stayed longer on this visit, but his impact as a guitarist on the local scene was negligible. He measured his musical earnings in nickels and dimes—even less than the few dollars a decent jukehouse player might have made back in the Delta. Soon he left Memphis behind, heading first for Knoxville, and finally settling in Cincinnati. Like other blues artists, Hooker "rambled," but on his arrival in a new location he sought out a conventional job, and his life during the Great Depression was far from glamorous. He earned his keep as a dishwasher or janitor, an usher or factory worker, whatever he could manage, dreaming perhaps of fame and fortune, but settling for ten dollars per week in wages. He played at a regular house party on the weekends, but made sure he was back on the job Monday morning. Hooker knew that Cincinnati boasted a strong local label willing to record black talent—King

Records, later famous as musical home of James Brown—but he didn't dare approach the company. "I wasn't known, wasn't even thinkin' about it. I didn't have a chance then."

Hooker finally hit his stride after he reached Detroit in the early 1940s, but even this decisive move was driven less by the musical attractions of Motown than by economic opportunities in the Motor City. Almost every car on every street in America was made in Detroit at that time, and Hooker arrived looking for better wages and a more stable work environment. With the exception of a very brief stint in the Army—Hooker claimed he was discharged when they found that he had lied on his enlistment papers, his fuzzy autobiography catching up with him for once—he earned his livelihood in the booming local factories, often as a janitor, occasionally on the assembly line. Work was readily available, and even if he got fired at one plant for sleeping on the job, he could quickly find another employer willing to hire him. And sleeping on the job became more common, because Hooker was increasingly spending the wee hours between dusk and dawn pursuing his second career as a blues musician.

Hooker continued to perform at house parties, as he had done in Cincinnati, but also began exploring other venues for his music. The posher Detroit nightclubs rarely offered blues, and certainly not the raw, down-home music played by Hooker, but many working-class bars were receptive to his kind of music. Without a reputation, or any records to his name, or even a union card testifying to his professional status as a musician, Hooker had to rely on persuasion and persistence to get his music heard. He would bring his guitar and ask if he could play a song, eventually parlaying these spontaneous jams into real gigs. In time, Hooker's boogie proved to be a stronger calling card than any he might have secured from the local American Federation of Musicians. He was performing many of the songs that he would later record to great acclaim, "Boogie Chillen" and "Sallie Mae," "Crawlin' King Snake" and "Hobo Blues," and as his following grew, the part-time blues guitarist found himself welcome at more and more nightspots. The Apex Bar, the Caribbean Club, Henry's Swing Club, the Sensation, and other similar venues became platforms for his distinctive style. In time, people in the music business started hearing about a remarkable new talent on the scene.

Elmer Barbee, who owned a record store on Lafayette, learned of the promising guitarist, and paid a visit to the crowded Apex Bar to see for himself. Hooker was playing in a trio with pianist James Watkins and drummer Curtis Foster, and Barbee was deeply impressed by their music. As Hooker recalls it, Barbee told him: "You are the best I ever heard." Hooker began visiting the small recording studio Barbee had set up in the back of his store. Here, over a period of months, they recorded a number of acetate disks featuring Hooker, sometimes performing alone, in other instances joined by accompanists. Several of these acetates survive, and they present a mixed picture. When supported by piano, Hooker lets the keyboard establish and drive the song's pulse, and the results are lackluster. But when Hooker performs unaccompanied, a potent energy is palpable in the music.

An amateur recording made by Hooker at a house party around this same time offers an even more dramatic revelation of the hypnotic power of his music. Gene Deitch, a cartoonist and illustrator, had recently moved to Detroit from Los Angeles, where he had hosted performances in his Hollywood bungalow. Now he attempted to recreate the same informal musicmaking in his new home. A friend told him about John Lee Hooker's incendiary work in the local clubs, and soon the guitarist was playing at Deitch's dining-room table, sometimes with a DuKane tape recorder capturing the proceedings. This music, which ranks among the finest blues work recorded during the 1940s, was almost lost to posterity. The tapes themselves eventually found their way to Czechoslovakia, and were not released commercially until 2004. Fifty-five years had passed, but the music had lost none of its vitality.

In the parlance of the music's fans, this is "deep blues," blues stripped of all extraneous matter, played for an audience but almost as if listeners were irrelevant, drawing on a passion within, rather than responding to expectations from without. Even when Hooker played requests at Deitch's house—and the range of his repertoire here is striking, including spirituals, folk songs, and old country blues alongside his own compositions—he reconfigured them into a distinctive personal statement, as though tapping some hidden inner reserve of feeling. Almost like the Method actors of that same period, Hooker was revealing that the most personal and deeply felt emotions could be a springboard for public performance. At the close of the 1940s, this "deep blues" had almost disappeared from the commercial music world, gone with Charley Patton and Robert Johnson, now dead, or with Son House and Skip James, who had seemingly disappeared off the face of the earth. But the increasing slickness of the music industry created a hunger among record buyers for precisely this type of music, songs that cut through the extraneous, the ribbons and bows with which producers bedecked their paltry offerings, revealing the beating heart within. The postwar record industry had developed a successful formula of taking promising talent, and improving it through packaging, elaborating on it, surrounding it with the right session musicians and the hippest new material. The concept of taking raw music and keeping it raw must have been as foreign and unappetizing to the mind-set of Barbee and his peers as a sushi restaurant would have seemed in the midst of Motown, circa 1948. Yet Barbee and his protégé gradually realized that the less they tinkered, the less they beefed up the Hooker sound, the better it sounded.

Recall that the American music audience—indeed, the whole cultural climate—was on the verge of an extraordinary change, one that first emerged with the bohemian currents of the 1950s, and then deepened into full-fledged rebellion in the 1960s. Slick packaging became suspect, and the search for authenticity would emerge as a vision quest for the vanguard of the new paradigm. The primal energy of a young Marlon Brando, the untrammeled freedom of Jack Kerouac's prose in *On the Road*, the aloofness of cool school trumpeter Miles Davis, the naïve idealism of Holden Caulfield in Salinger's *The Catcher in the Rye*: all of these, despite their individual differences, announced a different cultural tone on the horizon, an iconoclastic mind-set in which the refinements of the past were seen as so many chains binding us to a mind-numbing conformity.

The blues had an important role to play in this transformation. The music's troubled history; its dubious social status; its role as a vehicle of expression for the nation's most oppressed underclass; its lack of superficial polish and sophistication: these had perhaps been seen as limitations or flaws in the past, but in the topsy-turvy new worldview, they emerged as salient virtues, as guarantors of *real*-ness, of the much prized authenticity that would become an obsession of the entertainment industry, an elusive quality which always threatened to disappear, Midas-like, the moment the execs put their hands on it. At the close of the 1940s, even the blues had lost much of its down-home verisimilitude, as record companies had domesticated it for their servile purposes. But the success of Lightnin' Hopkins, a short while before Hooker emerged on the scene, showed—to the surprise of many industry insiders—that the older blues could find a new audience.

Hopkins had arrived in a recording studio in postwar Los Angeles almost as though out of a time warp, playing music that had more affinity with long dead Blind Lemon Jefferson than with the swing or bop or R&B that crowded the local airwaves. The success of his "Katie May," recorded at his debut session, must have struck many as a fluke novelty hit, but it revealed something more profound: a fault line in the oh-so-slick music industry, one that would rupture in the future, sending the polished pop idols tumbling, making room for a grittier, hard-wrought sound that made no apologies for its poor pedigree or rough manners. And almost at the same moment that Hooker had his similar breakthrough, Muddy Waters was shaking up Chicago with his first hit releases, unlikely successes that seemed too old-fashioned to appeal to big city listeners. Coincidence? Not really. Although the deepest of the blues always resists the trends and pressures of the music industry, its commercial success is created, at least in part, by the vacuum in the cultural soundspace—a vacuum formed by the music industry itself in its zeal to commoditize its product. Hooker, Waters, and Hopkins were all part of this same vanguard, a return to the roots that was truly a "back to the future," a revelation of how the blues' past would shape the sound of the next generation.

3. everybody in the record business is crooked

Captivated by his new discovery, Elmer Barbee brought Hooker to Bernard Besman, a hard-nosed businessman who was a big fish in the small pond of postwar Detroit music. Together with his partner Johnny Caplan, Besman had built Pan American, a struggling record distributor, into a strong regional player, and now aimed to establish his own Sensation label. Like the Chess brothers, Besman was an immigrant whose family had come to the United States in the 1920s—in his case from Kiev, via London. The young Bernard Besman had shown some knack as a pianist, but he soon found greater success booking the bands of other, more talented musicians. He eventually parlayed his initial six-thousand-dollar investment in Pan American into a substantial business that allowed him to retire comfortably in California as a millionaire.

Much of that wealth walked in the door in the fall of 1948 when John Lee Hooker was ushered into Besman's presence. Besman had never dealt with such a big talent before, and never would again. Yet he deserves some credit for how he recognized and parlayed the opportunity at hand. One of the first things Besman noticed was the bluesman's pronounced stutter. The mannerism seemed to disappear when Hooker sang, but many label execs would have shut the door at that moment, refusing to put their money behind a vocalist with a speech impediment. Besman took the opposite approach, deciding not only to record Hooker as a singer, but also to allow him to include long spoken monologues in his performances. Moreover, Besman was determined to present his new discovery on disk without additional accompaniment. Hooker had frequently performed with a trio or quartet, but now would be featured as a solo act. And instead of asking Hooker to stop tapping his foot so loudly (the invariable request of producers and engineers since the birth of recorded sound), Besman decided not only to let the foot *tap*, but to have it *pound*. He even arranged the miking so that the sound came into the forefront of the music.

Perhaps most remarkable, Besman did not even expect Hooker to perform the blues—at least, not by any traditional definition of blues music. Instead, he let the guitarist riff on a single chord while improvising a narrative. Hooker's boogie sounded *bluesy*, no mistake about it, but there was no formal blues structure, no shift to the subdominant chord, no twelve-bar repetitions, no A–A–B lyrics, no bottleneck sounds. To be honest, these weren't even songs, just freewheeling grooves, without a clear beginning, middle, or end. They concluded after around three minutes each, but that was imposed by the limitations of a 78rpm record. When Hooker got into a groove, it sounded like he could go on for an hour or a day, or maybe stop for a meal or a nap, and pick up again in the same place. Many listeners have assumed that Besman had no choice in all these matters, that he simply took Hooker's music as he found it. But the Deitch recordings from this same period show Hooker quite capable of playing the old blues—"Trouble in Mind" or "Catfish Blues"—in fairly recognizable forms. In truth, Besman's lack of experience in recording the blues may have made him more forgiving of these eccentricities, in a way that, say, the Chess brothers would never have been.

On two gripping takes of "Sallie Mae," Hooker hovered close to traditional blues form, although cavalierly ignoring the rule that the A and B lines should rhyme. Yet the rhythmic flow more than compensates for any limitations in the words. At moments like this, Hooker showed that no one surpassed his *feel* for the medium-slow blues. "Poor Slim" is taken at an even slower tempo, lingering at that liminal point where a rhythm seems on the verge of collapsing into a free rubato. But Hooker and Besman also experimented with faster tempos, albeit lightly played, a pulsation rather than a beat, the sound of the musician's foot interacting with the vibrations of the guitar, all underpinning a rambling narration, half-spoken, half-sung. In performances they called "Henry's Swing Club" and "Johnny Lee's Original Boogie," the musician and producer contrived nothing less than a modern-day evocation of a one-man band. Finally, on a track they named "Boogie Chillen," everything came together in one of those magical moments that sometimes happen in nightclubs, in the heat of a performance, but rarely in the sterile environment of a recording studio.

Joe Bihari and his brothers, owners of the large Los Angeles–based indie label Modern, were so excited by "Boogie Chillen" that Besman agreed to license the master to them. Modern's strong distribution in the South was invaluable in fueling and filling the growing demand for Hooker's boogie. One Nashville deejay played the record twelve straight times, and the phone soon started ringing from fans demanding to hear it again. B.B. King, who was working as a disk jockey on WDIA in Memphis, constantly featured the hot new song. Buddy Guy heard it in Louisiana, Albert Collins in Texas, the next generation of blues players galvanized by the new sound coming out of Detroit. By February 1949, "Boogie Chillen" had climbed to the top position on *Billboard*'s R&B charts. Besman would later deny the frequently mentioned claim that the record sold a million copies—*he* never got paid for a million units, Besman grumbled, and he certainly didn't pay Hooker royalties on anywhere near that number. But by any reasonable standards, "Boogie Chillen" was a sensation, and while it was still leading the charts, Besman brought his hot property back in the studio to make additional records.

A more experienced producer than Besman might have struggled to find the right recipe for a follow-up hit. Directing Hooker in the studio was not like producing other acts. Talk about artistic inspiration as much as you want; but *economic reality* demands that most bands arrive at a session prepared to play well-rehearsed material which, over a series of takes, they refine into polished, finished performances. Not so for Hooker: a second take would produce, likely as not, a substantially different song. The kind of methodical production that, say, Muddy Waters received at Chess—where the guitarist might go through twenty takes before everyone was happy—would never have worked for the young John Lee Hooker. He would have covered the whole history of the blues in twenty takes, and be no closer to a definitive version of a specific song. Yet Besman understood the essence of Hooker's talent perhaps better than any of the bluesman's later producers. He didn't want polished performances; he wanted to capture the heat of the moment. He went with the flow, and if take two sounded like a different song, Besman simply accepted that it was a new creation, and assigned it a separate title.

Hooker flourished in this environment. He played with the same freedom and spontaneity with which he would have performed for intimate friends. Record buyers intuited the spontaneity of this off-the-cuff hipness, and responded with their wallets. During the summer of 1949, "Hobo Blues" climbed to number 5 on the charts, *and* the flip side "Hoogie Boogie" also charted, reaching number 9. In December, "Crawlin' King Snake," a hypnotic, slow blues that bobbed and weaved at a measured pace slightly above 70 beats per minute, made it to number 6. Hit records may be commonplace in the music industry—but nothing is rarer than charting with the B side of a disk, except perhaps making a top ten slot with a slow blues on unaccompanied guitar—yet here Hooker and Besman achieved both! They must have understood that, given the nature of Hooker's peculiar muse, breaking all the rules was their surest path to success.

Hooker was breaking other rules too—legal ones relating to contract law—in a flagrant manner far less to Besman's liking. Rival record companies wanted to jump on the boogie bandwagon, and using Elmer Barbee as an intermediary, arranged to bring Hooker into the studio to record under different names. The practice was not unusual in the industry, although few exploited it more relentlessly than Barbee and Hooker. And small labels rarely took legal action to protect their prerogatives, since it might expose their own shady contracts and sham royalty agreements to scrutiny in a court of law. "Everybody in the record business is crooked," Besman admitted to Charles Shaar Murray in a 1994 interview. "Everybody. I don't care how big they are, or how small they are." But after a moment of reflection, he added: "I'm not talking about *me*. I don't count." Of course, Hooker knew he was in violation of his agreement with Besman, but he justified his activities as payback for the legitimate royalties from "Boogie Chillen" he never received.

For a few hundred dollars—paid in cash—Barbee could deliver the hot new blues artist for a surreptitious late night session. And many took him up on the offer. Hooker recorded as "Texas Slim" for the King label. He laid down tracks as "Birmingham Sam and his Magic Guitar" for Savoy. For Acorn Records, Hooker was "The Boogie Man." For the Danceland label, he performed as "Little Pork Chops." For Regent, he played as "Delta John." Blues fans might puzzle over other releases by John Lee Booker or John Lee Cooker—again, Hooker, hiding under the flimsiest pseudonyms. For the uninitiated, it seemed that a whole new style of blues had hit the scene, with a half dozen different exponents. Yet a single man was behind this mini-industry in boogie blues. Like Delta floodwaters bursting the levee, a torrent of music was pouring out of one individual, a coming-of-age both remarkable and unprecedented in the history of the music. During the first five years of his recording career, John Lee Hooker appeared on some two dozen different labels, under almost as many names—recording more music in the studio than Robert Johnson, Son House, Willie Brown, Tommy Johnson, and Skip James had done *combined* during their entire lives.

Hooker claims that he often composed his songs while driving to the session. Such a cavalier attitude would lead to disastrous results if practiced by other artists. But Hooker was different. "I can go into a studio and in two hours' time I can record five or six songs," Hooker boasted in 1992 to Jas Obrecht. "I can make ten albums in a year, and they come out perfect too." Maintaining a studio schedule that would deplete the creative energy of almost anyone else, Hooker forged a body of work during these early years that he would never surpass. And though the hectic pace led to a certain amount of repetitiveness and self-parody, the music never sounded stale. Texas Slim and Delta John and all the other aliases never released a ho-hum, workaday performance. Like those shamans of the non-Western world whose magical rhythms cause altered states of mind and a pathway to a higher realm of consciousness, Hooker seemingly channeled at will some powerful cosmic force, a primal boogie, that never let him down.

But the flurry of recording activity threatened to overwhelm Hooker's fans with a surfeit of boogie. By a conservative count, twenty-two Hooker records were released on the market in 1950, under a confusing array of names and by a host of labels. Deejays and record buyers rebelled, and only one song, "Huckle Up Baby," came close to matching Hooker's previous record sales, topping out at number 15 on the *Billboard* R&B chart. Hooker ran the risk of becoming, at age thirty-three, a novelty act whose time had come and gone. Besman continued to make records with his star performer, but most of them sat on the shelf unreleased, and the prospect of another number one hit seemed more and more remote. Despite his successes, Hooker had done very little to improve his day-to-day situation. The record companies had pocketed most of the money from his hit records, and Hooker was still playing in the blue-collar clubs where he had first made his name, unable to break into posher venues. Meanwhile, places like the Apex and Caribbean could hardly pay him much more than they had before—even if an extra hundred people showed up to hear the famous John Lee Hooker on any given night, most of them would be turned away, since the clubs had always been packed.

Hooker himself would have had good reason to feel depleted, creatively exhausted by the non-stop recording schedule of the last two years. Yet toward the end of 1951, just when it seemed that his career had reached a plateau, Hooker burst out with another inspired recording that shot to number one position on the *Billboard* R&B chart. "I'm in the Mood" revealed that Hooker's voice could prove as hypnotic as his guitar beat. Built around an echoing over-dubbed vocal and a slow, throbbing rhythm, the song evokes a late night eroticism that lingered at the border of what was permitted on radio airwaves, circa 1951. Hooker, for his part, proved that his talent was anything but one-dimensional, that his range of musical expression could move far beyond conventional blues material. "I'm in the Mood" has more in common with the soul music of the 1970s than with the Delta blues tradition. One senses that Hooker might easily have branched out in a different direction at this point in his career—much like two other former Clarksdale, Mississippi, talents, Ike Turner and Sam Cooke, who soaked up the blues and gospel music of the Delta only to climb the charts as soulful pop artists. Eddie Kirkland, a Jamaica-born guitarist who was a frequent accompanist to Hooker during this period, and a participant at the "I'm in the Mood" session, made exactly this transition, eventually joining Otis Redding's band. Living in the midst of the musical melting pot that would see the birth of the Motown sound some years later, Hooker could have done the same on a much larger scale. Instead, he maintained an allegiance to the blues that may, for a time, have limited his audience, but which he eventually parlayed into a much grander renown as one of the last keepers of the flame, the authentic voice of the Delta tradition.

By mid-1952, Hooker had recorded more than two hundred performances in a recording career that had spanned little more than three years. And the burden of creativity had fallen clearly on his shoulders: most of the performances featured Hooker as singer, instrumentalist, composer, arranger, and solo performer, a jack-of-all-trades in the studio. On those rare occasions where sidemen joined him—Eddie Kirkland on guitar, or James Watkins on piano, or Eddie Burns on harmonica—Hooker still tended to drive the performance, set the tone, push the beat, create the energy force that gave his recordings their special appeal. In truth, accompanying Hooker was not an easy task: when he brought some regulars from his Detroit club engagements into the studio in December 1952 to add saxophone, piano, and drums into the mix, the results were a crazy game of "find the downbeat." "It's Been a Long Time Baby" was probably intended to be a standard twelve-bar blues, but Hooker completes the first chorus in nine and a half bars, compresses the form into nine bars for the next chorus, then stretches out, at least comparatively speaking, for ten bars on the third chorus. At that point, Hooker drops out for a sax solo, and the band immediately settles into the standard twelve-bar blues form; one can almost hear the collective sigh of relief as the sidemen finally know with confidence where the bar lines and chord changes are supposed to fall. As a solo performer, Hooker could give free rein to these rhythmic eccentricities, and the song would still possess an organic feeling of wholeness, but with his colleagues he merely sows confusion.

On his road tours, which became an increasingly important source of income for him as the decade progressed, Hooker typically traveled with just one partner, guitarist Kirkland, who did everything except tuck his boss into bed at night. Kirkland drove the car, fixed it when it broke down, acted as informal business manager and personal bodyguard, even recruited women to come back to Mr. Hooker's hotel room. Along the way, Kirkland also showed a sure instinct for weaving his guitar and background vocals into the inner workings of Hooker's music, letting the blues forms implode or expand, following the feeling of the moment rather than a formal structure. Kirkland would prove to be Hooker's most reliable collaborator on recordings during this period, and at times Hooker even lets his versatile sidekick take a lead vocal or release a performance under his own name, with Hooker stepping into the background.

Life on the road was often preferable to the turmoil that awaited Hooker at home. He would stay with Maude Mathis, whom he had met in 1944, for most of the next quarter century. But the longevity of the relationship should not be mistaken as a sign of its tranquility or stability. The fights and arguments at home sometimes spilled over into the nightclubs where Hooker played, and fans might witness on-stage spectacles that left them speechless. Hooker was surprised during one Toledo performance by Maude's unscheduled arrival—she had arranged for a ride all the way from Detroit—when she grabbed his guitar and broke it over his head. Fortunately Hooker was playing an acoustic instrument instead of his solid-body Gibson Les Paul that evening! But Maude Hooker was not hesitant about inflicting permanent damage. To the end of his life, Hooker was unable to flex one of his fingers, where his wife had cut a tendon during an especially bitter fight. But often the pain was merely psychological, as in her harangues over Hooker's inability to translate his fame into a larger income. She ridiculed his guitar as a "starvation box," and told him repeatedly that his music career was going nowhere. Hooker, for his part, confided to an interviewer that his real home was on the stage, where he found the most unconditional acceptance and his happiest moments. Fans were sometimes surprised to hear Hooker refer to his guitar as his "wife," and though they liked to think that this merely reflected his love of the music, it was an even more telling reminder of which relationship had proven the most stable and predictable during the course of the bluesman's life. The six strings were constant; the four wives came and went.

As did record producers. Hooker's relationship with Besman ended in 1952, when the latter sold his business and moved to California. In addition to the money he made from his label, Besman retained valuable revenue streams as publisher and co-composer of Hooker's output. To critics who contested his right to these profits, Besman pointed out that Hooker arrived in the studio unprepared—and given his poor musical education, couldn't even write down a song if he had composed one. Only Besman's intercession, the producer insisted, helped transform the ramblings of this unschooled musician into hit material. Besman's justifications fall flat, and his ways of doing business (albeit not unusual for the time) would strike many observers as exploitation, plain and simple. Besman, for his part, claimed to make more money from his next initiative in the world of arts and entertainment—selling paint-by-number kits on the West Coast! For most people, the shift from producing hit records to peddling hokey art kits to worse-than-amateur painters would have seemed a disgraceful step down in the world. But as Besman told Charles Shaar Murray, "music didn't inter-est me. Money is the thing that interested me."

In an ironic twist, Besman's disregard of the finer points of respecting intellectual property returned to haunt him. When the band ZZ Top bor-rowed from "Boogie Chillen" for their 1973 song "La Grange," it came to light that Besman had never filed for a copyright on the Hooker composi-tion at the time of initial release. Lawyers for ZZ Top argued that the release of the original record in 1948 constituted publication, hence the implied copyright would have expired in the mid-1970s. Expensive legal proceed-ings led to a court decision that determined that the song was in the pub-lic domain. The U.S. Supreme Court was asked to overrule the decision, but declined. The furor in the music industry was so great that a host of influential players—including ASCAP and BMI—lobbied successfully for a congressional bill that countered the court's verdict, legislation eventually signed into law by President Bill Clinton. Hooker, of course, merely watched as a curious spectator. He had lost all publishing rights to this music a long time ago! Nonetheless, his spontaneous performance in a recording studio had led to a substantial change in U.S. intellectual property law.

Even after all this litigation, we are hardly able to unravel the legal com-plexities of Hooker's early catalog. Joe Von Battle, an African-American who operated a record store on Hastings Street with a modest studio in back, recorded Hooker, emulating Besman's techniques—miking the tap-ping foot, sometimes over-dubbing the vocal. Many of these performances found their way onto the Chess label. But Battle also sold recordings to Mod-ern, infuriating Besman, who had also been supplying the Bihari brothers with material from Hooker. Modern, in turn, would sign Hooker to a direct contract superseding, or perhaps supplementing, deals with other labels. Then, while continuing to record for various outfits, Hooker signed another contract in April 1954, a one-year agreement with Specialty Records, a small R&B label out of Los Angeles. The Specialty relationship, however, soon went sour. Nine songs were recorded over two days, but owner Art Rube was unimpressed with the results—or perhaps with the fact that Hooker had not severed his ties with the Modern label—and only one single was issued before the contract lapsed.

Finally, in 1955, after almost seven years of sowing his musical seed wher-ever he could, John Lee Hooker must have sensed that something had to change. He was making more first-rate blues records than anybody else, but had overwhelmed the market with a glut of product released in a manner that seemed almost deliberately designed to confuse and mystify fans. Record companies saw no long-term benefit from building his career—he would simply run off to another, more lucrative deal elsewhere. Nor would the most tightly written contract deter him from his philandering ways. Besman had moved away; Rube had lost interest; the seemingly endless opportunities to make extra cash from surreptitious late night sessions were now drying up. And to make matters worse, the musical tastes of the country were shifting. In 1955, the public got its first taste of rock and roll, and began a love affair with the music that continues to this day, sending releases by Chuck Berry, Bill Haley, and other kindred spirits up to the top of the charts, lionizing artists who were stealing not only blues licks and songs, but much of the blues audience in the process. At a crossroads, Hooker decided that he needed to settle down, at least in his record making, into a mostly monogamous relationship. The industry trade journals made the news public right before Christmas 1955: John Lee Hooker had signed with the Vee-Jay label in Gary, Indiana.

4. boom boom boom boom

Until the ascendancy of Motown in the 1960s, Vee-Jay would stand out as the most successful black-owned independent label in the country. Record store proprietors Vivian Carter and James Bracken combined the initials of their first names to create the label's identity, and financed their first release with five hundred dollars borrowed from a pawnshop. Their first successes in the blues field came through the surprising popularity of guitarist Jimmy Reed, born in Dunleith, Mississippi, in 1925, who had come to Chicago in the early 1940s. Here Reed was turned down by the Chess label, and the mid-1950s found him working at the Armour meatpacking plant in Gary. When his Vee-Jay release "You Don't Have to Go" took off in early 1955, Reed walked off the job, never even returning to pick up his last paycheck or drop off his butcher knife.

Reed failed to achieve the fame or critical recognition in the blues world accorded to Muddy Waters or Howlin' Wolf, but he outsold both of them handily during the late 1950s and early 1960s, reaching the charts with no fewer than fourteen songs. Like Hooker, Reed made his mark with a boogie beat, but purified of the quirky rhythms of his Detroit-based rival. You could set your clock by the steady boogie patterns of "Baby, What You Want Me to Do," "Bright Lights, Big City," "Take Out Some Insurance," "Honest I Do," and so many other Reed performances. Blues fanatics might carp that this was a watered-down version of the real Delta sound, but few guitarists ever settled into a more comfortable, pleasing beat, especially in a medium-tempo groove—"betwixt and between, wasn't fast enough or slow enough," Reed modestly described it in an interview shortly before his death—and its crossover appeal drew in record buyers who would have been mystified by Son House or Charley Patton.

Reed's predictable, settled music hid a turbulent, out-of-control life. His alcoholism caused him to stumble through gigs, or miss them entirely. Calvin Carter, Vivian's brother who worked for Vee-Jay, reportedly engaged a policeman friend to "arrest" Reed before important recording sessions, and keep him in the slammer for the night—this being the only way to guarantee that their star guitarist would arrive sober at the studio. But the alcoholism also prevented a timely diagnosis of Reed's epilepsy: it was all too easy to attribute his seizures to delirium tremens. After leaving Vee-Jay in 1964, Reed continued to record with ABC-Bluesway, but he failed to recreate the successes of his earlier efforts, and by the close of the decade, he had abandoned music. From 1969 to 1972, Reed was institutionalized, first in a VA hospital in Downey, Illinois, and later in a convalescent home. He attempted to revive his career after his release, but these efforts were cut short by his death, due to respiratory failure caused by a seizure, on August 29, 1976. He may have seemed like a spent old man, yet Reed was only fifty years old at the time.

If the owners of Vee-Jay thought that Hooker's boogie was similar to Reed's, they soon learned otherwise. At the first session in October 1955, they brought Reed and his longtime collaborator Eddie Taylor, along with bassist George Washington and drummer Tom Whitehead, into the studio to back Hooker. Here two different conceptions of time clashed head-on: Reed and Taylor try to hold the music into symmetrical, Mondrian-type boxes, and Hooker bursts forth with unbridled energy, an abstract expressionist who refuses to allow form to dominate content. In this battle—as in all such confrontations—the formalists retreat in confusion: Hooker imposed his own quirky beat on the band, and everyone else danced around his eccentric orbit.

"Mambo Chillun," an attempt to merge Hooker's sound with a trendy Latin rhythm, achieved respectable sales. But when Hooker returned to the studio in March 1956, Reed was nowhere in sight, although the rest of the band returned from the previous session. Hooker's beat is no more domesticated this time around, but the other musicians have become adept at anticipating his capricious moves. Each chorus of "Dimples" sounds like a twelve-bar blues with a few beats amputated—always around bar 8—imparting a lopsided feeling to the whole performance. Yet this peculiarity was precisely the "hook" that gave the song its odd appeal—if Hooker's sense of time was hopelessly flawed, his feeling for rhythm was impeccable. As a result, Hooker enjoyed another hit on the R&B charts, and "Dimples" even briefly appeared in the pop rankings.

The success reinforced Vee-Jay's decision to record Hooker with small combos. At a follow-up session in June, they added piano and saxophone, but the four songs recorded that day were not released at the time. Calvin Carter, who handled most of the Vee-Jay sessions, complained of the difficulties presented by his star talent. Other musicians struggled in adapting to Hooker, and if they figured out how to match what he played on the first take, they could be sure that he would do it differently on the second take. Even within a single performance, Hooker's form would contract or expand, depending on the inspiration of the moment. The words Hooker sang were no more predictable—the only sure bet here is that they would not scan or rhyme like a Tin Pan Alley song. Yet Carter persisted in viewing Hooker as a bandleader rather than a solo performer. The painstaking efforts Besman had taken to record Hooker's stomping foot as the underlying percussion beat, to let his quirky guitar set the texture and pace of the performance, to give Hooker's vocals free rein to stretch out into impromptu performance art: all these inspired decisions, which captured the essence of Hooker's artistry, were given up by Vee-Jay in the quest to squeeze his talent into the confines of a more conventional Chicago blues sound.

The Chicago influence was inescapable, especially since Hooker came to that city for his Vee-Jay recording sessions, and also performed regularly in the local nightclubs, where a host of other Mississippi natives dominated the blues scene. Here he also caught up with his first cousin, Earl Hooker, then making his own mark on the Chicago scene. Another Clarksdale native, Earl Hooker had moved with his family to Chicago while still a child. Although both Hookers found inspiration in the Delta tradition, their respective approaches were sharply opposed. Earl Hooker was an indifferent singer, and would never have been satisfied recording stream-of-consciousness, rambling vocals such as "Boogie Chillen." Yet he created singing lines with his fingers on the fretboard, employing methods that other blues musicians disdained, most notably in his use of the wah-wah pedal, that much maligned invention which extracts vocal inflections from an electric guitar. Above all, Earl Hooker earned respect for his mastery of the slide guitar, a technique cousin John had never fancied. In Chicago, known as the adopted home of the best slide guitarists in the world—Muddy Waters, Robert Nighthawk, Elmore James, and so many others—Earl Hooker ranked among the finest. Yet he never achieved the widespread popularity of his older cousin. Earl Hooker recorded for more than a half dozen labels during the 1950s, never staying with any one company long enough to build a catalog or establish a home base. In the 1960s he continued on the same path, moving from label to label, sometimes recording his best work for outfits too small to do much with it, such as Chicago's Chief / Age, which only released a handful of singles each year for its whole roster, and Cuca, which tried to build its artists into stars out of its home base in Sauk City, Wisconsin. In 1970, Earl Hooker died of tuberculosis, not long after celebrating his fortieth birthday.

Unlike his unfortunate cousin, John Lee Hooker had finally found a stable relationship with a record label. Recording sessions, which took place every few weeks at the start of the decade, were now better organized events, scheduled once or twice per year. Vee-Jay also worked to update the Hooker sound, in songs like "Little Wheel" and "Maudie," which anticipated the rock music of the 1960s—the latter tune was later covered by Eric Burdon with the Animals—and "I Love You Honey," which attempted to remake John Lee Hooker into Jerry Lee Lewis. But only the last number figured on the charts, briefly appearing in the top thirty. Before the close of the 1950s, Vee-Jay was beginning to shift its strategy. The label increasingly asked Hooker to record the same songs he had made earlier in his career, and even decided to imitate the minimalist sound of his efforts with Besman, including the foot-pounding beat. These reworkings of "Boogie Chillen," "Crawlin' Kingsnake," and "I'm in the Mood" rank among Hooker's better performances for the label, yet they were unlikely to make anyone forget the classic versions.

The first stirrings of the blues revival were in the air—Samuel Charters was publishing his path-breaking *The Country Blues* around this same time—and Hooker was perhaps more valuable as a representative of the music's past than as a harbinger of its future. Accordingly, Vee-Jay built Hooker's first long-playing album *I'm John Lee Hooker* around already released material, including the remakes of his early hits. But another label would understand even better than Vee-Jay the potential for highlighting the traditional elements in Hooker's music. When his Vee-Jay contract expired, Hooker was asked by Riverside to record songs associated with Leadbelly, the great blues singer who had passed away a decade before. As it turned out, Hooker was not very familiar with Leadbelly's music, and instead drew mostly on other traditional material for the resulting release, offering moving renditions of "Pea Vine Special, "How Long Blues," and "Bundle Up and Go." On "Tupelo Blues," Hooker recorded one of his most memorable performances, a gripping story song that recounts the circumstances of the great Mississippi flood of 1927. The stark sound favored by producer Bill Grauer was perfectly suited for the music: Hooker is accompanied solely by his acoustic guitar, and he favors simple fills and stays closely rooted to the tonic chord. His tapping foot can be heard, but only softly in the background. The beat unfolds leisurely, more a canter than a boogie. Above all, Hooker's voice is featured front and center, and he sings with more pathos and intensity than on any of his Vee-Jay sides. This understated approach was unlikely to produce hit singles, but reviews for the resulting album, *The Country Blues of John Lee Hooker*, were ecstatic. The blues world was in the process of developing its own metaphysical systems, hierarchies of duespaying, in which fans sought to measure artists by their "authenticity"—an attribute no less important for all its intangible vagueness. But Hooker had passed the ultimate test here. His music was judged to be the "real thing," and a new stage in his career was underway.

At the 1960 Newport Folk Festival, Hooker played before the largest audience of his career, accompanied only by bassist Bill Lee (father of filmmaker Spike Lee), and again he abandoned the R&B and dance leanings of his Vee-Jay work in favor of more traditional material. Hooker also continued to record for Riverside, and even entered into a daring meeting-of-the-minds with two jazz musicians, bassist Sam Jones and drummer Louis Hayes, world-class players then anchoring the rhythm section in Cannonball Adderley's band. But Hooker was not ready to abandon the label that had nurtured his career over the last several years, and on March 1, 1960, he returned to the studio for Vee-Jay, accompanied by an understated trio

consisting of drummer Jimmy Turner, bassist Sylvester Hickman, and guitarist William "Lefty" Bates. The performances were issued as *Travelin'*, and
reflected a halfway point between the driving group sound of the label's
earlier combo recordings and the more underproduced style featured on
the Riverside country blues release. The most successful effort, "No Shoes,"
found Hooker singing a tear-jerker blues ballad—"no food on my table and
no shoes on my feet"—over a slow, lilting 12/8 groove. The song briefly
hit the R&B charts, and proved that Hooker's foray into old-time country
blues did not prevent him from garnering airplay with more up-to-date
material.

But Vee-Jay, like all of Hooker's previous labels, found that the artist's
promises of exclusivity and fidelity were meaningless. Hooker was back to
his old tricks, recording for several labels, taking whatever deals came his
way. Henry Stone, who had recorded the artist as John Lee Booker in the
early 1950s, taped some new Hooker material, and sold the lot to Atlantic,
which released the best of the music as *Don't Turn Me from Your Door*. Vee-
Jay was able to put legal pressure on Prestige, and take ownership of some
masters Hooker had recorded for that label. The company also secured the
tapes of Hooker's Newport performance from the Vanguard label. Songs
acquired from these two labels were combined with some additional tracks
to make *The Folklore of John Lee Hooker*, which ranks among the artist's
finest Vee-Jay albums, despite the cut-and-paste method of assembling the
project. Still there was little Vee-Jay could do about the glut of older Hooker
material appearing on LP during this period. Chess had acquired a considerable number of recordings made by Hooker in the early 1950s, and issued
these as *John Lee Hooker Plays and Sings the Blues*; King Records released
some of the older sides recorded by Joe Von Battle as *John Lee Hooker Sings
Blues*; and Modern's Crown label brought out *The Blues*, which featured the
best of Hooker's collaborations with Besman.

But Hooker again showed that he could deliver a new hit, despite the
intense competition from his own catalog—just as he had done with "I'm in
the Mood" in 1951. "Boom Boom" brought Hooker together with the finest
band he would front during his Vee-Jay years. Pianist Joe Hunter, whose spirited keyboard work had helped propel Hooker's earlier "I Love You Honey"
onto the charts, had since established himself as one of the key studio musicians forging the Motown sound back in Detroit. Hunter now returned for
the "Boom Boom" session and brought with him the cornerstones of the

Motown rhythm section: bassist James Jamerson, drummer Benny Benjamin, and guitarist Larry Veeder, along with saxophonists Hank Cosby and Mike Terry. Hooker would never sound more uninhibited or more relaxed in front of a combo. He growls, hums, whispers, croons—and mostly keeps strict time—in a performance that continues the distinguished Delta tradition of songs about firearms. Skip James had sung about his lover, "I'll get my 22-20, I'll cut that woman half in two," and Robert Johnson had made virtually the same promise in his "32-20 Blues." Howlin' Wolf had built a celebrated recording around the pain in his shoulder from carrying his gun so long, and Son House had sung about killing Vera Lee. Now Hooker made his own contribution to this genre: "Boom boom boom boom. Goin' to shoot you right down." Fans were delighted by Hooker's expedited alternative to relationship counseling, and the song reached number 16 on the R&B charts in June 1962. Vee-Jay featured the performance on its *Burnin'* LP as well as a greatest hits compilation released as *Best of John Lee Hooker*. Another song about gunplay was *de rigueur*, given Hooker's success, and for the follow-up LP, *The Big Soul of John Lee Hooker* released in early 1963, the artist obliged with "She Shot Me Down."

At the same time that Hooker was dipping into the Motown sound, he was increasingly appearing in coffeehouses, working the folk music circuit, where these hard-driving funk songs were out of place. Yet Hooker delighted in the opportunity to play before a reverent, attentive audience, where no alcohol was served, no fights broke out, and late-arriving fans waited like pious parishioners until the end of a song before they were seated. Even when recording for Besman, Hooker had hoped to sing ballads, but the producer had steadfastly refused. He may have worried about losing Hooker's core audience, or justifiably doubted the guitarist's ability to navigate through the complicated chord changes of these songs—or perhaps merely resented giving up the publishing royalties by recording pop standards. But the desire to express a kinder, gentler side of his musical personality never left Hooker. Indeed, shortly after the success of "Boom Boom," he left blues fans dumbfounded when he recorded an adaptation of "I Left My Heart in San Francisco." What was next, some must have wondered, perhaps "Bei Mir Bist Du Shon" or maybe "On the Good Ship Lollipop"? Yet the coffeehouses allowed Hooker to present more nuanced performances, perhaps not schmaltzy pop ballads, but at least the hear-a-pin-drop slow, acoustic blues that Hooker played so masterfully.

Hooker was now mixing in different circles. At Folk City, Bob Dylan served as Hooker's warm-up act, and sometimes the two guitarists would hang out at the bluesman's hotel room, talking and playing music. (Some years later, Dylan would offer a devastating parody of Hooker as part of his "basement tapes" sessions.) In 1962, Hooker made his first visit to Europe as part of the American Folk Blues Festival, and was dazzled by enthusiastic, standing-room-only audiences in Germany, Italy, France, Denmark, Sweden, Switzerland, and the United Kingdom. In Manchester, Mick Jagger, Keith Richards, and Jimmy Page were among the fans who traveled all the way from London to witness the event. While overseas, Hooker recorded "Shake It Baby," and enjoyed an unexpected hit on French radio.

Once he experienced the adulation of the European audiences—and especially of his more attractive female admirers—Hooker was hooked. He would make several more transatlantic trips during the early 1960s, performing more often in England than in most major U.S. cities during this period. He complained bitterly about the warm beer, the limited offerings of British television, and blue laws that kept the shops (and pubs) closed during many of his finest hours. But Hooker kept coming back for more, building his audience and reputation with each return visit. When "Dimples" was released in the United Kingdom—eight years after it was a hit in the United States—it stayed on the charts for ten weeks. Only a few years earlier, record companies had felt that blues releases would only sell well in the Southern states, and a few cities—Chicago, Detroit, Los Angeles—with large numbers of African-Americans recently arrived from that region. Now John Lee Hooker was finding his most receptive audiences on the Northeast folk music circuit, and across the Atlantic.

But as London town grooved to Hooker's beat, his record label lacked even the foggiest notion of how to produce and promote its star blues artist. Vee-Jay too often chose to imitate the trends other record companies were setting, rather than allow Hooker to establish his own sound. The results were rarely successful, sometimes amusing, occasionally disastrous. Fans who were deeply moved by, say, Hooker's emotionally charged live performance of "Tupelo" would purchase a Vee-Jay album of the artist to find any number of travesties—a lame Tony Bennett knock-off, a crypto-bossa disaster like "No One Told Me," a half-baked imitation of "Green Onions," or watered-down soul music. When Vee-Jay tried to capitalize on Hooker's popularity on the coffeehouse and college circuit, they released *On Campus*—which, despite the name, was a cobbled-together work drawn from disparate studio sessions. Finally with *John Lee Hooker: Concert at Newport*, issued in 1964, Vee-Jay offered fans a legitimate chance to hear what the bluesman could do in performance. But by then it was too late for the label to benefit much from its newfound appreciation for Hooker's on-stage charisma—he was back to his practice of recording for other companies.

And Vee-Jay had other things to worry about by this time. The company had been the first U.S. label to feature the Beatles, after Capitol refused to release the mop-top band recorded by their British affiliate EMI. During the course of one month, Vee-Jay sold more than 2.5 million records by the hot Liverpool act. But Capitol soon reconsidered its folly: the label took control of new material by the Beatles, and entered into a series of legal and negotiating battles to limit Vee-Jay's use of the older masters. In the fall of 1964, Vee-Jay lost its right to release any of its Beatles music, and over the next year and a half, the company struggled with the resulting cash flow and debt problems. In May 1966, Vee-Jay closed its doors and dismissed all of its employees.

The collapse of the longest stable relationship in his recording career did little to slow down the steady stream of Hooker LP releases. But the frequency of his studio sessions offered no guarantee of their success in the marketplace. Hooker's collaboration with the British blues rock band the Groundhogs was released in 1965 by Verve-Folkways as . . . *And Seven Nights*, but was soon deleted from the catalog. Hooker was handed an even greater opportunity when he became the first blues artist featured on the ABC Impulse label—the most prestigious home for black music of the period. During the early and mid-1960s, Impulse released classic sessions featuring John Coltrane, Ray Charles, Duke Ellington, Quincy Jones, Charles Mingus, Coleman Hawkins, and others, and now it was looking to expand its musical horizons to encompass Hooker's inimitable boogie. *It Serves You Right to Suffer*, issued in 1966, put the bluesman on the same footing as this elite roster, and promised to further expand Hooker's audience. But the record, a mismatch of Hooker with a seasoned jazz rhythm section, would also prove to be the last blues release on the ABC Impulse label. Without missing a beat, Hooker teamed up with the Chess outfit that already owned some Hooker masters from the 1950s. Chess was aiming to capitalize on the revival of traditional blues, and entitled its new Hooker release *The Real Folk Blues*. Once again, the positioning in the marketplace did not match the music in the grooves. Instead of digging into *real* folk blues, Hooker works his way through a nice mix of dance songs, pensive mood tunes, and even makes another attempt at covering a pop standard. "I Cover the Waterfront" is best known as a vehicle for Billie Holiday, but Hooker dishes up a free-association, Rorschach test version of the lyrics over pared-down chords that few fans would ever have recognized as Johnny Green's classic tune if Hooker had not occasionally let slip a reference to the title during his rambling vocal.

Early in his career, the best Hooker was pure Hooker, undiluted by session musicians, horn parts, professional songwriters, and all the other trappings that record producers see as their brilliant contribution, as their obligation even. But Hooker inevitably ran smack into the perennial love-hate paradox of the entertainment industry: it thrives on talent, the lifeblood of the global media behemoths who transmute creativity into a marketable commodity; yet it rarely trusts this talent to stand alone and unaided, but constantly tinkers and trivializes, prefers the safety of formulas and packages to the uncertainty of artistry. Hooker, more than most musicians, suffered from this constant interference. He didn't fit into the package, he didn't adapt to the formula. Like the temperamental child at the preschool, Hooker deserved a report card which spelled out in large block letters: NOTE: DOES NOT PLAY WELL WITH OTHERS.

Yet, in a strange transformation, Hooker reversed course for the last half of his career. During the 1960s, Hooker becomes the great collaborator, the team player who starts dishing out assists after a career hogging the ball. This generosity of spirit was most assuredly *not* inspired by a sudden conversion experience or a new attitude of altruism. Rather, as the *quality* of his partners improved, Hooker's own collaborative skills became more evident. The success with the Motown sidemen on "Boom Boom" was perhaps the first sign of this new side of Hooker. He no longer feels compelled to lead the band, but rather jumps into its flow. His live peformance at Café au Go-Go in Greenwich Village backed by Muddy Waters's band, which Hooker recorded for his new label, ABC-Bluesway, in August 1966, reveals this same revitalized artist, one who feeds off the energy of the world-class rhythm section bumping and grinding to his rear. In time, Hooker would enjoy a similarly productive meeting-of-the-minds with Carlos Santana, Bonnie Raitt, Van Morrison, and others. And as the sixties came to an end, Hooker would embark on the most fruitful, and perhaps unlikely, collaboration of his career, alongside a group of young white rockers, ambitious lads who had formed a band under the blues-inspired name (taken from a Tommy Johnson song title) Canned Heat.

Al Wilson and Bob Hite, respectively the Prince Hal and Falstaff who founded and gave impetus to Canned Heat, were no strangers to the blues world. "There would not have been a rediscovery of Son House in the 1960s without Al Wilson," Dick Waterman once remarked. And though Waterman's claim that "Al Wilson taught Son House how to play Son House" perhaps goes too far, the description at least helps us appreciate Wilson's deep knowledge of traditional blues at a time when few guitarists had mastered this body of work. Oddly enough, Wilson's music was everything that the blues—at least in its most typical forms—was not: his singing had an effete, feminine quality that defied the macho stereotypes of the genre; his stage presence was cool and stoic in a form that thrived on the bacchanalian; his analytical mind, which delighted in learning the Latin names of every tree and plant in the world (a typically quixotic, Wilsonian endeavor), had no counterpart in the music's traditions; even his nickname, "Blind Owl," hinted at a wisdom that was unconnected to the empirical give-and-take of the here-and-now, the situated reality that forms the cornerstone of blues imagery and, some would say, the source of its vitality. Yet by negating all the *idées reçues* of blues rock, Wilson took it to a higher level than anyone else at the time, forging a sound that was at once as old as the grooves in a Paramount 78, but also fresh and original, no mere knock-off played at untold decibels, but a new take on the great Delta tradition.

Bob Hite, known affectionately as "The Bear," served as the counterbalance to Wilson, the large body whose gravitational pull holds all smaller satellites in its orbit. If Wilson was Rodin's Thinker with a harmonica thrust between hand and mouth, Hite was Keats's dream "for a life of sensation rather than of thoughts" embodied in a massive frame, shaking, shouting, swearing, partying, putting his life force on stage as much as his music. Along with a changing group of sidemen, Wilson and Hite took the rock world by storm during the last half of the 1960s. Even before their debut album on the Liberty label hit the charts, Canned Heat had dazzled an enormous audience at the Monterey Pop Festival—the high point of the Summer of Love, with two hundred thousand people in attendance. Their 1968 hit single "On the Road Again," with a throbbing beat reminiscent of Hooker's Detroit-era boogie, further expanded their following. And the following year, Canned Heat took the stage at Woodstock, making history at the most celebrated, define-the-era-today and tell-it-to-the-grandkids-tomorrow concert of the century. What to do as an encore at the dawn of the 1970s? For Canned Heat, it was obvious: embark upon a collaboration with John Lee Hooker.

Under different circumstances, Hooker might have connected with Canned Heat much earlier, perhaps even joined the band on the world-changing stage at Woodstock, but the brilliant minds managing the blues-man's career knew better. "It took over two years for us to get permission from Hooker's label, ABC-Bluesway, to record with him," recalls Fito de la Parra, who joined the band as drummer toward the close of 1967. "It was a very long, very arduous ordeal involving a tangle of legal issues that had to be resolved." Not that Hooker was helping matters: still thinking in terms of his late night sessions masquerading as John Lee Booker or John Lee Cooker, the artist wasn't looking for rock stardom but cold hard cash, pref-erably paid in advance. When he heard that the collaboration might result in a two-disk release, his immediate response was all too revealing: "If it's gonna be a double album, you're gonna have to pay me double money."

These were turbulent years for the artist. In 1970, Hooker caught wind of the California dream, and though he had few friends or musical contacts in the San Francisco area, he headed west with a carful of belongings and twelve thousand dollars in spending money. His ABC recordings had done little to advance his fame or booking prospects, and increasingly Hooker risked becoming a historical figure, coasting on the waning momentum of past achievements. Shortly before his move, ABC had recorded him with his cousin for the *If You Miss 'Im . . . I Got 'Im* LP, but Earl Hooker was already enervated by the tuberculosis that would soon contribute to his death. As a result, the project seemed just one more backward glance, celebrating a partnership that once might have been a promising start but was now merely a sober valedictory.

Yet John Lee Hooker was not ready to become a past master, a portrait on the wall in the Blues Hall of Fame. In his early fifties, Hooker was younger than the other Delta players working the blues revival angle during their golden years. He still played an aggressive boogie on the guitar. His singing was more soulful than ever. And his experiences with Vee-Jay and ABC had taught him how to adapt his sound to a wide range of settings. In short, Hooker was at a turning point in his career, and the opportunity to enlist with the commercial rock juggernaut of Canned Heat was a heaven-sent match, driven not just by the money angle—which has always tempted old blues players to hang out with young rockers—but even more by the compatibility of musical visions. Canned Heat, more than any rock band of its day, thrived by getting the groove just right. And with Hooker on hand, it was sure to stay in the pocket.

Whatever hesitancy Hooker might have had before the session, whether over the dollars or the sense of the project, was overcome by the sheer power of the music. As the number of successful takes mounted, Hooker quipped that he might need *triple* money for a *triple* album. Hooker's relationship with Alan Wilson would be short-lived—the latter died of a drug overdose, possibly a suicide, before *Hooker 'N Heat* was even mixed—yet this would rank as perhaps the most sympathetic partnership of Hooker's long career. Wilson had studied Hooker's music and now inhabited it with an uncanny rightness, putting it on like some secondhand-store suit that magically fit all the contours of his own physiognomy, channeling John Lee Hooker through his guitar, his piano, and especially his harmonica. His give-and-take with Hooker to close "Drifter" is like a reunion of blood brothers, with none of the awkwardness or contrived feeling endemic to so many of these first-met-today-in-the-studio collaborations of the mutually famous. Hooker, for his part, would later laud Wilson in generous phrases, praising his playing, his genius, his knowledge of the tradition, his ability to play music as an extension of his listening rather than just of his fingers. With the benefit of hindsight, Hooker cited *Hooker 'N Heat* as the finest project from the middle period of his career, not to be matched until his tremendous success with *The Healer*. From a purely financial perspective, the release did acceptably well—reaching number 73 on the pop album charts—but as an artistic statement, staking out the potential for a true meeting-of-the-minds between rock and the blues, *Hooker 'N Heat* ranks as one of the finest recordings of the era.

In the afterglow of this release, ABC tried to put together other marketable rock-oriented projects for John Lee Hooker. But the label's overproduced—and appropriately named—*Endless Boogie* release thrust Hooker into unrehearsed, sink-or-swim encounters with a changing cast of session musicians and name players. The best known, Steve Miller, later lambasted the apparently aimless management of the project, and Miller even tried to nudge the proceedings in a direction more conducive to Hooker's artistry. But this LP needed more than a nudge; one suspects that nothing short of a power outage would have been sufficient to convince the ABC honchos that Hooker only needed six strings and his God-given talent as studio support. Instead, Hooker is relegated to serving as an innocent bystander at this accident, his guitar lost in the mix, his once succinct boogie bogged down in a compendium of generic blues and rock textures. Follow-up sessions for additional projects, conducted at Wally Heider's studio in San Francisco, pursued a similar formula, a shake-and-bake recipe matching Hooker with a number of greater and lesser talents. Sometimes this produced a promising mixture, found for instance in the surprising affinity between the Delta blues legend and the Celtic-tinged folk rocker Van Morrison on the title track to *Never Get Out of These Blues Alive.* But the serious blues fan is ultimately disappointed by how little John Lee seems to influence and drive the music. Hooker had made his name as a one-man-band marvel, singing, plucking, stomping, taking charge of the session from start to finish. Now he figured as a bit player, moving to the rhythms that others set, even if his name was featured in large print on the LP cover.

It is tempting to view much of the period between *Hooker 'N Heat,* from the dawn of the 1970s, to *The Healer,* recorded in 1988, as Hooker's lost years. Rather than climb the charts, Hooker's LPs were more likely to sink into the cut-out bins. No visionary record producer stepped forward to reignite Hooker's once surefire studio magic. Hooker had always found record companies vying for his services, but after leaving ABC in 1974, no major label wanted to take a chance on him. He moved from the big leagues to the distinctly farm-team atmosphere of Tomato Records, where expectations were far lower, and bunts and strikes more likely than hit singles. Yet what the discographies and thumbnail bios fail to capture is the in-person proselytizing of this period, the persistence with which Hooker went on the road and electrified audiences night after night. Airplay was hard to come by, not just for Hooker but for most blues acts, during this dry spell, but his visibility on the bandstand was far greater than on the bandwidth. True, his records circa 1950 were better than those circa 1980, but the gray-haired Hooker—at least one assumed what was left of it was gray; his obsessive seclusion in wide-brimmed hats and oversized sunglasses turned the top half of his head into a mysterious, uncharted realm—beat his younger self hands-down when measured by ticket sales, audience draw, or road miles accrued.

Hooker's active touring life was balanced by tumultuous activity on the homefront. Although he had divorced Maude, she rejoined him in California, and his children also gravitated to the San Francisco Bay Area. Hooker's daughter Zakiya left Detroit after her husband got caught up in drug problems, and arrived on her father's doorstep. His sons Robert and John Junior, and his daughter Diane, also found their way west. Here they often stayed under Hooker's roof, or in houses that he would pay for, in whole or in part. Hooker's generosity in these instances was remarkable. He helped his ex-wife purchase a house, and when Maude decided to move back to Detroit and get remarried, he let Zakiya take over the residence. But Maude came back, and Hooker again put up money for another home. The bluesman was equally active at the car dealership, keeping his family in wheels. But not all Hooker family reunions were happy ones, despite ongoing subsidies from the paterfamilias. John Lee Hooker, Jr., who nurtured musical aspirations of his own, had problems with drugs and the law that eventually sent him to prison. Robert Hooker also dealt with substance abuse issues, but got his act together, with the help of his strong religious faith. Their father's relentless touring during these years may have contributed to the volatility on the homefront, but the cause-and-effect most likely went the other way. The road had always been an escape, a safe haven for the bluesman. And, at times, the example Hooker set at home with his own late night partying made him a less than exemplary role model even when he shared a roof with his offspring.

The best perspective on Hooker's music from the lost years comes from the occasional live recording, where the machinations of producers and record execs were held in check. *Live at Soledad Prison*, recorded in 1972, and *Alone* from 1976 reveal an artist increasingly focused on evoking a mood, an intensity of feeling, rather than kicking the music into overdrive with his guitar. The classic Hooker boogie still appears, but in more judicious doses. The stamina and urgency that distinguished his earliest recordings are clearly diminished in these later recordings, but Hooker had honed the dramatic qualities of his voice over the previous two decades. In 1949,

Hooker's guitar work had served as the riveting focal point of his music; a quarter of a century later, he was a blues singer, first and foremost. Like Muddy Waters and Howlin' Wolf, Hooker had learned that he could hold an audience even if he wasn't holding a guitar.

By the time of his breakthrough comeback recording of *The Healer*, in 1988, Hooker was content to let Carlos Santana do the heavy lifting on the six strings for the title track. Hooker chants, hums, and sings, while Santana adds a gripping performance on electric guitar. Hooker's vocalizing is equally effective in his duet with Bonnie Raitt from this same project. The pair resurrect his 1951 hit "I'm in the Mood" and recraft it as a boy-meets-girl mutual seduction piece. For other performances on the CD, Hooker adds his own guitar into the mix, even accompanying himself alone on a National steel guitar for "Rockin Chair," although with a free, rubato tempo that bears little resemblance to the taut rhythmic excursions of his earlier days. Mike Kappus, who now actively managed Hooker's career, also brought in his other clients George Thorogood, Robert Cray, and Los Lobos for guest appearances on the project.

No major record label was interested in releasing *The Healer*, despite the famous names on the roster. Hooker's star had fallen so far, and reissues of his earlier work were so prevalent, that few industry insiders felt much enthusiasm for promoting one more project in the face of this glut. Kappus finally cut a deal with Chameleon Records in the United States and Silvertone in the United Kingdom—both modest outfits even by the low standards of independent labels. Yet the sales were anything but modest, with *The Healer* first taking the UK by storm, and then pushing its way onto the U.S. pop charts. Hooker's road tour on the heels of this success grossed around $3 million. Now approaching his mid-seventies, John Lee Hooker was more in demand than ever before—proving once again that in the topsy-turvy world of the blues, fans like their musicians well-aged, and just when an artist seems the most out-of-date and over-the-hill, the smart money bets on a stunning comeback.

Hooker followed up with *Mr. Lucky*, another all-star collaboration, which brought back Carlos Santana and Robert Cray from *The Healer*. But there was no shortage now of other prominent musicians interested in collaborating with a Delta legend whose box office power was at its apex. Van Morrison, who had passed on *The Healer*, helped Hooker revisit "I

Cover the Waterfront," and Keith Richards assisted at the resurrection of "Crawlin' Kingsnake." Elsewhere on the disk, Ry Cooder, Albert Collins, Johnny Winter, and John Hammond contributed their talents. In the entertainment industry, where commercial artists are invariably judged by the company they keep, Hooker had reinforced the turnaround story of *The Healer*. Established stars were coming to Hooker not so much to increase their record sales—Hooker's own audience may have been large for a blues artist but still was minuscule in comparison with the mass market followings of a Keith Richards or Carlos Santana—but to enhance their credibility. Hooker's image as the elder statesman of boogie, as a primal source for blues feeling, was further cemented when Miles Davis collaborated with him on music for the Dennis Hopper film *The Hot Spot*. Davis essentially fills the role that a harmonica player would in a conventional blues band, imparting a darker, more nuanced ambience to a landmark soundtrack recording.

Fans were grateful for these all-star collaborations, but many wondered whether they would ever hear Hooker record again in the unaccompanied format which had produced his earliest hits. Here was an odd state of affairs. The greatest innovators in the history of this music—Muddy Waters, Howlin' Wolf, John Lee Hooker, B.B. King—seemed destined to end their celebrated careers as window-dressing for young rockers. Hooker's fame was greater than ever at the dawn of the 1990s, yet forty years earlier, when he was still largely unknown and unproven, he had much more freedom to present his own music in his own manner. The bluesman's 1992 release *Boom Boom* went some way toward rectifying this situation. Many of the tracks were leftovers from the sessions that had produced *Mr. Lucky*, but in order to fill out the project, producers Roy Rogers and Mike Kappus allowed Hooker to perform unaccompanied on several tracks. Listeners expecting a return to the fiery guitarist of the Truman administration, the one-man rhythm section who neither needed nor wanted bass or drums, were likely to be disappointed with Hooker's loose and impressionistic performances of "I'm Bad Like Jesse James" or "Sugar Mama." Yet these efforts probe an emotional depth that one does not find in the boogies and dance grooves of the Besman era. Hooker, like Billie Holiday and Dizzy Gillespie before him, had learned over the passing years how to compensate from his heart for what he may have lost in technique.

Hooker was cutting back his activities by this time, preferring home life to the excitement of touring. Even when *Boom Boom* was nominated for a Grammy, Hooker declined to travel to New York for the ceremony. He continued to record, albeit at a more measured pace than before. For the most part he remained loyal to the recipes that had worked for him in the past. *Chill Out* finds him accompanied on the title track by Carlos Santana, while on the follow-up release *Don't Look Back*, Hooker relies on Van Morrison as producer on all but one of the tracks. "The Healing Game," written by Morrison, who also performs a soulful vocal duet with Hooker, even tries to pick up on the therapeutic angle of "The Healer." But if Hooker was covering familiar territory on these final projects, the music is never merely formulaic. During his seventies, Hooker did not make a single bad record. At an age when many artists fade away, or tarnish their reputations by lingering too long in the limelight, Hooker added to his oeuvre and further solidified his reputation.

During the last half-decade of his life, Hooker further reduced his commitments, but the honors continued to come his way. *Don't Look Back* was awarded a Grammy in 1998 as Best Traditional Blues Album, and the title track garnered another Grammy for both Hooker and Morrison as Best Pop Collaboration with Vocals, beating out stiff competition from Barbra Streisand, Celine Dion, and Stevie Wonder. The National Academy of Recording Sciences followed up with another award for "lifetime achievement," and the Rhythm and Blues Foundation did the same. Hooker's name was ensconced on the Los Angeles Rock Walk, the Bammies Walk of Fame in San Francisco, and Hollywood Boulevard's Walk of the Stars. Even his song titles found lasting fame in surprising ways. An enterprising San Francisco nightclub owner set up John Lee Hooker's Boom Boom Room, which continues to host roots music for appreciative Bay Area audiences. And the old songs managed to find new audiences. A final recording, *The Best of Friends*, was mostly a greatest hits compilation from the previous decade, but it also celebrated Hooker's half century as a recording artist with a new version of "Boogie Chillen" featuring Eric Clapton. A few months later, the Recording Industry Association of America selected the original recording of "Boogie Chillen" as one of the "Songs of the Century."

Hooker cancelled a tour in 2000 after being diagnosed with a debilitating vascular condition, although he continued to play occasional gigs in the San Francisco area until a few days before his death. A show in Santa Rosa,

California, some two hours away from his home in Los Altos, would be his final appearance on stage. Five days later, on June 21, 2001, he died quietly in his sleep. Another show, in Saratoga, was scheduled for ten days after his passing, and ads for it continued to run in the same newspapers that featured his obituary. Yet even in death, Hooker was a sure draw. Almost two thousand people attended his funeral service in Oakland.

The obituaries tried to clear up the contradictions and obscure facts of Hooker's life, most of them preferring the 1917 birthdate—making the bluesman eighty-three years old at the time of his death—and tabulating his survivors at eight children, nineteen grandchildren, and "several" great-grandchildren. No fewer than three of his children have pursued careers in music with some success: Zakiya Hooker, who made her first public appearance alongside her father in 1991, and has continued an active career as a performer and recording artist; keyboardist Robert Hooker, who has recorded with Van Morrison; and John Lee Hooker, Jr., who has worked to put his substance abuse and legal troubles behind him, and earned a Grammy nomination for his debut CD release *Blues With a Vengeance*.

But no headcount, however accurate, could adequately encompass all the musical progeny of this seminal blues artist. Nor can the still active John Lee Hooker Foundation—a rarity here: a blues musician who can start a charity in his final days, and not require one!—do more than add a few footnotes to this musician's legacy, no matter how commendable its philanthropic efforts. Indeed, the sheer global breadth of Hooker's lineage is unlikely to be matched by any future blues artist. Half a world away from Hooker's land of birth, in Mali, Ali Farka Touré became a leading force in African music by drawing on Hooker's powerful influence, just as the most celebrated Hispanic musician of his day, Carlos Santana, found inspiration in Hooker's groove. The leading rock-and-roll band of the late twentieth century, the Rolling Stones, looked to Hooker's early recordings as a precursor to their own sonic revolution, just as the most famous American folk rock singer, Bob Dylan, was mesmerized by Hooker's much different persona as a coffeehouse performer during the early 1960s. Van Morrison felt that his "Celtic soul" music was refreshed by his Delta mentor, and a host of others, from Bo Diddley to Bonnie Raitt, experienced similar feelings. And who could even begin to gauge the influence Hooker has exerted within the more insular world of the blues? Perhaps Carlos Santana summed up these sentiments best, saying of Hooker, "When I was a child, he was the first circus I wanted to run away with." John Lee Hooker, the man-child so anxious to escape from Mississippi during his youth, served paradoxically as the escape vehicle for so many other musicians, seekers who hoped to reach beyond the limitations of their own upbringings—in Mali, or Liverpool, or Jalisco—and tap into the primal forces that gave shape to the Delta blues.

Howlin' Wolf

chapter nine

smokestack lightnin'

1. the greatest thing you could see

One day in mid-1951, a middle-aged black man strolled into the cramped front office of Memphis Recording Service at 706 Union Avenue. He had no appointment, but it wasn't hard to guess what he wanted. Like almost every other stranger who showed up to sweet-talk secretary Marion Keisker, he came seeking an audition with the boss.

At least he had found his way to the right place, a door worth knocking on, or trying to force down, if necessary, in pursuit of the golden opportunities that lay inside. This nondescript storefront, which had formerly housed a radiator repair shop, certainly looked like an unlikely setting for a cultural revolution. But during the course of the decade, proprietor Sam Phillips would achieve just that, and do it moreover with a cast of characters—Elvis Presley, Jerry Lee Lewis, Carl Perkins, and Johnny Cash, among others—who would first enter the door on Union Avenue as unknown quantities, yet be transformed by some magical alchemy of the location into world-beating stars. If Memphis had any right to challenge Chicago or New York or Los Angeles as a change agent for America's listening habits, it would be due to the activities that took place within these four walls. In time, many aspirants came knocking, hoping that some of the magic might rub off on them.

But this visitor was something different. He was far older than the dreamy-eyed teenagers who usually gravitated to the recording studio. He spoke very little, too; but he was a man who didn't need many words to make his presence felt. His size alone caught your attention. When Keisker brought him back to the studio, Sam Phillips judged his visitor's height to be about six foot six, and his feet were larger than any the record producer had seen before. The stranger filled out this tall frame, his bulky build seemingly better suited to wrestling or construction work than to music. When he pulled out a harmonica, the contrast between the huge man and the tiny instrument was almost comical. He seemed just as likely to swallow it up in a gulp as to extract music from the humble harp—a perception the musician sometimes reinforced by ostentatiously licking the harmonica during his performances, as though it were a succulent morsel.

Phillips showed no surprise at the visitor's arrival. Ike Turner had already told Phillips about this man, who had been christened by his parents as Chester Burnett, but now went by the very odd nickname of "Howlin' Wolf." Phillips had even had a taste of Wolf's music over the airwaves of KWEM, broadcasting from West Memphis, and had sent out word that he would welcome a chance to meet him. And if Howlin' Wolf caught Phillips's attention when he entered the room, he riveted the studio owner to the spot when he started to sing. "I tell you," he recalled years later, "the greatest thing you could see to this day would be Chester Burnett doing one of those sessions in my studio. God, what it would be worth to see the fervor in that man's face when he sang. . . . How different, how good!" Phillips would later claim that Wolf had the greatest talent of all the celebrated artists he had worked with—an extraordinary claim given the star-studded associations of the Memphis Recording Service and the Sun Records label that it spawned.

At a time when the great creative awakening of the Delta blues during the pre-Depression years was just a dim memory, when its treasures had seemingly been exhausted, its shining moments a matter of distant history, here came another huge talent confirming the untapped riches of this musical Mecca. Many Delta bluesmen far younger than Howlin' Wolf had already established themselves while he continued to hone his craft in obscurity. Younger men such as Muddy Waters and John Lee Hooker had become nationally recognized stars. Even Sam Phillips had already recorded B.B. King, fifteen years younger than Burnett, and Ike Turner, more than two decades his junior. Burnett was from a different generation, almost a different world: he had learned the blues alongside Charley Patton, and had refined his craft as part of the remarkable collection of guitarists who lived in the vicinity of Drew, Mississippi, in the 1920s. While Patton and other long dead bluesmen had built their careers during the administration of Herbert Hoover, Howlin' Wolf had waited patiently, and now was about to do the same in the 1950s, competing with his down-home blues against the nascent sounds of rock and roll.

Less than two hundred miles separated Howlin' Wolf's birthplace in White Station, Mississippi, from this historic recording studio in Memphis, but it had taken him more than half a lifetime to cover the distance, to rise above the oppressed conditions of his earliest years, and assert his talent on a regional and national stage. Even by the woefully low standards of rural Mississippi, Burnett's background had been impoverished and soul-crushing, leaving him ill-prepared for anything except the most abject menial labor. As a youngster he would roam barefoot and in rags alongside the train tracks, looking for scraps of food the railroad workers might have left behind. Lacking even the most basic schooling, he could barely read or write, or do simple arithmetic, at the time of his Memphis recording debut. The greatest aptitude he had developed as a child, he would sometimes relate, required neither alphabet nor figures: it was merely to *run*, to avoid the whippings and beatings that seemed inevitably in store for him.

Burnett was painfully aware of the limitations this background imposed on him. In an interview he gave to Michael Erlewine shortly before his sixtieth birthday, the bluesman repeatedly lamented, "I am not a smart man," adding, "I don't have no education, see. Now you can take my sense and put it in a paper bag and it'll rattle like two nickels." What Wolf did not mention, however, was his own dedication in compensating for these limitations, how he painstakingly learned the rudiments of reading and math at adult education classes in the 1950s, and continued to take courses almost until his death. Fans who followed Howlin' Wolf's circuit in the Chicago nightclubs during the height of his career might scarcely believe it, but they could have also found their main man, had they only known, in a host of quite unlikely settings—at Crane High School on the West Side (during the late 1950s and early 1960s), at Wendell Phillips High School on the South Side (during the mid-1960s), or Jones Commercial Evening School in the loop (during the late 1960s and early 1970s). At a time when he had achieved substantial fame on an international level, with a large crossover audience from the rock world now flocking to his performances, Chester Burnett was still determined to make up for the poor schooling of his Delta childhood.

The son of sharecropper Leon "Dock" Burnett and Gertrude Jones, a cook and maid, the future Howlin' Wolf was born Chester Arthur Burnett on June 10, 1910. The name came from the twenty-first president, the seldom commemorated Chester Alan Arthur, who served less than four years in the nation's highest office but, as a young lawyer, had helped desegregate New York's streetcars and railroads. The child's maternal grandfather gave him the nickname "Wolf"—as part of a recurring family jest, derived from the Little Red Riding Hood story, that the wolf would get him if he was bad. When he misbehaved, family members would chase after the young Chester Burnett, howling in wolflike pursuit, and the child would hide under the bed. Before long most of his acquaintances called him Wolf, although it would not be the only alternate identity he would adopt. For much of the 1920s, he went by the name of John D. At other times, he was known as Foots, or Bigfoot, or Buford, or Bullcow, or John D. Burnett, his various aliases selected perhaps more to distance himself from the travails of his childhood than for any new affiliation they might represent.

His parents separated when Burnett was only one year old, and mother and child relocated to Monroe County. Gertrude Jones was an eccentric woman, who sang spirituals of her own composition on the streets and would try to sell copies to passersby. She and her son also sang in the church choir, and Burnett's early love of music no doubt developed under his mother's tutelage and example. But while he was still a young child, she turned him out, forcing him to find some other home. The reasons for this sudden separation remain unclear, although several motives have been offered. Wolf himself gave varying accounts of the event, explaining to his wife that his mother could not accept his abandoning spirituals in order to sing the blues, but telling a friend that Gertrude, light-skinned, of partial Native American descent, objected to her son's darker coloring. In other instances, he attributed their separation to his unwillingness to labor in the fields for fifteen cents per day. Another account, coming to us at third hand, relates that Gertrude Jones had a new man in her life, one who didn't want the child of his predecessor under the same roof. Perhaps his mother's apparent mental instability also caused or contributed to the rupture. But if we lack a clear understanding of the causes, there can be no mistaking the results of this event. For all intents and purposes, Chester Alan Burnett was little better than an orphan during this period of his life, without parent or sibling to protect or help him, yet still at a tender age where he could hardly survive on his own.

He hiked across many miles of frozen terrain that day. Lacking shoes, he fended off the cold by tying burlap sacks around his bare feet. He made his way to the home of his great-uncle Will Young. Young took in the youngster, but exacted the cost of room and board in the backbreaking labor imposed on the newcomer. But the long hours picking cotton or pulling corn were perhaps the easiest part of Burnett's time in the Young household. Will Young was "the meanest man between here and hell," according to Priscilla Swift, who knew Burnett at this time. Feared by family and neighbors alike, Young meted out punishment on the slightest provocation—not just with a wooden switch, but sometimes using a leather plow-line, which served him as a makeshift bullwhip. Chester Burnett was singled out for special humiliation, forced to sit apart at meals, not allowed to attend school, often poorly fed, invariably ill clothed and shod.

The solitary time in the fields gave the boy the chance to sing. Plowing with a mule, wearing a straw hat and bib overalls, he would pace his labors with various songs he knew or made up for himself. For the young Howlin' Wolf, the timeless work song of the cultivator, a venerable tradition dating back thousands of years, merged seamlessly into the distinctive blues idiom of early twentieth-century America. This new music—with its deeply personal expressions of loneliness, complaints against hard luck and troubles, wistful longings to leave for some better place—could hardly have been better suited to the boy's situation and temperament. And even if the youngster neither read nor wrote, his vocal mastery was obvious to all. "He was sad but he could sing," Swift recalls. "He'd sing so pitiful and so sweet. . . . He was a good-hearted person and he would teach us how to sing."

Burnett assembled his own makeshift set of instruments. A tin bucket became his preferred accompaniment, and he would beat out time on it while he sang. At other moments, he would rely on pots and pans as ready-to-hand percussion instruments. He also constructed a diddley bow—the traditional one-string instrument of rural Mississippi, but resembling similar chordophones found in Africa—from planks and baling wire. His only "legitimate" instrument—made in a real factory, not cobbled together at home—was a harmonica, which could be purchased for a modest fifteen cents at the time. Burnett would not own his first guitar until he was seventeen years old, but its arrival represented such an extraordinary event that he long remembered the exact date: January 15, 1928. The crops had been successful the previous year, and for a short period a few luxuries would supplement the bare necessities of life. With his large, rough hands, the teenage plowman struggled with such a subtle, delicate instrument. But gradually he found that he could control the strings much like he did his own voice, drawing from them the proper support for his blues singing.

By then, Burnett had left the Young household. At age thirteen, he ran away, pursued by Will Young, who aimed to give the boy a "whuppin'" —according to one account for killing a hog without permission, while another version tells of Burnett incurring Young's anger by spilling a glass of water. Burnett eventually reunited with his father Dock Burnett, who was living with his new family on the Young and Morrow Plantation in the heart of the Delta, between Ruleville and Doddsville on the Quiver River. Some forty families sharecropped this large parcel of land, encompassing more than one thousand acres. Here Burnett earned his living working a plow, picking cotton, pulling corn, fixing fences, and other such chores, continuing in the same workaday activities he had learned under Will Young. Given his skills and circumstances, these promised to be Chester Burnett's lifelong activities, a toilsome and uncertain existence, dependent on the vagaries of the weather, the soil, and the (mostly falling) price for cotton.

But a pathway to a different life was at hand, even if Burnett scarcely realized it at the time. In the 1920s, this sparsely populated region in America's poorest state was the center of the most intriguing musical development one could find anywhere on the globe. Less than five years after Burnett's arrival at the Young and Morrow Plantation, the first widely heard traditional blues recordings would announce to a larger audience the powerful currents of musicmaking in the African-American communities of the rural South. But before the rest of the world knew about this music, it thrived in its own quasi-secret environment. And the young Chester Burnett was situated at the epicenter of these happenings. Within a few mile radius of where he now labored behind the plow, most of the future legends of country blues were either residing, or would soon do so, or at least would pass through, sharing their music and learning from the others gathered together at this important nexus point.

Charley Patton, residing nearby on Dockery's plantation, made the most powerful impression on the teenager. "He had a voice like a lion," Wolf would recall almost a half century later. "You'd hear him in a house, you'd think it's a man in there big as all us put together. Wasn't nothin' but a little rascal." The youngster would track down Patton wherever he played, listening rapturously to "Pony Blues," "Banty Rooster Blues," "Spoonful," and the other trademark songs of this blues pioneer. When Burnett began learning guitar, Patton offered instruction and encouragement, even inviting the aspiring musician to join him in performance. This association would prove invaluable in advancing Burnett's own musical development. But above all, he learned the art of showmanship from Charley Patton, the ability to captivate an audience and keep it mesmerized by his every move. Patton was the flashiest of the Delta bluesmen, playing the guitar behind his back or between his legs, constantly bantering, joking, holding court like a king who had deigned to visit a humble jukehouse. Years later, when Howlin' Wolf made his mark on the Chicago blues scene, drawing large crowds who came as much to experience his persona as to hear his music, the legacy of Patton could be felt in his every move.

By the close of the 1920s, Howlin' Wolf began looking to free himself, at least in some degree, from the demands of farm life by earning money as an itinerant blues musician. He would play at house parties or juke joints, or just out on the street, working his way through various Delta communities, or back to his hometown of West Point. Sometimes he would cross over to the Arkansas side of the river to perform in West Memphis or Pine Bluff or Brinkley. The powerful impression he made on audiences is perhaps best conveyed by Johnny Shines, who saw him performing at Saturday night fish fries in Arkansas during the mid-1930s. "I was afraid of Wolf. Just like you would be of some kind of beast or something. . . . Well, it wasn't his size. I mean, what he was doing, the way he was doing, I mean the sound he was giving off. That's how great I thought he was." Shines even speculated that Wolf might have sold his soul to the devil in order to achieve such a larger-than-life talent.

Yet Burnett's escape from the farm was far from complete: even during this period, he would periodically return home to help his father with farming, especially in the spring when plowing needed to be done. This continued even after the Burnett family moved to Arkansas in 1933, first residing in Wilson, and then moving the following year to Parkin. "Wolf never dodged no work," commented David "Honeyboy" Edwards, who worked with Burnett around this time. "He was a hard-working man. Howlin' Wolf didn't get no rest till he come here to Chicago, and started recording for Chess."

Wolf strived to improve his harmonica playing during these years. And just as he had learned guitar from Charley Patton, he relied on a legend-to-be for tutelage on this instrument. "It was Sonny Boy Williamson—the second one, Rice Miller—who taught me harmonica," Wolf attested to Pete Welding in 1967, a claim he repeated in many other settings. "He married my sister Mary in the '30s." Wolf's biographers James Segrest and Mark Hoffman see no reason to doubt the assertion, although their research failed to identify Mary, sometimes described by the bluesman as a half sister or stepsister. "See Sonny Boy married my stepsister Mary," Wolf told Peter Guralnick. "Maybe by my being around so much they didn't stay together long, but anyhow I was over all the time pestering him to show me how to play that mouth organ. Sometimes I think he'd show me something just to get me out of the way." In any event, Wolf came to rely increasingly on his harmonica playing during the 1930s. "He discovered for himself that he wasn't going to make a good guitar player with them big old fingers," Honeyboy Edwards remarked. "Then he took up the harmonica and made headway with it. . . . Wolf had his own style with harmonica and that big voice of his. That set him apart. That made him Howlin' Wolf."

Yet private lessons with Charley Patton and Sonny Boy Williamson II represent only the smallest part of Howlin' Wolf's blues education, which in toto may have been unique in the history of the music. He traveled and performed periodically with Robert Johnson—a claim supported by Johnson's stepson Robert Lockwood, who learned of Wolf through Johnson—over a two-year period. In Robinsonville, he played with Son House and Willie Brown. He also worked alongside Honeyboy Edwards, Johnny Shines, Jimmy Rogers, and a range of other talents, greater and lesser, during the course of the 1930s. In the Delta, where blues playing was largely an aural / oral tradition handed down from master to student, such affiliations were, much like Ishmael declares of his time on a whaling ship in *Moby-Dick*, Wolf's "Yale College and his Harvard." And if anyone could boast of an Ivy

League caliber education in Depression-era blues, it was Chester Burnett, that private man so self-conscious about his lack of formal schooling.

By the start of the next decade, Wolf was ready to move beyond this apprenticeship period, and present his talents on a larger stage. He was now in his thirties, and any chance to establish himself as a commercial performer in a larger market would have to happen soon or he would be dismissed as too old. Popular music celebrates the cult of eternal youth: even established stars struggle to keep their audience as they age, and for an unproven act, any signs of advancing years are taken as harbingers of certain failure. For Howlin' Wolf, the obvious choices were Chicago, Memphis, St. Louis, Detroit, perhaps even Los Angeles or New York. But his next destination proved to be none of these. Instead, he found himself booked for a long-term engagement with the U.S. Army.

2. the wolf is comin' at you, baby

Wolf was inducted some eight months before Pearl Harbor. He later claimed that vengeful white plantation owners forced him to join the Army because he had been unwilling to work for them. But, as we have seen with his sudden departure from home as a child, Wolf's explanations for events could vary depending on who was asking the questions. As it turned out, anything Chester Burnett was running away from could hardly have been as bad as the new troubles he was courting.

His lack of education presented constant problems. Burnett was initially given a lowly job as a kitchen orderly, but America's entry into World War II required that he develop more advanced skills. He was assigned duty as a Technician Fifth Grade in the Army Signal Corps, and expected to master the various requirements for battlefield communications. But the new trainee's progress was so slow that he was sent to a school for instruction in reading and writing. He made strides, as measured by letters he wrote home during this period, but these probably came at the cost of punishments and disciplinary measures inflicted by his overzealous superiors. Wolf's health began to suffer, and he experienced bouts of dizziness or physical exhaustion. By the fall of 1943, he found himself placed in a military hospital near Portland, Oregon. The medical staff was alarmed by his violent outbursts, and a doctor considered a range of possible diagnoses, dismissing epilepsy, but landing on either syphilis or psychoneurosis as likely explanations.

Unable to rehabilitate their errant soldier, the U.S. Army finally released him with an honorable discharge on November 3, 1943. He had never seen combat, but Wolf's psyche was so unsettled by his service that family and friends insisted he suffered from "shell shock."

In the aftermath of this disastrous interlude, Wolf was not seeking stardom, merely stability. He settled down briefly with Lillie Crudup in Lebanon, Tennessee, but after they broke up he returned to the Phillips Plantation, north of Parkin, Arkansas, where his father still lived. He resumed the lowly farm labors that had been his mainstay in previous years. Another short-lived relationship, with Blanche Ship, brought him to Penton, Mississippi, and here he continued as a farmer for another two years. He played music in his spare time, but the crops always came first. Wolf's diligence paid off when he was appointed overseer of a farm, and his responsibilities increased when he inherited a patch of land near Walls, Mississippi, from his grandfather. His marriage to Katie Mae Johnson in 1947—a sometimes tumultuous relationship that would last a half-decade—helped further settle the once rambling bluesman into a workaday life.

But with the postwar economic boom cooling off in 1948, prospects in Mississippi looked worse than ever. Although 1948 is often remembered as the beginning of the "baby boom," Mississippi's population was steadily declining and would continue to do so until the 1960s, when welfare programs, not a robust job market, would finally halt the migration. During the 1940s, the state's black population declined by 8 percent—but in Michigan it increased by 112 percent, and in California by an extraordinary 272 percent. Mississippi had ranked last in the nation in per capita income before the war, and it tenaciously held on to this distinction after the war. Even for Howlin' Wolf, cautious by nature and concerned whether his poor education would prevent him from earning a living in the big city, the implications were clear. His prospects in rural Mississippi—whether as a musician, or a farmer, or merely as a black man hoping to be treated with some decency and respect—were meager, and unlikely to improve anytime soon.

Even so, Howlin' Wolf was not a risk-taker. "California," he would sing at one of his first sessions, "*that's* the place I want to live." But when it came time to choose the destination for his own personal migration, Wolf did not select the West Coast, or even the closer beacons of opportunity in Chicago or St. Louis. He made a much more tentative step, not even to Memphis, but to West Memphis. This community, less populous even than Clarksdale, had been founded as a logging camp in 1910, and was known as Brag's Spurt until 1927, when it was incorporated under its new name. Compared to the larger city of Memphis across the river, West Memphis was a fast-and-loose community where vices of various sorts—gambling, drinking, prostitution—flourished with little interference from the police. Such environments have usually proven hospitable to the blues, and though Wolf quickly found a job in a factory, the many clubs, bars, and cafés in the area had been a major attraction drawing him to the city.

Wolf formed a band, with Willie Johnson and M. T. Murphy on guitar, Willie Steele on drums, Junior Parker playing harmonica, and piano player William Johnson who went by the colorful name of "Destruction." Sometimes guitarist Pat Hare or harp player James Cotton would play with the group. After arriving in West Memphis, Wolf acquired an electric guitar, and his group relied heavily on amplification in forging their hard-edged sound. While Muddy Waters was tearing up Chicago with his modernized and electrified Delta blues, Howlin' Wolf was doing the same on the smaller stage of West Memphis. But if his success was less prominent than Waters's, his audience was just as enthusiastic, and crowds packed into the small venues where the House Rockers—Wolf's name for his band—played their loud, wild music. "Between 1948 and 1950," in the words of critic Robert Palmer, "Wolf molded his musicians into the most awesome electric blues band the Delta had seen."

The band had a mean streak, a roughshod sound far more primitive than anything the Chess brothers would have let Waters attempt at the time. Steele thrashed the drums like they were stubborn mules unwilling to pull the plow, while Johnson delighted as much in the distortion and feedback of his guitar as in the blues notes he tore from its strings. With the benefit of amplification, the harmonica, that lowliest of the wind instruments, now took on the wallop of a freight train heading down the tracks. And on piano, Destruction was . . . well, destruction, pounding and slashing away at the keyboard, filling in whatever gaps were left in this miasma of hot blues sound with riffs and grooves. Above this commotion, Howlin' Wolf strutted and preened, the master of all he surveyed. His singing transfixed audiences, who thought they had discovered the meaning of the bluesman's lupine nickname in the howls and wails, the raw, feral energy of his vocalizing. Even by the topsy-turvy standards of the Delta, where songs were prized like bulls bred for the rodeo, loved for their grit and toughness, even in the wake of all the blues shouters and hollerers who had hit this town long before him, Howlin' Wolf was something special. He had surrounded himself with a cacophony of amplified sound that might well make the walls shake, but his voice cut through the clash and clang, in all its sinuous and abrasive beauty.

Many have tried to unlock the secrets of Howlin' Wolf's singing voice. Some have suggested that he constricted his throat, much like the famous herders of Tuva in Siberia, who employ this method to produce overtones, creating two distinct notes simultaneously, a low drone akin to a bagpipe and an ethereal, flutelike harmonic. Others have sought a medical explanation, linking Wolf's distinctive singing to a childhood case of tonsillitis that permanently damaged his vocal cords. Others have given up on comprehending the origins of the sound, and merely reach for metaphor in trying to circumscribe it—for example, the rockabilly great Ronnie Hawkins, who described Wolf's voice as "stronger than forty acres of crushed garlic." *Newsweek*, in turn, compared his singing to "a runaway bucket of nails." Certainly many have tried to imitate Wolf's voice, either in parody or, like the famous radio deejay Wolfman Jack, as a life-changing career move. But for all this, Howlin' Wolf's sound resists assimilation into the mainstream, and eludes those who try to recreate its magic, their efforts never approaching the vigor of the original. Some sixty years after he first shook up the West Memphis nightlife, his sound retains all of its hypnotic and unsettling allure.

Wolf parlayed his notoriety in the clubs into an opportunity to broadcast his music over the airwaves. The local West Memphis station KWEM had lost some of its audience to WDIA in Memphis following the latter's switch to a format playing black music targeted at the metropolitan area's large African-American population. Other stations in the region had enjoyed similar successes, most notably the pioneering KFFA in Helena, which first broadcast its *King Biscuit Time* blues show on November 21, 1941. *King Biscuit Time* continues to this day—making it the longest running daily radio show in the country. KWEM had avoided the blues in the past, but in 1949 the station took a chance on Howlin' Wolf. Wolf, for his part, did everything he could to ensure his radio program's success. He went from store to store, finding sponsors, selling advertising, and building goodwill in the community. He started advertising various seeds—corn, oats, wheat, and such—and worked his way up to higher-ticket goods, plows and tractors and tools. Here his more than two decades of experience in farming must have been an asset as he chatted with the vendors of agricultural products who would support his newfound, albeit limited notoriety as a radio star.

This fame came in small doses. Howlin' Wolf's show lasted a mere fifteen minutes each day. But he made the most of the time available to him. "Aoooooh," he would holler like a wolf, then change to his grit-in-the-throat speaking voice, a strange sing-song that both fascinated and repelled his audiences. "This here's the *Wolf* comin' at you, baby." He would be sure to announce his band's performances at the conclusion of each broadcast, and when the musicians arrived at their gigs, they often encountered fans waiting who had heard about the engagement on KWEM. The station had a large audience in the rural areas surrounding the city, and Wolf found his services increasingly in demand at jukehouses and parties out in the country; but he also brought his band on the road, where he could make three times as much for a performance per night as in West Memphis, sometimes supplementing his band with three horn players—a rarity in the Delta blues, where often one or two guitarists were sufficient for the evening's entertainment. Yet Wolf understood the value of delivering more than what his fans expected, and he looked for any opportunity to stand out from the crowd.

As his fame increased, so did the legend. People told stories about Howlin' Wolf, and who knew if they were true? Sometimes the tales dealt with Wolf's music, but more often they reveled in his primal energy and sheer cussedness. An attacker had pulled a knife on him, some said, and Wolf had used his brute strength to grab the man, twist his arm, and stab the assailant with his own weapon. Another time, Wolf took on two or three men at once, and left them badly beaten and with broken bones. Outside a club, he had supposedly lifted the whole back end of a car while a flat tire was changed. Some musicians stayed away from him, having heard that Howlin' Wolf would beat a man for playing a song the wrong way. Wolf's on-stage persona was so overpowering, many quickly gave credence to even the most extraordinary tales of his off-stage prowess.

One day in 1951, a disk jockey from West Memphis told Sam Phillips, then hoping to make his mark as a record producer, that he needed to listen to Howlin' Wolf's show on KWEM. Phillips had opened his Memphis Recording Service the previous year, with the intention of tapping the musical riches found in Memphis and the surrounding region, talent neglected by the major record companies. He had already had a measure of success with "Rocket 88," which many would later acknowledge as the first rock-

and-roll record. Although "Rocket 88" had been credited to Jackie Brenston, a saxophonist who sang the vocal, the mastermind behind the new sound was Ike Turner, another Delta transplant from Clarksdale, Mississippi, who had taken a standard jump blues, and by incorporating a harder backbeat and a distinctive fuzz guitar sound—perhaps the chance result of damage to a speaker while the band was driving down Highway 61 to their Memphis destination—had concocted a hit that became the second best selling song on the R&B charts that year. Now Phillips heard another talent from the Delta, with even more promise than Turner, in Phillips's estimation, but also more peculiar and less polished.

Although Phillips sent out word that he would welcome a visit from the KWEM radio star, Howlin' Wolf did not show up for a few days. Wolf was skilled at selling himself, but he did more listening than talking on his initial visit, perhaps trying to take the measure of this odd young white man from Alabama, fourteen years his junior, who proposed they plan a record session together. Wolf agreed, and on May 14, 1951, he cut two sides for Phillips, embarking belatedly on a recording career at an age when many of his contemporaries had long ago put away their harmonicas and guitars.

But if Wolf was no longer a young man, the music he recorded for Phillips gave no sign of it. "Moanin' at Midnight" opens with an eerie wordless vocal, wavering between B flat and B natural, a sound effect for a graveyard scene in a Hollywood scare flick. This unaccompanied introduction is of uncertain tonality, but hints at the major and minor third in the key of G. When Willie Johnson's guitar enters, vamping aggressively in E, the shift is unsettling. Wolf now rises to a penetrating howl on the ninth interval, rich in vibrato, a hoot owl in the cemetery giving a warning call, then he resolves momentarily into the tonic note. But almost without pause or breath, he is blowing hard on harmonica now—it sounds like he is playing directly into the recording mike, forcing everything else into the background—and the intensity of the music ratchets up a notch. Johnson responds on guitar with jagged notes that disrupt the vamp, then settles back into the groove, only to do the same for the rest of the song, alternating between a predictable rhythmic figure and acerbic interjections that push and prod Wolf in his bristly vocal. "Well, somebody knockin' on my door," he bellows, and though he refuses to tell us who is calling, we sense unmistakably that this is an unwanted visitor, more likely a dark raven than the lost Lenore. "Well, I'm so worried, don't know where to go," and for once the perennial pop song complaints of anguish and torment seem all too believable. In an age of icky sweet ballads and jive dance tunes, this throbbing paean to bipolar disorder was an unlikely hit, but Phillips was transfixed. "I can take one damn record like 'Moanin' at Midnight' and forget every damn thing else that the man ever cut," he would later proclaim. "That is a classic thing that nobody can improve on."

But Wolf would be called on to do just that, not only in his boogie-driven "How Many More Years" from the same session (with Ike Turner, perhaps, joining on piano), but in a knock-off of "Moanin' at Midnight" recorded at his follow-up session in September under the similar title "Morning at Midnight." Wolf released competing versions of his song due to the awkward situation of being under contract to two different record labels. Phillips had sent the results of the May 14 session to the Chess brothers, who were excited by the music and quickly rushed it into production. By the fall, both sides of the Chess release, "Moanin' at Midnight" and "How Many More Years," had reached the top ten on the *Billboard* R&B chart. The Bihari brothers also wanted Howlin' Wolf for the RPB subsidiary of their Modern label, and arranged their own recording session around the time of the Chess release. They released "Morning at Midnight" with "Riding in the Moonlight" on the flip side, and followed up with additional records, including "Crying at Daybreak," which looked back to Charley Patton and anticipated Wolf's later hit "Smokestack Lightnin'." But the recordings Wolf made for Phillips had the upper edge. Their sound quality was superior to the RPM efforts, and Phillips, who later claimed that he never enjoyed any sessions more than those with Wolf, was a sympathetic and supportive producer who elicited the best out of the assembled musicians. Phillips brought Wolf back into the studio in December and in January 1952, which resulted in two memorable Chess releases, the first matching "The Wolf Is at Your Door" with "Howlin' Wolf Boogie," and the second pairing "Getting Old and Gray" and "Mr. Highwayman."

The dueling record companies finally reached a settlement over Wolf's conflicting contracts. The Bihari brothers gave the bluesman over to Chess in exchange for four Rosco Gordon masters and acknowledgment that they could keep the Wolf sides they had already recorded. Chess got the best of this deal. By the mid-1950s, Gordon had departed from RPM, and a few years later he left the music industry to run a dry cleaning business. But Howlin' Wolf would become one of the core assets for Chess, staying with the label for over two decades and recording more than one hundred fifty performances, many of them still solid sellers today.

Yet Howlin' Wolf was an unlikely crossover star in an era of bobbysoxers and tailfins. Wolf's age was an obvious factor, likely to limit his audience appeal, but the antiquity of his songs must have seemed an even greater obstacle to widespread popularity. Almost at the same time that Hollywood was launching its first major 3D movie, Chess had to peddle "Saddle My Pony," a song Wolf had learned from Charley Patton, and a composition that had struck audiences as primitive back in the 1920s, when ponies and mares were already losing out to the Ford Model A. Yet the record sold well, reflecting perhaps the growing undercurrent of rebellion against the oppressive slickness of all the popular arts during this period. Wolf was anything but slick, and evoked a paradoxical hipness by being so un-hip. Indeed, listening to his unreleased recordings from this period, one is inescapably struck with just how out of touch Mr. Burnett was. On his "California Blues," he sings about moving to "Beverland Hill"—even Jed Clampett knew better than that! His music was no more sophisticated: on "My Troubles and Me," Wolf sets up a musical train wreck, veering repeatedly from the straight twelve-bar form his rhythm section is supplying, and stubbornly evoking those ancient Delta blues where bar lines and strict meter were dispensed with as unnecessary restraints running counter to the feeling of the music.

But Wolf, for all his limitations, was moving up in the world. He now played the better clubs on Beale Street, with higher visibility and heftier paychecks. It was no longer a question of who had the hottest blues band in Memphis, but rather whether anyone on Beale Street had *ever* played with more fire or intensity. Wolf was recording regularly, and his releases not only sold well in the South, where the blues market was strong, but even up north fans were starting to take notice. In this environment, he could have settled in for the long haul, like Furry Lewis and Gus Cannon before him, enjoying the diverse nightlife of the Memphis area, and perhaps occasionally going on the road to supplement his income. But the Chess brothers had bigger plans for the blues act they had fought so hard to retain. They wanted Wolf in Chicago, where he would be near at hand, and more easily marketed in America's second largest city.

The move was a painful one. Burnett's wife Katie Mae did not come with him, and she died a few years later. He would seldom see his mother and father again. He left his farm, inherited from his grandfather, in the hands of his brother-in-law. He also left behind the musicians who had helped build his band into a major force on the blues scene. And when he arrived in his new locale in the winter of 1954, he was moving on to the home turf of another Mississippi transplant, Muddy Waters, who had already established himself as king of the Chicago blues scene.

3. why don't ya hear me cryin'?

Howlin' Wolf wanted to arrive in Chicago, in his words, "like a gentleman." In the fifteen years since Robert Johnson had sung "Sweet Home Chicago," many Delta musicians had made the 600-mile trip northward to try their luck in the largest market in middle America. But few had done it in such style as Chester Burnett. Instead of taking a bus or train, Wolf drove an expensive two-tone DeSoto, and carried several thousand dollars in cash on his person. He was no raw talent hoping for a break, but a proven star with hit songs and a record contract, and he wanted the world to know it. In short, he had everything he needed to set up shop in the Windy City, except for a roof over his head. But Leonard Chess obliged his new artist by finding him a place to stay—in this instance, the home of Chess's star act, Muddy Waters!

The two musicians had never met, but certainly knew each other by reputation. Waters was inclined to help out Chess in a pinch, and opened his doors for the newcomer. But Wolf paid for his room and board—and took pride in doing so. In time, these two blues legends would feel some rivalry, and it may have first stirred during this period. Yet Waters acted with generosity in making Wolf feel at home in his new surroundings, introducing him into the local blues scene, bringing him to clubs, and setting him up as a replacement when Waters took his own band on the road.

At his first Chicago session in March 1954, Wolf showed that he could replicate his West Memphis success in this new setting. "No Place to Go," a one-chord vamp with a loping, start-and-stop beat, imparted a mesmerizing background to Wolf's throaty recitative and harp playing. Backed by "Rockin' Daddy," a bouncy dance tune, this release hit the charts in May and stayed there until July. By then, Chess had already brought Wolf back into the studio, where he contributed another hit, the classic "Evil Is Going On." Penned by Willie Dixon, this song proved to be the perfect vehicle for Wolf's abrasive and doleful voice, so suitable for dire warnings such as the title admonition. The ever vigilant Wolf warns the jealous husband a "long way from home" that "another mule is kickin' in your stall."

That's evil, evil is goin' on wrong.
I am warnin' ya brother, you better watch your happy home.

"Evil" stayed on the charts from midsummer through Thanksgiving, not only selling well in strong blues markets like Memphis and Atlanta, but also finding a ready audience in Nashville, Cleveland, and Detroit.

At his first engagements in his new hometown, Wolf had played with various musicians, usually borrowed from other bandleaders; but he wanted to make a big splash on the Chicago scene, perhaps even challenge the great Muddy Waters, and this would require a first-class working band with the same energy and drive that his West Memphis cohorts had shown. Guitarist Jody Williams was one of Wolf's first additions. Born in Mobile but raised in Chicago from the age of five, Williams had started out playing harmonica as a youth. An encounter with fifteen-year-old Bo Diddley at a talent show changed his life. Diddley taught Williams the rudiments of the guitar, and the two musicians were soon performing together. Their first band featured two guitars and a washtub and played on a street corner. Williams parlayed this relationship into prominence as one of the hottest guitarists on the Chicago scene during the mid-1950s. On piano, Wolf initially relied on Otis Spann—who had played with Williams and was a mainstay of Muddy Waters's band—whenever he could. But Spann's first allegiance was to Waters, so Wolf sent to West Memphis for Hosea Lee Kennard, a polished young keyboardist who admired and emulated Nat King Cole. Kennard would keep the band anchored with his solid grooves; and his versatility—his range of moods stretched from the quasi-Latin tinges of "Who's Been Talking" to the ethereal undercurrents of "Smokestack Lightnin' "—made him an ideal partner for Wolf. In search of a drummer, Wolf had tried to convince Willie Steele to move to Chicago. But Steele joined the Army. Instead, through Muddy Waters's intercession, Wolf was able to enlist Earl Phillips, a transplanted New Yorker who had apprenticed playing jazz and swing styles. In his new setting Phillips would craft an invigorating and original style of drumming, sensitive to the space between the beats, yet forging the hypnotic, repetitive rhythms essential to the success of Wolf's music.

Wolf's most important addition would prove to be another Delta native, Hubert Sumlin, born in Greenwood in 1931, whom he had known for over a decade. Like many other Delta guitarists, Sumlin had been introduced to music through the diddley bow. His older brother took baling wire from a broom and nailed it to the wall. "Stuck my momma's snuff bottle in there and pulled it down 'til he got this tone off the wire." His first guitar was short-lived: the bossman found Sumlin playing it when he should have been plowing, and broke the instrument across the tractor wheel. When he got a second guitar, the youngster took care to keep it out of the fields, and instead practiced at home, often in the company of another future Chicago blues journeyman, harmonica player James Cotton.

Sumlin's first encounter with Howlin' Wolf could easily have been his last. He was only eleven or twelve years old when he climbed on top of soda bottle cases outside the back window of a juke joint where Wolf was playing—a location that gave the youngster a perfect view of the proceedings inside. "Well these coke cases started to come unbalanced and I fell through the window into the club, in the middle of a song. Over on the old Wolf's head I landed—right on the dude's head." Wolf was famous for his short temper, but in this instance he showed compassion for his young fan. "He said, 'Let him stay, let him stay. Bring him a chair,'" Sumlin would later recall. "That's right, I sat there. . . . That's the first time I saw the Wolf and I followed him ever since." Now in his mid-twenties, Sumlin found himself enlisted as guitarist in Wolf's Chicago band. The relationship would be tumultuous—the two argued, sometimes even threw punches at each other, and when tensions reached a boiling point, Sumlin would leave the band. Despite these outbursts and separations, they always patched it up, and Sumlin would remain Wolf's closest associate until the latter's final days.

With his new band in place, Wolf shook up Chicago with a flashier style of blues performance than the city had ever seen before. Most Chicago musicians sat down while they performed. Muddy Waters and other blues acts relied on highback chairs on stage almost as much as they did on their instruments and microphones. The music might reach a fever pitch of intensity, but the musicians themselves rarely seemed responsive to the danceable rhythms they were making. Wolf changed all that. When he took over Muddy Waters's engagement at the Zanzibar, he came with a microphone on a cord as long as a basketball court. Wolf was now free to prowl the entire length and breadth of the club. At the Zanzibar, he would dance through the audience, hollering and moaning, or walk the large oval bar that spanned the establishment. At the 708 Club, he even brought his music out the door and down to the corner, singing and blowing his harmonica, and causing so much commotion on the street that the police escorted him back to the bandstand.

"Muddy never had the energy Wolf had, not even at his peak," asserted saxophonist Eddie Shaw, who played with both bandleaders during the late 1950s. "Muddy would rock the house pretty good, but Wolf was the most exciting blues player I've ever seen." Robert Palmer describes the unforgettable experience of watching Howlin' Wolf in performance: "He would dart around the stage, chanting a key phrase over and over, his face bathed in sweat, eyes rolling back in his head, while the band riffed one chord and the audience swayed as if in a trance." Wolf was fifty-five years old at the time Palmer saw him at a Memphis performance, but neither age nor indifference had slowed him down. He played guitar "while rolling around on his back and, at one point, doing somersaults." Then, when a signal from off stage indicated that his performance was running too long, Wolf

> counted off a bone-crushing rocker, began singing rhythmically, feigned an exit, and suddenly made a flying leap for the curtain at the side of the stage. Holding the microphone under his beefy right arm and singing into it all the while, he began climbing up the curtain, going higher and higher until he was perched far above the stage, the thick curtain threatening to rip, the audience screaming with delight. Then he loosed his grip and, in a single easy motion, slid right back down the curtain, hit the stage, cut off the tune, and stalked away, to the most ecstatic cheers of the evening.

The sexual energy of Wolf's performances sometimes crossed boundaries that few entertainers broached during these years. At times, he would crawl around on all fours, howling like a wolf on the prowl, and might even entice an overly-excited female fan to climb on his back for an impromptu ride—or two or more women would get on simultaneously. In other instances, he would tell credulous audiences that he had a tail like a real wolf, inciting the more curious to try to get a peak at the anomalous appendage. After the release of his recording "Spoonful," Wolf added an enormous cooking spoon to his on-stage arsenal, which he brandished like a phallic symbol in a pagan fertility rite—not even toning down his act for the white wives of Ole Miss alums at a university event that people still talked about years later. His most outré stunt found Wolf shaking up a Coke bottle, and slipping it down his pants. Walking up to the microphone, he would unzip his fly, pop the top of the bottle, and spray the audience with the resulting fizz. But just as much as he pushed the limits on the bandstand, Wolf knew where to draw the line off stage, especially with the members of the band. When drummer S. P. Leary whistled at a white woman from the car while the band was on tour in Mississippi, Wolf pulled the automobile over to the side of the road, took out a gun, and threatened to shoot him on the spot. Wolf knew that his performance antics might shock, but in the less tolerant world of "real-life" Mississippi, liberties of this sort could get you killed—and, if there were any shooting to do, Wolf preferred to be the one pulling the trigger.

No blues performer had shown such a mastery of showmanship, could create such a carnival atmosphere in a nightclub or auditorium, or work audiences into such a fine peak of frenzy. But the music never faltered, never became a mere soundtrack for Howlin' Wolf's on-stage shenanigans. Wolf might be willing to push the envelope with his feral on-stage persona, but in his songs he kept to the basics, extracting new life from the oldest traditions. The Delta blues had always captivated listeners through its incisiveness, through the brutal simplicity of its musical onrush. This had been true in its earliest days—while the big city stars were learning to play the blues with larger ensembles and tight band charts, the Delta pioneers built their legacies with one or two guitars, and arrangements as flimsy as the tumbledown shacks where they had been born and bred. But even in the modern era, the Delta blues players stayed true to this minimalist aesthetic as they brought their music to the major urban markets and on to the *Billboard* charts. John Lee Hooker showed that a single musician vamping on a primitive riff could still achieve a chart-rockin' hit record in the nuclear age. Muddy Waters did the same, teaching the Chess brothers that less could be more, earning his first big hits with reworkings of the simple field recordings he had made for the Library of Congress back on Stovall Plantation. Now Howlin' Wolf was reinforcing the point, building a series of hits from songs that were little more than vamps, a wisp of harmony backed by a bump-and-grind beat, tunes you didn't so much hear as feel. In any other setting, the Wolf's rolling on the floor, his seizurelike attitudes, would have seemed like corny theatrics, but with this throbbing, unrelenting music getting folks hot and bothered, in the seething intensity of the moment, the bandleader's excesses seemed a natural expression of what everyone in the room was feeling.

Wolf recorded little during late 1954 and 1955, devoting most of his energies to his Chicago performances, and taking his band on the road. An October 1954 session produced only one release, pairing "Forty-Four" and "I'll Be Around." Although they sold respectably, making the *Cash Box* "hot charts" for Memphis and New Orleans, Chess only brought Wolf back into the studio one more time over the next fourteen months. But the road trips exposed thousands of new listeners to Wolf's larger-than-life presence, an experience that no record or radio broadcast could adequately convey. In Cleveland, Wolf's show attracted audience members Little Richard and James Brown to join in the on-stage commotion, and create some of their own. In New York, Wolf dazzled the crowd at the legendary Apollo Theater with a show that garnered extensive media coverage, and inspired owner Frank Schiffman to proclaim: "I haven't seen anything like it in my thirty years with the Apollo." Everywhere he went, Wolf left behind true believers, and despite his infrequent visits to the recording studio, *Cash Box* named him one of the top twenty-five R&B vocalists of the year.

Wolf was primed to make more records, and when a session was finally scheduled in January 1956, he responded with one of the landmark performances of his career. "Smokestack Lightnin'" had been germinating in Wolf's repertoire for many years, much of the song drawing on material he had played when first learning the blues in the Delta. The piece was little more than a two-bar repeating phrase, a medium-tempo groove in the key of E, with the guitar jumping into a minor third, like a knife thrust, on the second beat of every other bar. One might think that this was merely the introduction to the song, that something more formal and structured would emerge from this jabbing rhythm. But no, the groove was the song— just like John Lee Hooker had done with "Boogie Chillen" or Son House with "Dry Spell Blues" back in 1930.

Wolf's "Crying at Daybreak," recorded for Sam Phillips back in Memphis, had been a first attempt to build a hit record out of this ancient formula. Now with "Smokestack Lightnin'" everything fell into place, not so much a song as a mood, an evocation of a late night, bluesy feeling that resists deep analysis. The lyrics are little more than a collection of images, some of them timeless blues fare—trains and no-good women—but creating a powerful overall effect. Literary critics once called this an "objective correlative," the precise ingredients, the phrases, objects, events, that immediately draw the audience into an intense emotional state. But for Wolf, this was no technique learned from Shakespeare or Keats but, one suspects, the channeling of his own feelings of loneliness and isolation as a child, his sense of abandonment from his mother, his despair at the brutal beatings of his greatuncle Will Young. "Why don't ya hear me cryin'?" is the recurring phrase in his chant, followed by his characteristic howl, "whoo-hooo, whoo-hooo, whooo"—not a predatory baying at the moon, more a mournful yowl, full of painful memories. The song ends:

> *Whoa-oh, who been here baby since I been gone, a little bitty boy?*
> *Girl, be on.*
> *A-whoo-hooo, whoo-hooo, whooo.*

The intimacy of the performance, the vagueness of the events recounted, did not prevent "Smokestack Lightnin'" from becoming a hit with the general public. The record appeared on the *Billboard* R&B chart in March 1956, and peaked at number 11.

Despite his growing success, Wolf had problems with band personnel, who resented his application of techniques learned as a farm overseer to the management of a musical ensemble. He sometimes hit or slapped his sidemen, and was known to threaten them with a knife or gun for especially egregious offenses. But a thousand-dollar penalty imposed by the musicians' union proved to be even more effective than a course in anger management; afterwards, Wolf preferred to fine or suspend rather than assault the offender. Wolf was frugal, despite his growing income, and this too led to friction with his band. After Jody Williams left in a dispute over pay, Wolf hired his old West Memphis guitarist Willie Johnson. But Wolf's temper and Johnson's drinking made this relationship as tempestuous off stage as it was productive on the bandstand. After "Smokestack Lightnin'," Wolf and Johnson briefly parted ways, and guitarist Mighty Joe Young joined the group, but his stay was also short-lived.

The biggest blow came when Hubert Sumlin left to join Muddy Waters's band. Losing sidemen in a huff was part of a bandleader's life, but the departure of his closest associate to Wolf's crosstown rival amounted to nothing less than betrayal. Waters offered Sumlin three times what Wolf was paying him, and also gave the guitarist a respite from the bandleader's constant needling and put-downs. "[Wolf] would say, 'Look here, Hubert, I think you're good. I like you, but you ain't great. Don't never let nobody tell you that you're the best in the world. 'Cause in my book, you all right, but guitar players are a dime a dozen.'" Wolf hired Willie Johnson back to replace Sumlin, who stayed with Waters for around a year. Finally, the demands of life on the road with Waters—sometimes a thousand miles separated one gig from the next—took too much of a toll on Sumlin. After a draining tour of forty one-night stands, Sumlin and Waters got into a fight, and the guitarist phoned up his old bandleader from the club, asking for his job back. Wolf came to retrieve his returning bandmate, and told Waters: "Next time you do that man, I'll kill you over him."

Wolf followed up "Smokestack Lightnin'" with "I Asked for Water," another no-good-woman song built around one of the most striking, if disquieting, images in the annals of American popular music:

> I asked her for water, ohhhh, she brought me gasoline.
> That's the terriblest woman, oh, that I ever seen.

The image is a recurring one in the blues—Tommy Johnson had made the same claim about his woman in 1928, and Furry Lewis may have dated the same lady, for he repeated the accusation in a song recorded the following year. Although "I Asked for Water" did not match the success of "Smokestack Lightnin'," it sold well, and reached the local charts in Cleveland, Atlanta, St. Louis, Newark, and Memphis. Wolf had no qualms about continuing to borrow from largely forgotten prewar blues to build his Sputnik-era career. His recording of "The Natchez Burnin'," from the same session, was probably as close as Wolf would get to contemporary stylings, commemorating, as it did, a news event that was only sixteen years old—a devastating nightclub fire from April 1940 that killed more than two hundred people. For "Bluebird," recorded a few months later in December 1956, he drew on an old Sonny Boy Williamson song; and although Wolf recorded little in 1957—only eight songs at two sessions—he again turned to some of the oldest material in his repertoire. "Poor Boy" is among the earliest Delta blues standards, dating back to the turn of the century, while "Sittin' on Top of the World" had been a hit for the Mississippi Sheiks at the start of the Great Depression. "Howlin' Blues" from his next Chess session was reminiscent of the same song, although the tempo is slower and the words different. But even when he recorded newer material, Wolf retained the primitive feeling of old-time blues, drawing on one-chord vamps or old-fashioned shuffles, his vocals harkening back to the field hollers of a bygone day.

Since separating from Katie Mae Johnson when he moved to Chicago, Wolf had not enjoyed a close, lasting relationship with any woman. Lillie Handley, whom he met in the late 1950s, would change this, serving as a stabilizing influence on Wolf for the rest of his life. A widow, whose first husband had died in 1952, Handley was an educated woman who owned properties in Chicago and Alabama, and didn't need a man to support her. Handley initially resisted Wolf's overtures—even giving him a fake phone number when he asked how he could get in touch with her. But Wolf's persistence eventually paid off. They began dating, and Handley moved in with him in 1958. The couple married in a civil ceremony in May 1964, and Wolf reportedly told his bride: "I wish I had had you the first day I ever howled."

Wolf was almost fifty when he settled down with Lillie Handley, and just shy of his fifty-fourth birthday when they got married. Of course, Wolf had always done things later than most folks, whether starting his recording career or learning the basics of reading and arithmetic. His performances gave few signs of his advancing years: his singing was strong; his bands well suited to his music; and his stage antics as unpredictable as ever. Yet his compositions rarely broke new ground now. When Wolf resurrected an old blues tune, unknown to most of his audience, this might not pose a problem. But with increasing regularity, he was imitating his own hit records. "Moanin' for My Baby" from April 1958 revisits the familiar territory of "Moanin' at Midnight," and at his next session in September, Wolf took the same riff as the basis for "You Can't Put Me Out." The band would not return to the studio until the following July, but here Wolf's "Mr. Airplane Man" combines music from "Smokestack Lightnin'" with lyrics adapted from "Bluebird." The Chess execs further complicated matters by promoting Wolf's first long-playing album around this same time, *Moanin' at Midnight*, a compilation of his various hits from the decade—making it even clearer to blues fans how derivative his latest efforts were.

Fortunately, Wolf's record label had the solution to this problem at hand. Willie Dixon had proven himself indispensable to the Chess brothers over the years, first as a bass player, but increasingly as an adviser, an informal (and often uncredited) producer, and especially as a songwriter. Dixon had made Muddy Waters into the "Hoochee Coochee Man," and had composed many of the defining songs of the Chicago blues style, including one of Wolf's biggest sellers, "Evil Is Going On." Despite the success of this release, Wolf had shown little interest in recording more of Dixon's tunes. He had several reasons for this reluctance. Wolf's poor reading ability made it difficult for him to learn and perform new lyrics—especially the complicated kind Dixon crafted. Wolf may also have resented the loss of songwriter royalties, which often amount to substantially more money than the recording artist receives. But, above all, Wolf had a suspicion that Mr. Dixon offered his best songs to Muddy Waters. Dixon understood the rivalry between the two, and used it in his favor, pretending that the songs he showed Wolf were intended for Waters. "He would be glad to get in on it by him thinking it was somebody else's, especially Muddy's. They seemed to have a little thing going on between them so I used that backwards psychology." After years of relying on his own skills as songwriter, Wolf now turned about completely: from 1960 through the end of 1963, Dixon composed the vast majority of the material Wolf recorded.

The strength of this pairing was evident almost from the start. Wolf only recorded three songs at his June 1960 session, all of them Dixon compositions, and each a classic performance. Wolf reportedly disliked "Wang Dang Doodle" at first hearing—it reminded him of old-time levee camp songs—and it had proven difficult for him to learn. Dixon needed to stand next to him at the session, whispering the words into Wolf's ear, hoping he wouldn't garble the tongue-twisting patter lyrics.

Tell automatic Slim, tell razor-toting Jim,
Tell butcher knife toting Annie, tell fast-talking Fanny,
We're gonna pitch a ball . . .

"Wang dang" referred to a good time in Southern parlance, and the song evokes the Saturday night fish fries of the Delta, although the "wang dang doodle all night long" of the refrain—sung with gusto by Wolf on record—also conveys the pointed sexual overtones that always helped sales. (And not just for Wolf: Koko Taylor's cover of "Wang Dang Doodle" in 1965 climbed to number 4 on the *Billboard* R&B charts, becoming a million seller, and standing out as one of the last great Chess R&B hits.) Chess paired Wolf's version of this song with another Dixon classic, "Back Door Man," an even more direct evocation of late night promiscuity, which aimed to do for Wolf what "Hoochie Coochie Man" had done for Muddy Waters. "Spoonful" from the same session recalls Charley Patton's "A Spoonful Blues" of a generation before, that dark evocation of the taboo topic of cocaine addiction. But in Dixon's song, the cause of addiction is more elusive, the lyrics referring to a spoonful of diamonds or gold, or of a woman's love. At a follow-up session, Dixon again returned to Wolf's Delta mentor for inspiration with "The Red Rooster," a slow blues in the tradition of Patton's "Banty Rooster Blues." Wolf's collaborations with Dixon formed the foundation of Wolf's second LP, *Rocking Chair*, released in 1962.

But if Dixon's credentials as a hitmaker, for blues bands and rock-and-rollers alike, are beyond dispute, the musicians who recorded his songs nonetheless carped that Dixon took too much credit for arrangements, which often built on the spontaneous contributions of the sidemen. It is hard to imagine Dixon's "The Red Rooster" succeeding half so well without Wolf's sly slide guitar work, or "Shake for Me" without Sumlin's hard-grooving dance rhythms. In general, Wolf's band during the early 1960s was the finest of his career, and the Dixon material benefited from the skills of this ensemble. The addition of Sam Lay as drummer helped solidify the rhythm section, and Sumlin was at a new creative peak. The guitarist was drawing on a quirky combination of fills, licks, chords and grooves, harmonics, percussive jabs—an unpredictable arsenal of sounds, but ideally suited to supporting Wolf's voice and propelling the band.

A humiliating public moment may have been the decisive turning point in Sumlin's musical development. Wolf had fired him on stage one night, in front of a large audience. He sent Sumlin packing, advising him to learn to play with his fingers not his picks. When Sumlin returned, he had abandoned the pick, but also came fired with a new zeal, driven as much by his desire to prove himself as to please his boss. Wolf would still occasionally rely on two guitarists during this period—especially at recording sessions where his band sometimes included Buddy Guy, Jimmy Rogers, and possibly Freddie King (although his participation on the "Wang Dang Doodle" session is disputed). But increasingly Wolf felt comfortable with Sumlin holding down the guitar spot alone. And when he had to learn Willie Dixon's sometimes confusing songs, Wolf preferred to work on the music with just Sumlin before bringing in the rest of the band.

In short, few sidemen in the history of the blues would exert more influence, and in time a bevy of rock stars would count themselves among Sumlin's most passionate fans. Jimi Hendrix came in homage to one of Wolf's performances, telling Sumlin, "You're my favorite guitar player." When Eric Clapton encountered Sumlin at Wolf's high-profile London session with an all-star band of rockers, he almost turned around and left, exclaiming: "What do you need me for? I mean, you got Hubert in there. You don't need me." After Wolf's death, Keith Richards stepped in as Sumlin's producer and session mate, and the aging bluesman would even find himself invited to sit in with the Rolling Stones on stage.

Dixon's music during this period often sounds as though it were composed with Wolf and Sumlin in mind. Yet two crowd-pleasing songs about Wolf's sizable girth—"Built for Comfort" and "Three Hundred Pounds of Joy"—were actually written for Dixon to sing himself. A big man who could challenge Wolf pound-for-pound, Dixon didn't have a chance to record them; but they proved to be perfect vehicles for Wolf, contributing to his larger-than-life persona, and also served as excellent settings for Sumlin. "Goin' Down Slow" also sounded like a personal statement from Wolf, but it too was borrowed—from Jimmy Oden, who had recorded it for Bluebird in 1941. Wolf talks, chants, sings, and howls his way through this rambling retrospective about his life and times, with his sidemen offering a catalog of guitar and piano fills in the background. But just when it seemed Wolf had given up songwriting, content to rely on the well-crafted contributions of others, he recorded his own "Killing Floor" in August 1964. The song built on material Wolf had recorded on an unreleased track eight years earlier called "Break of Day." But the newer version was more incisive, with a rock-oriented rhythm that managed to reach out to younger listeners without losing the deep blues feeling that stood as the cornerstone of Wolf's sound.

Wolf's biggest opportunity to bring his music to a larger rock audience came to him the following May in a most unexpected way. The Rolling Stones were engaged to perform on the ABC television show *Shindig*, and they reportedly demanded that the show's producers also feature either Muddy Waters or Howlin' Wolf. Wolf was hired, and for the first time in his storied career, the celebrated bluesman performed on a national television broadcast. Wolf toned down his act for mainstream America—leaving his cooking spoon, Coke bottle, and other rude props behind. He wore a conservative suit and tie (in contrast to the more casually attired Stones) and neither crawled nor strolled far from the center-stage microphone. But even a strait-laced Wolf was more than what most TV watchers expected. He sang

"How Many More Years" with a passion and intensity that seemed incongruous with the laid-back, good-time ambiance of major network entertainment, all the while shaking, pointing, and gesticulating with a violence that
suggested nothing less than a boxer taunting a smaller opponent. At least at
first—then came the change mid-song from fighter to lover. Thrusting his
hips, contorting his knees, gyrating from the waist down, Wolf took all the
licentious choreography that had accompanied Elvis Presley's appearance
on *The Ed Sullivan Show*—when the producers, fearing a scandal, made sure
that their cameras never showed the singer's lower body—and did it one
better. Wolf apparently thought little of the performance: when the show
was broadcast, he surprised his family by refusing to get out of bed to watch
it. As for what the network executives thought . . . well, no one made any
public statements, but one can surmise much from the fact that the great
Howlin' Wolf never appeared again on a network television show.

4. still poor and scuffling like a dog

By the mid-1960s, Howlin' Wolf's career had reached a new level. Indeed,
he was now as much a legend as an entertainer. The blues revival was in full
swing, and the music of many of Wolf's Delta contemporaries was finding its way onto LPs and, after years of neglect, attracting an enthusiastic
audience among the baby boomer generation. Obscure figures from the
past—Son House, Bukka White, Skip James, Mississippi John Hurt—had
been forgotten, or written off as dead, but now reappeared on the concert
and nightclub circuit, lauded as celebrated icons of America's musical heritage. Wolf's prestige and reputation grew in tandem with this new state of
affairs. In February 1966, *Newsweek* published a profile of the bluesman,
highlighting Wolf's "mean old blues" sung in a "hoarse rasping voice"—
comments which, a decade earlier, might have sounded like criticism, but
with the changing tastes of the younger generation, now stood as praise of
the highest order.

Chess jumped on the bandwagon, releasing a collection of Wolf's singles
as *The Real Folk Blues* around this time. Wolf continued to record occasional new material for Chess—a few weeks after the *Newsweek* article he
was in the studio resurrecting "New Crawlin' King Snake" and "My Mind Is
Ramblin'," both adaptations of older songs. But his career from this point
on would be more about celebrating his legacy than trying to break new

ground. Invited to perform at the Newport Folk Festival that year, Wolf arrived on stage wearing boots, bib overalls, a work shirt, and a straw hat. The bandleader who had dressed like a banker on *Shindig* now was attired like a Delta farmhand!

But Wolf knew what the audience wanted. The blues revival had rubbed up against a large number of emerging notions and fantasies in the minds of the younger generation—of a return to the roots, getting in touch with the land, sensitivity to the environment, righting the wrongs of racial oppression and poverty, and, yes, finding authentic music that cut through the glitz of pop stardom. Wolf sensed that an evocation of his own background plowing the cotton fields had more value now than an acre of fuzz boxes, wah-wah pedals, and Moog synthesizers. Younger blues artist Taj Mahal was so impressed with Wolf's appearance that he adopted a similar wardrobe in performance and on the cover of his 1969 classic *Take a Giant Step*. Never before had sharecropping seemed quite so . . . glamorous. But the pattern itself was vaguely familiar. Once again—as perennially happens in the history of the American music—what was old, borrowed, and blue sounded fresher and more immediate than the newest releases by the latest acts.

The executives at Chess could have done more to build on Wolf's stature as a keeper of the flame, as one of the last survivors of the Delta generation who had mastered their craft before the Great Depression. But Chess itself was no longer a stable environment for its artists. Other labels—Motown, Atlantic, Stax—seemed more in touch with the tastes of African-American consumers. Yet as Chess faltered in the marketplace, it continued to plan for expansion, moving into a spacious new headquarters in April 1967—seven times as large as the company's previous home. The additional overhead required a comparable increase in record sales. Accordingly, when Chess brought Wolf into the studio a few weeks later, the label tried to remake him into a soul singer with the halfhearted "Pop It to Me." The follow-up *The Super Super Blues Band* was a notch higher in quality, full of lighthearted banter; yet its combination of Wolf with Muddy Waters and Bo Diddley might have produced so much more than this encounter, little more than a jam session tossed off without much forethought.

The worst was yet to come. The electric and psychedelic *Howlin' Wolf*, recorded in 1968, stands as the low point of the bluesman's career. Just as Chess had done with Muddy Waters on the disastrous *Electric Mud* release, the label forced Wolf into an incongruous setting that would have been comic had it not been so disrespectful. And just as Waters had publicly criticized *Electric Mud*, Wolf denounced his rock release in an interview with *Rolling Stone* magazine, dismissing the music in the journalistic venue that might have done the most to build sales and credibility. In one of the oddest public relations moves of the decade, Chess was inspired to place a disclaimer on the cover of the album, stating: "This is Howlin' Wolf's new album. He doesn't like it. He didn't like his electric guitar at first either." Record buyers apparently shared Wolf's sentiments, and the release was both a financial and critical disaster. At the same time he was working on this project, Wolf recorded some breathtaking acoustic music, evoking what he must have sounded like back in the Delta during the days of Charley Patton. But Chess did not think these songs were worth releasing at the time.

Chess itself was not the same company any more. In the midst of the *Electric Mud* and *Howlin' Wolf* fiasco, the label was sold to GRT, a Silicon Valley outfit that made blank tape and believed that more money could be made from owning the music rather than the medium. An incorrect assessment, in retrospect, since the new owners erased most of the value in the Chess label over the next six years and were forced to resell the business at a loss. Had Leonard Chess still been alive, the family might have repurchased the assets, but he had died suddenly at the age of fifty-two. Wolf often complained about the Chess family. "They taken advantage of me. They got thousands, millions of dollars off me, and I'm still poor and scuffling like a dog trying to live." Yet in the aftermath of the sale of the label and Leonard Chess's death, Wolf may have learned that an impersonal corporate owner could well be worse than the paternalistic family-owned business that had nurtured his career for so many years.

Wolf's own health was faltering now. On the way to a 1969 gig at the University of Chicago, he suffered a heart attack and slumped over onto the dashboard of the car. Hubert Sumlin, who was driving, pulled over to the curb, where he found a two-by-four lying at the roadside, and in an inspired moment never taught in a CPR course, slammed it forcefully into the bandleader's back. The force of the blow brought Wolf back to his senses, and Sumlin rushed him to a nearby medical facility. Wolf spent much of the next few months in and out of the hospital, where he was also diagnosed with hypertension and severe kidney problems. Yet he continued to make occasional performances, in defiance of doctor's orders that he stay home and follow a strict regimen that included abstinence from cigarettes, alcohol, and other staples of the blues life.

In this precarious condition, Wolf was invited to England to participate in an all-star session featuring many of the most famous rock performers of the day. The resulting release, *The London Howlin' Wolf Sessions*, stands out as perhaps the finest of the many attempts to pair aging blues stars with their younger rock admirers. The word-of-mouth sensation caused by Wolf's presence in town was so great that when Rolling Stones drummer Charlie Watts missed one of the sessions, Ringo Starr of the Beatles showed up as his replacement. But the session could easily have collapsed under its own weight. The rock stars' egos were larger than London's Olympic Studios could hold, and Wolf tried at first to match them attitude for attitude. Wolf also rebelled against producer Norman Dayron, less than half his age, and twice as tenacious. Dayron pushed and prodded everyone in attendance, including Mick Jagger, who incurred the producer's ire by asking to sit in with the band as a tambourine player. Dayron also feuded with engineer Glyn Johns over recording techniques—the former wanting a rougher, Chess-oriented ambiance, the latter aiming for a cleaner, crisper sound. The accumulated pressures of the session may have contributed to Wolf's collapse in a studio bathroom stall at the close of day. Dayron called an ambulance, but Wolf refused to be taken to the hospital, and returned to his hotel room.

At this point, not only the album but Wolf's health seemed to be hanging precariously in the balance. Yet the following day, in a simple, gracious move, Eric Clapton defused many of the tensions and seemed to set the project back on course, when he asked Wolf to show the band how he played a guitar lick on "The Red Rooster." This deference to the older man's musicianship placated and calmed Wolf, and helped bring cohesiveness to the whole session. Clapton was more than just a peacemaker: he plays at top form throughout, and Wolf's singing and harmonica work are exemplary as the ensemble worked through a dozen classic blues numbers. Upon its release, some critics carped at the commercial angle of the project, but *The London Howlin' Wolf Sessions* has held up well with the passing years and deserves to be considered one of the finest blues albums of the era.

Wolf would never achieve such success in the studio again. For his next project, Chess concocted another disaster, *Message to the Young*, which continued in the same schlock-rock vein as the earlier *Howlin' Wolf* and *Electric Mud* releases. A live album from January 1972 showed the Wolf could still deliver the goods in front of paying audiences, but this tough, authentic side of his musical personality was no longer nurtured inside the recording studio. By the time of his last Chess release, *The Back Door Wolf*, recorded in August 1973, the new owners of the company had still not learned their lesson. Here they mix in electric harpsichord, and prod Wolf to sing about current events, such as Watergate and space travel.

Wolf had suffered another heart attack in May 1971, and his kidney problems were so severe that he now needed regular dialysis treatments. His doctors urged him to retire from touring and public performances, but Wolf continued relentlessly, working clubs, festivals, even serving as opening act for second-tier rock stars and their sometimes unappreciative audiences. As one, small concession to his condition, he agreed to stay seated while performing—a far cry from his earlier days of prowling and crawling around the stage and nightclub—yet even this restriction proved unenforceable, and audiences found him rolling on the floor and putting on a spirited show for the patrons.

A car accident on New Year's morning 1973 further aggravated Wolf's kidney problems, forcing him to increase his dialysis treatments from once to three times per week. After each session, he felt good for perhaps a day, then soon began to flag. The mounting cost forced him to rely on Veterans Administration hospitals where he was entitled to free treatment—belated recompense for his short, disastrous stint in the military. By now his road trips needed to be restricted; he could only perform out of town if there was a nearby VA hospital. He would make no more records. Yet even under these daunting conditions, Wolf continued to work—at Joe's Place in Cambridge, Massachusetts, Max's and the Village Gate in New York, Grendel's Lair in Philadelphia, Paul's Mall in Boston, and elsewhere. During this same period, Wolf mounted a legal battle against Chess and ARC, the publisher of his music, over royalties. In time, Willie Dixon and Muddy Waters would initiate similar suits.

Wolf eventually won his court battle, but he would not live to reap the benefits. During 1975, his health continued to deteriorate, his eyesight faltered, his thinking often grew confused. He spoke frequently of his mother, and finally asked his wife Lillie to call her. In one of his tours of Mississippi a few years before, he had encountered Gertrude in Clarksdale, but when he tried to give her some money, she spat on it, threw it on the ground, and stepped on it. The embittered mother refused any gift tainted by the evil blues music that had corrupted her child. Wolf walked away in tears, and Sumlin later recalled how his boss, so often a paragon of toughness, sobbed all the way to the band's next stop in Memphis. Now Lillie Burnett phoned Gertrude and tried to convince her to come visit her son in his final days. Gertrude listened to the message, but made no response. A moment later, a man's voice came on the line, telling Lillie that Wolf's mother refused to come back to the phone. After Wolf heard of this, he no longer asked about his mother.

On January 7, 1976, the doctors diagnosed a brain tumor, and suggested that Wolf's only chance of survival would be an immediate operation—although the condition of his heart made such a procedure highly risky. The operation took place the following day, but Wolf's heart failed during surgery, and the team struggled to revive him with a heart pump and resuscitator. The doctors kept his heart beating through this intervention, but saw no chance of Wolf recovering. After conferring with family, the doctors turned off the equipment that kept their patient alive. Chester Burnett died at 3:00 p.m. on January 10, the cause of death attributed to metastatic brain carcinoma.

A memorial service was conducted six days later, on a bone-chilling Chicago day. Despite the freezing weather, the funeral chapel was overwhelmed with a crowd that spilled outside, and the city was forced to close off the street. More than ten thousand people came to view the body of Chicago's fallen bluesman. Television monitors were set up outside for those who could not get into the building to pay their respects to the great Howlin' Wolf.

For all his acclaim, Wolf's record sales had been modest by the standards of popular music. Only one of his albums—the London sessions, helped by the prominence of his rocker cohorts—had ever reached the *Billboard* top 200 list, and only five of his many singles sold well enough to make that periodical's national R&B charts. Yet Wolf's indirect influence would prove incalculable, not just in the blues world, but even more in the wider sphere of contemporary music, where British rockers, Seattle grunge bands, on-the-fringe experimentalists like Captain Beefheart, singer-songwriters like Tom Waits, even Wolfman Jack, that performance artist disguised as a radio deejay, would all partake in the lupine legacy. The Rolling Stones sold far more copies of their version of "The Red Rooster" than Wolf ever did with his. The Yardbirds and the Animals and Soundgarden brought "Smokestack Lightnin'" to countless fans who never knew Wolf's original. Jim Morrison and the Doors did the same with "Back Door Man," just as Koko Taylor did with "Wang Dang Doodle," and Cream with "Spoonful"—along with Stevie Ray Vaughan, Led Zeppelin, Jimi Hendrix, Rod Stewart, Jeff Beck, and others who covered Wolf songs. The list could go on and on, many of the most distinct and original stylists of the last several decades drawing inspiration from Howlin' Wolf in shaping their own original musical personas.

His tombstone refers to him simply as Chester Burnett, and only the engraved images of a guitar and harmonica remind visitors of the man's career as Howlin' Wolf. Yet the nickname told all. The wolf has been a potent symbol throughout human history, but the symbol has always conveyed such contradictory, such paradoxical beliefs. In Native American cultures, and other traditional societies, the wolf is the pathfinder, the spirit teacher of new ideas, yet also the antagonist that terrorizes the community. The wolf is a creature of instinct and violent impulse, but also crafty and intelligent, operating from sly plans and careful reasoning. The wolf is to be feared as the silent attacker, yet also pitied as the lonesome outcast howling at the moon. And, in dream psychology, taming the wolf of our nocturnal visions represents nothing less than channeling our own tumultuous emotions into world-building and inner healing. For American music, Howlin' Wolf was all of these: the trailblazer, the aggressor, the cunning interloper, the teacher, the reconciler, but above all, the sad and mournful voice we still hear wailing into the dark.

B.B. King

chapter ten

riding with the king

1. dust my broom

The grandeur of the Delta blues during the middle years of the twentieth century came not merely from a growing appreciation of its past—after all, many traditional forms of music have found their adherents and celebrants—but even more from a surprising recognition of its varied futures. Here was an intriguing paradox: how could a style of performance captivate one set of fans for its evocation of old-time ways, and impress another group as a blueprint for new sounds and attitudes never before seen? But the very simplicity and malleability of the blues structure allowed this freedom, ensured its adaptation. In the Darwinian world of the entertainment industry, where survival of the fittest is practiced on a weekly basis with each new release of the *Billboard* charts, the blues thrived through its rugged, cast-iron constitution, immune to the predators who picked off the more effete stylings of Cold War pop music.

Everywhere one looked, the intoxicating spirits of the Delta were being poured into capacious, new bottles. When music critic Nat Hentoff first heard Elvis Presley on the radio, he was convinced that he was listening to Mississippi guitarist Arthur "Big Boy" Crudup, who had made his reputation around Clarksdale before journeying to Chicago, circa 1939. Presley's starting point was so close to Crudup's end point that fine distinctions, at the time, between Delta blues and Memphis rock were almost too subtle to define. Ike Turner and Sam Cooke, both Clarksdale natives—if soundscapes were as tangible as buildings, grand pyramids and skyscrapers would rise high above the 38614 zip code—would also draw on their Delta roots in cutting through the complacencies of the hit parade with insistent, new melodies and grooves. At midcentury, Robert Johnson was largely forgotten, an obscure name for all but the most obsessive record collectors; but another Mississippi musician, Elmore James, dusted off Johnson's "Dust My Broom," translated it into the language of the electric guitar, and enjoyed a stunning hit. Other native sons of Mississippi would have an even greater impact on popular genres: Little Milton and Bo Diddley, and in an overpowering torrent, the great Presley himself, a white boy born in a humble two-room home in Tupelo in 1935, who would channel the power of the Delta idiom into a new form of performance art, and bring it places where no black man was allowed to go in these years. But even if we take for granted the impact of the Delta tradition on the musical ambitions of Memphis, Chicago, New York, and Los Angeles, we are left in amazement by a world-changing sound born and bred in Liverpool, England, which turned to Muddy Waters and Howlin' Wolf for inspiration, borrowing from their down-home melodies to transform everything in its path. Yes, the venerable heritage of the Delta blues may have been old news by the midcentury mark, but over the next twenty years it would work grand miracles that even Charley Patton and Robert Johnson, in their most visionary moments, could never have foreseen.

Arthur Crudup was an unlikely instigator of the rock-and-roll idiom, yet Elvis recorded several of his songs and developed his own Ed Sullivan–shocking, jailhouse-rocking approach at least in partial emulation of the older bluesman. But Crudup's whole career seemed to move according to a larger destiny in which chance—or perhaps that even more mystical pixie dust the blues singers called *mojo*—outweighed all the best laid plans of Forest, Mississippi's, most celebrated guitarist. Born in 1905, Crudup spent his youth in various rural occupations, and found musical expression only in the confines of the church choir. He gave no early signs of a special affinity for the blues, and did not learn guitar until the age of thirty-two. As such, Crudup missed the great wave of blues recording during the late 1920s, and refined his craft at a later date, when allegiance to the country blues was a one-way ticket to obscurity for a working musician. When he arrived in Chicago, Crudup held no starry-eyed dreams of stardom; mere survival was a pressing enough concern. His break came when he was living in a packing crate beneath an L-train track, and earning spare change performing for pedestrians. Destiny intervened in the person of Lester Melrose, the legendary mover and shaker in the highest spheres of Chicago blues, who heard Crudup and signed him to the prestigious RCA-Bluebird label.

Crudup's first recordings give little promise of important things to come. Long after Robert Johnson sang of the metaphorical virtues of his Terraplane, the high-performance automobile that set numerous records for power and speed during the Great Depression, Crudup was still asserting the superiority of his "coal black mare," drawing on thematic material that had struck listeners as old-fashioned when the first country blues guitarists had recorded during the 1920s, and now seemed positively anachronistic. Crudup's guitar playing never dazzled; he kept mostly to barebones, on-the-beat chords that circled through the standard twelve-bar form. Yet his singing was smoothly insinuating, gliding in relaxed, mellifluous phrases over these simple harmonic structures. Crudup boasted a powerful voice—he would have been a stand-out blues shouter in the days before amplification—but his sound never became clamorous, never lost its inherent sweetness even at volume levels that would have left other singers barking and braying.

Crudup's style slowly evolved during the course of the decade. At a follow-up session from 1942, he switched to electric guitar, although his manner of playing the instrument still kept true to the traditions of the country blues. During the mid-1940s, his singing often took on a more insistent quality, pushing the beat rather than lingering behind it; sometimes he clipped his phrases, adopting mannerisms we associate with R&B or later rock stylings. Crudup's version of "Dirt Road Blues" from 1945 is a revelation in this regard. The basic material of the song draws from Tommy Johnson's 1928 recording of "Big Road Blues," but Crudup starts rocking and rolling from the outset, and in the second chorus shifts into "That's All Right"—destined to be a Crudup classic, recorded in its own right the following year, and

later a hit single for Elvis—before returning to Johnson's road anthem. The
whole song proceeds in this schizophrenic manner, jumping ahead into the
rock idiom, returning to the Delta tradition, all backed by a clangorous,
abrasive guitar. If the blues, as Muddy Waters would later assert, "had a baby
and they named the baby rock & roll," this song could very well have been
played during the unholy coupling.

Crudup benefited little from the rock revolution he helped ignite. He
battled with Melrose over royalties, and eventually returned to Mississippi,
where he made money for a time as a bootlegger. Although he toured and
recorded during the late 1940s and early 1950s, Crudup never found a large
audience, and he had mostly abandoned the musician's life by the mid-
1950s. He gravitated to the menial farm labor that had supported him long
before he had learned to play the blues, even while Elvis exposed millions
of new fans to Crudup's music. He returned to the stage in the 1960s, and
found his niche in the blues revival movement of the period, even bringing
his act overseas to England and Australia. He continued performing until
his death in 1972, having firmly established his reputation as one of the
seers of the blues idiom, whose prescient recordings blazed the trail for a
later generation of megastars.

In 1949, Crudup had revived "Dust My Broom," the Robert Johnson
song that would become a runaway hit for Elmore James three years later.
In an odd bit of emulation, spurred by record label rivalries, Crudup would
later record under the name Elmer James for the Trumpet label in Jackson,
Mississippi. Crudup readily expressed admiration for the younger guitarist. "Now I wish I could sit down and play guitar like Elmore," he told an
interviewer. "To tell you the truth, I met a whole lot of people playin' guitar
and could really play most anythin' you wanted, but I have never run into
another man could play a bottleneck like Elmore plays it. That's the truth."

The Trumpet label, during its half-decade history, attempted to resurrect
H. C. Speir's approach from the 1920s. Lillian McMurry's introduction to the
music industry, like Speir's, came through retailing race records from a store
on North Farish Street in Jackson, Mississippi. And like Speir, McMurry was
struck by the potential for recording some of the state's homegrown talent,
a treasure trove near at hand for those who knew where to look. During the
label's brief run, McMurry was able to secure the services of, among others,
Sonny Boy Williamson II, Big Joe Williams, Arthur "Big Boy" Crudup, Little
Milton, Willie Love, even B.B. King in a cameo role. But McMurry's role in

advancing Elmore James's career stands out as the label's defining moment, just as its inability to capitalize on James's early success and develop it—as Chess did with Muddy Waters and Howlin' Wolf—may have determined Trumpet's ultimate failure.

McMurry had been introduced to James through Sonny Boy Williamson II, but the unassuming guitarist made little impression on her until he performed a spirited version of "Dust My Broom" during a rehearsal at McMurry's store. Surprised by the forcefulness of the vocal and the driving power of James's guitar attack, McMurry offered him a contract on August 4, 1951, and recorded the song during a Williamson session the following day. McMurry didn't like releasing cover versions of older blues material, and would likely have scrapped the project if she had known about the earlier recordings of "Dust My Broom" by Johnson and Crudup. Even with her support, the single almost died through lack of a flip side. After waiting for two months for James to come up with another performance to pair with "Dust My Broom," McMurry decided in desperation to use "Catfish Blues," recorded by Bobo Thomas, who adopted the pseudonym Elmo James for the occasion. The release of the recording at the close of 1951 proved the wisdom of McMurry's persistence. "Dust My Broom" rapidly climbed the charts, first in Dallas, and then spreading around the country, to Denver, to Oakland, to New Orleans, and Chicago. By April, it had reached the top ten of *Billboard*'s national R&B rankings.

Once again, a Mississippi guitarist was pointing the way to the future. In the late 1960s, the guitar would become a visceral instrument, felt as much as heard, but definitely heard too, with its cranked-up volume and raw, metallic clash-and-clang. The gentle six-string musings of its past would be all but forgotten, replaced by a new vision of the guitar as a high-energy work tool, brandished proudly in a campaign to assault the ears, move the feet, and penetrate the minds of those brave enough to listen. No one, circa 1951, embraced this vision with more certainty or daring than Elmore James. James takes the hints of 12/8 rhythm in Johnson's original, where they alternate with a dotted eighth boogie feel, and makes them more insistent, firing out a machine-gun triplet beat that would become a defining sound of the early rockers. Williamson's harmonica plays along, almost acting like a member of the rhythm section, sending out a stream of pulsations that mesh perfectly with the sound of the guitar. James's voice matches the energy of the band, staking out a brassy, assertive independence unusual in an unknown artist at his first leader date, but perfectly suited to the words of the song. "Dust my broom" signifies packing up one's bags and leaving—much like the biblical passages about shaking the dust off one's feet—and the song has come to symbolize in twelve-bar form the rambling ways of the blues musician. James captured the free-spirited wanderlust of the song perfectly; and at a time when many Mississippians were "dusting their broom" and heading to the more tolerant urban centers to the north, the music took on depths of meaning hardly foreseen by Robert Johnson.

James himself would take to heart the message of the song. In the spring of 1952, he moved to Chicago. Trumpet lost its rising star, and learned the hard lesson that the label's location might give it an advantage in finding talent, but put it at a distinct disadvantage in retaining it. Several companies were vying for James's services even before he left town, and his new affiliation with the Modern label found him in breach of his contract with McMurry, who instigated legal action to hold on to her wayward discovery. Yet only a few months into his supposed three-year agreement with Modern, James also signed with the Chess label, and the following year he recorded for Atlantic. Much like John Lee Hooker was doing during this same period, James was taking advantage of his newfound fame, and had few scruples about double-crossing the record companies whose own shady dealings were legendary. Trumpet, for its part, had no qualms about recording Crudup as Elmer James, in a move that may well have sent a signal to their departed artist—hey, we can play hardball, too!—but only at the price of deceiving its own customers.

James's fame is often seen solely in the light of this early hit performance. And James himself did much to encourage this portrait of the artist as a one-hit wonder, renaming his band the Broomdusters, and re-recording the same song, or close approximations, time and time again. Yet James, more than almost any other blues performer of his generation, had the potential to take his music in many different directions. James Meredith, in his memoir *Three Years in Mississippi*, describes Elmore James working the crowd into a frenzy at Mr. P's, a humble juke joint, with a thirty-minute version of "Shake Your Moneymaker." "There was no dance floor as such," Meredith writes; "the dance floor was everywhere." Meredith struggles to find the right category or general term to describe the performance, which represents a type of music, in his opinion, that "has not yet been documented by writing or record." He considers a number of possible labels—"gut-bucket, down-in-the-alley, back in the woods"—before settling on the simple, broad claim that "to me it is folk music of the highest order. . . . I have learned more about the Negro from listening to and digesting this music than from any other source."

But James was also unsurpassed at crafting a deeply felt blues tearjerker, like "The Sky Is Crying," "The Sun Is Shining," or "Sho' Nuff I Do." His sandpapery vocals, cracking and sometimes overwrought, the phrases sliding so slowly into the tonal center that the blue notes risk becoming mere dissonances, could easily convince you that James had stopped weeping just moments before the session began. But his fingers were as expressive as his singing. James's slide work on performances such as "Madison Blues" or "Done Somebody Wrong" exerted a tremendous influence on later guitarists. James also knew more about the subtleties of amplification than most sound engineers, having worked as a radio repairman and spent countless hours tinkering with and modifying his equipment. In the age of rock and fusion, he almost certainly would have been at the forefront of new developments.

But James died from a heart attack in 1963, at age forty-five. His promising future was curtailed, yet even his significant past risked being obscured by this early demise. James was a mystery man, having given only one documented interview during his career—and that little more than a casual chat during a break between sets with two visitors from France. Newspapers and magazines paid little attention to James during his life, and no U.S. periodical saw fit to offer an obituary at the time of his death. Many of the individuals, bandmates or friends, who knew James passed on before they could be interviewed, and those who were contacted often had little to offer, since even close acquaintances found James a private person, little prone to self-disclosure or autobiographical monologues. Even the music, James's most permanent legacy, tended to languish in obscurity. At the time of his death, most of his recordings were either out of print or sitting unreleased. Yet his cult following grew, and in time dedicated researchers—Marc Ryan, Ray Topping, Steve Franz, and others—rounded out the details, and made possible a more complete assessment of this seminal figure.

In the final years of Elmore James's life, the Chicago blues scene found itself revitalized by another new movement with strong Mississippi roots. The so-called West Side Sound drew on the rural electric blues tradition of Muddy Waters and Howlin' Wolf, but also found inspiration in the more fluid guitar stylings of B.B. King, the innovations of jazz, and the emerging sounds of rock and roll. With its insistent, danceable grooves, and its confident, unapologetic attitudes, the West Side Sound appealed to a younger audience, and seemed the perfect adaptation of the blues spirit to the developing sensibilities of the 1960s. Here, the acoustic bass was discarded in favor of the electric bass; the saxophone sometimes usurped the role previously held in blues bands by the harmonica; and amplification, even to the point of distortion, served as the inevitable calling card of this in-your-face and in-your-ears music.

Again, Mississippi exiles played a decisive role in taking the blues into this next phase of its evolution. Magic Sam, born as Sam Maghett in Grenada, Mississippi, in 1937, had moved to Chicago in 1950, and by the close of the decade was recording for the Cobra label. His *West Side Soul*, made for Delmark in 1967, stands out as a major landmark in modern blues and a defining statement of the West Side style, but Maghett had little opportunity to build on this success. In December 1969, he died of a heart attack at the age of thirty-two. A few months older than Magic Sam, Jimmy Dawkins hailed from Tchula, Mississippi, and arrived in Chicago in 1955, where he worked in a box factory and made music on a West Side street corner. But Dawkins gradually established himself as one of the most expressive guitarists on the local scene, and around the time of Maghett's death released his *Fast Fingers* on the Delmark label, which earned a "Grand Prix du Disque" and opened up opportunities for touring and further sessions. Other late sixties offerings from Mississippi natives active on the West Side—such as Otis Rush's *Mourning in the Morning* and Albert King's *Born Under a Bad Sign*—further reinforced the point that urban blues could still sound fresh and up-to-date during the Age of Aquarius.

The significance of the blues as a forerunner of rock makes for such a powerful, appealing story that we often risk missing out on the other great strides made by Delta artists at the midcentury mark. In time, the blues sensibility would filter into virtually all forms of popular music. At the close of the 1950s, Antonio Carlos Jobim's song "Desafinado" would help inaugurate the bossa nova movement in Brazil, and though the impressionistic harmonies might mask the blue notes in the melody, they could not hide the spiritual ties to idiomatic African-American music. The following decade, a whole host of other styles—Motown, reggae, even surf and modern folk—crafted unique, individual identities that could stand on their own, yet the

Delta tradition was an inescapable part of their genetic code. Soundtracks and commercial jingles drew on blues material, relying on it to set a mood, fill a space, sell a product. Youngsters at piano lessons found blues slipped into their songbooks, alongside the great German masters of classical music. The Delta legacy was no longer just one more genre, relegated to its own section in the record store. By fits and starts, it had infiltrated the other bins, transforming all other styles in its wake.

But the blues itself had to adapt as part of this process. Musicians working in other genres often could not assimilate the simple guitar vocabulary of, say, a Son House or John Lee Hooker, stylists whose contribution seemed a matter more of feeling than of notes and chords. They needed a different role model, a blues visionary who was as skilled playing single-note lines as in laying down harmonies and grooves. They needed a blues that could be elegant as well as raw; a blues that had learned the lessons of modern jazz, and could also blend seamlessly with pop, country, gospel stylings; a blues that felt at home in the juke joints, but wasn't out of place in tux and tails; a blues that could swing with a big band, glide over strings, or mess it up with just a bass and drums. In short, the music world needed one more towering Delta master. And it found it in the guise of a humble farmworker turned guitarist named Riley B. King.

2. listened harder than anyone in the history of listening

Albert Lee King had two inspirations for the first name of his baby boy, born on September 16, 1925, between Indianola and Greenwood in a house on the bank of Blue Lake. His dead brother Riley may have been first in his mind, but his employer, a white plantation owner named Jim O'Reilly, had been a fair boss to the elder King, and had helped secure a midwife for the delivery. So when the landowner asked Albert, shortly after the birth, what the boy would be named, he replied, "O'Reilly." In time the "O" was dropped—because the child didn't look Irish, Albert King quipped—and Reilly became Riley. The "B" never stood for anything, although in time, B.B. King, as the young musician became rechristened (the initials deriving from his nickname "Blues Boy") would come to stand for almost everything and anything having to do with postwar blues.

B.B. King's enormous influence—his blues licks went off patent long ago, and have been appropriated everywhere from garage bands to TV jin-

gles—should not obscure his role as the farsighted assimilator, the brilliant
synthesizer, the mastermind who heard the changes shaking up American
music at midcentury and instinctively knew which elements could bring the
blues to the next level. He became the great teacher, but only by first being a
great student. We have already seen how many Delta guitarists learned from
recordings, but none of them surpassed King for his sheer persistence at
the turntable. King would eventually amass a collection of thirty thousand
recordings—many later donated to the University of Mississippi. But even
as a youngster, he spent countless hours in attendance at his aunt Mima's
crank-up Victrola, a "machine that changed my life," he would later assert,
without a trace of exaggeration. Here King kindled his early devotion to the
music of Blind Lemon Jefferson and Lonnie Johnson—two of the greatest
early blues performers, but neither of them from the Delta. In time, King
would also learn from the great talents of his native soil, Robert Johnson
and Muddy Waters, and many others, but even these were experienced primarily through recordings.

To the historian of the Delta blues as a regional style, it is sobering to
contemplate how technology tended to eradicate the boundaries of time
and space almost from the first documented stirrings of the music. When
sketching the story of a rock band in Liverpool, for example, we accept that
their blues will be absorbed via recordings, but for a boy coming of age in
the Delta during the prewar years, the same forces are easy to underestimate. And with B.B. King, we need to be especially sensitive to influences
from afar.

There were many brilliant guitarists living within a few miles of the King
household, but none of them would have exposed the youngster to the fluid,
cosmopolitan stylings that he would discover in Lonnie Johnson's oeuvre.
Johnson, born at the close of the nineteenth century in New Orleans, liked
to refer to his music as "urban blues"—almost delighting in the refinements
that separated his performances from the rougher products of the Delta.
But he could easily have disdained the blues label entirely. Johnson was,
without question, one of the finest jazz guitarists of his generation, as testified by his recordings with Louis Armstrong and Duke Ellington, among
others, but perhaps demonstrated most clearly in his collaborations with
the white guitarist Eddie Lang, which are remarkable for both the music
they made and the racial barriers they preferred to ignore. In many ways,
Lonnie Johnson would prove to be a better role model for B.B. King than

either of the other Johnsons—Robert or Tommy—with deeper Delta ties. B.B. King would break through many barriers of his own and, like Lonnie Johnson, cross stylistic divides that few dared to traverse. For the destinations he had in mind, even the great legacies of the Delta masters were insufficient guides.

The sound of Blind Lemon Jefferson was more familiar to the youngster—this music reminded King of the songs he heard in the cotton fields. But other recordings in his aunt's collection would have been a revelation, opening up pathways to exciting spheres of music from far-distant worlds: the jazz performances of Duke Ellington; the classic blues of Bessie Smith and Ma Rainey; the country yodeling of the "Singing Brakeman" Jimmie Rodgers. Authentic Delta blues also were heard in the King household, especially when Booker "Bukka" White, King's mother's first cousin, visited his relations twice a year, at midsummer and Christmas time. White was a genuine recording star, whose "Shake 'Em On Down" was one of the most widely emulated recordings—in the Delta or elsewhere—when King was first beginning to listen to the blues.

Soon King aspired to do more than listen. Reverend Archie Fair, a visitor to the house who would bring along his guitar, taught the boy a few chords, and served as a countervailing influence to the famous blues-singing cousin. Fair explained that music was a precious gift, meant to express a higher love than the carnal sort celebrated in blues songs. Inspired by this mentor, King aimed to be a guitar-playing minister, and in his zeal began teaching younger children at Sunday School. But by the time King received his first guitar, a cherry red Stella purchased secondhand for fifteen dollars—an entire month's wages for the twelve-year-old, who earned his keep as a houseboy—his whole life had been infected with a bitter tragedy that put an end to his innocent childhood dreams.

In the early morning hours, on a winter day a few months after his ninth birthday, King was awakened by his grandmother. She traveled with the boy on a horse-drawn wagon to a distant shack where King's mother, only twenty-five years old, lay on her deathbed. Nora Ella King's eyes were misted over, and she could not see her child as he entered the room; she held out her hand, but lacked the strength to grasp his own. She told her son that she loved him, and that she would always be with him. King was taken away, and within a few hours, his mother was dead. His parents had already separated when he was four years old, and now he stayed in the care of his grandmother. But she too died a short while later. King was still just a boy when he found himself living alone in his grandmother's former home in Kilmichael, and earning his living as a farmworker.

His father came back into his life, unannounced, around the time King was fourteen. He told his son to pack up his belongings and load them in the back of the truck Albert King had borrowed for the day: they were heading to Lexington, some fifty miles away, where the youngster would meet his "new mama" as well as three stepsisters and a stepbrother. His new home had electricity and indoor plumbing—innovations so startling to the boy that he had to be shown, to his embarrassment, how to operate the flush handle on the toilet. The most miraculous piece of technology of all was the family radio. King enjoyed the country music on station WSM, but station WLAC, with its blues music and homegrown Delta fare, was even more to his liking.

King did not stay in Lexington for long. Perhaps he was overwhelmed by the rigid rules of home and school, or the uneasy dealings with a family mostly comprised of strangers, or the body of the black man he saw, one Saturday afternoon, hanging from a platform in the courthouse square—for whatever reason, King took off on his bicycle and, without telling anyone, returned to the humble cabin in Kilmichael. King only stayed here a short while before moving on, in 1942, in search of better wages on the cotton plantations of the Delta. On Johnson Barrett's farm, some eight miles outside of Indianola, the teenager developed a reputation for his determination and hard work. King claimed he once picked 480 pounds of cotton in a single day—enough fiber to make over 300,000 hundred-dollar bills, but which generated less than two dollars of pay for the youngster—and he also plowed, chopped wood, baled hay, and planted corn and soybeans.

King saved up twenty dollars to purchase a guitar, and joined a gospel group that modeled itself on the Golden Gate Quartet and the Dixie Hummingbirds. The group's honeyed harmonies made them welcome at many churches, although a few ministers cancelled performances when they learned that the musicians planned to bring a guitar into the sanctuary of the Lord. King's group called itself the Famous St. John Gospel Singers, but the performers never achieved the renown announced in their name. Their finest moment came when they were enlisted to perform on a Greenwood radio station, singing gospel songs and promoting a local furniture store. Yet King nurtured his ambitions—he was determined to find fame, one way or another—and soaked up the music that came his way.

The sound of the blues was pervasive in the Delta, as dependable and cherished as the cotton crop. King found, when he played music on street corners, that he made more money with the blues than with any of his religious songs. But King also heard jazz, on the airwaves, and in person when Count Basie played in Indianola. The boy was too young to gain admission, but he pressed up against the building in order to look through a crack in the side wall of Johnny Jones's Night Spot, where the *truly* famous—legends such as Jimmy Rushing, Lester Young, Freddie Green, and the Count himself—deigned to grace the humble stage. "I believe I listened harder than anyone in the history of listening," King later asserted. On separate occasions, the same venue offered the youngster an invigorating dose of Jay McShann, Pete Johnson, Aleck "Rice" Miller, Robert Lockwood, and other celebrated performers. But a far greater shock came when King peered one day through the viewer of a ten-cent vending machine, a Delta novelty that played a grainy film clip of a black guitarist performing in the midst of a white swing band led by Benny Goodman. King never forgot the impression that Charlie Christian made on him that day. He didn't know which represented the greater achievement: the dazzling single-note lines and complex harmonies Christian played on his guitar, or the symbolic resonance of an African-American musician working his magic as part of the most celebrated ensemble in the nation. In time, King would benefit from both lessons.

But for the most part, these were uneventful years. King put in thousands of miles following the mule-drawn plow—six days a week for half the year, sometimes for twelve hours in a day. Unwilling to lose the skills of such a dedicated laborer, King's boss Johnson Barrett arranged for an exemption from military service. The local planters had an agreement with the Selective Service that allowed certain essential workers to be released from military duty because of their importance in providing materials needed by the troops. King also married Martha Denton around this time, a legal commitment that may have been spurred, at least in part, by his boss's advice that a wife at home would help in securing his exemption from the Army. If King nurtured dreams of leaving the Delta and realizing his musical aspirations in a major city, he put them on hold during the war years, when combat in Europe or island-hopping in the Pacific loomed as the most likely alternative to farming.

By 1946, King had no more excuses for remaining in Mississippi. He bragged to his fellow workers that he would one day be a famous musi-

cian, but they teased and taunted him in return. Still he hesitated, and may
have stayed on the farm indefinitely if he had not been involved in a tractor
accident that destroyed part of a barn. Fearing the anger of his boss, and
the heavy financial penalty that lay ahead, King decided to leave before the
damage was discovered. He hurried home, grabbed his guitar and all his
money, a meager $2.50. And without telling anyone—not his wife, not his
fellow workers, certainly not Mr. Johnson—he decided to make his way to
Memphis.

3. sniffed around in Memphis

The migration of the blues from Mississippi to Chicago has often been celebrated as a coming-of-age for this simple folk music, now thrust upon the
stage in the largest metropolis in Middle America. But artistic movements
rarely follow strict itineraries in their travels; and other destinations, detours,
and stopping-off places intrude into our history of this music. Above all,
Memphis can stake a valid claim as the pathway by which this country-bred
music was channeled into the wider streams of global pop music. Trying to
encapsulate this history in an aphorism, Peter Guralnick has quipped that
"the blues came out of Mississippi, sniffed around in Memphis and then
settled in Chicago where it is most likely it will peacefully live out the rest
of its days."

Indeed, the final destination of this tradition is more the world-
conquering beat of rock and roll rather than the urban blues of Chicago,
the journey moving from Son House to the house of Sun Records then on
to the great globe itself, the sounds rising from the Delta lands finally residing in the deft hands of countless aspiring rock guitarists. But Memphis still
plays a decisive role as the linchpin in this alternative version of the dissemination of blues music. In truth, Memphis always had its blues, and never
really relinquished them. We have already seen how W. C. Handy developed
his own skills as a blues composer in Memphis. The most famous blues
hymn about *any* city, Handy's "St. Louis Blues," was composed not in St.
Louis, but in a rented room off of Beale Street in Memphis. But even before
this, Frank Stokes, one of the earliest documented blues singers—Stokes
was three years older than Charley Patton and fourteen years senior to Son
House—made his home in Memphis and established himself as a familiar
presence on the local music scene.

Stokes was playing on the city streets at the turn of the century, and for the next half century he earned money entertaining at various social functions, dances and picnics and other events where an appreciative audience might congregate. Some have suggested that better known performers, as diverse as W. C. Handy and Jimmie Rodgers, learned from Stokes's example. Stokes, for his part, never secured more than the smallest taste of fame and fortune, and labored as a blacksmith for more than three decades. Later in life, he roamed farther from this home base, and we hear of him performing in traveling shows or playing in Clarksdale—an odd destination given that community's surfeit of notable guitarists, where constant exports, not imports, of blues talent were required. Stokes's musical career ramped down a few years before his death, from a stroke, in 1955. He was a largely forgotten figure at the time of his passing, but had he survived another decade he almost certainly would have been celebrated by a new generation of fans as a founding father of the Memphis blues tradition.

The pathway from the heart of the Delta to Memphis is a short one, a few train stops away, or less than a day's journey by horse. But even this modest change in latitude seemed to affect the temperament of the blues. The languorous melancholy of the Delta is replaced by a sunnier disposition; the dark corners of the music are cast in sudden illumination; songs aim to move the audience's feet even more than their feelings, and a holiday spirit prevails, an escape from drudgery and despair. We can hear these qualities in Stokes's recordings from the late 1920s. Stokes's eleven-bar blues, "How Long," seems to hark back to an earlier age, when blues co-existed on familiar terms with more diatonic folk material. Stokes just as often leaves the blues form far behind, as in his elaborate patter song "You Shall," which seems more akin to the declamations of preachers and street barkers than to the music of the plantations and juke joints. But even when he digs deeply into the twelve-bar blues, Stokes softens its rough edges, and makes us forget the field hollers and levee camp songs that contributed to the music's evolution. In his hands, the blues gains consciousness of itself as a performance art, and the drive for self-expression is now tempered by an equally powerful desire to entertain and divert.

Furry Lewis, our next Memphis blues pioneer, was born in Greenwood, Mississippi, probably before the turn of the century. Several different birth years have been offered, from 1893 through 1899 (the Social Security Death Index tells us 1895), although the March 6 birthday is generally accepted.

Lewis's late-in-life fame shows us the kind of reception Stokes might have enjoyed had he lived longer. In his final years, Lewis was fêted on *The Tonight Show*, opened for the Rolling Stones, and, in general, achieved a celebrity that stood in stark contrast to his earlier obscurity. Lewis had apprenticed as a performer in medicine shows, but his rambling days were curtailed by a devastating 1916 accident, when he lost a leg while trying to hop a freight train. A job offer in 1923 from the Memphis Department of Sanitation gave Lewis a secure position that he held on to for the next forty-five years. Lewis seized the opportunities to record that came his way in the late 1920s, and though he sang about romantic failure and low-down feelings, he was more renowned as master of the celebratory blues, perhaps most notably in his braggadocious "I Will Turn Your Money Green," where he promises to show his woman more money than "Rockefeller ever seen." Despite his brief notoriety as a recording artist, and the claims of this song, Lewis held on to his day job—a move that proved prescient when the Great Depression toppled the hopes and dreams of musicians far more famous than him. He would not record again for another three decades. But Lewis, in his sixties, boasted a voice as strong, fingers as sure, a slide technique as expressive, as in his thirties, and he made the most of the performing and recording opportunities that came his way in these later years, before his death in 1981.

The recordings of Stokes and Lewis still hold the power to delight and uplift us today. But the exuberant sensibility of African-American music in Memphis is perhaps best experienced in the legacy of the jug bands that flourished there in the 1920s and 1930s. Even in the midst of the Depression, a half dozen jug ensembles worked the city and its environs, and both black and white audiences flocked to hear them. African-American communities had long demonstrated tremendous ingenuity in extracting music from the humblest household items—the baling or broom wire transformed into a diddley bow; the bottleneck or pocket knife adopted to play slide guitar; the various other makeshift string instruments, constructed from cigar boxes, pie pans, shoeboxes, washtubs, and other extraneous items. The jug band took this celebration of the everyday to a new level. The 1902 Sears, Roebuck catalog demanded $1.75 for a banjo and $2.75 for a guitar—half a week's wages for an unskilled laborer at the time—but a jug could be purchased for a mere twelve cents. In the hands, or rather face, of a sufficiently breathy *artiste*, this capacious receptacle could produce notes or phrases that, in other bands, might be played by bass or tuba. The neck of the jug served as a resonator, amplifying with a pleasant accompanying buzz the tones blown across the aperture. Of course, the jug required more effusive melodic riches to ornament its simple offerings. But instead of the cornets and trombones that graced the New Orleans ensembles of this same era, we find kazoos and harmonicas filling comparable roles in the jug band, swinging their bluesy phrases in syncopated splendor over the ground beat. At the heart of the music, offering harmonic support and rhythmic momentum, one or two string instruments invariably prevailed—typically guitar or banjo or mandolin—holding the performances together, and imparting a touch of respectability to ensembles that otherwise disdained any instrument that might be found in the parlors or music rooms of the patrician class.

Memphis cannot claim to be the birthplace of the jug band. The early Louisville tradition, which dates back to the turn of the century, is far better documented, and other cities no doubt shared a fascination with these colorful ensembles. Gus Cannon maintained that he introduced the jug band to Memphis. A decade older than Stokes, Cannon was born on September 12, 1883, in Red Banks, Mississippi, but he was in his mid-forties when his recording career took off in earnest—although he claimed to have made primitive cylinder or disk recordings during the early years of the century. Cannon devised a harness, utilitarian in function and delightful to see, that allowed him to perform on the jug or kazoo while playing the banjo. He was self-sufficient as a one-man band, but Cannon often worked with a guitarist and sometimes a harmonica player as well. Noah Lewis, a Tennessee native twelve years younger than Cannon, filled the latter role admirably, adding to the spectacle with his trick of playing two harmonicas simultaneously, one with the mouth, the other with the nose. The recordings made by Cannon's Jug Stompers from 1928 through 1930 fail to convey the visual delight of these ingenious performers at work, but they effectively capture the carefree ambiance of the music, a perpetual holiday stroll in sound, invariably taken at a relaxed, ambling pace.

Like Furry Lewis, Cannon found himself back in the limelight in the 1960s after decades of obscurity. "He was the yardman for an anthropology professor," recalled Jim Dickinson, who met Cannon around this time. "Gus had told this family that he used to make records and he had been on RCA and they'd say, 'Yeah Gus, sure, cut the grass.'" But when the Rooftop Singers enjoyed a surprise number one hit in 1963 with their version of Cannon's "Walk Right In," the eighty-year-old yardman found that he was a celebrity of sorts. Journalists, musicians, and fans now walked right into his life, seeking firsthand exposure to this elder statesman of the Memphis musical scene. Cannon obliged them with songs and stories, and even a charming comeback recording, *Walk Right In*, which finds him in the company of Milton Roby on washboard and Will Shade on jug. But even this late flowering of Cannon's talent seemed destined to remain hidden from view. Only five hundred copies of the LP were pressed at the time of initial release, and it was not until its reissue on CD, years after Cannon's death in 1979, that this magical music became widely available to fans of the jug band idiom.

Back in the 1920s, Shade's Memphis Jug Band had been even better known than Cannon's Jug Stompers. Shade handled the business arrangements for his jug ensemble, led the rehearsals, played guitar adequately, sang even better, could handle a jug with aplomb, and deserves our respect as perhaps the most underrated of the first generation of blues harmonica players. Ralph Peer of Victor discovered the Memphis Jug Band in 1927 and recorded the group at a temporary studio set up in the McCall Building on February 24—the first commercial recording session held in the state of Tennessee. The band's popularity led to a number of follow-up sessions, continuing into the early 1930s, when the novelty of the jug band sound had worn off, and the economy's precipitous decline forced record companies to retrench. Shade tried to adapt the jug band concept to the changing tastes of the times, but rarely with much commercial success. His 1963 recording with Cannon marked a final moment of glory for the Memphis pioneer. Shade died of pneumonia three years later.

The lessons of Stokes, Lewis, Cannon, and Shade are sobering ones. The great pioneers of African-American music in Memphis, their careers were marked by long dry spells, decades passed in draining day jobs, and belated acclaim that either arrived posthumously or so late in their lives that they hardly had strength to enjoy it. Little wonder that many musicians followed the lead of W. C. Handy, and left Memphis for more promising opportunities elsewhere. For Mississippi musicians, Memphis—and increasingly West Memphis, across the river in Arkansas, during the postwar years—was best viewed as a way station, not a final destination, in any career that had potential to reach the highest rung. The arrival of Sam Phillips and his Memphis Recording Service in 1950, which would serve as the foundation for the celebrated Sun label, should have changed all this. But Phillips found himself developing million-dollar talent for the major labels in the larger cities: Elvis Presley moving to RCA, who purchased his Sun recording contract in 1955; Johnny Cash signing with Columbia in 1958; Howlin' Wolf settling down with Chess; Jerry Lee Lewis reviving his career with Mercury. The talent that passed through Memphis was staggering; the talent that stayed and thrived negligible by comparison.

When B.B. King arrived in Memphis in 1946, he went looking for his cousin Booker "Bukka" White, the bluesman whose 1937 "Shake 'Em On Down" stood out as one of the most imitated Delta standards, and whose March 1940 sessions rank among the finest landmarks of the blues idiom. But in Memphis, such achievements were only a ticket to occasional gigs supplemented by—that venerable local tradition—a tiring day job. White now worked as a "fit-up man" for the Newberry Equipment Company, a position that required him to set out and prepare the large pieces of steel that the welders made into tanks for the U.S. military. White helped his cousin make contacts on the local music scene, but offered more immediate help by securing him a job at Newberry as a welder at sixty dollars per week. White provided King with a place to live, purchased a new Gibson guitar for his cousin, and also co-signed on notes to finance the acquisition of an amplifier and speaker.

King stayed in Memphis for less than a year before reasons to return to Indianola—to see his wife Martha; to make amends with Johnson Barrett; to reunite with his gospel group—proved too hard to resist. He found himself once more sharecropping and driving a tractor, and paid off his debt for his earlier tractor mishap. But he also put aside money, hoping to embark on one more attempt to establish himself on the Memphis scene. Toward the end of 1948, King made his move. This time he headed to West Memphis, where he waylaid Sonny Boy Williamson #2, who was then promoting a tonic called Hadocol on KWEM—the same station that would soon help boost Howlin' Wolf to local prominence. King managed to convince Williamson to let him sing a number on the radio, and the modest taste of fame—and opportunities to gig—that it produced were a revelation to the young guitarist. As a result, he was determined to secure a radio show of his own.

4. how blue can you get?

The next interlude in B.B. King's personal odyssey has often been recounted, celebrated as the turning point that took a determined young man and started him on the path to stardom. Hearing that a new radio station, WDIA, based in Memphis, was featuring black music on the airwaves, King took a bus downtown, bringing his guitar along in hopes of securing an impromptu audition. But the day was cold and rainy, and when King arrived in Memphis, he discovered that the radio station was located some twenty blocks away. He hugged the guitar close to his body, the strings pressed against his chest, trying to protect his instrument from the damaging rain. King made a sorry sight when he finally arrived, but his ambitions were undimmed by the inclement weather, and he announced to deejay Nat D. Williams that he wanted to be on radio and make records. Williams explained that WDIA didn't make records, only played them; if he wanted to be on the radio, he needed to talk to Bert Ferguson, the station owner who made programming decisions.

Ferguson gave King an audition on the spot, and enlisted him to promote one of the station's new advertisers, Pepticon—a powerful elixir consisting of five minerals, six vitamins, and (perhaps most important for its loyal users) 12 percent alcohol—which competed directly with Sonny Boy's Hadocol. A jingle was quickly composed for the young guitarist to sing on air:

Pepticon, Pepticon, sure is good.
You can get it anywhere in your neighborhood.

And B.B. King left station WDIA that day as the star of his own ten-minute daily radio show.

King proved to be a dedicated advocate for Pepticon, and for his own career. He would sometimes spend his Saturdays out with the company sales reps, and perform the Pepticon jingle from the back of a flatbed truck. King was soon given more time on the radio, allowed to spin records for listeners near and far—WDIA's strengthened signal now carried as far as New Orleans on a clear night. He gigged regularly, and every week without fail entered the amateur night competition at the Palace Theater on Beale Street, but never once won the first prize of five dollars. Despite his constant failure in this contest, King was enjoying a degree of fame in the area. He was known over the airwaves as the "Beale Street Blues Boy," sometimes shortened to "Blues Boy," and eventually abbreviated to the simple "B.B." that would become his lasting identity.

Martha had joined him soon after he started his show at WDIA, and when King had a chance to make his first recordings for Bullet Records his most heartfelt performance came on the song "Miss Martha King," written for her. The record opens with a few characteristic solo blues licks on the guitar, before settling into a demonstration of King's ample vocal range, especially his searing power in the upper register. But these early releases did little to expand King's audience beyond Memphis, and Bullet was soon out of business. Yet Ike Turner had alerted the Bihari brothers, owners of Modern Records, to the up-and-coming artist making his name in the Memphis area, and when they came to town they arranged to meet with King. Before long, King was recording for the Biharis at the famed Memphis Recording Service, with Sam Phillips working the control board. The Bihari-Phillips relationship would not last long, but King's allegiance to the former would endure most of the decade, and the guitarist would rise to stardom on the roster of the Biharis' RPM label.

In later years fans would honor B.B. King as the representative of a time-honored blues tradition, a walking-and-talking museum piece drenched in the authentic heritage of the most primal style of African-American music. But in the early 1950s, King was anything but a traditionalist, and his records often strayed from the styles prized by blues purists. Muddy Waters had deeper blues roots than King at the time, as did Howlin' Wolf and John Lee Hooker and a legion of the other urban bluesmen from the Delta. These other musicians reminded listeners of their rural heritage with every note they played. But B.B. King strayed from his geographical roots, sometimes adopting the persona of a modern rhythm-and-blues performer—at his audition for WDIA he chose to imitate Louis Jordan, that master of the slick jump blues—just as he also knew how to mimic the smooth pop stylings of Nat Cole or adopt the mannerisms of a jazz artist. Moreover, King was a gifted ballad singer with a flair for dramatic delivery, and also knew how to shout it to the back of the house over the loudest big band. Yet, with only the slightest modifications in his style, King might have been a rock-and-roll icon, a teen idol with a crossover audience. He was only a year older than Chuck Berry, and a few months younger than Bill Haley, and with his stage presence and guitar licks, King would have been a formidable rival to the first generation of rockers. In truth, none of the Delta pioneers were as versatile as B.B. King, and while other musicians often played the down-home blues because they couldn't do much else, King faced an abundance of choices.

At this stage of his career, King may have learned the most from T-Bone Walker, a native Texan transplanted to the West Coast, who shook up the blues world during World War II and the years that followed, stirring the pot with his endless repertoire of licks and figures. Walker did more than anyone to change blues guitar from a rhythmic to a melodic instrument, and make electricity an essential part of the mix. Walker could take a jazzy solo, sing a ballad, blend effortlessly with horns, swing or rock or boogie, or just stick to the basic, unadulterated blues, going wherever the spirit moved him. In short, Walker broke through all the stultifying barriers that kept blues performers in a cultural ghetto, held apart from the other currents of American popular music at the midcentury mark. Many others benefited from the path-breaking efforts of this pioneer, but no one more so than B.B. King. Here the younger guitarist found not just tasty blues licks, but also a compass that allowed him to navigate through currents far afield from the confluence of the Yazoo and Mississippi, and yet still feel always at home, the blues vocabulary no longer staying down on the farm as a regional style, but proving to be a passport that allowed access across all musical borders and boundary lines.

King's first hit for the Biharis, "Three O'Clock Blues," showed what he had learned from Walker. King introduces the piece with a soulful single-note guitar line that settles into a moody ballad, at a 65 beats per minute tempo, slower than a lover's heartbeat. The harmonies—as well as the title—clearly indicate that the song follows a standard blues structure, but the performance probably struck most listeners at the time as a classic tear-jerker, a slow dance right before the band packs up and heads home. King pulls out all the emotional stops: the song's lyrics start out as an insomniac's lament, but end up with a weepy farewell more suited to a suicide note. In the middle, King offers a wake-the-dead solo, somewhat out of keeping with the mournful attitude presented by the lyrics, but clear evidence that this balladeer could wipe away his tears and play a mean guitar before ending it all.

The recording made for an unlikely hit. The song was a retread, borrowed from a 1948 Lowell Fulson record. The audio quality was a step down from the standards set by Sam Phillips—the Biharis had separated from him by now, and were forced to use a room at the Memphis YMCA as an improvised studio. King himself was still an unknown commodity outside of Memphis, and his previous records had shown little promise of building a national following. But the dreamy despair of "Three O'Clock Blues" touched the listeners' heartstrings. The record ranked as the number one R&B song in the nation at the close of 1951, and stayed seventeen weeks on the charts.

King's "You Know I Love You" also reached the top spot on the charts in September 1952. This was another weepy ballad, with no obvious ties to the blues idiom. The performance sounds saccharine and hollow, almost as though electric guitar lines and background vocals were left out by mistake. Ike Turner tinkles desperately at the piano, trying to fill the void. But King's voice carries tremendous authority, even on this piece of fluff, assaulting the high notes of the final chorus with ease. Record buyers must have again found solace in channeling their own romantic frustrations through King's paradoxical persona, which conveyed extraordinary strength even when the lyrics wallow in a crying-in-my-pillow malaise. But before fans could type-cast King as a sentimental fool, he hit the top of the charts again with "Please Love Me," a raw blues workout on electric guitar which borrowed heavily from Elmore James and Robert Johnson.

Audiences could be forgiven for wondering who the real B.B. King might be. And future releases did little to answer the question. Was he the master of the dance beat that propelled "Woke Up This Morning," which reached number 3 on the charts in 1953? Was he the proto-rocker who burnt brightly on "Please Hurry Home," recorded later that year in Cincinnati, a song which peaked at number 4? Was he the soulful blues guitarist who pushed "You Upset Me Baby" to the top of the rankings in 1954? Was he the hard-luck-and-troubles storyteller who made "Ten Long Years," recorded a year later, into a top ten hit? Or the master of the deep, slow blues who thrust "Sweet Little Angel" into the number 6 slot during the summer of 1956? Or finally the doo-wop master who glides over "On My Word of Honor," which reached number 3 a few weeks later? In truth, King was all these and more. His guitar could be sweet or hot, a gospel testifying in tongues or a devil's celebration of more carnal impulses. His voice was even more flex-ible, strong in all registers, whether the lyrics were sheer poetry or mere doggerel. By the mid-1950s, everybody knew what B.B. King *could* do, but what he really *wanted* to do was another matter completely.

Yet no one could dispute King's popularity. The success of his records made it possible for him to tour anywhere in the country, and King's deter-mination transformed the road life into a personal imperative. In 1955, he bought a bus to transport his band on their incessant touring, and the fol-lowing year he played an astonishing three hundred forty-two one-night stands! Even King couldn't maintain this pace, but he rarely fell much below it. For a period of more than half century, he would average two hundred seventy-five concerts per year—an extraordinary test of stamina and endur-ance which has brought him face-to-face with millions of fans at more than ten thousand engagements during his storied career. These performances have encompassed the lowest of the lows and the highest of the highs. King has performed at the White House and the Vatican, but adapted just as easily to Cook County Jail or San Quentin, where he recorded two of his finest live albums.

Often the humblest engagements were the most memorable. At a gig in Twist, Arkansas, the music was interrupted when a kerosene space heater was knocked over during a fight between two patrons, who were battling over the affections of a woman. The resulting conflagration required an immediate evacuation of the room, but King returned when he realized that his prized guitar was still inside. Dodging the flames, King retrieved the instrument, but berated himself silently for his foolhardiness. When he learned that the fight had started because of a woman named Lucille, King decided to rechristen his guitar with that name, to commemorate the event and remind himself to avoid such crazy heroics in the future. The name stuck, and King has gone through countless versions of Lucille, the mysterious woman embodied in his Gibson guitar; she has become almost as famous as King himself, a talisman and trivia answer well known to blues fans.

The road and its many attendant temptations had led to the end of King's first marriage in 1952. He married Sue Hall in 1958, who resisted the role of stay-at-home wife. She often joined her husband on tour, keeping an eye on his business affairs, and the other eye on the lookout for less savory affairs. On the rare occasions when both Mr. and Mrs. King were at home, their new residence was South Pasadena in the Los Angeles area, where the guitarist enjoyed the temperate weather and the proximity of the recording industry. But the new location also meant that King was often working even when he was home. Most of his sessions now took place in Los Angeles, where he continued his relationship with the Biharis, under the auspices of their Kent label.

The rigors of touring had this compensation: when King brought his band into the studio, they were already a tightly knit team requiring little preparation. A 1958 session produced two hit singles for Kent in "You've Been an Angel" and "Please Accept My Love." The former piece represents King's late 1950s work at its finest. Other singers have managed to holler with authority in the high register, but somehow King keeps his voice rich and pure even when shouting at the top of his lungs, rarely falling below high C in this instance. His most powerful moments almost always come with this honeyed exterior, like those potent cocktails that mask their bang behind a deceptive sweetness and a tiny umbrella laden with fruit. His guitar work is much the same, probing for the sensitive blue notes, showing teeth and threatening to gnaw or bite, before subsiding into a vibrato-laden held note, soothing in its trembling vulnerability. But King still dipped into a rhythm-and-blues bag on occasion, achieving a top ten hit with his 1960 Kent single "I've Got a Right to Love My Baby." Yet King's strongest play was always the soulful slow- or medium-tempo blues, as he demonstrated on his "Sweet Sixteen," which climbed to the second position in the charts on its Kent release, and was a modest hit again when King later recorded it for the ABC label.

If the Biharis managed to keep King's singles in rotation at America's radio stations, they were less skilled at packaging the bluesman's work in long-playing albums. "When I went into the record stores and looked at everyone else's stuff—Ray Charles or Joe Turner—they'd have liner notes and beautiful photographs on the cover," King would later recall. "The albums would cost $3.99. But the Biharis' labels—RPM, Modern, Kent and Crown—would be thrown in the cut-out bin. You could buy practically any B.B. King album for 99 cents." Instead of fancy artwork and informative notes, the Biharis used the back album cover to promote their other releases. To save on costs, the company had generic album covers printed with this standard backing, and added a slick sticker on the front to differentiate their various LPs. The whole effect was cheesy and unprofessional, justified only by the few pennies it added to the bottom line. Yet, at the dawn of the sixties, economizing in this manner was a major mistake: in the past, hit singles would create sales for LPs and set the image for a traveling act, but over the next decade, the roles would be reversed. From now on, album sales would dominate the music industry, not just measured in pure dollars and cents, but even more as a psychological imprint of an artist's ethos.

King had other reasons to be unhappy with the Biharis: they balked at paying more than three or four thousand dollars as an advance for an album, only caving in when King received a five-thousand-dollar offer from the Chess label. They also held on to the publishing royalties for his songs; and they foisted mysterious names as co-composers—Taub or Ling or Josea—to divert more money from King's wallet. When King finally left to sign with ABC-Paramount in 1961, he received an upfront guarantee of twenty-five thousand dollars—a sum that would have taken years of recording and bickering to secure from his previous label.

But though King had severed his ties to Kent, they had not ended their interest in him, and the company continued to release new recordings under his name for almost another decade. True, some of these were only super-ficially new: an older track over-dubbed with horns, as in "Worry, Worry" from 1968, which updated the 1959 version; or with a new bass and drum part, which "enhanced" the 1958 cut of "The Woman I Love" to make it more suitable for the musical tastes of 1968. Kent sometimes even managed to push these retreads into minor hit status—the latter recording reached number 31 on the R&B charts. But even when sales were lackluster, these stale releases managed to confuse the marketplace and serve as payback to the ABC execs who had stolen the Biharis' star act.

Despite these complications, the move to ABC provided a clear boost to King's career, and finally allowed him a platform that would bring him in front of a larger audience. Indeed, this switch in labels was an essential step in securing King's later successes. Even after his string of hits in the 1950s, King saw few white faces at his engagements, and his songs lived an equally segregated life, restricted to certain radio stations, bins in the store, and charts in the industry trade journals, carryovers from the marginaliz-ing "race records" mentality that had accompanied the blossoming of black music as a commercial presence in American life. And the country's musical tastes were a-changing. Blues and R&B were passé. Rock and, soon, soul styl-ings would completely reconfigure the sound of black music and broaden its market appeal. A host of independent labels—Stax, Motown, Atlantic—were at the forefront of this movement, although ABC was quickly adapting to the new sensibility, taking Ray Charles away from Atlantic, and picking up Fats Domino from Imperial around the same time that King came on board. But ABC not only wanted to steal talent; the label was also intent on grooming it and taking it to the next level. In this environment, King found himself surrounded by a team of handlers—arrangers, lyricists, marketers, producers, and various know-it-alls—who took in hand many of the deci-sions that the Biharis had either ignored or left up to the artist.

The new level of professionalism was most evident in the slick produc-tion values, the well-crafted arrangements by Johnny Pate, the superior sound quality of the releases. Yet ABC still seemed uncertain of the way to position this new addition to its roster, and King's very versatility once again made this a complicated issue. On "Sneakin' Around" from 1962 he showed his incomparable skill in fronting a large horn section, while "My Baby's Comin' Home" from this same period is an unabashed rocker, and "Help the Poor" from 1964 dispenses entirely with King's guitar, instead asking him to sing his way over an emasculated Latin groove and incongruous female gospel choir. King transforms all of these into palatable performances; but he really shined when given a chance to tackle a slow- or medium-tempo blues, as demonstrated on his classic 1963 rendition of "How Blue Can You Get?" Here King's lazy, loping guitar intro paves the way for two simmering choruses, hot and bothered with the burner on low, before the song bursts into a vehement stop-time interlude, a nay-saying of the no-good woman who inspired this bruised hue of blue:

I gave you a brand new Ford; you said "I want a Cadillac."
I bought you a ten dollar dinner; you said "thanks for the snack."
I let you live in my penthouse; you said it was just a shack.
I gave you seven children, and now you want to give them back.

If ABC was looking for a formula to attach to B.B. King, here it was. And it required little packaging or producing. Just put the artist in front of a road-tested band amidst an appreciative audience and let him work his magic on these uncluttered grooves. The label did just that on November 21, 1964, at the Regal Theater in Chicago, and the result was one of the finest blues recordings of the decade. After years of constant touring, King had developed a sixth sense of how to communicate to an audience, how to pace a show, how to segue from song to song, when to hold back and when to pull out all the stops, and he demonstrated this mastery in front of an enthusiastic audience at the Regal. From the opening bars of "Every Day I Have the Blues," King has his fans in a near frenzy. But the following medley is a tour de force. King courses masterfully through three different slow groove blues—his former hits "Sweet Little Angel," "It's My Own Fault," and "How Blue Can You Get?"—capturing a perfect rightness, not too fast, not too slow, not too hot, not too cool, and holding it for an extraordinary ten minutes. Next he pushes up the tempo, kicking off "Please Love Me" with a slashing guitar solo, first unaccompanied, then prodded by an insistent drum backbeat. Finally, the horns come in, at first supporting King's vocal and guitar with gentle nudges, then raising their volume, becoming more relentless in their braying riffs. King can do no wrong now, the audience has entrusted him with their heart and soul, but the artist on stage does not relax his hold on them. King still has familiar hit songs to share, unfailing crowd-pleasers from his road repertoire, such as "You Upset Me Baby" and "Woke Up This Morning," that maintain the bluesy mood. On "Worry,

Worry," King whines mournfully in a raw falsetto, then launches into a bit
of storytelling, a classic talking blues, that settles the audience and creates
an intimate parlor ambiance, palpable even when experienced secondhand
on the turntable. Here, as on every track on *Live at the Regal*, we never stray
from this standard blues progression, and no concession is made to those
who might prefer a taste of rock or soul or R&B. Yet there is no ennui of
repetition here: these are not so much blues songs as an uninterrupted blue
mood, glorious amidst its melancholy. King's musical identity was solidified, here at the Regal a few days before Thanksgiving in 1964. The musician who was so versatile at age thirty has identified his strongest play, his
straight-to-the-basket move, just shy of his fortieth birthday.

   This should have been the start of a great new era in King's career. His
music was stronger than ever, and was finally being recorded in settings
that did justice to it. The section on the bluesman in Charles Keil's 1966
book *Urban Blues* further contributed to King's midcareer revitalization,
and addressed head-on the bias against modern, electric blues among many
fans, at a time when the traditional acoustic sounds were seen as more
authentic. In truth, B.B. King's life was every bit as anguished and blue as
the songs he sang on the stage of the Regal. The Internal Revenue Service
charged him with underpayment of taxes and, in 1966, placed a $78,000 lien
against his income. His wife filed for divorce and his second marriage came
to an end almost at the same time as the tax authorities were hounding him.
Even life on the road, where King usually felt master of his own fate, proved
problematic. Thieves made off with his bus after it broke down in Augusta,
Georgia, and it was never recovered. King was not insured against theft, and
the loss hit him hard at a time when he was least prepared to cope with it.

   Yet his fans remained loyal, and King hit the charts with "Don't Answer
the Door," another in-the-pocket slow blues, while the world around him
collapsed. But expectations were growing even faster than his sales. When
King was recording with the Kent label, a release that sold fifty thousand or
one hundred thousand copies was viewed as a tremendous success; but ABC
hoped to bring the bluesman to an even larger audience, much as they had
already achieved with Ray Charles, whose hit singles could rack up sales of
1 million units or more. Although he had started to attract a small white
following at his engagements, King still found himself playing the same
chitlin circuit he had been working for years, and the owners of these venues
balked at his attempt to raise his rates. Yes, King might well be more popular

than ever before, but he was constantly reminded of how much he still fell short of the mark.

5. never make your move too soon

King would return frequently to the live format for his recordings during the next three decades. It proved to be the most conducive environment for his creative energies during the middle years of his career, just as he would later focus his efforts on studio projects with famous guest artists—the preferred recipe for aging blues stars, according to the music industry execs who decide such things—when he entered his seventies. Whether entertaining inmates at Cook County Jail and San Quentin, or introducing new fans to the blues in Japan or London, or bringing his band into clubs such as the Village Gate in New York or the International Club in Chicago, King somehow managed, time and again, to evoke the same bluesy atmosphere he had created at the Regal. He frequently relied on the same songs—dependable standbys such as "Every Day I Have the Blues," "Sweet Sixteen," "Worry, Worry," and "How Blue Can You Get?"—but these became less a repetition than a ritual, an invocation to the blues spirit that presides over such occasions. And like a ritual, the thousandth performance is perhaps even better than the first or the hundredth, having now the long tradition behind it that adds to the meaning, that deepens the emotional connection.

But King was not without his dreams of crossover success, of reaching an audience that would never browse in the blues bins at Sam Goody. He went on the road as part of a revue featuring soul music acts, hoping that the exposure to younger fans would broaden his appeal, but was deeply hurt one night when he heard boos from the crowd in response to the emcee's introduction. The teenagers had come to hear other performers, and the very idea of the blues may well have seemed tired and old to them. King won them over, digging deeply into "Sweet Sixteen," teaching the youngsters where soul music had originally found its soulfulness.

In time, the roles would be reversed, not because King changed his style, but because the musical tastes of the younger generation began to evolve, to broaden out in surprising new ways. The middle-aged bluesman might well have been puzzled when he heard that John Lennon had expressed his admiration—the Beatle had commented that he wished he could play guitar like B.B. King. For his own part, King could hear little of his own influence in the music of the Liverpool rockers. But Lennon's praise was more than an isolated opinion. Other expanding minds in the 1960s found their way back to the blues. In February 1967, King was engaged to play an unlikely, but career-changing, gig at the Fillmore in San Francisco on the same bill as Moby Grape and Steve Miller. When he arrived, King was puzzled to see a gathering crowd of long-haired, white rock fans, and was convinced that there had been some mistake in the booking. But promoter Bill Graham knew what he was doing, and brought King on stage to tumultuous applause. Carlos Santana, who was in attendance, would later recall:

> B.B. King got a standing ovation before he hit the first note and he started crying. I mean he just started crying, he just lost it, you know, and I remember, because all you could see—he went to wipe his tears and all you could see was the diamonds shining from this [ring on his] hand and the tears.... But when he hit the note to bring the band in, my whole life was changed again. When I saw B.B. and I heard that note for the first time like that, I could see what Michael Bloomfield and Eric Clapton and everyone else could see in him.... When you play like that, you heal yourself and you heal other people.

Santana's enthusiasm was apparently shared by the rest of the attendees, who lavished adulation and applause on the bluesman to a degree he had never seen before from any young audience, white or black.

Doors were now opening for King that had long remained closed. He began playing at rock venues, meeting and jamming with a new generation of megastars. His guitar summit with Jimi Hendrix at the club Generation is still talked about in hushed terms, and perhaps the tape Hendrix made that night will someday find its way into a commercial release. Eric Clapton finagled an introduction, and later described his meeting with King as the highlight of his first tour of the United States with the rock band Cream. The Rolling Stones engaged King as an opening act for a U.S. tour. But King also found himself welcomed at the Newport Jazz Festival or at the highest-class Las Vegas showrooms. Spurred by the excitement of these broadened opportunities, the guitarist moved to a New York apartment at 66th and Central Park West, and immersed himself in the Manhattan music scene. He did commercials and endorsements, and in general settled into a comfortable second career as a living legend.

Record sales had been healthy, but still lagged behind the more marketable offerings of the young rock musicians whose circuit and audience were increasingly becoming King's own. King was now recording with Bluesway, the label established by ABC in 1967 as a home for the company's growing roster of blues artists. King's first offering on Bluesway, *Blues Is King*, found him again performing in front of a live audience in Chicago, a strong outing if still a notch below the classic *Live at the Regal*; and he followed up with five more Bluesway releases during the next three years. Under the guidance of ABC, King sometimes adopted a slicker, funkier sound, but one that meshed well with his own musical roots. King added to his list of classic performances, with solid recordings of "Paying the Cost to Be the Boss," "Lucille," and "Why I Sing the Blues." These sold well—the latter proclamation of King's blues roots was a minor R&B hit—but gave little indication of the big success waiting just around the corner.

At a late night session in Manhattan, King pulled out an old blues song, one Roy Hawkins had recorded almost twenty years earlier, called "The Thrill Is Gone." Producer Bill Szymczyk had put together a young rhythm section, and their work evoked a midnight mood more soul-oriented than bluesy. Paul Harris's work on the Wurlitzer electric piano behind King's vocal was especially effective, and after the session, Szymczyk decided to add a subtle string track. The producer later recalled:

> The energy was there. BB started playing the song riff in that minor key and Paul picked up on it immediately on the Wurlitzer electric piano. It fell into its groove in minutes. I was freaking out, that's how good it was. Then I got the idea to put strings on it. I called BB and he hesitated a bit. But I called in a great arranger who wrote this killer, hypnotic chart and we put it down. That was his breakthrough record.

The song first started receiving airplay on black music stations in early 1970, then was picked up by more mainstream deejays, and finally climbed into the top twenty of the pop charts—an unprecedented success for King, and one he would never surpass.

The song earned the bluesman his first Grammy, and further expanded his audience. For his follow-up recording, *Indianola Mississippi Seeds*, King brought younger pop icons Leon Russell and Carole King into his orbit. He now could demand five thousand dollars for a regular gig, but also found his band increasingly booked at special engagements, large rock festivals, ballparks, or downtown arenas where paydays—and sometimes the fans—

were getting higher and higher. King continued to tour relentlessly, and finally brought his act overseas, finding to his amazement that he could fill a hall with devoted admirers in Japan, Australia, Europe, or Africa. His long-standing British admirers knew his old hits even better than people back in the States, yet King also had a following with fans who were still in diapers—or nappies, as the case may be—when "Three O'Clock Blues" first charted. When he recorded in London, King was accompanied by Ringo Starr, Steve Winwood, and Dr. John, and the resulting album made clear that the blues pioneer was not out of place amidst this aggregation of prominent rockers. He brought his act to the Soviet Union, and worked a new circuit—Azerbaijan, Georgia, Moscow—marveling at how much the simple rural lives and pervasive poverty reminded him of his own Delta upbringing. King could now fit in anywhere, entertaining Middle America on *The Ed Sullivan Show* or chatting with Johnny Carson on *The Tonight Show*. At the same time, he never forgot the fans who had the deepest blues in their life. King took his band inside Cook County Jail in Chicago for a memorable live recording. He also helped establish the Foundation for the Advancement of Inmate Rehabilitation, dedicated to the improvement of living conditions for prisoners, and showed his personal commitment to the cause in periodic appearances for those in confinement.

Of all the Mississippi masters working to please younger fans during this period—Muddy Waters, Howlin' Wolf, John Lee Hooker, and other lesser lights—King's talent was the most flexible, the best suited to grooving with a modern dance beat. Sometimes the attempts to cross over did a disservice to B.B.'s king-sized sound. He should have resisted, for example, the producer who prodded him into doing a cover of Lovin' Spoonful's "Summer in the City." In contrast, his recordings with Bobby Bland were great artistic and financial successes, and King should have demanded more collaborations with true peers who could match his deep blues roots. But for the most part, King thrived as part of the pop music scene during these years. In particular, the decision to join forces with the Crusaders might have been a disastrous one for a lesser talent. Indeed, one can hardly imagine another blues artist from King's generation who could have made this move so smoothly. But for B.B. King, this setting provided a hospitable musical environment and one more opportunity to expand his following.

This seasoned band had been around almost as long as King himself. In 1954, pianist Joe Sample had teamed up with saxophonist Wilton Felder and drummer Stix Hooper in Houston to form a band called the Swingsters.

The group evolved into the Modern Jazz Sextet, and finally changed into the West Coast–based Jazz Crusaders. The musicians dropped the jazz from their name, and to some extent from their repertoire, in the early seventies, and emerged as a big draw in the growing market for funk and fusion music. Yet King felt at home in this setting. "I heard funk as a hopped-up variation on the blues," he remarked. For their collaboration on *Midnight Believer*, King relied heavily on the Crusaders, and especially on keyboardist Joe Sample, for compositions and arrangements, and the effort generated strong airplay for "Never Make a Move Too Soon" and "When It All Comes Down (I'll Still Be Around)." King closed the seventies with a follow-up release in the same vein, *Take It Home*. He had shared a label with the hit band Steely Dan for most of the decade, and now seemed to have borrowed a page out of their songbook. This repackaging of King as a contemporary artist continued with his 1981 offering *There Must Be a Better World Somewhere*, where his vocals blended nicely with the slick horn parts and studio savvy rhythm section. King earned a Grammy for this release, as well as for his *Blues 'n Jazz*, from 1983, which kept the emphasis on the horns, this time played by a crack jazz ensemble that included trumpeter Woody Shaw and saxophonist Arnett Cobb.

Despite these efforts to experiment and broaden his appeal, King would not earn another radio hit that approached the success of "The Thrill Is Gone." Most of his releases during the 1980s and early 1990s were compilations of older material, supplemented by the occasional live recording, which invariably relied heavily on time-tested songs from back in the day. He had moved to Las Vegas in 1975, a city that loves world-class entertainers—especially ones like King with a fondness for games of chance—but also tends to celebrate past triumphs rather than create new chart-busters for the aging warriors who work its premier rooms. King had started his Vegas experience decades before, playing all-black clubs on the outskirts of town, but he moved up to the top casinos by the mid-1970s. His talent and name recognition opened doors for him, but King also enjoyed a little help from a couple of admirers named Frank and Elvis, who had some clout with the local proprietors.

In short, King had settled into a comfortable existence. He had paid off his debts to the IRS. He could earn a living off the afterglow of old achievements, without worrying about changing fads and fashions in the music industry. He could work near home, with countless opportunities to gig waiting just a limo drive away; or listen to his massive record collection, a lifetime's worth of activity in that alone; or just polish up his Grammy awards (eventually more than a dozen) on the mantelpiece. His place in American music was secure, even if he never made another record. An honorary degree awarded by Yale seemed to reinforce the point, as did the first of many books about him, Charles Sawyer's *The Arrival of B.B. King*, published by Doubleday in 1980. The title said it all: King had arrived; the poor farm boy from Indianola, Mississippi, was living it large as his home state's most famous native son.

King could have settled into comfortable retirement. But at an age when his contemporaries were cashing Social Security checks, he still looked to expand his horizons. This zeal for constant improvement was no late addition to King's character, but a long-standing drive, similar to the impetus that kept Howlin' Wolf attending evening school classes long after he was a world-famous musician. The legacy of Mississippi for its least fortunate—a sizable portion of the state's population, at last count—is too often a sense of inadequacy, a felt need to compensate, for the lack of schooling, nurturing, preparation for the challenges ahead. King never lost his sense of early deprivation, and always looked to make up for it. He was mostly an absentee father to his fifteen children, but he wrote checks to cover their education, and for his more than fifty grandchildren, with a sense of pride. Yet he kept tabs on his own education, as well, boasting that he liked to learn something new every day. On his travels, he could hardly pass a bookstore without peeking in to find another volume to add to his shelves. King continued to study music at a point when other players consider themselves fortunate if they remember what they once knew, and his cherished volumes of *The Schillinger System of Musical Composition* were constant traveling companions, as were the tapes of other performers, which King listened to with a student's ear, seeking out nuggets of inspiration that he might apply to his own work. He learned to sight-read on the clarinet; he played scales on the violin; he made headway on the electric bass; and experimented with various keyboards.

Fans never saw these undertakings, private labors hidden from their view, but they witnessed King's work ethic firsthand in his continual touring. His globe-trotting during his golden years brought King face-to-face with fans in Brazil, Uruguay, Lithuania, Latvia, Australia, China, Japan, Singapore, Spain, France, Germany, England, Holland, Italy, Austria, and throughout the United States, among other locales. The 1950 tour bus trips measured in hundreds of miles now seemed simple subway stops in comparison. But a 1987 performance in Dublin may have been the single biggest factor in keeping King at the forefront of the global music audience. The Irish rock group U2, the most popular band on the planet at that juncture, was in attendance, and the meeting between blues icon and pop superstars initiated an extraordinary partnership.

King performed "When Love Comes to Town" with U2 on stage in Texas during the latter's *Joshua Tree* tour, and was invited back for the final concert of the road trip in Arizona. King appeared in a documentary film on U2, *Rattle and Hum*, as well as in the recording and video that accompanied it. He now was reaching a new generation via MTV, a senior citizen let loose in the chosen crib of the youth culture. King's enlistment as U2's opening act on a four-month tour solidified the relationship, and brought him in front of audiences no other blues artist had ever reached.

Collaborations of this sort would serve as the foundation for many of King's strongest late vintage recordings. Sessions in Memphis and Berkeley in early 1993 brought him into the studio with some of the greatest living blues artists—including John Lee Hooker, Robert Cray, Buddy Guy, Albert Collins, and Koko Taylor—to produce the exceptional *Blues Summit* release. King moved into a different sphere with his *Heart to Heart* collaboration the following year with jazz vocalist Diane Schuur. The project put King in the spotlight as a singer of pop and jazz material, but he handled the role with ease, and soon found himself in another unaccustomed spot when the release rose to the top position on the *jazz* charts. But King raised the ante in 1997 with the all-star roster for *Deuces Wild*. It is hard to pick the best performance here: the combination of King with the Rolling Stones on "Paying the Cost to Be the Boss"; Joe Cocker joining in on "Dangerous Mood"; or the other pairings of the blues master with Eric Clapton, Van Morrison, Tracy Chapman, Willie Nelson, Bonnie Raitt, Dr. John, or even the unlikely Heavy D. Yet one fact was clearly established: when matched up with these heavy hitters, King lived up to his own legendary status.

By now, King's admirers among the rich and famous went far beyond the realm of music. His Majesty Carl XVI Gustav of Sweden presented the bluesman with the Polar Music Prize—one King to another, so to speak—in the same room where Nobel Prizes are awarded. President Clinton invited him to the White House, and when he told the guitarist that he had once heard King play in concert, his visitor was skeptical, thinking the president was merely trying to be polite; but Clinton proceeded to describe the details of a performance from years before, given in tandem with Bobby Bland at

Robeson Auditorium in Little Rock, establishing his credentials as the highest ranking fan in the land—which he further solidified by inviting King back on a half dozen more occasions. In a private audience with Pope John Paul II, King gave the pontiff one of his guitars, having heard that the spiritual leader played the instrument, and was delighted by the warm response and blessing he received in return. (Although we are perhaps justified in doubting the claim, made by King's bandmates, that they heard the Pope playing "The Thrill Is Gone" as they were leaving the room.)

King's biggest challenge during this period came off stage and outside of the public arena. He collapsed while on tour in April 1990, and was diagnosed with diabetes. After a period of hospitalization, he resumed performing, but paying strict attention to medication and diet. King's diabetes as well as his high blood pressure were aggravated by his excessive weight, and in 1994 the bluesman began making annual two-week visits to the Pritikin Institute, a clinic specializing in the treatment of obesity. Determined to find some good in his affliction, King took on the role of public spokesperson, with the goal of raising awareness of diabetes. His road tours now took on additional meaning, not just as a way of earning a livelihood or entertaining blues fans, but showing millions of people suffering from this ailment how the condition could be controlled and not impede an active life.

The success of *Deuces Wild*, which remained atop the *Billboard* blues charts for three months, confirmed the wisdom of pairing King with well known guest artists. Record labels are fond of these collaborations for aging blues artists—yet serious blues fans lament the fact that their musical icons are often validated only as attendant lords in the palace of the rockers. King, at least, refused to abdicate his throne, and insisted on the centrality of his own music and his own roots. His 1998 release *Blues on the Bayou* was a modest studio session featuring the guitarist's road band; but it showed that B.B. King needed no famous rock artist in tow in order to present music of the highest caliber. He followed up with a tribute to one of his own role models, Louis Jordan, whose music served as the centerpiece for King's 1999 release *Let the Good Times Roll*. Rather than celebrating the youth culture, King looked back to a figure older than himself, and dead for almost a quarter of a century. Yet the choice was inspired: the spirit of Louis Jordan lives on in the popular music of today, and King showed that he was a perfect interpreter for this material.

King published his autobiography in 1996, the candid and moving *Blues*

All Around Me. Books had dealt with King before, but now the floodgates seemed to open. When Charles Sawyer was seeking a home for his 1980 work *The Arrival of B.B. King*, he was turned down by fifty-two publishers—out of the fifty-three he approached. But in his seventies and eighties, King was a hot property in print, just as he had long been on disk. Richard Kostelanetz edited a collection of writings, *The B.B. King Companion*, drawing on a half century of commentary on the artist. Dick Waterman worked with King on an elegant coffee table volume, *The B.B. King Treasures*, which offered not just the usual text and photos, but also elaborate inserts and pouches stuffed with memorabilia. David Shirley wrote a King biography for youngsters. David McGee contributed *There Is Always One More Time*, a study of the bluesman that paid particular attention to his rich legacy of recordings. In addition, method books, transcriptions, discographies, interviews, critical assessments, and reviews round out the picture of this celebrated, and now well documented, life.

King took the new millennium in stride. He continued to play some two hundred dates per year, extraordinary by any measure, except perhaps by his own past standards. His recordings maintained a very high level of quality, measured not just by the famous names, who grace *Riding with the King*, his stand-out collaboration with Eric Clapton, or the star-studded *80*, a celebration of the dawn of the Delta legend's eighth decade, which brought on board new friends, including Elton John, Sheryl Crow, and John Mayer, but also by King's own mature musical vision. So many of the greatest performers falter long before becoming octogenarians, and even those who survive rarely want to venture in public and match up against the memories, and recordings, of their past greatness. But King somehow defied the odds, remaining a riveting presence and a commanding performer. Who knows why? Perhaps the relentless touring prevented the fingers, the vocal cords, the musical mind from atrophying. Perhaps King's lifestyle, his vegetarian diet and abstinence from alcohol, gave him an edge over the more self-indulgent. But it's likely something simpler and more primal: King's deep soulfulness, his full-of-soulness, his commitment to a music of emotion, played on the heartstrings as much as on the six strings, is what has kept this music so fresh, this performer so vital, and fans still grooving to the last surviving superstar of the Delta tradition.

Mississippi John Hurt

chapter eleven

the blues revival

1. as remote as kurdistan

Our story should be ended. If it were like most tales from the music world, it would be. The reader would have little to do now except rummage through the footnotes and pick over a bibliography. But the Delta blues singers never abided by the rules that held others in check. And if they defied convention in their prime, they did so even more in their senescence—in a manner as gratifying as it is odd. The final episodes in this narrative are, to be sure, the grandest ones of all.

Few events in the annals of American music are more surprising than the blues revival of the 1960s. Career resurgences of any sort are unusual in the popular arts. Most entertainers lose their audience, in whole or part, with the passing years. Many are reluctant to perform their craft beyond a certain age, anxious about unflattering comparisons with their younger selves. And the few who insist on continuing in their chosen field invariably find their opportunities much diminished. Even rarer are those careers with celebrated final inning spurts, stars that go out blazing, matching or surpassing the achievements of earlier decades. How many public figures enjoy such curtain calls? One in a hundred? One in a thousand? F. Scott Fitzgerald came closest to the truth here, when he wrote: "There are no second acts in American lives."

But, in this light, what are we to make of the Delta blues revival? Musicians who had never enjoyed substantial fame in their youth, who had not been household names, whose records had hardly *survived*, so don't even ask how they *sold* . . . how could a whole cohort of these forgotten figures suddenly find themselves in the limelight, lauded as great figures, treated not so much as premier entertainers, but even more as legendary artists and cultural icons? They no longer even thought about making records, and now they were told they were making history. This is too much, even for the made-for-TV-movie. A closing chapter of this sort is even less plausible than the final fifty pages of those thick Victorian novels, where a steady stream of coincidences and contrivances set all wrongs to right, and deliver us a happy ending, all wrapped up in a bow and shiny paper.

But precisely this happened to the surviving Delta blues musicians in the last years of their lives. In the 1950s, no one even knew if Son House, Skip James, Bukka White, and others of their generation were still alive. Even more to the point, hardly anyone cared; no one remembered their artistry, or longed for their return. Their anonymity was assured by that most certain guarantor of privacy: the utter indifference of everyone surrounding them. A few dozen record collectors may have recognized these names, and actively sought out surviving 78s, but even for these cognoscenti, the artists in question were only names—the most avid blues fan would hardly have noticed Son House if he had moved in next door—enigmas without faces or histories, shadowy figures as mysterious as their disks were rare. This music, as Peter Guralnick recalls, "seemed as remote as Kurdistan and destined always to remain so."

James McKune stands out as the most influential of the first generation of traditional blues record collectors. McKune kept his precious disks in cardboard boxes in the single room at the Williamsburg YMCA where he lived for a quarter of a century. His passion for these recordings dated back at least to the early 1940s, and McKune's enthusiasm eventually shaped the views of other collectors, such as Bernie Klatzko, Nick Perls, Pete Whelan,

Lawrence Cohn, and Don Kent. Cohn remembers McKune as "a very with-drawn, shy individual," but acknowledges his preeminence. "He was way ahead of us when it came to collecting and appreciating country blues." McKune would only rarely attend the gabfest gatherings of these early blues collectors, instead typically imparting his views privately with one or two of the fraternity, who would then pass them on to the rest.

The influence of these record collectors on our perceptions of tradi-tional blues has often been noted, and sometimes lamented—most recently in Marybeth Hamilton's *In Search of the Blues: Black Voices, White Visions*. Hamilton looks with skepticism on the role of these individuals "who set themselves up as cultural arbiters, connoisseurs whose authority rested on their powers of discernment," attitudes which she sees as linked to their "fears and obsessions." *Perhaps* it would have been better for academics such as Hamilton to take the lead on this process during these years of neglect—although other fears and obsessions might have emerged in this case. But the issue is moot: college professors had *no* interest in the blues at the time. Moreover, the record collectors were the only people who had access to this music, most of which was available solely on the original 78s in which it had first been presented to the public. As such, we must temper our criticism of these enthusiasts with at least a measure of gratitude for the music they were able to track down, preserve, and share with those open-minded enough to appreciate its virtues.

The reissue of traditional Delta blues recordings on the Origin Jazz Library label in the early 1960s is often seen as a major turning point, the moment when this music was once more made available to the American public. But the reception to these releases at the time was far from encour-aging, and only the most starry-eyed optimist would have seen it as the start of a movement. The label's first blues reissue had a pressing run of just five hundred copies—and it took close to two years to find buyers for those! When a second reissue was ready for release, owner Pete Whelan decided again to press five hundred albums. After all, the label was little more than a hobby for him—no one in their right mind would do this and expect to earn a decent living—and Whelan needed to minimize his expenditures. Around half of the sales were made overseas to fans in Europe. In the entire United States, it seemed, only around two hundred people, at best, were willing to pay money to listen to this forgotten, old music.

But a revival took place—five years after Whelan founded his label, traditional Delta blues had developed a passionate following, especially among younger listeners—and to understand the reasons for it, we almost need to look to the great religious revivals of the past. For the blues resurgence, like those moments of spiritual rebirth, reflected less the genius and determination of a few individuals in the limelight, but rather a change in the air, a cosmic shifting of attitudes and aspirations that made a new worldview both possible and desirable. In such instances, the leaders of the movement seem to multiply, but only because so many are now willing to be led, people who would have resisted the same change in an earlier day. The blues musicians themselves did almost nothing to set this revival in motion. For the most part, they were unaware of it until it literally came to their doorsteps. This shift in cultural perceptions and imperatives was in the air as the 1950s gave way to the 1960s, a transformation signaled in books and movies, politics and cultural values, but above all in music, preeminently in music. There had been social revolutions before, but none with such painstaking attention to the soundtrack.

To some degree, the songs changed first, and took the rest of society along for the ride. The hit parade of the early 1950s boasted its own equivalents of polyester and TV dinners, its syrupy arrangements and slick studio performances, designed and packaged for mass consumption. The bigger budgets of the major record labels made possible a fastidious refinement that often drowned out the emotional core of the performance. In the late 1950s and throughout the 1960s, musicians and their listeners of the new generation jettisoned all this overboard in search for their own first principles, their own reclaiming of a more authentic past, a golden age that none of them had been around to experience firsthand. They found this authenticity—perhaps a romanticized or spurious one, at times—in old blues music, which they cherished with a fervor unknown to the previous generation.

At the same time, the first stirrings of the civil rights movement had emerged in the 1950s, gaining momentum throughout the decade and into the 1960s; and though its mandate was essentially political and social, changes of this sort inevitably cast a diffused light over music and the popular arts. The dismantling of segregation in schools and voting booths served gradually to broaden cultural sensibilities, and to legitimize the old blues disks as more than just "race recordings," more than just a way of serving a niche market. They now offered much needed testimony to the often neglected artistic contributions of America's least favored citizens. The (mostly white) music industry execs who had recorded this music in the 1920s and 1930s had not been looking to right wrongs, or address grievances—in some instances, they were decidedly close-minded in racial matters—but the body of work they preserved could hardly be heard a generation later without being filtered through the transformed racial consciousness of the nation.

Samuel Charters took little notice of these larger currents when he settled into a one-room basement apartment in the spring of 1959 and, during the course of thirty-six feverish days, wrote his book *The Country Blues*. True, Charters was an ardent civil rights advocate, and well immersed in the bohemian currents of the decade—his wife Ann would establish herself a decade later as a leading expert on Jack Kerouac and the Beat Generation—but these sensibilities were hardly evident in the book he was writing at a furious pace, a work which exuded, on every page, the passion of a music fan and the flowing prose of a natural storyteller. Charters had little reason to hope that his personal interest in this music would be shared by a wider public. Like Whelan, he had been involved in reissuing old blues music, and was well aware that these albums were purchased by a fringe within a fringe, not even a market by any real definition, more just an oddball community. Yet Charters's enthusiasm for the music, married to his skillful pen, would prove infectious, moving even those unfamiliar with traditional blues.

Charters left several sample chapters at the offices of Rinehart, a New York publisher, and four days later he was offered a contract and a small advance. In retrospect, we can mark the publication of *The Country Blues* in the fall of 1959 as a signal event in the history of the music, a moment of recognition and legitimization, but even more of proselytization, introducing a whole generation to the neglected riches of an art form. Very little information was available on early blues singers at this time, and Charters's success in telling their stories, despite these limitations, stands as a major achievement. His own diligent research, based on his persistence in tracking down 78s and his fieldwork in Mississippi, Texas, Tennessee, Georgia, Missouri, Illinois, and Louisiana, enabled him to jump confidently into the void and pull together the first extended history of traditional blues music. Where facts failed him, Charters relied on his sympathetic listening and his acute sensibility to the spirit of the music; and this deeply felt commitment no doubt played the key role in inspiring his readers, a number of whom made their own decisive contributions to blues research over the next decade. Although Charters would write half a dozen more books on the blues in later years, none surpassed the popularity of *The Country Blues*. The book has consistently stayed in print during the half century since its initial release, and has served as a guide to several generations of blues fans.

Paul Oliver, an indefatigable British researcher with wide-ranging interests—his work on architecture is almost as influential as his music writing—published *Blues Fell This Morning* the next year. Although this was primarily a view of the blues from afar, a sociological assessment based on a close study of the lyrics of these songs, Oliver followed up with extensive field research during the summer and fall of 1960. Oliver and his wife Valerie journeyed to various communities in the South, as well as to major urban centers such as Chicago, Detroit, and New York. These travels resulted in his follow-up book *Conversations with the Blues*, and the thoroughness of Oliver's oral histories—the work drew on interviews with over sixty-five musicians—showed how much of the music's past could be uncovered by those willing to go on the road and knock on doors. Oliver would continue to publish extensively on the blues, and his works, alongside those of Charters, sold well and paved the way for the reemergence of traditional blues as a commercial enterprise during the course of the decade.

A native Mississippian would be best equipped to undertake this research, but only one rose to the challenge during the early 1960s. Gayle Dean Wardlow began going door-to-door in black neighborhoods in March 1961, seeking out old blues recordings. His initial interest was in trading these 78s to other collectors in exchange for Roy Acuff recordings. Wardlow had some familiarity with blues music, but his initial reaction had been dismissive. "I had met John Fahey in 1960 at a folk jam session in Washington, D.C.," Wardlow recalls. "Fahey found out that I was from Mississippi, and he played me some of Charley Patton's music. But at the time, it sounded too primitive to me. But later, when I started listening to the blues, I came back to Patton and became very interested in his music." Fahey had visited Clarksdale in the late 1950s, and had even made some inquiries about Patton, but it would be left to Wardlow to undertake the first extensive research into the guitarist's life and times, as well as to gather many of the basic facts about the careers of other pioneering Delta musicians. In 1962, Wardlow moved from Meridian to Jackson, Mississippi, and his job for Orkin Pest Control gave him entrée into many African-American homes. Residents were more than happy to sell their dusty stack of old 78s to this unusual exterminator who seemed more interested in blues music than in their infestations. Wardlow's typical offer was a quarter per side, although for choicer items he would raise it to fifty cents or even a dollar. Eventually his methodical approach to canvassing neighborhoods enabled Wardlow to amass a treasure trove of rare blues material.

Hunting for records naturally broadened into a search for the mysterious musicians who had made them. In 1963, Wardlow was knocking on doors in Jackson, when a gentleman told him that Ishmon Bracey was still alive and residing in the area. "After that, I checked the city directory, and there he was, listed as Reverend Ishmon Bracey," Wardlow explains. Under other circumstances, this find might have brought Bracey back into the limelight as a performer of traditional blues. "But Bracey wouldn't play blues music. He had terrible guilt about the blues and the blues life." Wardlow helped Bracey record a few religious songs, but they were unable to interest a record label in releasing them. Unlike Reverend Robert Wilkins, who successfully made the transition from secular to religious music, Bracey had removed the telltale blues licks from his songs. Even if the blues world would take him back with open arms, Bracey refused to compromise.

Almost from the start, these efforts to track down the "lost" blues musicians from the 1920s and 1930s took on a sense of urgency. The researchers themselves felt that they were in a race against time. J. D. Short—who had made a handful of 78s as Joe Stone and Jelly Jaw Short in the early 1930s—was recorded and interviewed by Samuel Charters in July of 1962; less than four months later, he was dead. This gritty musician was a walking history book of the Delta tradition—he had heard Charley Patton in 1910, and had lived in Clarksdale from 1912 to 1923. Had Short survived a few more years, he might have played a prominent role in the blues revival, but instead he passed away a few weeks shy of his sixtieth birthday. Other times, researchers were even less fortunate. Gayle Dean Wardlow attempted to trace the whereabouts of Blind Joe Reynolds, who had recorded a few choice blues songs in 1930, over a period of several years in the mid-1960s. But when Wardlow finally found Reynolds's home near Monroe, Louisiana, he was just a few weeks too late—the blues singer had died of pneumonia.

Of course, other record collectors had taken notice of Wardlow's activities by this time, and one of the more dedicated aficionados, New Yorker Bernie Klatzko, visited him in August 1963. Klatzko had encouraged Wardlow to learn more about the musicians who made this music, and now the two of them journeyed to Dockery's plantation. Only a few weeks before, Wardlow had heard from one of his informants that Charley Patton had died on the plantation. The statement proved incorrect, but the trip was invaluable, and Wardlow and Klatzko met several people who had known Patton. The visit enabled Klatzko to pen a thumbnail biography of the Delta legend as part of the accompanying notes to a reissue, *The Immortal Charlie Patton*, released the following year.

Other researchers now began making the trek to Mississippi for greater or longer periods. Nick Perls and Stephen Calt traveled from New York to visit Wardlow in the summer of 1964—a dangerous time for Northerners to canvass the state given the recent murder of civil rights advocates in the area. Calt eventually teamed up with Wardlow, helping the latter complete a biography of Charley Patton, and later writing his own book on Skip James. Perls was a flamboyant New Yorker—actually his preferred term of self-appraisement was "outrageous"—who worked indefatigably to reissue blues recordings on his Yazoo Records label until shortly before his death from AIDS in 1987. Perls came from a wealthy family, owners of a prestigious art gallery, and was known to pay as much as twenty thousand dollars for a single collection of 78s. But he shared generously the music he tracked down, and his lovingly produced reissues serve even now, decades after his passing, as the backbone of many blues fans' record collections.

David Evans, a native Bostonian and magna cum laude graduate from Harvard, had made a brief visit to the Delta while heading out west in 1965 to pursue graduate work at UCLA, and soon found himself undertaking frequent field trips into the region as he prepared his master's thesis on Tommy Johnson and his dissertation on traditional blues. In the late 1970s, Evans settled in Memphis, where he currently teaches at the University of Memphis—a rare setting for a blues researcher, most of whom operate outside the academic world, but also a convenient location for a scholar focused on the Mississippi tradition. Between 1967 and 1976, William Ferris undertook field research in the Delta, first for his dissertation at the University of Pennsylvania, and later in preparation for his 1978 book *Blues from the Delta*. Steve LaVere relocated from Southern California to Memphis in 1970, where, in addition to promoting artists, producing recordings, and running a record store, he followed the trail of missing blues musicians. His biographical research on Robert Johnson, included with the 1990 reissue of that artist's music, has proven to be especially influential. Even earlier,

Texan Mack McCormick began his field trips into the Delta and other parts of the South. During the 1960s and 1970s, McCormick would embark on dozens of these expeditions, firsthand sleuthing that would enable him to compile a treasure trove of ten thousand photographic negatives, some 10 million words of notes, as well as original recordings, documents, and other unique items—but, alas, none of it resulting in the long-awaited books that could perhaps answer so many unanswered questions about early blues.

The rediscovery of Mississippi John Hurt by two intrepid blues fans in 1963 showed that these research trips might generate much more than just books and articles. Indeed, the musicians themselves could be found, and initiate new stage in their previously stagnant or neglected careers. Before Hurt, the hunt for forgotten blues guitarists may have seemed like a quirky pursuit of a few fanatical fans. Now it promised to turn into a real commercial enterprise. Hurt, born in Teoc, Mississippi, in 1892, had recorded a handful of sides for OKeh in 1928 before disappearing into his quiet life as a working musician in his native region. These rare disks, featuring Hurt's spry, syncopated guitar style, would eventually captivate Tom Hoskins, a blues fan based in the D.C. area. With the encouragement and support of his friends Richard Spottswood and Mike Stewart, Hoskins decided to track down the bluesman, although they had only one firm clue to go on—and that clue was thirty-five years old! In his 1928 recording of "Avalon Blues," Hurt sang: "Avalon's my home town, always on my mind." Could Avalon be a real place on the map? And might it be Hurt's actual hometown? And would anyone there know more about the musician, or perhaps even be able to locate him?

Mack McCormick was the first to follow up this slim lead. In 1962, he identified the location of Avalon, Mississippi, just outside the Delta region, relying on a map in a prewar edition of the *Encyclopaedia Britannica*. "I phoned Avalon, and spoke to a woman in a general store. She was the local operator. I asked her whether she knew a musician named John Hurt. She said, 'John was just here. Do you want me to get him?' I agreed to phone back a short while later. When I did, I spoke to Hurt. He wasn't very talkative, but he did provide me with some answers to my questions." McCormick told a few individuals about his discovery, and he believes it is possible that Hoskins and company heard about it. In any event, it would be left to them to take the decisive steps that resulted in Hurt's extraordinary "second career," the touring and recording that marked the final years of his life.

Hoskins and Spottswood also faced the challenge of identifying the location of Avalon. They first began studying maps of the South picked up at the Automobile Club of America, and the discovery of Avalon, Georgia, was an exciting lead, but would prove to be a red herring. Then a Rand-McNally atlas from the nineteenth century revealed the existence of the small community of Avalon, Mississippi, north of Greenwood and near Grenada. Whereas McCormick had settled for a phone call, Hoskins decided to visit Avalon in his pursuit of the legendary guitarist—a brilliant decision, as subsequent events would prove. On his way back from a visit to New Orleans for Mardi Gras, Hoskins drove up to Stinson's, the town's main emporium, a combination general store, gas station, and post office. He asked the first people he encountered about Mississippi John Hurt and, to his amazement, was directed to travel another mile and stop at the third mailbox up the hill.

If Hoskins was startled to find Mississippi John Hurt in the flesh, still living in Avalon, Hurt was alarmed at the unexpected visit by a white stranger from the nation's capital. He concluded that Hoskins represented the FBI, or some other intrusive government agency. Hoskins only stayed briefly on this trip, before returning home. But soon he had traveled back to Avalon, and presented the bluesman with a novel and unnerving proposition: Hurt should come back with him to Washington, D.C. The aging bluesman eventually agreed . . . but one can only wonder at what he anticipated upon his arrival.

Yet the reception to this long forgotten musician was as extraordinary as his rediscovery was unexpected. Hurt found himself fêted and celebrated. His charm and gentleness, evident in his music as much as in the on-stage demeanor of the elfin performer, endeared him to audiences who might have been put off by the more tormented and anguished blues of the Delta tradition. Hurt was now presented with opportunities, at age seventy-one, that he had hardly dreamt of as a young man. He delighted fans at the Newport Folk Festival, captivated younger listeners on college campuses, and signed a record contract with the Vanguard label. And though he may have had only the foggiest notion of who Johnny Carson was—after all, Hurt didn't own a television set—the *Tonight Show* host had learned about the bluesman, and invited him onto the prominent late night program.

Hurt did not fit neatly into the Delta tradition—although many fans tend to overlook this and usually consider him as a representative of it. Avalon may have been only a few miles outside the Delta region proper, but Hurt's

music was a world apart from the raw and impassioned strains characteristic of Charley Patton or Son House, Robert Johnson or Muddy Waters.
Hurt aimed for precision and refinement, a sense of control and restraint.
His delicate stylings were almost the opposite of the Delta tradition, that
primal blues where the Id trampled on the Superego, content overran form,
and guilt and transcendence were as common as the love and courtship
conventions in a Tin Pan Alley song. Hurt may have had little experience
in front of large audiences—his hometown gigs had paid a couple of dollars, and the whole population of Avalon could not have filled some of the
venues he was now playing. But one would hardly guess it from his relaxed,
folksy demeanor in front of his newfound fans. Hurt's three-finger picking
style, and seesaw alternating bass, with its overtones of the rag tradition,
imparted an amiable, bouncy exuberance to his music. He kept to medium
tempos, and he held them better than the Delta stalwarts, who were erratic
timekeepers at best. He sang with a marked sensitivity to enunciation, dic-
tion, and volume, mostly eschewing the shouting and hooting, yodeling and
growling, testifying and whispering that, in the Delta tradition, sometimes
make performances seem less songs than ecstatic monologues.

Hurt's 1928 recordings for OKeh had found admirers for these very qualities. Harry Smith had included two tracks from Hurt in his quirky but influential compilation *Anthology of American Folk Music*, issued by Folkways in
1952. When he returned to the recording studio in the 1960s, Hurt took off
exactly where he had left off more than a generation before, and listeners felt
privileged to hear the purity of a traditional stylist who seemed to have paid
no attention to the profound changes in guitar music of recent decades.
Hurt had spent the intervening years farming, or logging, or building roads
and levees, supplemented by occasional gigs, at picnics and dances, rarely
journeying far from home. Perhaps Hurt was an anachronism, but in an
age that was reexamining all of the supposed benefits of modern life, this
throwback to a simpler era, with its implicit renunciation of almost everything contemporary popular music represented, was electrifying in spirit,
even if unplugged on the stage.

Hurt enjoyed this celebrated second career for only three short years
before dying quietly in his sleep on November 2, 1966. In this brief period, he
recorded and toured extensively, and proved that the sounds of prewar Mississippi could be relevant amid the turbulence and national soul-searching
of the 1960s. Nonetheless, Hurt's rediscovery raised many questions. Was

the favorable reception of modern audiences to this once obscure musician an anomaly? Did it signal a reevaluation of traditional blues, or was it driven more by the charisma and stage presence of this specific individual? Above all, what would happen if a real Delta player, a haunted soul with less folksy material—someone like Son House or Skip James or Bukka White—suddenly reappeared on the scene? Would fans accept their troubled and troubling music with the same enthusiasm that had greeted Hurt?

Blues fans had little time to mull over such questions. Within a few months of Hurt's reemergence, all three of these Delta legends reappeared, ready to present their dark, introspective music to a new generation raised on rock and roll: Booker Washington White, the former Parchman inmate whose 1940 sessions, with their impassioned blues, had captivated fans before the musician himself disappeared into an impenetrable fog of anonymity; Son House, another Parchman alum, who had served as inspiration for Robert Johnson and Muddy Waters, also missing from the music scene since the early 1940s; and Skip James, the master of the tormented minor blues, whose last known recording had been made in Grafton, Wisconsin, in 1931.

2. songs come down from the sky

A clue from an old song provided the link with White, much as it had with Mississippi John Hurt. In 1940, White had recorded a song called "Aberdeen Mississippi Blues," and in 1963 guitarist John Fahey, then a student at the University of California at Berkeley, sent a letter to White, relying on the evidence from this title for an address. The missive was marked for delivery to:

> Booker T. Washington White (Old Blues Singer)
> c/o General Delivery
> Aberdeen, Mississippi

Of course, White had left Aberdeen long ago, and had spent most of the previous two decades residing in Memphis. As we have seen, he helped his cousin B.B. King get established in that city, but White's own music career languished in the years following his final Chicago session. His rural blues were too old-fashioned to fit in with the tastes of the postwar period, and though he tried his hand at electric guitar, White found few listeners. He performed only sporadically, and his income came mostly from his long-standing job as a "fit-up" worker at the Newberry Equipment Company. But unknown to White, his old recordings had developed a cult following—only a few months before Fahey wrote to him, Bob Dylan had featured White's "Fixing to Die Blues" on his debut album. Now, for the first time in ages, a fan letter was about to arrive on his doorstep.

The U.S. Postal Service worked hard to earn the nickel stamp affixed to the hope-laden letter. White still had relatives in Aberdeen, and they were able to provide a forwarding address in Memphis. A short while later, Fahey was amazed and delighted to receive a written response from White, thanking him for his interest and expressing a willingness to meet in person. Although Fahey's friend ED Denson is often cited as a collaborator in writing the letter, Denson himself clarifies that it "was entirely John's idea and his plan. I actually didn't find out about it until Bukka responded. At that point John had no idea what to do about it." But Fahey and Denson quickly contrived a plan. Within a few hours of receiving this unexpected response, they had left town on a 2,000-mile journey to see—and, they hoped, to hear—the blues legend in person.

"We drove in John's car," Denson recalls, and—as often was the case when Fahey pursued one of his visions—the trip itself took on surrealistic overtones. "[John] was studying for his German finals so each day we stopped somewhere and he would conjugate German verbs loudly while sitting on a bench or the steps of a building. I recall one child watching and listening in complete bewilderment. As we got down south we would occasionally see a turtle crossing the road. John would stop and take it out of danger." After several days on the road, Fahey and Denson arrived triumphantly in Memphis, and met White in his rented room, where they found, to their satisfaction, that he played guitar as adeptly as on his old recordings.

One of the youngest of the prewar Delta pioneers, White was only in his early fifties, and still robust and healthy. "He was completely unaware of the folk revival, or of any interest in the old blues at all," Denson explains. "For him it was really old-fashioned stuff which no one wanted to hear anymore. I can't imagine what he thought of us—two young men just out of their teens really—with an old car." But White was determined to seize the opportunities presented by his surprising visitors. Fahey had mentioned in his letter that he was willing to pay White one hundred dollars for a recording session, and this no doubt contributed to the bluesman's cordiality.

"Bukka was living in a small upstairs rental in a house, as I recall," Denson continues. "We tried recording him there, but the setting and the equip-ment gave us poor results so we went to a recording studio for the sessions. The engineer liked the music, which gave us great hope." White responded with spirited versions of many of the same songs he had performed as a young man. Fahey and Denson would later release White's music on their Takoma label, and their activities were distinguished not only by the qual-ity of work they presented but also by their insistence on copyrighting the material under the name of their artist—an all too rare scrupulousness in the blues field, well known for its exploitative practices.

White decided to follow his visitors back to the West Coast, and in the fall of 1963 he arrived by train in Northern California, where he settled into a Berkeley bungalow. Here he delighted students by performing at folklore classes, playing engagements, and participating in a live broadcast on sta-tion KPFA. "He was a bit nervous about being on the radio anyway," Denson explains, "and so he gave it everything he had. As the song intensified, so did his playing. Finally with one downward swipe of his hand he broke 3 of the 6 strings on the guitar. Not missing a beat he went on to finish the piece on the remaining 3 strings."

While performing at The Cabale, a local folk music club, White met with Alan Lomax, and the two conferred in the small backstage area—perhaps they reminisced over Alan's father recording White back at Parch-man twenty-five years earlier. In any event, Lomax told Denson afterward that he should encourage White to play old blues rather than attempt more contemporary songs. But reining in White's performances was a futile, and perhaps pointless, endeavor. The rediscovered blues artist was a free spirit on stage, an improviser who wandered far afield from the short, highly structured renditions of familiar tunes known to blues aficionados from his classic recordings. Sometimes a set might include only three or four songs, and White would weave in stories and "talking blues" narratives, stretching out any given piece into a mini-epic. Night after night, the same song might evolve in different directions. When Chris Strachwitz decided to record White for his Arhoolie label, Fahey and Denson recommended that, if he wanted standard three- or four-minute performances, he should tap the musician on the shoulder when he needed him to wind down; otherwise a single take might go on indefinitely.

But Strachwitz had other ideas. He saw himself as a "documentor" rather than a "producer," and raised no objections when White offered to compose new songs for his Arhoolie releases, or when a performance went over a few minutes' duration. If Strachwitz asked about a certain type of music—say, gambling songs or a particular tuning—White typically offered to compose a new piece in that style or format, rather than wrack his brain to recall old material from the prewar years. Like the shamans of traditional society, White claimed that the songs came down to him from the sky. All he needed to do was to reach up and pull them down.

Soon, Strachwitz had enough material for two LPs, available today on the single CD *Sky Songs*. If Fahey and Denson had been successful at bringing White's music from the 1930s and 1940s back to life, Strachwitz showed that the imaginative capabilities of his recording artist were not limited to these old songs. Yet this degree of spontaneity and self-reliance presented an embarrassing mismatch with the marketing angles of the blues revival. Old blues musicians were expected to sing old blues. In truth, Booker White had never cared much for traditional songs, and had always been at his best when presenting his own recent compositions. Recall that when White recorded his famous Vocalion sides for Lester Melrose in 1940, the artist had apparently composed most of the music during a two-day burst of creativity—so even as a young man, the guitarist had perhaps looked up to the sky to capture the inspiration of the moment.

Yet White's career prospered even if he defied the expectations of some fans. In 1967, he participated in a European tour as part of the American Folk Blues Festival. He would return overseas several times, and leave behind a cadre of devoted fans as well as the more tangible legacy of films and recordings. The following year, White sang at the Olympic Games in Mexico City. In 1969, he recorded with an even older Memphis resident, Furry Lewis, and the two musicians, along with a number of other blues players, later formed the Memphis Blues Caravan, which toured under the direction of Steve LaVere and Arne Brogger. An even more emotional collaboration took place in 1973 when White joined B.B. King on stage, and reminded his famous cousin of the day he had given him his first guitar, a big red Stella. King looked down, his eyes brimming with tears, before embracing his older relative to the thunderous applause of the onlookers.

White continued to branch out, whenever producers allowed him the freedom to do so. For the Blue Horizon label he recorded a number of tracks featuring a blues combo—a rarity among the traditionalists who came back into the limelight at this time—and even on his last studio release, for Biograph, he was trying to introduce new material to his fan base. A series of strokes limited White's activities in the mid-1970s, and he died of cancer in 1977. But he had enjoyed a fourteen-year run, a whirlwind of musicmaking that solidified his historical importance and broadened his audience, following his rediscovery by two enthusiastic devotees who had tracked him down with little more than a song title as direction.

Fahey's success in finding White inspired him to follow the trail of other missing prewar blues musicians. Northern California offered few resources for sleuths seeking information about the early Delta blues, yet in Oakland Fahey encountered K. C. Douglas, who had previously lived in Jackson, Mississippi. In the 1940s, Douglas had known Tommy Johnson—a figure whose rediscovery would be a major find. But Douglas dashed Fahey's hopes when he said that Johnson was almost certainly dead. Even back then, Johnson's health had been destroyed by his drinking, and the once powerful blues singer had deteriorated into a feeble, emaciated figure—hardly someone who would survive to enjoy his late sixties. Douglas offered another suggestion. Ishmon Bracey, the blues singer turned minister, might still be alive back in Jackson. Perhaps Bracey could help Fahey find some of the other older Delta guitarists.

Fahey needed little more encouragement than this. Accompanied by Bill Barth and Henry Vestine, he journeyed again to Mississippi. Here he found Reverend Bracey willing to help—for a price. In exchange for thirty dollars, Bracey agreed to answer his visitors' questions, for at least a couple of hours. Bracey's recent encounter with Gayle Dean Wardlow may have alerted the minister to the financial value of his position as an elder statesman of the blues, and he was now determined to make at least some money off his sinful past. Bracey's answers were often vague, but when asked about Skip James, the singer of the eerie blues who had influenced Robert Johnson back in the 1930s, he provided a useful clue—as in the case of Hurt and White, the name of a city. James came from Bentonia, Bracey claimed; although he may well have merely been repeating what he had recently heard from Wardlow, who had traced James to this same location, and had mentioned this fact to the minister.

The three blues fans drove the thirty miles to Bentonia, but found few recalled James in this hamlet of five hundred citizens. Wardlow had visited the community earlier in the year, following a tip from James's old companion Johnny Temple, but encountered no one there who had seen the bluesman during the last decade. Fahey had little better luck, at least at first. He questioned a county clerk and a postal worker, neither of whom knew James. Then the three fans took to stopping random individuals and going door-to-door, seeking out the oldest residents, who might be most likely to remember the musician. Fahey was finally directed to James's aunt, Martha Polk. When her husband came home, he supplied a fresh clue: James had attended his father's funeral in Birmingham the previous year, and was now residing in Dunbar, a community near Tunica in the northern part of the state.

Fahey's map failed to show a Dunbar, but at this point the intrepid fans were unwilling to be discouraged by such a minor obstacle. They headed north, hoping that either Dundee or Dubbs, both located a few miles from Tunica, might be the current home of Skip James. Dundee initially proved to be another dead end; no one there had any information on the missing bluesman. But on the way to Dubbs, the trio stopped at a gas station and asked whether anyone there knew a musician by the name of Skip James. A young black man at the station recalled an older fellow, somewhat intoxicated, whom he had met one night at Benny Simmons's barbershop in Dundee. This man had bragged that he played guitar and piano and had made records—claims no one took seriously. Fahey and company tracked down the barbershop and were directed to a nearby shack.

They had arrived at their destination, but obstacles still remained. Here Mabel James, Skip's wife, at first denied any knowledge of the former Paramount recording artist—she thought these odd visitors might be government agents. (This suspiciousness was, as we have come to see, a recurring pattern to these fan-meets-artist encounters. Though one wonders, what government agency would have hired such oddball bohemians to implement its devious plans?) But as they spoke to her, the young fans revealed a devotion to old blues music, and an idiosyncratic knowledge of long forgotten records, that no revenuer was likely to possess. After some persuasion, she agreed to take them to see Skip James, at the Tunica County Hospital, where he was recovering from an embarrassing ailment—"a woman was the cause of it all," was his preferred explanation of the genital tumor—and about to be released. James should have been more concerned about what was likely the real underlying cause of his ailment, not an old girlfriend, rather the cancer that would lead to his death five years later. At the time,

James thought this medical problem was behind him, and was getting ready to return home.

If the three blues fans were awestruck by meeting Skip James in the flesh, the bluesman himself was blasé to an extreme. They proudly displayed a discography, which compiled all of James's known recordings, and he replied, "Now isn't that nice"—a patronizing dismissal such as a severe schoolteacher might give in response to the votive offering of an apple from a seven-year-old. After returning home, he agreed to play some music in response to his visitors' entreaties. His guitar technique might be clumsy— he had not touched the instrument in seven years—but his voice was seemingly unchanged from the 1930s, soaring with choirboy purity above his mournful minor chords. With a little bit of practice, James would be ready for the footlights and the recording studio.

But James had little interest in practice. The days passed, yet he seldom picked up the instrument—he preferred to hear his young visitors play for him. James was equally apathetic when the discussion turned to plans for a musical comeback. Instead, he spoke about the hogs he kept out back of his shack, or drank the moonshine he secured from a local bootlegger. Fahey tried to rouse James's interest in musicmaking by showing him a contract that would pay him if he recorded for the Takoma label. But this complex legal document only made James all the more wary of his visitors. James asked a local white planter, S. A. Arnold, for advice on the contract, and was referred to Arnold's lawyer, a state senator, who picked over the clauses with punctilious care and finicky disdain. Finally James relented, prodded by his wife, and advised by Arnold, who told him not to be a fool and to grab the opportunity to reignite his music career. In truth, James never got completely comfortable with the contract; besides, he was too smart to put much faith in these pieces of paper. It was the commitment of his patron that gave him the confidence to proceed. "If anybody mess with you," Arnold had promised, "I'll see the sonofabitches pay you what you deserve."

3. breathless expectation in the air

Only one month later, on July 25, 1964, Skip James stepped onto the stage at Newport, to perform at a Saturday "blues workshop" held on the third day of a folk festival that would attract almost seventy thousand spectators during its half-week of musical activities. James had not been part of the original lineup, and the last-minute decision to feature him meant he was *not* booked for a high-profile evening concert, but for this relatively low-key afternoon event. Yet even those who had hardly heard of James a few weeks before felt the buzz of raised expectations, and understood that his return marked a signal event.

James showed the signs of his recent hospitalization. He looked "gaunt and a little hesitant," Peter Guralnick would later recall, and some fans wondered whether he would actually perform that day. Perhaps James would merely step forward for an introduction, and accept the applause of the audience, before retreating back into the obscurity that had kept him from view for some thirty years. But James sat down at a chair toward the front of the stage, fumbled briefly with his guitar, adjusted the tuning, then launched into the same song he had used for his audition with H. C. Speir, half a lifetime ago:

> *I'd rather be the devil*
> *Than be that woman's man.*

The mood was hypnotic as James continued on, with his powerful imagery, telling how his mind got to ramblin' "like wild geese from the west," his voice sinuous and feminine, a striking contrast with the grim-faced man on stage in his undertaker's suit and broad-rimmed preacher's hat.

James would play for less than ten minutes that day, but the audience was transfixed by this mini-performance. Over a hundred artists were featured at Newport's six concerts and nineteen workshops that year, including Bob Dylan, Joan Baez, and Muddy Waters, but many attendees would remember James's short time on stage as the highlight of the festival—indeed, as one of the greatest moments in Newport's history. Bruce Jackson would later recall the opening of James's set as "one of those rare electric moments when things manage to connect and coalesce perfectly. . . . You could see so many of those young faces frozen as they listened, were taken up, and began to feel something of what it was all about." "As the first notes floated across the field," Guralnick would later write, "as the voice soared over us, the piercing falsetto set against the harsh cross-tuning of the guitar, there was a note of almost breathless expectation in the air. . . . As the song came to an end and

Skip, who had gradually been gaining confidence while he played, peered out at his new audience, the field exploded with cheers and whistles and some of the awful tension was dissipated."

"That was the high point of the man's career," Dick Waterman, also on hand that day, would say to Guralnick. "He came and conquered. It was high drama. . . . If he had come, played, conquered and quit right there, there could have been no greater legend in this entire world than Skip James." In time, James would enjoy a few more inspired moments in front of audiences—but only a few. Mack McCormick described to me another instance: "I remember Skip James performing at a free concert in Washington. There was something about the clear voice singing 'Cherry Ball' that captured people's attention. It was a magical moment. He was upset that day—he was always upset—but when he was on stage and started singing, he was beyond comparison."

In a more casual setting, a coffeehouse or nightclub, James was less prepossessing. Unlike Mississippi John Hurt, who could charm an audience, make them feel like close friends he had invited into his home to hear some music, James was an aloof performer. His distrust and scorn, soon apparent to those who spent time with him off stage, came across to fans in these intimate venues. The coffeehouse circuit, for all its importance in developing music careers at the time, was *not* just about playing songs; a certain open, bohemian sixties ambiance took root there, and people came to soak up the sensibility as much as the sounds. If Skip James was aware of the happening groove, the blossoming of love and peace and other metaphysical concepts that flourished in these settings, he gave few signs of it to the customers who paid their money to see him. And the owners of these venues also noticed this odd dynamic, or at least its impact on receipts. James failed to make much money for the proprietors of the Fret in Philadelphia, Ash Grove in Los Angeles, the Gaslight in New York. Booking agents grumbled that his forlorn music depressed the fans, who ordered less food and drink as a result. James, for his part, viewed himself as an artist rather than a mere entertainer—even those who had never met him might have picked this up from his prewar recordings with their refinement and otherworldliness—and made only the smallest concessions to the niceties of stagecraft, the smiles and banter, practiced by other working blues musicians. Perhaps another factor, James's religious scruples, also contributed to the emotional distance of his performances. At one point, James confided to Stephen Calt that playing the blues was sinful and that, as a result, he never did it with complete commitment. He had decided that performing this music as an intellectual exercise, rather than with his heart and soul, was an acceptable compromise, a manner of coming to grips with his personal legacy that might please his fans but not lure them into emulating his fallen path.

Yet James's personality is not solely to blame for his failure to capitalize on the momentum of Newport. His health also faltered soon after his comeback, his cancer sapping his strength and forcing him to return to the hospital. He commemorated this visit in his song "Washington D.C. Hospital Center Blues," which ranks among the best of James's new compositions from the 1960s. The song was perhaps the only positive outcome of his experiences at this facility, where they diagnosed his cancer and performed a surgical castration that may have slowed, but failed to halt its spread. With more robust health, James might have achieved much more during this second act of his career. But he was weakened in body and indifferent in spirit; he rarely practiced during this period, and although this had little negative impact on his singing, which still retained the exquisite beauty that had distinguished his earliest recordings, his guitar work and especially his piano playing suffered. He frankly admitted that he could no longer play "I'm So Glad" with the fervor of his 1931 version, and sometimes he was forced to slow down the tempo when attempting various older songs. As his health deteriorated, he turned much of his attention to folk healers and herbalists, but they were no more effective than the surgeons in curing him. The costs of these various treatments consumed much of his income from making music. From this perspective, the 1966 release of a rock version of James's "I'm So Glad" by Cream, featuring Eric Clapton, was a godsend. Cream (unlike many other rock bands that covered old blues songs) freely credited James, and the money he received in royalties—which may have approached ten thousand dollars—enabled him to continue his medical treatment and cover his living expenses.

Other disruptions in his life were brought on by James himself. He left his wife Mabel, and moved in with Lorenzo Meeks, the stepniece of Mississippi John Hurt. James was equally restless in his dealings with record companies and management, and here too John Hurt provided direction. James began relying on Dick Waterman, who was successfully booking Hurt, and now tried to bring his new client into many of the same venues. But it soon became clear that James could not match Hurt as a draw on the circuit.

James might make a hundred dollars for an appearance in a coffeehouse, and perhaps three hundred for a performance on a college campus. But work was sporadic, and paychecks unpredictable. His income was so low at one point that James qualified for welfare support, but Meeks objected to the disgrace of such a move, and refused to consider it as an option.

Despite all these troubles and afflictions—or perhaps because of them, if one can believe the conventional wisdom that links the blues to just such travails—James managed to make a number of recordings of haunting beauty during these comeback years. He recorded for several labels, and even if he lacked the strength or technical command he had enjoyed as a young man, he showed that he had lost none of his skills as an artistic visionary, as a painter of ethereal soundscapes. These late offerings often sound very fragile, but it is this tenuous quality, the rarefied air of his music, that many listeners find most moving. James's late work is much like those crafts whose very medium—in porcelain or glass or wax—extracts a gentleness and delicacy from the creative spirit. He often drew extensively on songs from his Paramount recordings, and fans who listen to all of James's 1960s sessions will encounter much repetition. Yet these reprisals of earlier works such as "Hard Time Killin' Floor Blues," "Devil Got My Woman," "Cherry Ball Blues," or "Cypress Grove Blues" can proudly stand alongside the classic version of a generation before, and to some degree compare favorably— certainly for the sonic fidelity, but also for an intangible, world-weary quality, hard to define yet clearly present in the grooves, a sense of seeing beyond the vagaries of this life that makes these songs almost more appropriate for an old man to deliver than for a younger one.

Only a few weeks after his Newport appearance, James recorded for Fahey, Denson, and Barth in the basement studio of Gene Rosenthal's home in Silver Spring, Maryland. He is more energetic and vivacious here than on many of his later recordings, especially on faster songs like "I'm So Glad" and "All Night Long." He recorded the latter piece for Dick Spottswood only a few months later; but the tempo by then is much slower, and James is in a much gloomier frame of mind, as demonstrated by two newer compositions recorded that day: "Sick Bed Blues" and "Washington D.C. Hospital Center Blues." On the whole, however, Spottswood's session was quite productive; instead of completing the eight tracks envisioned for an LP release, James produced fourteen songs during a single day, enough for two albums. It almost seems as if James were picking up where he left off in 1931, when

Arthur Laibly of Paramount had asked him how many songs he was ready to record that day; and James had smugly replied: "As many as you want."

But Fahey or Spottswood, for all their enthusiasm, could hardly support James's career the way a larger label might. James's decision to record for Vanguard in January 1966 marked a major step forward in his comeback. Founded in 1950 by Maynard and Seymour Solomon, the "Vanguard Recording Society, Inc." (as it ostentatiously labeled itself) had a large impact on the cultural front despite its small size and modest budget. It backed the careers of blacklisted artists, such as Paul Robeson and the Weavers, and lived up to its name as a vanguard for the new currents of the 1960s with its promotion of Joan Baez, Mimi and Richard Fariña, and Buffy Sainte-Marie, artists who valued social consciousness-raising as much as record sales. Maynard Solomon had supported the comeback of Mississippi John Hurt, and he now embraced Skip James as his latest project. At the conclusion of the efforts that resulted in the landmark album *Skip James Today*, he confided to the artist that it stood out as the best session he had been involved with during fifteen years of making records.

Solomon, a trained musician and scholar, brought his perfectionist tendencies to bear on this noteworthy collaboration. No one would ever do a better job of recording James. Even the slightest wavers and nuances of his singing come across clearly, and the guitar is equally well miked. James sounds extraordinarily relaxed, yet also charged with powerful emotions, a Delphic oracle brought into the studio to pass judgment on the vanity of human wishes. If the essence of James's artistry were to transmute blues into art song, this project stood as perhaps the highest realization of his goal. James returned again to his familiar standards, "Hard Time Killin' Floor," "Cypress Grove Blues," and others, but with a heartfelt immediacy that makes it hard to believe that these were old songs from a bygone era.

Skip James Today, for all its artistic merits, sold poorly. But Solomon, who knew more than anybody that the impact of Vanguard could hardly be measured in sales, pronounced himself pleased with the results, and began preparing for a follow-up recording. For this project, released as *Devil Got My Woman* in May 1968, Solomon demonstrated an even greater mastery of the studio environment. Stephen Calt, who accompanied James that day, has noted that the guitarist "bungled song after song." James was experimenting with a less structured, free-flowing approach, relying more on the spontaneous inspiration of the moment. As Calt recalls it, James would "begin a guitar riff à la Blind Lemon Jefferson, that is, have no idea where he was going with it, and (unlike Jefferson) proceed to go out on a limb, sound discordant or hesitant notes indicating his confusion, and then regroup and conclude the interlude with the ubiquitous tonic chord." Yet "Solomon appeared delighted with every take"—and the finished release showed why. Solomon somehow managed through careful splicing to create polished performances, perhaps the realization of some Platonic ideal that James could never have created live in concert. The producer had managed to deliver a dramatic musical document, and even if his methods may upset purists, they were modest in their manipulations compared to the studio pyrotechnics and wizardry commonly practiced in the present day.

In the fall of 1967, James was able to realize his ambition to perform in Europe; but this was one of his final triumphs. His health continued to deteriorate, and the following September he took ill after an engagement in Bethel, Pennsylvania. He spent much of October confined to his bed, and often drank to alleviate his chronic pain. When he finally sought treatment at the University of Pennsylvania hospital, he was told that his cancer was inoperable. He had no recourse except to return home and wait to die. James lingered on for almost another year, until his death on October 3, 1969. During the final months, he sometimes wondered whether his affliction were somehow due to his blues playing. According to Calt, James promised that, if the Lord favored him with a return to health, he would restrict his performances to religious songs.

Many fans might have thought that the conflict between blues and religion would have been resolved, or dismissed entirely as an issue, by the 1960s, when supposedly more enlightened—or at least more secular—views prevailed. But James's anxieties were by no means unusual, as testified by the similar concerns that prevented Ishmon Bracey, Robert Wilkins, and others from taking advantage of opportunities to resume their careers as blues singers during the decade.

Yet the most dramatic example of the psychological complexities of this conflict of values among practitioners of the Delta blues would be found in the figure of Son House, a source of inspiration to Robert Johnson and Muddy Waters and a man who had been dealing with his misgivings about the sacrilege of blues singing since he was an adolescent. Now House would bring his deep sense of foreboding to modern audiences—for he too now emerged from his obscure past and burst onto the national stage at virtually the same moment that Skip James was rediscovered.

4. i'm trying to build me a church

"The search for these old-time bluesmen has always had a note of urgency about it," *Newsweek* magazine reported to its readers on July 13, 1964. "No wonder then the excitement last week when it was learned that both Son House and Skip James had been found." A week earlier, the magazine's readership would hardly have been able to identify these two names, but now they were assured that they had been "the only great country blues singers still lost."

More than two decades had elapsed since Alan Lomax had tried, unsuccessfully, to lure Son House to New York to perform and potentially launch a new phase of his career. As it turned out, House had moved to New York around the time of Lomax's last letter, but settled in Rochester, far afield from the musical currents of Manhattan. Wardlow, Fahey, and others realized the potential value of finding this seminal figure in the history of the music, but House's considerable distance from the Delta communities where he had made his reputation kept him out of reach of the blues detectives who scoured Mississippi in search of the forgotten blues players of the prewar years. "When last heard of he had left the Delta for the North," Simon Napier wrote in *Blues Unlimited* in April 1964, "and reports several years ago now, indicated that he was in Chicago, but this was never confirmed." Only a few weeks before the *Newsweek* article, Stephen Calt, acting on information that House might be living in New York, pressed a family member who worked in the state's social services bureaucracy to try to use her access to confidential information on welfare recipients to see if House's name and address might be listed. But Calt's contact balked at this request, and another path needed to be found if the mystery of Son House were to be unraveled. And, as with Hurt, James, and White, a single, almost insignificant clue proved the missing link in determining the bluesman's whereabouts.

In April 1964, Booker White had traveled to Boston for an engagement; during his visit, he resided with Al Wilson and Phil Spiro at the house they shared on Roberts Road in Cambridge. Wilson would not launch the band Canned Heat for more than a year, and at the time, his living conditions were only a step above squalor. "We had about two nickels to scrape together," Spiro recalls. "We had a shotgun house arrangement. I had the back bedroom and Al had the front one. Booker White was staying with us. So Al brought in two trash cans and a shovel and cleaned up his room and gave it to Booker.

"Booker and Al had nothing to do all day, and Al had an untapped genius for getting other people to talk about their music. He would play recordings for Booker and get him to talk about them." White's preferences soon became apparent. He had little positive to say about Robert Johnson—due, it seemed, to Johnson's singing in a higher register than White thought was appropriate for the blues. He listened with more enthusiasm to Charley Patton, whom he had long admired. But in time, the conversation turned to the subject of Son House, and White became very thoughtful. He recalled that a friend of his had mentioned seeing House coming out of a theater in Memphis the previous year.

This was a stunning revelation. Blues fans had been on the trail of House for years, and now a clue seemed to point in the direction where the elusive guitarist might be found. "Now I long thought that Al Wilson was the person who asked Booker about Son House," Spiro clarifies—and, indeed, Spiro himself was the original source of this account. His article in *The Broadside of Boston* from July 22, 1964, has long served as the most detailed published description of the rediscovery of Son House, and it gave Wilson credit for probing White's knowledge of House. "But it turns out to have been Dave Evans [who was still a student at Harvard at the time]," Spiro continues. "Evans is an extraordinary person, and maybe it is going too far to call him ego-less, but just imagine: he was the person who spurred the rediscovery of Son House, and he lets forty years go by and never tries to take credit for it!"

Wilson and Spiro were determined to travel immediately to Memphis and pursue this promising lead. But neither of them drove a car. They needed a third member of the team, preferably one who could navigate the roadways and get them to Memphis. Evans had academic commitments. Spiro contacted Tom Hoskins, who was unavailable but suggested Nick Perls, only Spiro didn't know him. While this was unfolding, Spiro ran into Dick Waterman at a cafeteria near Harvard and explained the situation to him. Waterman expressed his willingness to join the expedition, and before long the three fans had stuffed their suitcases, two tape recorders, a camera, and sleeping bags into a red Volkswagen and began their journey to Tennessee. They would spend the next sixteen days on the trail of America's most wanted bluesman.

The promising clue that initiated their journey led only to a dead end. White's friend in Memphis, blues singer Lillian Glover, had in fact seen House, but did not know where he lived. Forced to find another road map to House's door, the threesome decided to enlist the services of Reverend Robert Wilkins, whose number was in the phone book—based on the assumption that Wilkins might have some connections who could help or, at a minimum, that the participation of an African-American minister in their midst might loosen lips among those who had useful information. "The smartest thing we did was to get in touch with Robert Wilkins," Spiro reminisces—and without his assistance it is hard to see how the three fans could have overcome the many obstacles that still lay in their path. Wardlow and Klatzko, while researching Charley Patton, had learned that House had lived in Lake Cormorant, Mississippi, and here the group focused their efforts. Wilkins knew the area well, and was able to make inquiries which led to Fiddling Joe Martin, who in turn put the seekers onto Benny Brown, Jr., who then pointed them in the direction of Grace Strong, mother-in-law to House's stepdaughter, who gave them the address of her son J. W. Smith in Detroit, who, when they phoned him, provided—yes, finally—an address for the old blues legend in Rochester, New York. No phone number was available for House, so a telegram was sent to his address, relaying a simple request: "If you are the Son House who recorded for Paramount in the thirties and the Library of Congress in the forties, please call person to person collect in Memphis . . ." Even at this point, their efforts were thwarted. There was a mistake in the address, and the telegram could not be delivered. Another call to Detroit fixed the error and a new telegram was sent. Finally, on Father's Day, 1964, the spiritual father of so many later blues musicians spoke to his devoted fans on the phone.

House's immediate reaction was . . . puzzlement. Nobody had shown any interest in his music in over twenty years, and he wondered how these youngsters even knew about it. He mentioned that he hadn't played the guitar in some four years, but that he still could. The trio of devotees now started on the last leg of their journey, driving to Rochester where—more than two weeks and some four thousand miles after they set out on their vision quest—they encountered House sitting on his apartment stoop. The man seemed too small to be the legendary blues player. They envisioned a big man to match the larger-than-life voice; but the thin gentleman of medium height was the only person around, so they asked him if he knew which apartment belonged to Mr. House. "This is him," he replied.

Finding House was one thing; putting him on the stage was another. House suffered from a pronounced hand tremor—so severe when the trio found him, he sometimes struggled to use a pencil or a fork, let alone a guitar. His propensity for drinking required constant supervision by those around him if he were to stay sober enough to perform, and only the smallest amount of liquor seemed to incapacitate him. Above all, House had always harbored doubts about the morality of singing the blues, and if he had been unwilling to seize the opportunities offered by Lomax in the 1940s, he was hardly more enthusiastic about following a similar path in the 1960s. In short, America might be ready to welcome Son House the long-lost blues singer with open arms, but did House want to participate in the lovefest?

Even if the medical and moral obstacles were overcome, musical ones remained. The initial tapes made of House by Nick Perls were far from promising, and the decision not to release them commercially at the time, despite their obvious importance, testifies to how much the Delta legend's playing had deteriorated. The conventional story, as it is commonly told, is a striking one: just as Willie Wilson had taught him guitar almost forty years before, now another Wilson—Alan Wilson—needed to step in, tutoring House on how to render his own legendary blues compositions. The scene is striking: one of the most influential guitarists in the history of American music, apparently so little concerned about his music that he no longer remembers how to play it, tutored by an up-and-coming rock legend. It is a colorful tale but, alas, somewhat exaggerated. Phil Spiro emphasized this point in my interview with him: "It is said that Al taught Son House how to play Son House. What really happened was that Al sat down with Son in our apartment, playing records and hearing Son's reactions. He played Son his old recordings and also played for him on the guitar. He was reminding Son of what he had done in the past, *not* teaching him how to play. It was more like 'remember this song.' Al was *not* showing Son where to put his fingers, and how to play his songs."

Even more than Wilson, Dick Waterman played the decisive role at this point in jump-starting House's career. He dealt one by one with all of the issues standing in the way of a comeback. Waterman's father was a physician, who sent House to Mass General for neurological testing for the guitarist's hand tremor. Waterman arranged for the high-profile article in *Newsweek*—the music editor at the publication, Hubert Saal, was his brother-in-law—that introduced House to the broader public. Waterman guided House through the complexities of resuming a record career, and while the other rediscovered blues players found themselves promoted by small labels operated by fans, Waterman helped secure a contract with Columbia, the most powerful record company in America, with the famous John Hammond acting as producer. Waterman also stepped in as booking agent for House, a role which demanded round-the-clock vigilance even more than managerial acumen. Waterman not only made the arrangements with club owners and concert promoters but also acted as personal escort and chaperone. In short, as Lawrence Cohn has suggested, Dick Waterman was "a man to whom House owed everything" at this stage of his career.

Although Waterman today is protective of House's reputation and prefers not to dwell on the pitfalls of the bluesman's problems with alcohol, he admits that booking this artist brought with it special responsibilities. "Son House was hard work—every day, every week, every month of every year," he told me during our conversation at his home in Oxford, Mississippi. Most managers might have sent House a bus or train ticket to get to an engagement, but Waterman knew that his only guarantee that House would arrive at the gig was to travel to Rochester and accompany the artist himself. House was typically more interested in finding a drink than in advancing his music career. He would pawn his guitar if that would help him secure money for alcohol. On stage, House could still be a dramatic performer. But getting him to the stage was fraught with risk. "If you turned your back on him," Waterman recalled, "he was gone."

The Columbia recording has since been re-released with the addition of almost a full hour of alternate takes and previously unissued tracks. As such, the project not only stands as the most important artistic statement by House during this final stage of his career, but also provides valuable insights into the challenges of reclaiming this music and presenting it for mass consumption to the record-buying public. House had never been an especially proficient guitarist, and the passing years had not improved his prowess on the instrument, yet his music is hardly held back by technical limitations on these late recordings. In truth, House showed no interest in extracting subtle or delicate sounds. He deals with the guitar in a manner reminiscent of those heavy-handed masseurs who pound your body mercilessly, and twist your joints into uncomfortable positions, an unabashed roughhousing that is almost a mockery of the craft—yet gives you a savage sort of relief, exhausted and drained, that a more nuanced practitioner could never have achieved. In the same way, House demands but one thing from his guitar: total submission. He strikes the strings with a passion that borders on ferocity, and the metal tube he wears on a finger of his fretting hand is akin to the brass knuckles that double the force of a sucker punch. There are awkward moments where a song seems about to falter, but House plays with redoubled intensity, either oblivious to obstacles or determined to overcome them by sheer willfulness. He is one of those rare artists—Miles Davis is another—whose missed notes seem to add to the emotional immediacy of the performance, and the listener is almost grateful for such lapses.

But House also needed to be seen, not just heard, for his intensity to be appreciated, and those in attendance at the Columbia sessions were transfixed by what they witnessed. "His eyes are closed, head reared back," Lawrence Cohn wrote in *Saturday Review* at the time, "and he gasps as he builds his song to a fever-pitched emotional level. He has a quality of becoming so totally immersed in his artistry that, by all indications, it appears that each song is a complete catharsis in itself." Record buyers could not experience the drama of the visual experience, almost ritualistic, of House entering what psychologists call the "flow state," that magical moment when the performer and the music become one. Even so, listeners sitting by their turntables in Middle America could have no illusions about this music. It was potent stuff, not prettified, not polished and packaged, not made more palatable for consumers in any way. For many, it must have been an unpleasant experience; for others, it was nothing short of a revelation.

Son House also brought this level of fervor to his live performances, and here blues fans from the 1960s got a sense of the powerful musical personality who had captivated Robert Johnson more than a generation before. House did not hold energy in reserve, did not calibrate his level of intensity depending on the venue or the size of the audience. He only knew one way of performing, and that way demanded his total commitment from first to last note. "Son House did it exactly the same for twenty or two thousand or twenty thousand [people]," Waterman explains. "He did it just exactly the

same. To see him just close his eyes, and get lost in performance, just lash-
ing out, full emotion, physical commitment, just raging, raging, to a fifteen
minute song, for about twenty, twenty-five people, was awesome."

House performed at Newport less than two weeks after *Newsweek*
reported on his rediscovery. He played Carnegie Hall, gracing the same
stage where John Hammond had told the audience more than a quarter
century earlier of Robert Johnson's death. He came to colleges and coffeehouses. Every audience received the same, impassioned performance—and
usually the same songs. House's repertoire was limited. He kept returning
to a handful of compositions, the same ones he recorded for Columbia—
"Death Letter," "Preachin' Blues," "Pearline," "Levee Camp Moan." Many of
these songs dated back to the earliest days of his recording career. In "My
Black Mama—Part 2," recorded for Paramount in 1930, House had sung:

I got a letter this morning, how do you think it read?
Oh hurry, hurry. Gal you love is dead.

This now becomes the central image of his "Death Letter," which House
featured at almost every concert, a macabre recital of events: the body laid
out on the cooling board, the scene at the burial ground, the coffin lowered
into the grave, the sun setting on this dolorous scene. For younger fans of
the 1960s, turned on to the blues perhaps through the gateway of rock and
roll, such stark performances showed how much the Delta style resisted
commercial pressures, how naturally it strayed from the typical topics of
pop songs and felt most at home in a landscape of gruesome detail and
psychological anguish.

But if the obsessive, unrelenting quality of the Delta idiom figured in
House's music, it came across even more insistently in the guitarist's long
monologues, which might take up a sizable portion of any performance. No
matter the setting, the mood, the makeup of the audience, House's remarks
tended to the subject that formed the large, looming tragedy of his life.
No, he did not talk about his time as a prisoner in Parchman; nor did he
seem bothered by his failed marriages, five in total; or the decades spent in
workaday jobs when he might have been a celebrated musician. Instead,
House lamented the sinfulness of the music he sang, and how the blues had
become his calling rather than the ministerial career to which he had once
aspired.

At an April 1965 Oberlin concert, captured on tape, Dick Waterman takes the stage and offers a long, erudite introduction, describing House's personal history, his technique with the slide guitar, the regional style he represents. But when the artist appears, he changes the subject before playing a single note. "I'm just an old, ordinary blues player," House begins, demeaning the very talent that has brought the audience together for this event. He continues:

> I won't say all the other things. Because I started off preaching. I preached for years and years. I done more preaching than I did *these things here* [said with scorn and sharp emphasis]. 'Cause it made me mad to see a guy with one of these things [obviously indicating the guitar]. Playing them old blues. Made me mad. And I'm trying to build me a church. Here he comes with a guitar swung on his shoulder. Whoa, I get so mad.

And on and on, some members of the audience occasionally laughing nervously, assuming these sentiments are offered as a bit of humor, others deathly quiet, apparently confused or put off by the unexpected homily. But for House, these rambling discourses must have served as something akin to the warning labels placed on packs of cigarettes or other unhealthy products: Use at your own risk, he told his fans. Listen to the blues but don't be swayed by its beguiling message. The failed preacher finally had a large congregation in front of him, and even if they did not come to hear the holy Word, he would make sure that they got a dose of religion in the process.

Sometimes, he would add a religious song into the mix. The one he chose most often was "John the Revelator," sung without guitar—only House's hands clapping out the rhythm in an impassioned performance. One is inevitably reminded of House's comment to an interviewer that, when he was younger, just placing his hands on a guitar seemed like a sin to him. Is this why he puts the guitar aside for this song? And the choice of the author of the Book of Revelation as the subject matter for House's song seems even more telling. It is the most mystical, the most apocalyptic book in the whole Bible, the richest in imagery, the hardest to interpret, sublimely poetic yet wedded into the harshest, most judgmental passages of the New Testament. In short, this book's relation to the rest of Scripture is much like the Delta style's relation to the rest of the blues—an intensifying of the whole in the part, a transcendence born in anguish and torment, an obsession conveyed in potent images. To some extent, House had always seemed to be quoting from the Book of Revelation—hear his "Dry Spell Blues" from back in 1930 with its end-of-world prognostications—even when he dealt with secular subjects. Now he simply made the linkages explicit for his younger fans.

House's audience changed during these comeback years. At first, the blues revival circuit relied on the same venues that hosted folk music acts, the coffeehouses and college campuses where a young and predominantly white audience encountered, often for the first time, an old blues singer like House or Booker White or Skip James. But in 1968 and 1969, the stirrings of an African-American roots revival brought a different audience to hear aging blues stars. House and others of his generation were able to secure gigs at black academic institutions, such as Howard University, Fisk University, and Spelman College. Around this same time, the first substantial festival focused solely on the blues was held in Ann Arbor, Michigan, and Son House played in front of what may have been the largest audience of his career. But at the close of the decade, House had a chance to reach an even more influential fan base, in essence an invitation to build a following in the world of rock and roll.

In 1967, B.B. King's career moved into overdrive after a memorable performance on a rock bill at the Fillmore in San Francisco. Around the same time, Muddy Waters found a new audience through his partnership with rocker Johnny Winter, just as John Lee Hooker did in conjunction with Canned Heat. Now a similar opportunity was presented to Son House. "Delaney Bramlett and his wife Bonnie were going out on the road," Waterman recalls. "Just a low key thing, [until] Clapton agreed to play rhythm guitar." He continues:

> Clapton would stand back in the shadows, and a couple times each set he would come forward and just take a wicked solo, and then step back. They were going to play the Fillmore East in the Lower East Side of Manhattan for Bill Graham. Bill calls me and wanted Son House to open for Delaney & Bonnie & Friends, with Eric Clapton. Bill said— and he was right—there were probably not two bigger Robert Johnson fans than Delaney Bramlett and Eric Clapton, and they worshipped Son House. If I could get Son House to do 15 or 20 minutes per night to open the show for Delaney & Bonnie & Clapton, they would see

him from the edge of the stage and it would inspire them to hit musical heights. . . . It's a win-win situation. Son House gets good money and he gets to play for three thousand people per night. And Delaney & Eric get to see one of their musical gods every night, and then follow him on stage.

But House was unable to make the gig. He had passed out in a snowbank back in Rochester, after drinking heavily one night, and lay there until dawn. He suffered a dangerous case of frostbite as a result and required hospitalization. House eventually recovered enough to resume playing the guitar, but his performances dwindled in the 1970s, and he retired completely in 1976. He moved to Detroit, where he lived quietly until his death from cancer of the larynx on October 19, 1988.

For the last twelve years of his life, Son House had little to do with the blues world, although it had not forgotten him. In 1980, he was inducted into the Blues Hall of Fame, and shortly after his death, the phenomenal, and unexpected, sales of Columbia's Robert Johnson reissue again drew attention to this seminal figure, inspiration to Johnson and so many other blues musicians. But for House, the periods of his life in which he had performed and recorded the blues were just passing interludes—he had spent more years working on the railroad and as a short-order cook or in other menial jobs. And all of them kept him from his true vocation, the pastoral calling that never was, but that still haunted him, and whose loss could hardly be compensated for by the applause, the recordings, and the awards.

5. bury my body down on Highway 61

Lesser and more obscure talents also basked in the light of the blues revival, and the dedication and enthusiasm of researchers, equipped with recording devices, gave many Mississippi musicians the opportunity to preserve their songs on tape or vinyl, some for the first time in their long careers.

The death of Tommy Johnson in 1956 had prevented one of the most talented blues musicians of the prewar years from participating in the revival. But many of the musicians who had known him filled the void with their own performances, some of them almost note-for-note replications of Johnson's songs. David Evans, who had completed a senior thesis on the Homeric epics while at Harvard, focused on Johnson for his master's thesis at UCLA, and later undertook a full-fledged study of a number of musicians in Johnson's orbit for his dissertation. Evans's shift in focus from Greek epics to Delta blues may have surprised outsiders, but to Evans it represented the continuation of his long-standing interest in the way oral traditions are shaped and preserved. The growing consensus—shaped by Albert Lord, Milman Parry, and others—was that the Homeric tales had been developed by a large number of forgotten individuals working within the confines of shared traditions, perhaps even in informal settings not entirely different from the jukehouses and small-scale entertainments where the Delta blues had first flourished. The borrowings of themes and material, their refinement during years of performance, the learning of novices at the feet of the masters—all the peculiarities of the Delta situation seemed to echo timeless practices from ancient cultures. Evans (who had studied with Lord at Harvard) came to believe that an inquiry into the roots of the blues music he loved offered a rare chance to trace the fascinating path by which a folk tradition coalesced into an artistic movement. He would eventually tape around seven hundred blues performances by more than eighty musicians as part of this research, which would result in the publication of his seminal book *Big Road Blues: Tradition and Creativity in the Folk Blues.*

Only a few of Evans's field recordings have been released commercially, and in truth they were not intended for mass market dissemination. Sometimes the skills of the musicians he tracked down had eroded significantly since the days of their youth, and many had perhaps never been especially talented. Babe Stovall, almost sixty years old when he met Evans, would quip when he performed in coffeehouses, "I ain't the best in the world, but I'll do till the best git here." Evans also made recordings of Houston Stackhouse, Mott Willis, Isaac Youngblood, Arzo Youngblood, Boogie Bill Webb, John Henry "Bubba" Brown, and Roosevelt Holts—all of whom had some connection to Tommy Johnson. Evans even recorded Johnson's brother, Mager (pronounced "Major") Johnson, another exponent of this same tradition. In some instances, the musicians he recorded had few direct ties to the Delta region—Stovall, for instance, spent most of his life in the southern part of the state and in Louisiana. But this, in itself, was interesting and provocative, demonstrating how musical practices may have been centered in the Delta, where the population density, so to speak, of important blues musicians was at its greatest, but they ultimately respected no city limits or state lines. We have experienced much the same throughout this study: the historian of the blues must exercise some judicious flexibility in drawing geographical borders, and sometimes activities centered a shorter or longer distance outside the proper limits of the Delta region have a tremendous bearing on our story. Evans studied this process in greater detail than anyone else, following the lines of influence and dissemination with a diligence and care that have made his writings a prime source for all future researchers into the Delta tradition.

Even earlier, Paul Oliver and Chris Strachwitz had sought out blues talent among the older generation of Mississippi residents. In 1960, they rediscovered Samuel Chatmon, then sixty-three years old, and though his music lacked the raw vigor of his (possible) half brother Charley Patton—indeed, Chatmon had long prided himself on performing for higher-class white audiences who didn't care much for the low-down blues—he proved to be a valuable source of information and insights into the prewar era. The visitors encountered more heartfelt performers at the Big Six Barber Shop in Clarksdale, where they met Wade Walton and Robert Curtis Smith. Wade would later give up the clippers and try his fortune as a performer in New York, and Smith later recorded for Strachwitz's Arhoolie label and the Prestige-Bluesville, but neither artist enjoyed much commercial success. Yet the very fact that even the local barber sang the blues in Clarksdale reinforced the romance and mystique of the ongoing quest for hidden talent in the Delta, and helped inspire others in their search for the next great discovery.

William Ferris also scoured the state in pursuit of neglected blues artists in the late 1960s and early 1970s, first in preparation for his dissertation, and later as he worked to complete his 1978 study *Blues from the Delta*. Ferris recorded Scott Dunbar, Lee Kizart, Lovey Williams, and James "Son" Thomas, among others, and studied his subjects' lives and times with a meticulous care unusual among blues researchers. In his book, Ferris included, among other exhibits, a map of Son Thomas's neighborhood, a diagram of his house, a reproduction of his handwriting, along with the usual photographs and transcriptions of lyrics. He also documented Thomas's music on film, and in other writings. Thomas seized the opportunities presented by this advocacy, and in time found himself performing on television, in concert overseas, even at the White House—a dramatic change for a man who had worked as a sharecropper and gravedigger, and had survived epilepsy, emphysema, a severe burn injury, and a shooting at the hands of his ex-wife.

Thomas's music was far more polished than his life, his voice warm and sinuous, and he played his guitar patterns and turnarounds with a precision and clarity of harmonic intent seldom found among Mississippi musicians of his generation. Even so, a subversive element always lurked beneath the surface, and when Thomas sang his unexpurgated version of the "Catfish Blues," delicate sensibilities were likely to be offended. Yet Thomas cannily understood his audience, keeping such renditions out of his White House repertoire, and in general offering folks only as much blue material in their blues as he thought they could handle. He never achieved substantial sales, and most of the music released during his lifetime came from field recordings rather than commercial projects. His final years were plagued with ill health, and he suffered a stroke that led to his death in June 1993 at age sixty-six. His tombstone, found at Bogue Memorial Cemetery, in Leland, Mississippi, offers a blues musician's philosophy in a recapitulation of one of Thomas's favorite lyrics:

Give me beefsteak when I'm hungry
Whiskey when I'm dry
Pretty women when I'm living
Heaven when I die.

Alan Lomax would, inevitably, also play a prominent role in the blues revival; although, unlike Evans or Ferris, Lomax was less interested in presenting a scholarly synthesis than in capturing the poetic essence of the Delta tradition. Lomax had been planning a book on the Delta since at least the early 1940s, and many must have given up hope that it would ever appear, when decade after decade passed without any news of publication. But finally, in 1993, more than a half century after the initiation of the Library of Congress and Fisk University project that provided the major portion of Lomax's research materials, he published *The Land Where the Blues Began*. This discursive, 500-page volume would win the National Book Critics Circle Award, and stand as Lomax's last substantial contribution to music studies—although one, as we have seen, not without its share of controversy.

Lomax's activities during the blues revival of the late 1950s and early 1960s were fairly low key—at least when measured by his past standards of prolific recording and promotion. He played little role in the rediscovery of the "lost" blues musicians of the prewar years, and it has been suggested that he actually slowed it down—by some reports, Lomax knew where Son House was living in Rochester, while others engaged in a prolonged hunt for news of the missing artist. But Lomax more than made up for this sin of omission by his discovery of a great neglected talent, Mississippi Fred McDowell, during fieldwork in Mississippi in 1959. Lomax recorded McDowell outdoors at night, with the aid of a flashlight, and was transfixed by the aged blues-man's music. He would later effuse that McDowell sounded "like a deep-voiced black herald of the *loi*, with a silver-voiced heavenly choir answering him from the treble strings." McDowell's own response, when he heard the playback, was equally felicitous, if more down-home. Lomax writes: "He stomped up and down on the porch, whooping and laughing and hugging his wife. He knew he had been heard and felt his fortune had been made."

And indeed it had! McDowell had never recorded during his younger years, and now he was determined to make the most of the chances that came to him late in life. Born in Rossville, Tennessee, most likely on January 12, 1904, McDowell offers us a case study in the odd paths a blues career might follow in the middle decades of the century, and his story further reinforces the point made above, namely, the difficulty of using strict geographical boundaries in delineating blues styles. McDowell grew up on the farm, where he helped his father work the twelve acres where they grew cotton, peas, and corn. He moved to Memphis around the time he turned twenty-one, and finally settled in Como, Mississippi, in the early 1940s. But his music was infused with the free-spirited intensity of the Delta tradition, even if his geographical connections to the heart of the region are weak ones at best, and his name is usually one of the first mentioned by blues fans when the conversation turns to the subject of their favorite Delta guitarists.

McDowell viewed with suspicion modern innovations of any sort, although he eventually embraced the electric guitar—but only because it was louder and easier to play; his fundamental approach was no different than on the acoustic instrument. His sound stayed true to prewar conventions, what McDowell called "the straight and natural blues," and he was quick to remind fans that he "did not play rock and roll." "The only way you can rock Fred," he quipped, "you have to put him in a rocking chair." Despite such admonitions, rockers would come, in time, to learn from McDowell; the Rolling Stones, in particular, would introduce many new listeners to his music through their cover of his song "You Got to Move."

But though many imitated, none surpassed McDowell's down-home sound and, especially, his skill with a bottleneck. He had learned the technique as a young boy from his uncle, who ground and filed down a steak bone to the proper size and wore it on his little finger. McDowell was mesmerized by the sound, and in time learned how to play the guitar with a pocket knife, a challenging technique that forced him to lay the instrument flat on his lap, thus restricting his ability to play chords. He later switched to a standard bottleneck, which he wore on his ring finger or little finger. He worked magic with this small implement, and McDowell could rightly brag that the guitar spoke when he spoke; sang when he sang. His tonal palette encompassed an endless variety of bending, vibrating, sliding tones, a return to that primeval time of innocence when there were no *notes*, but rather *sounds*, and instead of the twelve steps of our Western scale, musicians were blessed with an infinity of sonic colors, each unique and resisting reduction to the black and white spots held firmly in place on the cell bars of our staff paper. His standards of excellence derived from no textbook or school, but simply from his own fancy. "I don't care if it don't sound good to you," McDowell would maintain, "it sounds good to me."

Yet moral scruples—yes, again!—almost derailed McDowell's guitar career long before he was discovered by Lomax. "I went to church," he would explain. "You see I got religion. And I quit playing." Before she died, McDowell's mother asked him to give up the sinful instrument, and for a period of six years, he did not pick up a guitar. But by the time he encountered Lomax at the close of the 1950s, McDowell had come to terms with the blues. Even so, he kept a heavy dose of religious material in his repertoire, and even a secular song might take on an almost spiritual fervor, such as McDowell's intensely moving rendition of "Highway 61 Blues" recorded for Lomax. Here McDowell offers a tribute to the famous Delta roadway and adopts it as the peculiar setting for his envisioned last rites, a song that makes us forget all the stories of crossroads and midnight deals with the devil, here replaced by a true celebration of the byways and highways of the rambling blues life.

> *Lord, If I should happen to die, baby, before you think my time have come,*
> *Lord, If I should happen to die, baby, before you think my time have come,*
> *I want you to bury my body down on Highway 61.*

McDowell would live only a little more than a dozen years after Lomax jump-started his career, but he kept active during this time. Atlantic released some of the music Lomax recorded, and it caused quite a stir in the blues community; but McDowell soon sampled the opportunities presented by other independent companies, embarking on relationships with Pete Welding's Testament label and Chris Strachwitz's Arhoolie label. He even enlisted the support of a major company when Wayne Shuler at Capitol released McDowell's memorable stream-of-blues-consciousness album *I Do Not Play Rock and Roll*, later nominated for Grammy awards in both the traditional and ethnic-folk categories. McDowell played at Newport and on both coasts, ventured overseas, and delighted in his fans as much as they did in this walking-talking-and-rocking reminder of a bygone era. Yet he viewed his changed fortunes with a modest eye, and even held on to his job pumping gas in Como for thirty-two dollars a week when he wasn't traveling. The service station also doubled as McDowell's office, and the locals working there soon got used to the odd queries, from fans or from overseas promoters, though customers might be puzzled by the shout from inside— "Fred, Paris, France, is on the phone"—that would summon their venerable attendant away to handle his personal business.

McDowell stopped touring in November of 1971, when stomach pains forced him to cancel his performances and seek medical treatment. Although he told many people that he suffered from an ulcer, the real diagnosis was stomach cancer, and despite surgery, doctors were unable to halt its spread. He died on July 3, 1972, at the Baptist Hospital, and was buried—not on Highway 61, but at the Hammond Hill Baptist Church, between Como and Senatobia, Mississippi. He was reportedly laid to rest wearing a silver lamé suit, given to him by the Rolling Stones. But the adulation of the famous did little to prevent the guitarist's name being misspelled (McDewell) on the simple gravestone, an error that persisted many years before steps were taken to erect a more respectable tribute to one of Mississippi's greatest musical talents. On this newer memorial, we find again that a lyric—drawn from McDowell's best known composition—served as a fitting epitaph.

> *You may be high,*
> *You may be low.*
> *You may be rich, child,*
> *You may be poor.*
> *But when the Lord gets ready,*
> *You got to move.*

6. if you want a man who can flat lay down the blues

McDowell's brief career might well have signaled the end of an era; instead, it helped initiate one more—and perhaps a final—phase of exploration. The story of Lomax's discovery of the venerable bluesman showed that persistent researchers might still uncover significant new talent among the aged citizens of Mississippi. The locus of attention now turned to the hill country in the north of the state—an impoverished land which, as we have seen, lies just outside the fertile Delta area as strictly defined, but whose leading musicians are spiritual heirs of the legacy of Charley Patton and Son House, Muddy Waters and John Lee Hooker. Here, not far from McDowell's long-time home in Como, other musicians came to the attention of researchers, many of them playing in a very non-commercial, traditional style, sometimes evoking the African roots of the music to a surprising degree.

Alan Lomax had explored this area briefly in the early 1940s, and had been delighted by the musical versatility of old Sid Hemphill, born in 1876, who according to local repute was the "best musician in the world." Hemphill could play, as the mood suited him, guitar or banjo, fiddle or mandolin, snare drums or bass drum, fife or quills, even a little organ, and, if you left it in his hands long enough, almost anything else you might blow into, pluck, or pound. Hemphill made many of his own instruments, and though there were others thereabouts who might construct a passable fiddle or drum, he boasted of the superiority of his own craftsmanship. His performance of "Devil's Dream" on the quills—simple panpipes that Hemphill cut from reeds—ranks among the least Western-sounding music that Lomax ever recorded. With its simple melody that refuses to settle into a sonorous pentatonic—Hemphill took liberties with the standard intervals in the construction of his quills—and laced with monosyllabic, staccato vocalizations, this performance could pass for a field recording from Africa or South America. Lomax was so enchanted with this music, which represents a tradition that has now disappeared from black communities, that he sought out Hemphill again at the close of the 1950s and re-recorded him as part of the same trip that brought him to McDowell's doorstep.

Hemphill worked most often with string bands during his long career, but his fife and drum music captured the attention of the researchers and fans who scoured the hill country for new musical sounds. Many black soldiers had played fife or drum as members of the Union Army during the Civil

War, and at least one instance has been documented among the Confederate troops. But the musical tradition probably dates even farther back, perhaps to colonial times. The record labels who had promoted African-American music in the 1920s had missed this performance style—indeed, they had ignored musicians of all sorts from the northernmost region of the state. The drum and fife sound had flourished nonetheless at community picnics and holiday gatherings. When Lomax returned to this part of the state in 1959, he also recorded the Young brothers, Ed playing fife, Lonnie beating the bass drum, and G.D. joining in on snare drum. As Lomax preserved the music on his portable Ampex equipment, an impromptu dance began, with wives, cousins, kids, neighbors joining in the unplanned festivities. George Mitchell and David Evans would capture the same tradition in field recordings made in Tate and Panola counties during the late 1960s and early 1970s. They found the fife and drum music still alive and well in the persons of Napoleon Strickland and Otha Turner.

Turner had enjoyed a long career, marked by an improbable, if satisfying upswing in its final years. As a youngster he used a 50-gallon lard can as a makeshift drum, and in his mid-teens, around 1923, he began playing the cane fife. A bevy of researchers and enthusiasts—Alan Lomax, David Evans, George Mitchell, William Ferris, and Jim Dickinson, among others—eventually found their way to Turner's doorsteps. He was already an old man when he was fêted and recorded by these importunate visitors, but he managed to continue performing for several more decades. In 1992, the National Endowment for the Arts awarded him a National Heritage fellowship, but the eighty-four-year-old was far from ready to rest on his laurels. His 1998 release *Everybody Hollerin' Goat*, produced by Luther Dickinson, revealed that this superannuated music deserved respect as a commercial proposition, and not just as the subject of some scholar's field recording. *Rolling Stone* magazine would later laud it as one of the five best blues records of the nineties—no, the esteemed rock journal did *not* mean records made by musicians *in* their nineties—and the disk created the kind of buzz usually reserved for the up-and-coming, not the aged-and-infirm. Turner made his final recording, *From Senegal to Senatobia*, the following year, and could look back with pride on his almost single-handed role in passing on the fife and drum tradition to younger generations. At the time of Turner's death from pneumonia, at age ninety-four, on February 27, 2003, this performance style was vibrant and celebrated in North Mississippi—

although in other parts of the South it had all but disappeared. And almost every participant in the region had been personally trained by Turner, who had enlisted and drilled grandsons, cousins, neighbors, whomever might be willing to carry on the torch after the old man's inevitable departure.

Turner also provided the lead that brought Mitchell to R. L Burnside, the greatest of the North Mississippi bluesmen. George Mitchell was a devoted fan who had discovered the blues during the eighth grade when he heard a Muddy Waters record on Atlanta's WAOK. But in the summer of 1967, he wanted to do more than just listen to this music on record, and decided to spend his break from graduate school tracking down and recording old musicians in Mississippi. In Como, he stopped at a service station to ask for the whereabouts of Fred McDowell, and was surprised to find the blues guitarist, dressed in an attendant's uniform, pumping gas. McDowell welcomed the visitor with open arms, and invited him to a party he was hosting where the guests included a veritable who's who of North Mississippi musical talent, among them Otha Turner.

"If you want a man who can flat lay down the blues, I know who that be," Turner had boasted, and they arranged a time when the fife and drum master would take Mitchell to meet the guitarist. A long drive on a dirt road outside Coldwater, Mississippi, seemed to lead well beyond any possible neighborhood or residences, when finally a dim light ahead signaled that Mitchell had reached his destination. Here Burnside, his wife, and nine of his ten children shared a cramped, dilapidated house where virtually the only furnishings were a couple of beds, an old couch with springs coming through the cushions, and a box "upholstered" with some colored plastic. The youngsters sat on the warped, dirty floor, curious to learn what brought this unexpected visitor to their home. Burnside graciously accepted the stranger's invitation to play some blues, and after only one song, Mitchell knew that Turner's enthusiastic endorsement had not been empty praise. Here was the real thing, a throwback to the prewar tradition of one-chord blues, raw and unapologetic. "My jaw dropped when I heard his music," Mitchell recalled in our interview. "The first song he played was 'Goin' Down South,' which I hadn't heard before. I felt privileged to be in a position to preserve this music."

Robert Lee Burnside had been born on November 23, 1926, in Harmontown, Mississippi, and started playing the blues at age sixteen, first on the harmonica and later the guitar. He knew Fred McDowell and was distantly related to Muddy Waters—both of whom provided inspiration, as did John Lee Hooker, whose hard-grooving vamps are echoed in Burnside's persuasive solo guitar work. As a young man, Burnside earned his living sharecropping, fishing, and occasionally playing music. He spent most of the 1950s in Chicago, where he was eventually repelled by the violence that led to the death of his father, two brothers, and an uncle, and which spurred him to return to Mississippi at the close of the decade. Here Burnside himself got caught in a fatal encounter, shooting and killing (according to his account) a local bully who aimed to run him off his property. Like too many Mississippi musicians before him, he got ample time to meditate on the meaning of the blues at the government's expense while an inmate at Parchman.

In an entertainment industry where merit had its true reward, and real grooves prevailed over the usurpations of the drum machine, Burnside's initial recordings would have boosted him to fame and fortune as a middle-aged man. But Mitchell's discovery did not receive the international attention and fan adulation focused on Fred McDowell or John Hurt, Son House or Skip James. When Robert Palmer tracked down Burnside a dozen years later for his documentary *Deep Blues*, a collaboration with Robert Mugge, Burnside was hardly better off, or better known, than he had been before he first recorded. The footage shot for *Deep Blues* finds Burnside again at home, but the setting is so bleak—with its junked cars, broken-down appliances, stray farm animals, lean-to construction, and pervasive feeling of poverty and desolation—that one might justifiably suspect a carefully staged attempt by director Mugge to create a modern welfare state image of the blues life. But no, this was Burnside's real home, redeemed only by the music, as insistent and penetrating when played by the senior citizen as by the forty-year-old.

The next step forward for Burnside, and to some extent for the whole North Mississippi blues scene, required the unlikely intervention of Matthew Johnson, a former student of Palmer's at Ole Miss, who founded Fat Possum Records with the proceeds of a student loan and credit card borrowings in 1991. The company's financials would hardly be so bright again: despite its intermittent commercial successes, Fat Possum would eventually be beset by the veritable seven plagues of independent record labels: litigation issues, distribution bottlenecks, cash-flow problems, artist defections, artist deaths, artist incarcerations, and an out-of-sight-out-of-mind geographical presence in North Mississippi, where most folks think a Grammy is the old lady on a rocking chair on the back porch. Palmer had encouraged Johnson to record the largely undiscovered music around him; but the label's debut release, Burnside's *Bad Luck City*, sold only seven hundred copies and seemed merely to confirm the futility of promoting old blues in an age of rave parties and gangsta rap.

Yet Johnson persisted, and found that his best successes came through a devil-may-care assimilation of contemporary musical trends. He sensed astutely, perhaps instinctively, that the very rawness of the North Country blues gave it a spiritual kinship with the music of his own generation. Burnside had toured with the Jon Spencer Blues Explosion, a young white, New York–based band with an emphasis as much on the explosion as on the blues. Johnson gathered Burnside and Spencer's band at a rented hunting lodge near Holly Springs, where he recorded a loose, five-hour jam session over the course of a February 1996 afternoon. The tapes were spliced and diced into a surprising hit record, the ungrammatical, unpolished, and uncensored *A Ass Pocket Full of Whiskey*. Blues purists cringed, and some hurled accusations of exploitation—although it is hard to see the shrewd Burnside as a victim here. In truth, the guitarist was not playing at his best, his typically acute sense of rhythmic drive lost in the garage band ambience of the mix, his vocals mostly bellowing, shouting, and guttural sounds. But the sheer, unhinged energy of the music, its visceral impact, was a revelation. Here was something new in old blues. Sales were exceptional, and Burnside further expanded his cult following with *Come On In*, where a small dose of the blues is saturated with electronic sounds, loops, over-dubs, and a booming bass that takes no prisoners.

Johnson followed up on this success with other cross-generational pairings. Burnside served as opening act for the Beastie Boys, another white New York band who found an unlikely kindred spirit in the African-American bluesman from their fathers' generation. Junior Kimbrough, also featured in Palmer's documentary, signed with Fat Possum and soon brought his eerie, throbbing blues on the road with an unlikely companion, Iggy Pop. Even before this, Johnson had arranged for Palmer to record Kimbrough, and the resulting *All Night Long*, lauded in *Rolling Stone* as a masterpiece of the blues genre, gave notice of another major talent previously hidden from view in North Mississippi. The release was aptly named: Kimbrough captures a late night feeling, a floating, dreamy quality of that last stretch until dawn. The pulsations of the music are penetrating in a familiar way, almost like the rhythm of some organic process, the throbbing of a migraine or the beating of a heart, and over these Kimbrough's wailing voice expresses a litany of pains and indignities in simple, repetitive lines that often move in tandem with the notes of his electric guitar. This music was more accessible to mainstream blues fans than *A Ass Pocket Full of Whiskey*, but it was no less original than Burnside's release, a signal that Mississippi had not given up on forging innovative new paths for its blues music.

Born as David Kimbrough in Hudsonville, Mississippi, on July 28, 1930, the youngster first discovered the guitar through the neglect of his older sister. She watched Junior while their father was out working the fields, and should have stopped him from playing with the older Kimbrough's guitar. But he found a way to reach the high shelf where it had been put, supposedly out of reach, and soon made a habit of fooling around with the six strings when no one was watching. As a young man, Kimbrough reaped few of the benefits of the musician's life. He gave guitar lessons to future rockabilly legend Charlie Feathers, and watched as the latter's career ascended and his own languished. He worked at a John Deere dealership, or found employment as a mechanic or on the farm. But even when he decided to focus more on music, his determination to play his own compositions rather than well known cover tunes limited his prospects. Kimbrough spent time in Chicago and Memphis, and made sporadic attempts to launch a recording career, but his reputation never traveled far beyond his immediate environs. Yet over time he developed an enthusiastic following among those who chanced to hear him in person—such as researcher David Evans, who encountered Kimbrough at a juke joint in Holly Springs at the end of the 1970s, where a capacity audience crowded into the small room to hear his hypnotic songs. The bluesman managed to open his own juke joint, and Evans would arrange for him, and other North Mississippi talents, to record; but it was the later intervention of Johnson and Fat Possum that finally allowed Junior Kimbrough, at age sixty-two, to become a nationally known blues star.

Burnside and Kimbrough followed up on these successes, and broadened their audience among younger listeners, while older fans who felt out of touch with the Fat Possum sensibility also benefited from the reissue of earlier, neglected material by these artists, music which often stayed closer to traditional blues stylings. But fame arrived too late in life for these stalwart musicians, and they enjoyed too few opportunities to enjoy its perks.

Kimbrough's health was poor—he had survived a stroke, but his high blood pressure and weak heart made him reluctant to undergo the rigors of touring. Even so, many fans, including celebrities such as the Rolling Stones and U2, made their way to the door of Kimbrough's juke joint, Junior's Place, in Chulahoma, Mississippi. He died of heart failure on January 17, 1998, only five years after his Fat Possum release brought him to national attention.

Burnside underwent the first of his bypass operations in 1999, and suffered a heart attack in 2001. In his final years, he was in greater demand than ever, concert promoters willing to offer ten thousand dollars a night for a man who hardly made that in an entire year a decade before. But Burnside, too, had precious little stamina with which to respond to such offers. Yet in the summer of 2005, the guitarist agreed to travel to Davenport, Iowa, to be given the key to the city, amid a large gathering of his children and grandchildren. Burnside appeared in a wheelchair, and though he was unable to play, when given the microphone by his son Daniel, he offered his characteristic rejoinder to life's vagaries, good and bad: "Well, well, well." Two months later, on September 1, 2005, Burnside died in a hospital in Memphis at the age of seventy-eight.

7. gravesites and juke joints

After Junior Kimbrough's death, his family tried to keep his juke joint running as a hangout for local musicians and a destination for tourists. David Kimbrough, one of the guitarist's thirty-six children, often led the musical proceedings, trying to conjure the spirit of his departed father in his own music. But Junior's Place burned down in a fire, attributed to arson, on April 6, 2000. Similar fires also struck the houses of the bluesman's former bass player, Gary Burnside, and drummer, Kent Kimbrough.

Of course, blues fans had long grown familiar with both the symbolism and the substance of such senseless events. The history of their music has always seemed dictated by a fickle, often malicious, fate in which fire, flood, drought, illness, death, incarceration play far too large of a role. More than any other style of music, the blues has become conversant with such tragedies, even learning how to draw on them for strength and survival. But at the dawn of the new millennium, a century after W. C. Handy's legendary encounter with the lean, loose-jointed guitarist in Tutwiler, blues in Mississippi has been almost overwhelmed by the sheer accumulation of disasters, both impersonal and specific, that have decimated its ranks. While working on this book, it seemed that whenever I mentioned that I was writing about the Delta blues, I was asked about the devastation caused by Hurricane Katrina. Bad geography: the Delta region is far from coastal Mississippi, Biloxi and its casinos, where the hurricane wreaked its greatest damage. Yet my interlocutors' general sense was nonetheless true. Much of the authentic Delta blues tradition had been subject to devastation and destruction, only not by something as transient as a hurricane.

H. C. Speir's dream of a Mississippi-based record label that might promote the music of the region was rekindled sixty years on, as we have seen, in the efforts of Matthew Johnson, who grew up close to the location of Speir's old emporium. Johnson is perhaps the last living individual dedicated to finding and recording the hidden talent that still thrives in the neglected recesses of his native state. But his artist roster at Fat Possum seems cursed by a vengeful deity. The loss of Burnside and Kimbrough was perhaps more than any independent label could overcome. Under other circumstances, Robert Palmer, the critic and blues historian who had acted as an adviser and occasional producer for the label, might have served as a guide to other talent. But Palmer died in November 1997, only fifty-two years old, from liver disease.

Matthew Johnson persevered without his mentor, yet his own various attempts to promote Mississippi's greatest natural resource have been equally ill-fated. Johnson believed that Asie Payton, a full-time farmer from Holly Ridge where he had spent most of his life since his birth in 1937, might become a major blues act. Payton possessed an expressive voice and a high-energy performance style well suited to crossover success, but he died of a heart attack in 1997. Fat Possum was left to issue some demos and old tapes as a posthumous tribute to another major Delta star that might have been. A more recent discovery, Charles Caldwell seemed poised to become the next Fat Possum sensation, a raw and passionate North Country musician approaching his sixtieth birthday who had never made a record. Johnson signed him to the label, but midway in the preparation of his initial release, *Remember Me*, Caldwell was diagnosed with pancreatic cancer, and he was dead before the compact disk was issued. Johnson had better luck with T-Model Ford, a down-and-out bluesman whose hot-tempered language is well suited to appeal to the hip-hop generation—his love songs are laced with promises to "kick yo' ass" and "break yo' arm"—but which tends to keep his releases off the airwaves of Middle America. But James Lewis Carter Ford, as he was born (perhaps in 1924, he's really not sure), looks far too old and decrepit to carry out any of these threats, and with a rap sheet far longer than his discography, he is not the kind of artist around whom one can build a label's future. If Fat Possum were a stock, investors would be selling it short, if only because of inventory aging concerns.

The Fat Possum travails are far from unique. A host of other promising musicians from the region managed to make one or two recordings before death, illness, or an indifferent public intervened to cut short their careers. Lonnie Pitchford, born in 1955 in Lexington, Mississippi, seemed destined to emerge as the leading exponent of the local tradition among the baby boomer generation. He played the diddley bow with a consummate skill that defied the inherent limitations of this one-string instrument, and his expertise also extended to the guitar, piano, bass, and harmonica. A gifted carpenter, Pitchford was a throwback to earlier blues musicians who constructed their own instruments, and as a protégé of Robert Lockwood, he could claim a powerful blues lineage, dating back to Lockwood's own teacher (and stepfather) Robert Johnson. But Pitchford died of AIDS in 1998 at age forty-three, and as of this writing, his recordings are out of print—a sad legacy for a major talent whose music was insufficiently documented during his life and unfairly neglected after his passing.

Eddie Cusic finally released a compact disk in 1998, having spent most of his working life as a stonecutter working in a government quarry. Cusic had often performed around the Delta with fellow Leland resident Son Thomas, but until Matthew Block tracked down the seventy-one-year-old guitarist at his modest home located behind the city's old grain and feed store, he had never made a commercial record. Cusic's major claim to fame, at the time, had been his role in teaching much of what he knew about the blues to a future R&B success story, Little Milton. But Block was determined to make a recording of Cusic's own music, and the resulting *I Want to Boogie* made clear that the musical traditions of the prewar generation were still alive in the Delta region. Yet Cusic too, like so many other of these sexagenarian and septuagenarian blues discoveries, appears destined to be a mere footnote in the history of the Delta music, one more artist whose opportunities were too few and arrived too late.

Big Jack Johnson, born in 1940, is a youngster by comparison, and though he is beyond the age when, in most lines of work, retirement is mandatory, he is still often pointed to as a sign that the Delta tradition is alive and vital. Within the Delta, Johnson is something of a success story, and unlike many of his contemporaries he has several recordings to his credit, both under his own name and as a member of the Jelly Roll Kings. He possesses a big voice and a big heart. He knows the music's heritage, and his guitar work is a worthy continuation of the esteemed traditions of Clarksdale, home base for much of his career. In short, Johnson more than deserves the accolades that have come his way. But it is all too telling that his nickname, "the Oil Man," refers not to his on-stage achievements but to his longtime day job as an oil truck driver, which helped pay the rent until Johnson immersed himself full time in music in the early 1990s. This is the reality of the blues life for many of Mississippi's current generation, just as it was for Skip James, Son House, Booker White, and so many others who earned their living, through most of their lives, without a guitar in their hands. Big Jack Johnson, for his part, continues to serve as advocate for the Delta tradition; but how many younger musicians are there in the wings ready to step in and take his place?

Far better known than Johnson are baby boomers Keb Mo and Chris Thomas King, who have done more to introduce new listeners to the traditional Delta sound than any other musicians of their generation. But here we encounter a lesson in the vagaries of the modern entertainment industry, for both these artists earned their notoriety in the blues world as actors, before they achieved widespread fame as recording artists. At his birth, in Los Angeles in 1951, Keb Mo was christened with the less romantic name of Kevin Moore. In his youth, he learned trumpet and French horn, in addition to guitar. His first gigs were as part of a calypso steel drum band, but by his late teens he had switched his focus to R&B music. Finally a turning point came when Moore was cast as a Delta bluesman in a theatrical production called *Rabbit Foot*. His knack for play-acting was so convincing that it led to a further opportunity to portray Robert Johnson himself in the docudrama *Can't You Hear the Wind Howl?* Moore showed, on stage and on film, that he looked the part of a Delta performer. With the addition of a bluesier stage name, Keb Mo was now ready to assume the mantle as keeper of the Delta flame, real life imitating stagecraft. His resulting records have sold well, and have been the recipient of many awards.

A similar path was followed by Chris Thomas King, whose early musical interests gravitated to Jimi Hendrix, soul and rap. But the opportunity to play the Delta legend Tommy Johnson in the Coen brothers' successful film *O Brother Where Art Thou?* showed that he could convincingly put on the persona of a traditional bluesman. His recordings, like Keb Mo's, are consistently among the best-selling and most widely heard in the blues genre. Make no mistake, both artists are both exemplary musicians, who can play the old blues persuasively when they so desire—although the question of how much they desire remains to be answered; both seem reluctant to be too closely linked to traditional music and look for a larger "crossover" audience. But the irony here is inescapable: the most famous custodians of the Delta idiom, so prized for its authenticity and deep roots, are now apparently selected based on the whims of casting directors who have probably never laid foot inside the state boundaries of Mississippi.

But if the supply of celebrated, homegrown blues talent in the Delta is precarious, demand is on the rise, as the state's tourism industry focuses increasingly on this music as the centerpiece of its marketing efforts. Blues tour guides and maps are published, blues museums have been established, memorials erected, and more than a dozen blues festivals are held each year. Yet this ceaseless activity on the surface can scarcely hide the fact that younger African-Americans in the Delta show all too little interest in this tradition. The fan base that supports the economic viability of the Delta blues today is disproportionately white, well educated, and living outside the state of Mississippi. The most enthusiastic visitors to the blues museums and sacred locations of the Delta heritage are typically from afar—devotees trekking from Europe, Japan, Australia, and other distant locations, whose arrival on the spot serves perhaps as moving testimony to the global reach of this music, but does little to allay concerns that the history of the Delta's formative role in shaping the sound of American (and global) music is mostly over. Nor are fans reassured when they find that the maps and guidebooks highlighting the landmarks of the Delta direct them to more gravesites than juke joints.

Nonetheless, record companies have not lost interest in younger performers schooled in the Mississippi tradition. But, in truth, they often choose talent the way medieval societies selected their kings—namely, from the offspring of the most famous names of the last generation. A surprising amount of the publicity in the blues world in recent years has surrounded the recordings of various children, or grandchildren, of John Lee Hooker, Muddy Waters, R. L. Burnside, Junior Kimbrough, Sid Hemphill, and other departed masters of an earlier day. It would be wrong to dismiss this music simply because of the formulaic quality of the marketing effort put behind it, which stresses bluesiness as some sort of hereditary right or genetic capacity. Yet how peculiar that the blues, perhaps the most *ignoble* of America's cultural legacies, the least susceptible to the pretenses of pedigree—indeed, a true meritocracy in which depth of soul rather than genealogical descent is the true measure of a musician—how odd that here, of all places, the fame of the family name exerts such a strong claim.

The most successful of these second-generation bands has been, without question, the North Mississippi Allstars, built around the considerable talents of Luther Dickinson, a prepossessing slide guitarist and vocalist, drummer Cody Dickinson, and bassist Chris Chew. For a time, Dwayne Burnside, son of R.L., also added his guitar and singing talents into the mix. Luther and Cody, for their part, are the offspring of the legendary producer and musician Jim Dickinson, whose credits include session work with the Rolling Stones (hear his piano on "Wild Horses"), Arlo Guthrie (the same for "The City of New Orleans"), and various artists on the Atlantic label; his involvement with influential if sometimes obscure Memphis acts, such as Mudboy and the Neutrons; and personal ties to several generations of Memphis and Mississippi legends, dating back to his participation in jam sessions with the likes of Furry Lewis and Gus Cannon.

Luther Dickinson took an early liking to the musician's life and went to bed with a guitar in hand the way some children cradle a favorite stuffed animal, but his tastes at first clashed with his father's. The youngster's brief flirtation with punk rock settled into a deeper appreciation of the musical riches near at hand, and the North Mississippi Allstars built their repertoire around the songs—and sometimes the guest appearances—of R. L. Burnside, Otha Turner, and other representatives of the local tradition. When the band was formed in 1996, these artists were still alive; but with the gradual decline and passing of the older generation, the young Allstars have been promoted through the ranks until they now stand out as the leading representatives of the North Country heritage on the national stage.

Meanwhile, Matthew Johnson, whose Fat Possum business has not participated directly in this success—the Allstars currently record for their own label—works hard to keep his independent company afloat. In his zeal to discover neglected masters of Mississippi blues, Johnson has traveled to many out-of-the-way juke joints and waited at the threshold of countless strangers' homes—in a wistful moment, he says he wishes he had a dollar for every time he heard some kid shout, "White man at the door"—but he finds that, increasingly, the talent he records and promotes comes from outside the boundaries of his native state. The Black Keys, another promising act that eventually left the Fat Possum roster, may sound like an authentic Mississippi band, especially when they artfully cover the songs of Junior Kimbrough, but guitarist Dan Auerbach and drummer Patrick Carney hail from Akron, Ohio. Erika Wennerstrom, whose band Heartless Bastard is another Fat Possum act, also hails from Akron. Dax Riggs, the guiding light of Deadboy & the Elephantmen, is originally from Evansville, Indiana, while his musical partner Tessie Brunet grew up in Louisiana. In short, the homegrown Mississippi label no longer relies on homegrown talent.

In a way, Johnson's more expansive vision is perhaps the right one. The legacy of the Delta and North Country traditions can no longer be circumscribed by any border, no matter how loosely or tightly defined. In a real sense, the music's greatness can be measured by the vigor with which it permeates the global soundscapes, and its steadfast refusal to remain within the static definitions of a folk art or a local practice. The talent scout in search of the next great blues band might find it anywhere, in Bakersfield or Newark, Liverpool or Addis Ababa. Wherever it is found, the blood of the Delta founders will be running in its veins, the spirit of Robert Johnson will be hovering over its proceedings, and its imaginative genealogy will hail back to Clarksdale and Parchman, Tutwiler and the Yazoo River, no matter what actual place names show up on the musicians' birth certificates.

Yet we would be wrong to neglect the Delta itself, to write it off as a historical tourist site, akin to the old Civil War battlefields, where the action is over and just the memories remain. Only a short time ago, many jazz fans felt that way about New Orleans: its place in the music's history had long been eclipsed by Chicago, New York, Los Angeles, Philadelphia, Detroit, and other more vibrant urban centers. Tourists might imagine, after a few drinks, that the jazz in the French Quarter was first rate, but the more savvy listeners knew better. Yet the ascendancy of a new generation of New Orleans musicians—Wynton Marsalis and his siblings, Henry Butler, Harry Connick, Terence Blanchard, Nicholas Payton, and others—reasserted the centrality (and marketability!) of the New Orleans tradition a century after the births of Jelly Roll Morton and King Oliver. A similar resurgence might easily happen in the Delta, a blues revival that does not just mimic the past but takes the music into the future. Many of the same ingredients that contributed to the first flowering of the Delta blues—the sociological, demographic, and cultural fingerprint, so to speak—are still present today, shamefully so, in many regards. The same battle between spiritual and secular world-views looms large in the public consciousness, even if the balance has tilted somewhat toward the latter during the intervening decades. And no one will deny that folks here still have more than enough to be blue about, and have earned the right to put it into song. Above all, the fans are waiting for the fire to rekindle in the Delta, are half expecting it. Something tells me they will not be disappointed.

notes

chapter one: the blues and the old kingdoms

2   the most fertile to be found anywhere on the globe: For the fertility of the Delta soil, see James C. Cobb, *The Most Southern Place on Earth: The Mississippi Delta and the Roots of Regional Identity* (New York: Oxford University Press, 1992), esp. pp. 4–7. For poverty levels in Mississippi and the slow dissemination of modern technologies, see Ted Ownby, *American Dreams in Mississippi: Consumers, Poverty and Culture: 1830–1998* (Chapel Hill, NC: University of North Carolina Press, 1999).

3   Records have preserved the response of one white mechanic: See Charles S. Sydnor, *Slavery in Mississippi* (Baton Rouge, LA: Louisiana State University Press, 1966), p. 8. See also David J. Libby, *Slavery and Frontier Mississippi 1720–1835* (Jackson, MI: University of Mississippi Press, 2004).

6   "begins in the lobby of the Peabody Hotel in Memphis": David L. Cohn, *God Shakes Creation* (New York: Harper & Bros., 1935), p. 14.

7   "most suitable as the color of the interior life": William Gass, *On Being Blue: A Philosophical Inquiry* (Boston: David Godine, 1976), p. 76.

8   "In the intervals between their meals": Bryan Edwards, *The History, Civil and Commercial, of the British Colonies in the West Indies* (London: J. Stockdale, 1793), vol. II, p. 116, quoted in Dena J. Epstein, "African Music in British and French America," *The Musical Quarterly*, vol. 59, no. 1 (1973), p. 67.

9   "Things from the blues came from the tribal musicians of the old kingdoms": Samuel Charters, *The Roots of the Blues: An African Search* (New York: Perigee, 1981), p. 127.

11   "After I returned to the United States": John Chernoff, *African Rhythm and African Sensibility* (Chicago: University of Chicago Press, 1981), p. 54.

15   The dissemination of any innovation: The classic analysis of the spread of new cultural practices in terms of S-curves can be found in Everett M. Rogers's *Diffusion of Innovations*, 5th ed. (New York: Free Press, 2003), first published in 1962. I believe that applying this approach to an assessment of the spread of the early blues offers a number of insights—especially (as I discuss in the text) in showing that blues exhibited characteristics more often associated with a carryover from the past rather than attributes typically found with innovations. This approach may help us resolve the fascinating debate between Gayle Dean Wardlow, who argues that the early blues was the result of brilliant innovators such as Charley Patton, and David Evans, who prefers to describe the development of the blues in terms of traditional folk practices. See "Charlie Patton and the Scholastics," Appendix 3, in Stephen Calt and Gayle Wardlow, *King of the Delta Blues: The Life and Music of Charlie Patton* (Newton, NJ: Rock Chapel Press, 1988), pp. 301–18, and David Evans, *Big Road Blues: Tradition and Creativity in the Folk Blues* (New York: Da Capo Press, 1987).

chapter two: where the southern cross the dog

19   "an earth-born music": W. C. Handy, *Father of the Blues: An Autobiography* (New York: Da Capo Press, 1991), p. 75.

20   "I did more than cope with the crop": B.B. King with David Ritz, *Blues All Around Me: The Autobiography of B.B. King* (New York: Avon Books, 1996), p. 57.

20   "The weight of the damp earth": Charles Peabody, "Exploration of Mounds, Coahoma County, Mississippi," *Papers of the Peabody Museum of American Archaeology and Ethnology*, Harvard University, vol. III, no. 2 (Cambridge, MA: Peabody Museum, June 1904), p. 34.

21   "Busy archeologically, we had not very much time left": This and the quote below are from Charles Peabody, "Notes on Negro Music," *Journal of American Folk-Lore*, 16, (July–September 1903), pp. 148–52.

23   "On the whole the work songs of any country": John Storm Roberts, *Black Music of Two Worlds* (New York: Original Music, 1972), p. 29.

23   "like a conversation between second cousins": Alan Lomax, accompanying notes to *Roots of the Blues* (New World Records 80252-2).

24   "I have heard that many of the masters and overseers": Frances Kemble, *Journal of*

a Residence on a Georgian Plantation in 1838–1839, ed. John A. Scott (New York: New American Library, 1961), p. 164.

24 Only six years later, Frederick Douglass would denounce: Frederick Douglass, *Narrative of the Life of Frederick Douglass, An American Slave, Written by Himself* (1845; New York: Signet Books, 1997), p. 30.

24 "Very few of the Negro's ante-bellum secular songs": Howard W. Odum and Guy B. Johnson, *Negro Workaday Songs* (New York: Negro Universities Press, 1969), p. 18.

24 "Many of the most plaintive lines of blues yet recorded": Ibid., p. 6.

25 William Cullen Bryant, in an account from 1843: Cited in Dena Epstein, *Sinful Tunes and Spirituals: Black Folk Music to the Civil War* (Urbana: University of Illinois Press, 1981), p. 144.

25 accounts of slaves playing everything from the piano to the bagpipes: Ibid., pp. 139–60.

27 "every disease, human and inhuman": *Warren County Leader* (Iowa), June 15, 1871, cited in Brooks McNamara, *Step Right Up* (Jackson, MI: University of Mississippi Press, 1975), p. 12.

29 "was the genuine article, a real Negro minstrel show": Handy, *Father of the Blues: An Autobiography*, p. 34.

32 "There was little comparison": Ibid., p. 72.

32 "didn't head up a band, but handled Jim Turner's band": E-mail to the author from Stephen Calt, July 21, 2006. See also Stephen Calt and Gayle Wardlow, *King of the Delta Blues: The Life and Music of Charlie Patton* (Newton, NJ: Rock Chapel Press, 1988), pp. 107–08.

32 "when Handy came here": Interview on file at the American Folklife Center, Library of Congress, folder 67 of LOC / Fisk materials from the 1941–42 Coahoma County research project.

32 "A lean, loose-jointed Negro": Handy, *Father of the Blues: An Autobiography*, pp. 73–74.

34 "At first folk melodies like these": Ibid., p. 75.

35 "A rain of silver dollars began to fall": Ibid., p. 77.

37 "Well, they say life begins at forty": Ibid., p. 123.

37 "I know why the best blues artists come from Mississippi": John Lee Hooker, interview in *Melody Maker*, October 1964, quoted in Charles Shaar Murray, *Boogie Man* (New York: St. Martin's Press, 2000), p. 14.

38 "One of the phonograph companies made over four million dollars": Quoted in Daphne Duval Harrison, *Black Pearls: Blues Queens of the 1920s* (New Brunswick, NJ: Rutgers University Press, 1993), p. 43.

39 "I believe my audience wants to see me becomingly gowned": Quoted in ibid., p. 48.

41 the "singer of blues that are really blue": Quoted in Chris Albertson, *Bessie* (New Haven: Yale University Press, 2003), p. 45.

chapter three: dockery's plantation

47   He showed Wardlow and Calt around the farm: This and the quotes below from Joe Dockery come from e-mails from Stephen Calt to the author, December 11 and December 13, 2005.

48   "Lord God, he could holler": Quotes from Mack and other comments below from Stephen Calt and Gayle Wardlow, *King of the Delta Blues: The Life and Music of Charlie Patton* (Newton, NJ: Rock Chapel Press, 1988), pp. 15, 22, and 27.

48   H. C. Speir, the talent scout responsible for Patton's first recordings: Ibid., p. 13.

50   "*All* my folks came directly from the shores of France": Alan Lomax, *Mister Jelly Roll* (Berkeley: University of California Press, 1950), p. 3.

51   "That's the way he played": Calt and Wardlow, *King of the Delta Blues: The Life and Music of Charlie Patton*, p. 211.

52   If Son House can be believed: David Evans has contested House's assertion, indicating that in his discussions with Patton's sister, she claimed that her brother had a ninth-grade education. See David Evans, "Charley Patton, the Conscience of the Delta," in Robert Sacré, ed., *The Voice of the Delta: Charley Patton and the Mississippi Blues Traditions, Influences and Comparisons, An International Symposium* (Liège, Belgium: Presses Universitaires de Liège, 1987), pp. 109–214, and, in particular, p. 136.

53   "It was $150, and times was tight too!": From Gayle Dean Wardlow, "The Talent Scouts: H. C. Speir: 1895–1972," *78 Quarterly*, 8 (1994), p. 25.

55   "That's *pure* Delta there": This and the quotes below from Gayle Dean Wardlow, " 'Big Foot' William Harris," *78 Quarterly*, 3 (1988), p. 46.

56   "nothing is known about William Harris": Paul Oliver, notes to *William Harris and Buddy Boy Hawkins: Complete Recorded Works in Chronological Order (1927–1929)*, Document CD DOCD 5035 (1991).

56   Some have even doubted Harris's Delta ties: Stephen Calt, who tried to validate various details of the conventional Harris biography, tells me that he ultimately came to wonder whether the William Harris known to Gayle Wardlow's Delta informants was the same person who recorded blues for Gennett. The strongest piece of evidence linking Harris to the Delta remains Speir's reported testimony that he discovered the musician at a church picnic. But Calt recalls hearing Speir state that all of the musicians he sent to Birmingham from this picnic were white. Wardlow counters that he found solid evidence of Harris in Tallahatchie County, and remains convinced that Harris went from Mississippi to Birmingham, probably via the train route that linked Tupelo to Birmingham. Wardlow tried to uncover further information on Harris in Birmingham, mainly via city directories, but could not find any clear traces. Alas, such opaque biographies are all too common in the world of the Delta blues, where the most successful researchers have been forced to borrow the techniques of private investigators—E-mails from Stephen Calt to the author, December 4, 5, and 6, 2005, and interview with Gayle Wardlow, April 22, 2006.

57   "Ole Charlie [Patton] was the best I ever seen": Gayle Dean Wardlow, *Chasin' That Devil Music* (San Francisco: Backbeat Books, 1998), p. 127.

61   "There are twelve million colored people in [the] US": Quoted in Robert Dixon and John Godrich, *Recording the Blues* (New York: Stein & Day, 1970), p. 13.

65   "If it is possible for you to make arrangements": Quoted in John Fahey, *Charley Patton* (London: Studio Vista, 1970), pp. 8–9.

70   "just dry screwin'": Johnny Shines quoted in Calt and Wardlow, *King of the Delta Blues: The Life and Music of Charlie Patton*, p. 101.

chapter four: parchman prison

79   "I was more churchified": Jeff Titon, "Living Blues Interview: Son House," *Living Blues*, 31 (March–April 1977), pp. 14–22.

79   "I was there in that alfalfa field": Ibid., p. 15.

80   "It always made me mad to see": Son House with Julius Lester, "I Can Make My Own Songs," *Sing Out*, vol. 15, no. 3 (July 1965), p. 38.

80   "Well, I stopped, because the people were all crowded around": Ibid., p. 40.

80   "I could make [the guitar] say what I say": This and the quotes below from Titon, "Living Blues Interview: Son House," p. 16.

80   "I said, 'I ain't good enough for that'": House with Lester, "I Can Make My Own Songs," p. 40.

81   "I thought Son House was the greatest guitarist": From Jim O'Neal's interview with Muddy Waters in *The Voice of the Blues*, eds. Jim O'Neal and Amy van Singel (New York: Routledge, 2002), p. 160.

82   he "about done quit": This and the quotes below from Alan Lomax, *The Land Where the Blues Began* (New York: Pantheon, 1993), p. 17.

83   "all the moneymen, like a rattlesnake in his coil": E-mail from Stephen Calt to the author, December 21, 2005.

85   Stephen Calt relates his surprise: E-mail from Stephen Calt to the author, December 7, 2005.

85   Calt continues: "[House] told me he shot a man to death": E-mail from Stephen Calt to the author, December 10, 2005.

87   "Everywhere we heard of men working": This and the quotes below from Lomax, *The Land Where the Blues Began*, p. 258.

88   it would take "a volume of 500 pages": Nolan Porterfield, *Last Cavalier: The Life and Times of John A. Lomax, 1867–1948* (Urbana: University of Illinois Press, 1996), p. 299.

88   John Lomax lamented in a letter: John A. Lomax, *Adventures of a Ballad Hunter* (New York: Macmillan, 1947), p. 126.

89   White was probably twenty-nine years old: The most likely birthdate is November 12, 1909—supported by the 1920 census, which finds Bucker T. White, age eleven, residing in Itta Bena. However, the Social Security Death Index lists a birthdate of November 12, 1900. White's name is not found among the list of those who

registered for the draft in 1917 or 1918, although he would have been of age if the earlier date were correct. Some sources assign a 1906 birthdate.

90   "as good a land as a bird ever flew over": F. Jack Hurley and David Evans, "Bukka White," in *Tennessee Traditional Singers: Tom Ashley, Sam McGee, Bukka White*, ed. Thomas G. Burton (Knoxville, TN: University of Tennessee Press, 1981), p. 158.

90   "It was hoboing, sleeping on this railroad track": Ibid., p. 169.

91   Stephen Calt recalls White boasting: E-mail from Stephen Calt to the author, December 16, 2005.

91   "I just shot him where I wanted to shoot him": Quote from Hurley and Evans, "Bukka White," p. 171.

93   Muddy Waters would later recall: Robert Gordon, *Can't Be Satisfied: The Life and Times of Muddy Waters* (Boston: Little, Brown, 2002), p. 71.

93   "I never had a man, black or white": Hurley and Evans, "Bukka White," pp. 177–78.

95   "There is the weight of myth": Mark Humphrey's accompanying essay to *The Complete Bukka White* (Columbia CK 52782).

96   When Alan Lomax interviewed pianist Thomas "Jay Bird" Jones: Lomax and Jones can be heard on *Deep River of Song: Mississippi Saints & Sinners* (Rounder 11661-1824-2).

100 In 1965, Gayle Wardlow tracked down a death certificate: See Wardlow's essay, "Can't Tell My Future: The Mystery of Willie Brown," in Gayle Dean Wardlow, *Chasin' That Devil Music* (San Francisco: Backbeat Books, 1998), pp. 181–90. Wardlow mentions that Son House told Stephen Calt that Brown had died in the vicinity of New York. But Calt denies this—and thus actually strengthens Wardlow's claim. As Calt recalls, House believed Brown had died in Mississippi. This gives us greater confidence that the Willie Lee Brown listed in the death certificate is the musician who recorded for Paramount.

100 "was generally considered to be the best": David Evans, *Big Road Blues: Tradition and Creativity in the Folk Blues* (New York: Da Capo Press, 1987), p. 176.

101 "tall, lanky, silky-muscled": Lomax, *The Land Where the Blues Began*, p. 5.

103 "Several of my informants recognized the name": Evans, *Big Road Blues: Tradition and Creativity in the Folk Blues*, p. 194.

104 recalls seeing "two little guys": Quote from Joe Callicott in Wardlow, *Chasin' That Devil Music*, p. 120.

104 "I had three sources for Kid Bailey in Leland": Gayle Wardlow, interview with the author, April 22, 2006.

104 "a police officer shot and killed": E-mail from Stephen Calt to the author, December 23, 2005. Wardlow could not recall this incident when I asked him about him, but he did not dispute it. He noted that there were often clues that were rejected when they didn't seem to lead anywhere, and that this might have been one of them.

106 "Patton stomped both his feet": Quoted in Calt and Wardlow, *King of the Delta Blues: The Life and Music of Charlie Patton*, p. 222.

chapter five: hard time killin' floor

111   "It's a *thousand* musicians down there": David "Honeyboy" Edwards to Stephen Calt—E-mail from Stephen Calt to the author, November 18, 2005.

112   Henry Sloan: The comments from Gayle Dean Wardlow on Henry Sloan are from an interview with the author, January 6, 2007. For David Evans on Henry Sloan, see his *Big Road Blues: Tradition and Creativity in the Folk Blues* (Berkeley: University of California Press, 1982), p. 175. For Jim O'Neal on Henry Sloan, see his article "BluEsoterica," *Living Blues*, 123 (September–October 1995), p. 120.

113   "probably as good a musician as Brown": Evans, *Big Road Blues: Tradition and Creativity in the Folk Blues*, p. 176.

115   "That old lady stole him away": David Evans, *Tommy Johnson* (London: Studio Vista, 1971), p. 20.

115   "He had four wives": Quoted in ibid., p.28.

115   "tired of living a devil's life": Ibid., p. 30.

117   "didn't have nothing on but the top of their shoes": Ibid., p. 27.

117   "got to be a pretty good musicianer": Ibid., pp. 40–41.

119   "He was at a supper once": Ibid., p. 50.

120   "People'd walk five or six or ten miles to hear him": Jim O'Neal, "Houston Stackhouse," *Living Blues*, 17 (Summer 1974), p. 23.

124   "I'm going a long way this time I go": Quoted in Evans, *Tommy Johnson*, p. 85.

128   but Gayle Wardlow confirms that he asked Ishmon: Gayle Wardlow, interview with the author, April 22, 2006.

129   When researcher Paul Oliver tracked Carter down: Paul Oliver, *Conversation with the Blues* (New York: Horizon, 1965), p. 19.

129   Mike Bloomfield wrote a small book: Michael Bloomfield with S. Summerville, *Me and Big Joe* (San Francisco: Re/Search Publications, 1980).

130   "He wanted to work *no* way": David "Honeyboy" Edwards, *The World Don't Owe Me Nothing: The Life and Times of Delta Bluesman Honeyboy Edwards* (Chicago: Chicago Review Press, 1997), p. 42.

132   "We only know how good you are by your sales figures": Quoted in Stephen Calt, *I'd Rather Be the Devil: Skip James and the Blues* (New York: Da Capo Press, 1994), p. 330.

136   Peter Guralnick has described: See Peter Guralnick, *Feel Like Going Home: Portraits in Blues and Rock and Roll* (New York: Bay Back Books, 1999), p. 116.

137   "Skip was a born musician": Quoted in Calt, *I'd Rather Be the Devil: Skip James and the Blues*, p. 122.

137   "You can't put a price on a song": Ibid., pp. 142–43.

138   "He gave me a few lashes with his belt": Ibid., p. 47.

138   In his own words, he was a "mean bastard": Ibid., p. 48.

139   "I don't pattern after anyone or either copycat": Bruce Jackson, "The Personal Blues of Skip James," *Sing Out*, vol. 15, no. 6 (January 1966), p. 28.

139   "Skip taught hisself": Eric Mossel, "Skip James Talking," *Blues World*, 24 (July 1969), p. 14.

140   "If you stay where you are, I'm gonna catch up to you": Quoted in Calt, *I'd Rather Be the Devil: Skip James and the Blues*, p. 100.

142   "As many as you want": Ibid., p. 4.

chapter six: hellhound on my trail

151   "had been killed by his girl friend": John Hammond with Irving Townsend, *John Hammond on Record* (London: Penguin Books, 1981), p. 202.

151   "Father has written me several encouraging": Letter from Alan Lomax to Harold Spivacke, March 26, 1939, in the Alan Lomax correspondence files at the American Folklife Center, LOC.

151   "Almost nothing is known of his life": Samuel Charters, *The Country Blues* (New York: Da Capo Press, 1975), p. 207.

151   "a singer who walked hand-in-hand": Paul Oliver, *Blues Fell This Morning: Meaning in the Blues* (Cambridge: Cambridge University Press, 1990), p. 255.

152   "I mean he was amazing": Samuel Charters, *The Bluesmen* (New York: Oak Publications, 1967), p. 87.

153   Perhaps Wardlow's most important contribution: Gayle Dean Wardlow, *Chasin' That Devil Music* (San Francisco: Backbeat Books, 1998), p. 91.

154   Ike Zinermon: The name is usually spelled Zinnerman in blues literature, but Stephen LaVere clarifies that the musician himself used the spelling Zinermon—E-mail from Stephen LaVere to the author, September 24, 2007.

154   "in the neighborhood of seven figures": See Shawn Macomber, "The Tune Cop: Collecting Music Royalties Is This Exeter Guy's Business," *Foster's Sunday Citizen* (Dover, NH), August 31, 2003.

155   "Legend says this man sold his soul to the Devil": Quoted in Elijah Wald, *Escaping the Delta: Robert Johnson and the Invention of the Blues* (New York: HarperCollins, 2004), p. xvii.

156   "You hear people talk about they played with Robert": Larry Hoffman, "Robert Lockwood, Jr.," *Living Blues*, 121 (June 1995), p. 16.

159   "Such another racket you never heard": Son House with Julius Lester, "I Can Make My Own Songs," *Sing Out*, vol. 15, no. 3 (July 1965), p. 41.

159   "Here's to Robert Johnson . . . for being dead": Dick Waterman, *Between Midnight and Day: The Last Unpublished Blues Archive* (New York: Thunder's Mouth Press, 2003), p. 41.

160   "Now if Tom was living, he'd tell you": Quoted in David Evans, *Tommy Johnson* (London: Studio Vista, 1971, pp. 22–23.

161   to "get over the cliché": Wald, *Escaping the Delta: Robert Johnson and the Invention of the Blues*, p. 266.

161 Barry Lee Pearson and Bill McCulloch: For the quotes here and below, see Barry Lee Pearson and Bill McCulloch, *Robert Johnson: Lost and Found* (Urbana: University of Illinois Press, 2003), pp. 38, 39, and 102.

163 "My gut feeling is that Johnson": Mack McCormick, interview with the author, October 21, 2005.

164 "It may be Robert could have sold himself": David "Honeyboy" Edwards, *The World Don't Owe Me Nothing: The Life and Times of Delta Bluesman Honeyboy Edwards* (Chicago: Chicago Review Press, 1997), p. 105. For Edwards's comments on Johnson from 1942, see folder 4 of the Lomax—Fisk University files relating to the Coahoma County project, at the American Folklife Center, LOC.

164 "These designations gave Peetie a sense of power": Paul Garon, *The Devil's Son-in-Law: The Story of Peetie Wheatstraw and His Songs* (Chicago: Charles H. Kerr, 2003), p. 115.

167 "He had terrible guilt about the blues": Gayle Wardlow, interview with the author, April 22, 2006.

168 "The blues are true and the Truth shall set you free": See John Fahey's essay "Charley Re-considered Thirty-five Years On," accompanying the lavish set of CDs and documents *Screamin' and Hollerin' the Blues: The Worlds of Charley Patton* (Revenant 212), p. 52.

169 "He came out with such compelling themes": From the accompanying booklet to *Robert Johnson: The Complete Recordings* (Columbia C2K 46222), p. 21.

169 "I can't tell you how disappointed I was": Phil Spiro, interview with the author, November 23, 2005.

170 "simply showed that if you asked him": Mack McCormick, interview with the author, September 10, 2005.

171 "As far as musicians that he liked": I am indebted to Ed Leimbacher for providing me with the full transcript of Pete Welding's interview with Shines—See Pete Welding, "Ramblin' Johnny Shines," *Living Blues*, 22 (July–August 1975), pp. 23–32. The passage cited is at p. 29.

171 "I gave him a little instruction": Son House with Julius Lester, "I Can Make My Own Songs," *Sing Out*, vol. 15, no. 3 (July 1965), p. 42.

173 "Do you know how many Robert Johnsons there are?": Mack McCormick, interview with the author, September 10, 2005.

173 "I realized that the man done come": Quoted in Peter Guralnick, *Searching for Robert Johnson* (New York: Plume, 1998), p. 28.

174 "Robert was like a father to me": Quoted in Robert Palmer, *Deep Blues* (New York: Penguin, 1982), p. 179.

181 "No matter how many times I have listened to it": Guralnick, *Searching for Robert Johnson*, p. 45.

184 "See, Robert was a guy": Welding, "Ramblin' Johnny Shines," p. 30.

184 "He wasn't able to take care of himself": Ibid., p. 28.

184   "He loved whiskey and he was crazy about his women": Edwards, *The World Don't Owe Me Nothing: The Life and Times of Delta Bluesman Honeyboy Edwards*, p. 102.

184   In an interview conducted by Pete Welding: See *Nothing But the Blues*, ed. Mike Leadbitter (New York: Oak Publications, 1971), p. 139.

184   Mack McCormick, for his part: Interview with the author, August 26, 2006.

185   "Now this guy that Robert was working for": Edwards, *The World Don't Owe Me Nothing: The Life and Times of Delta Bluesman Honeyboy Edwards*, pp. 101–02.

185   "I talked with the white man": Gayle Dean Wardlow, *Chasin' That Devil Music: Searching for the Blues* (San Francisco: Backbeat Books, 1998), p. 91.

186   Rosie Eskridge, who claimed that her husband dug: I am indebted to Gayle Dean Wardlow, who interviewed Eskridge, for providing me with this information—Gayle Wardlow's interview with the author, April 22, 2006. Mack McCormick, who is skeptical about Eskridge's linkage to Robert Johnson, also offered me some valuable perspectives on this matter.

187   In a letter to Agent E. J. Connelley: This letter is part of the FBI files on John Henry Hammond, provided to me in response to a request under the Freedom of Information Act (FOIA).

chapter seven: i'm a rolling stone

192   the "only man on earth": Elijah Wald, *Escaping the Delta: Robert Johnson and the Invention of the Blues* (New York: HarperCollins, 2004), p. 229.

193   "Lomax was a very peculiar individual": From FBI files on Alan Lomax, provided in response to an FOIA request. See also my article "The Red Rumor Blues: Newly Released Files Reveal a Long-Running FBI Probe into Music Chronicler Alan Lomax," *Los Angeles Times*, April 23, 2006.

194   "name-calling, hostility, deception": The quotes here and below can be found in Robert Gordon and Bruce Nemerov, eds., *Lost Delta Found: Rediscovering the Fisk University–Library of Congress Coahoma County Study, 1941–1942* (Nashville, TN: Vanderbilt University Press, 2005), pp. xv–xvi.

196   "creative deployment of African style in an American setting": Alan Lomax, *The Land Where the Blues Began* (New York: Pantheon, 1993), p. xiv.

198   "whippin' never did him no good": Ibid., p. 15.

198   "I'm used to plowin' so many acres a week": Ibid., p. 17.

198   "I don't know where Son took me": Ibid.

199   Unpublished correspondence on file in the Library of Congress: Letters from Lomax to House, as well as a single letter from House to Lomax dated October 30, 1941—in which the blues musician requests copies of his recordings for the Library of Congress—can be found in folder 11 of the Lomax–Fisk University files from the Coahoma County project, American Folklife Center, LOC.

203   could "sing, blow a jug, play a guitar, beat a washboard": Quoted in Robert Gor-

don, *Can't Be Satisfied: The Life and Times of Muddy Waters* (Boston: Little, Brown, 2002), p. 4.

203 "Son House played this place for about four weeks": Quoted in Don DeMichael, "Father and Son: An Interview with Muddy Waters and Paul Butterfield," *Down Beat*, vol. 36, no. 16 (August 7, 1969), p. 12.

203 "When I heard Son House, I should have broke": Ibid.

209 Tommy was dark and had big eyes: David Honeyboy Edwards, *The World Don't Owe Me Nothing: The Life and Times of Delta Bluesman Honeyboy Edwards* (Chicago: Chicago Review Press, 1997), p. 32.

210 "In Chicago and New York, they don't use that word": The quotes here and below are from William Broonzy and Yannick Bruynoghe, *Big Bill Blues: William Broonzy's Story* (New York: Da Capo Press, 1992), pp. 141, 143.

211 "He was just a skeleton": Michael Bloomfield with S. Summerville, *Me and Big Joe* (San Francisco: RE/Search Publications, 1980), p. 6.

212 "He was popular all over Mississippi": From Jeff Harris's accompanying essay to *Robert Nighthawk: Prowling with the Nighthawk* (Document DOCD 32-20-6).

214 "It was unpleasant . . . just too tough": This and below from Pete Welding, "An Interview with Muddy Waters," *The American Folk Music Occasional* (New York: Oak Publications, 1970), p. 5.

215 "I thought that record was drownded": Gordon, *Can't Be Satisfied: The Life and Times of Muddy Waters*, p. 82. See also Jim O'Neal, "Muddy's First Chicago Record," *Living Blues*, 52 (Spring 1982), p. 4.

217 "Poor recording distorts vocal and steel guitar backing": Quoted in Gordon, *Can't Be Satisfied: The Life and Times of Muddy Waters*, p. 94.

220 As Gunnar Myrdal showed in his survey: Gunnar Myrdal, *An American Dilemma: The Negro Problem and Modern Democracy* (New York: Harper & Bros., 1944), pp. 587–88.

221 "many can play the blues better than me": DeMichael, "Father and Son: An Interview with Muddy Waters and Paul Butterfield," p. 32.

227 "That's a very good title": Ibid., p. 13.

228 "I think if he was livin'": Gordon, *Can't Be Satisfied: The Life and Times of Muddy Waters*, p. 209.

229 "We recorded most of the songs": Johnny Winter, interview with the author, April 17, 2006.

230 "I'm skeptical about the supernatural": Quoted in Gordon, *Can't Be Satisfied: The Life and Times of Muddy Waters*, p. 273.

chapter eight: hooker's boogie

235 "just vanished out of the world": Charles Shaar Murray, *Boogie Man: The Adventures of John Lee Hooker in the American Twentieth Century* (New York: St. Martin's Press, 2000), p. 43.

235   Even the guitarist, at his most truthful moment: Hooker's rhythms are fascinating. To unravel their mystery, Fernando Benadon and I have conducted a microrhythmic analysis that will be published in a forthcoming issue of *Popular Music*: "How Hooker Found His Boogie: A Rhythmic Analysis of a Classic Groove."

235   "What he picked up has got to come": Quotes from Richards and King in Jas Obrecht, "John Lee Hooker," in Obrecht, ed., *Rollin' and Tumblin': The Postward Blues Guitarists* (San Francisco: Miller Freeman, 2000), p. 284; see also p. 400.

235   "older than the earliest country blues records": Murray, *Boogie Man: The Adventures of John Lee Hooker in the American Twentieth Century*, p. 59.

235   "I'm the first person that really got": Jim O'Neal and Amy van Singel, eds., *The Voice of the Blues: Classic Interviews from Living Blues Magazine* (New York: Routledge, 2002), p. 204.

236   "I got that from my stepdad": Murray, *Boogie Man: The Adventures of John Lee Hooker in the American Twentieth Century*, p. 36.

236   "identical like me, identical": Pete Welding, "John Lee Hooker: Me and the Blues," *Down Beat*, vol. 35, no. 20 (October 3, 1968), p. 15.

236   Both David Evans and Gayle Wardlow: E-mail from David Evans, April 4, 2006, and interview with Gayle Wardlow, April 22, 2006. However, Evans notes a similarity between Hooker's playing and several blues players recorded in Shreveport, Moore's hometown—figures such as Country Jim Bledsoe and Clarence London, about whom very little is known. Can the roots of Hooker's famous sound be found in Louisiana rather than in the Delta? This might present an interesting angle for future researchers.

237   "I was a great gospel singer": Murray, *Boogie Man: The Adventures of John Lee Hooker in the American Twentieth Century*, p. 25.

238   "I know why the best blues artists come from Mississippi": Ibid., p. 14.

238   "I know, living in Mississippi": Steve Stolder, "John Lee Hooker: The Crawling King Snake Strikes Again," *BAM: The California Music Magazine*, vol. 14, no. 18 (September 9, 1988), p. 14.

240   "I wasn't known, wasn't even thinkin' about it": Murray, *Boogie Man: The Adventures of John Lee Hooker in the American Twentieth Century*, p. 43.

241   "You are the best I ever heard": Ibid., p. 106.

246   "Everybody in the record business is crooked": Ibid., p. 136.

247   "I can go into a studio": Jas Obrecht, "The Funkiest Man Alive! John Lee Hooker," *Guitar Player*, vol. 26, no. 8 (August 1992), pp. 29–30.

251   "music didn't interest me": Murray, *Boogie Man: The Adventures of John Lee Hooker in the American Twentieth Century*, p 169.

253   "betwixt and between": Quoted in Jas Obrecht, ed., *Rollin' and Tumblin': The Postwar Blues Guitarists* (San Francisco: Miller Freeman, 2000), p. 186.

262   "There would not have been a rediscovery of Son House": Waterman's comments, made to researchers for a PBS documentary, can be found in Francis Davis, *The History of the Blues* (New York: Hyperion, 1995), p. 219.

263   "It took over two years for us to get permission": Quotes here from Fito de la Parra
       with T. W. and Marlane McGarry, *Living the Blues: Canned Heat's Story of Music,
       Drugs, Death, Sex and Survival* (Nipomo, CA: Canned Heat Music, 2000), p. 172.

270   "When I was a child": Quoted in Andrew Dansby's obituary, "John Lee Hooker
       Dies," *Rolling Stone*, posted online on June 22, 2001, at www.rollingstone.com/
       news/story/5932751/john_lee_hooker_dies.

chapter nine: smokestack lightnin'

274   "I tell you," he recalled years later: James Segrest and Mark Hoffman, *Moanin' at
       Midnight: The Life and Times of Howlin' Wolf* (New York: Pantheon, 2004), p. 89.

275   "I am not a smart man": Michael Erlewine, "Howlin' Wolf at the First Ann Arbor
       Blues Festival," *Living Blues*, 183 (April 2006), p. 39.

277   "the meanest man between here and hell": Segrest and Hoffman, *Moanin' at Mid-
       night: The Life and Times of Howlin' Wolf*, p. 7.

277   "He was sad but he could sing": Ibid., p. 10.

279   "He had a voice like a lion": From Howlin' Wolf's interview with David Little,
       Peter Riley, and Dorothy Riley, conducted in Boston in 1973. My thanks to Mark
       Hoffman for providing a copy of this, and for arranging permission through
       David Little and Peter Riley.

279   "I was afraid of Wolf": Quoted in Peter Guralnick, *Feel Like Going Home* (New
       York: Back Bay Books, 1999), p. 100.

280   "Wolf never dodged no work": David "Honeyboy" Edwards, *The World Don't Owe
       Me Nothing: The Life and Times of Delta Bluesman Honeyboy Edwards* (Chicago:
       Chicago Review Press, 1997), p. 113.

280   "It was Sonny Boy Williamson": Pete Welding, "Howlin' Wolf: 'I Sing for the
       People,'" *Down Beat*, vol. 34, no. 25 (December 14, 1967), p. 21.

280   "See Sonny Boy married my stepsister Mary": Quoted in Guralnick, *Feel Like
       Going Home*, p. 154.

280   "He discovered for himself": Edwards, *The World Don't Owe Me Nothing: The Life
       and Times of Delta Bluesman Honeyboy Edwards*, p. 96.

283   "Between 1948 and 1950": Robert Palmer, *Deep Blues* (New York: Penguin Books,
       1982), p. 231.

284   "stronger than forty acres of crushed garlic": Quoted in Segrest and Hoffman,
       Moanin' at Midnight: The Life and Times of Howlin' Wolf, p. 72. *Newsweek* quote
       from "Mean Old Blues," *Newsweek*, February 21, 1966, p. 91.

287   "I can take one damn record": Quoted in Segrest and Hoffman, *Moanin' at Mid-
       night: The Life and Times of Howlin' Wolf*, p. 90.

291   "Stuck my momma's snuff bottle in there": Hubert Sumlin, "My Years with Wolf,"
       Living Blues, 88 (September–October 1989), p. 10.

291   "Well these coke cases started to come unbalanced": Ibid., pp. 12–13.

292   "Muddy never had the energy Wolf had" and the quotes that follow: Palmer, *Deep
       Blues*, pp. 232–33.

294   "I haven't seen anything like it": Quoted in Segrest and Hoffman, *Moanin' at Midnight: The Life and Times of Howlin' Wolf*, p. 129.

296   "[Wolf] would say, 'Look here, Hubert'": This, and below, from Sumlin, "My Years with Wolf," p. 15.

297   "I wish I had had you the first day": Segrest and Hoffman, *Moanin' at Midnight: The Life and Times of Howlin' Wolf*, p. 203.

298   "He would be glad to get in on it": Willie Dixon with Don Snowden, *I Am the Blues: The Willie Dixon Story* (New York: Da Capo Press, 1990), p. 149.

300   "You're my favorite guitar player": Quoted in Hubert Sumlin, "My Years with Wolf," p. 17. Quote from Clapton related by Norman Dayron in Segrest and Hoffman, *Moanin' at Midnight: The Life and Times of Howlin' Wolf*, p. 272.

300   The Rolling Stones were engaged to perform: *Shindig* host Jimmy O'Neill has claimed that the commonly told story of the Stones demanding Wolf's appearance on the show is wrong. Producer Jack Good, he asserts, brought Wolf onto the show as a surprise for the British rockers, because he knew they were admirers of his work. Yet anyone familiar with the booking policies of network TV is perhaps justified in remaining skeptical of this revisionist account. In contrast, the Stones' commitment to sharing the stage with old blues musicians is well documented elsewhere in this book—See "Shindig! Tapes Bring 1960s Rock Back to Life," *Los Angeles Times*, December 14, 1991.

301   In February 1966, *Newsweek* published a profile: "Mean Old Blues," *Newsweek*, February 21, 1966, p. 91.

303   "They taken advantage of me": Segrest and Hoffman, *Moanin' at Midnight: The Life and Times of Howlin' Wolf*, p. 263.

chapter ten: riding with the king

312   "Now I wish I could sit down": Mike Leadbitter, "Big Boy Crudup, Part 2," *Blues Unlimited*, 76 (October 1970), p. 18.

314   "There was no dance floor as such": James Meredith, *Three Years in Mississippi* (Bloomington: Indiana University Press, 1966,), p. 35.

318   a "machine that changed my life": B.B. King with David Ritz, *Blues All Around Me: The Autobiography of B.B. King* (New York: Avon Books, 1996), p. 23.

321   "I believe I listened harder than anyone": Ibid., p. 72.

322   "the blues came out of Mississippi": Peter Guralnick, *Feel Like Going Home: Portraits in Blues and Rock and Roll* (New York: Back Bay Books, 1999), p. 46.

325   "He was the yardman for an anthropology professor": Quoted in Robert Gordon, *It Came from Memphis* (New York: Pocket Books, 2001), p. 78.

333   "When I went into the record stores": King with Ritz, *Blues All Around Me: The Autobiography of B.B. King*, p. 201.

338   "B.B. King got a standing ovation": Quoted in B.B. King with Dick Waterman, *The B.B. King Treasures: Photos, Mementos and Music from the B.B. King Collection* (New York: Bullfinch, 2005), p. 89.

339   "The energy was there": Quoted in Dan Daley, "Bill Szymczyk," *Sound on Sound* (November 2004), available at http://www.soundonsound.com/sos/nov04/ articles/szymczyk.htm (August 2006).

341   "I heard funk as a hopped-up variation": King with Ritz, *Blues All Around Me: The Autobiography of B.B. King*, p. 263.

chapter eleven: the blues revival

348   "seemed as remote as Kurdistan": Peter Guralnick, *Searching for Robert Johnson* (New York: Plume, 1998), p. 1.

349   "a very withdrawn, shy individual": E-mail from Lawrence Cohn to the author, February 23, 2007.

349   "who set themselves up as cultural arbiters": Marybeth Hamilton, *In Search of the Blues: Black Voices, White Visions* (London: Jonathan Cape, 2007), p. 10.

352   "I had met John Fahey in 1960" and the quotes that follow: Gayle Dean Wardlow, interview with the author, April 22, 2006.

355   "I phoned Avalon, and spoke to a woman": Mack McCormick, interview with the author, August 26, 2006.

359   it "was entirely John's idea," and the quotes that follow: E-mail from ED Denson to the author, December 21, 2005.

360   "He was a bit nervous about being on the radio anyway": E-mail from ED Denson to the author, April 23, 2006.

363   "a woman was the cause of it all": Quoted in Stephen Calt, *I'd Rather Be the Devil: Skip James and the Blues* (New York: Da Capo Press, 1994), p. 236.

364   "Now isn't that nice": Ibid., p. 246.

364   "If anybody mess with you": Ibid., p. 248.

365   "gaunt and a little hesitant": Peter Guralnick, *Feel Like Going Home: Portraits in Blues and Rock and Roll* (New York: Back Bay Books, 1999), p. 113.

365   "one of those rare electric moments": Bruce Jackson's notes to *Skip James Today* (Vanguard VMD 79219).

365   "As the first notes floated across the field" and "That was the high point": Guralnick, *Feel Like Going Home: Portraits in Blues and Rock 'n' Roll*, pp. 113–14.

366   "I remember Skip James performing": Mack McCormick, interview with the author, August 26, 2006.

369   "bungled song after song": Calt, *I'd Rather Be the Devil: Skip James and the Blues*, p. 329.

370   "begin a guitar riff à la Blind Lemon Jefferson": E-mail from Stephen Calt to the author, dated September 1, 2006.

370   "Solomon appeared delighted with every take": Calt, *I'd Rather Be the Devil: Skip James and the Blues*, p. 329.

371   "The search for these old-time bluesmen": "Looking for the Blues," *Newsweek*, July 13, 1964, p. 82.

371   "When last heard of he had left the Delta": Simon A. Napier, "Eugene 'Son' House," *Blues Unlimited*, 14 (April 1964), p. 6.

372   "We had about two nickels to scrape together": Phil Spiro, interview with the author, November 23, 2005.

372   "But it turns out to have been Dave Evans": When Evans was contacted to confirm Spiro's crediting him with finding out about House from Booker White, he responded: "Yes, I recall being the one who actually asked Booker about Son House, though Al and I were talking with him together. I have no qualms about sharing any 'credit' with Al. He probably would have asked the same question eventually in the same conversation (and gotten the same answer)"—E-mail from David Evans to Phil Spiro and the author, December 9, 2005.

373   "The smartest thing we did was to get in touch": Phil Spiro, interview with the author, November 23, 2005.

374   "It is said that Al taught Son House": Ibid.

375   "a man to whom House owed everything": Lawrence Cohn's liner notes to *Son House: Father of the Delta Blues: The Complete 1965 Sessions* (Columbia Legacy C2K 48867), originally published in *Saturday Review*, September 28, 1968.

375   "Son House was hard work": Dick Waterman, interview with the author, November 16, 2005.

376   "His eyes are closed, head reared back": Cohn's liner notes to *Son House: Father of the Delta Blues: The Complete 1965 Sessions*.

376   "Son House did it exactly the same": Dick Waterman, interview with the author, November 16, 2005.

379   "Delaney Bramlett and his wife Bonnie": Ibid.

381   "I ain't the best in the world": Quoted in David Evans's accompanying notes to Babe Stovall, *The Old Ace: Mississippi Blues and Religious Songs* (Arcola A CD 1005).

384   "like a deep-voiced black herald" and "He stomped up and down": Alan Lomax, *The Land Where the Blues Began* (New York: Pantheon, 1993), p. 353.

384   "the straight and natural blues": Fred McDowell, notes to the CD *I Do Not Play Rock and Roll* (Fuel, 2000).

385   "I don't care if it don't sound good to you": This and below from Hoyle Osborne, " 'I Been Headed Up Ever Since': An Interview with Fred McDowell," *Sing Out*, vol. 19, no. 2 (July–August 1969), pp. 16–19.

389   "If you want a man who can flat lay down": Accompanying notes to *R.L. Burnside's First Recordings* (Fat Possum 80365-2).

389   "My jaw dropped when I heard his music": George Mitchell, interview with the author, September 12, 2006.

recommended listening:
100 essential blues performances

Most lists of recommended listening in music books refer readers to compact disks or LPs. I have offered here instead a list of one hundred *individual songs*, focusing on these specific performances instead of citing entire releases or reissues. My hope is that by suggesting a song instead of a CD, I will encourage closer and repeated listenings, and that this relatively modest amount of music—perhaps five or six hours' worth—will become deeply familiar to my readers. The listing of songs also offers practical advantages in this age of downloading and playlists, when many fans have bypassed the CD format entirely. Finally, such a guide continues to be useful even when specific compact disks go out of print, or are replaced by different titles, and is thus immune to the fickle decisions of entertainment industry executives. For each song, I have provided some additional identification, usually referring to the initial release number of the performance, to help guide the curious listener to the right source. Although my focus here is on the Delta blues, I have included a few tracks from outside the Delta region proper—from, for example, Blind Lemon Jefferson and Bessie Smith—to provide a broader context for our main areas of inquiry.

Artist	Performance	Release
Akers, Garfield (with Joe Callicott)	"Cottonfield Blues"	Vocalion 1442
Bailey, Kid	"Mississippi Bottom Blues"	Brunswick 7114
Bracey, Ishmon	"Saturday Blues"	Victor 21349
Brown, William	"Mississippi Blues"	Library of Congress, 1942
Brown, Willie	"Future Blues"	Paramount 13090
Brown, Willie	"Make Me a Pallet on the Floor"	Library of Congress, 1941
Burnside, R. L.	"Goin' Down South"	*First Recordings* (Fat Possum), 2003
Canned Heat (with John Lee Hooker)	"Drifter"	Liberty LST-35002
Cream	"I'm So Glad"	Polydor 623 031
Crudup, Arthur	"Dirt Road Blues"	Victor 20-2757
Delaney, Mattie	"Tallahatchie River Blues"	Vocalion 1480
Edwards, David "Honeyboy"	"Worried Blues"	Library of Congress, 1942
Handy, W. C.	"St. Louis Blues"	Black Swan 2053
Harris, William	"I'm Leavin' Town"	Gennett 6306
Hooker, John Lee	"Boogie Chillen"	Modern 20-627
Hooker, John Lee	"Boom Boom"	Vee-Jay 438
Hooker, John Lee	"Dimples"	Vee-Jay 205
Hooker, John Lee	"The Healer"	Chameleon D2-74808
Hooker, John Lee	"I'm in the Mood"	Modern 835
Hooker, John Lee	"Tupelo Blues"	Riverside 838
House, Son	"Death Letter"	Columbia 48867 (1965)
House, Son	"Dry Spell Blues"	Paramount 12990
House, Son	"My Black Mama"	Paramount 13042

Artist	Performance	Release
House, Son	"Preachin' the Blues"	Paramount 13013
House, Son	"Walking Blues"	Library of Congress
Hurt, Mississippi John	"Avalon Blues"	OKeh 8759
Hurt, Mississippi John	"See See Rider"	Library of Congress, 1963
James, Elmore	"Dust My Broom"	Trumpet 146
James, Skip	"Devil Got My Woman"	Paramount 13088
James, Skip	"Hard Time Killin' Floor Blues"	Vanguard 79219
James, Skip	"If You Haven't Any Hay Get On Down the Road"	Paramount 13066
James, Skip	"I'm So Glad"	Paramount 13098
Jefferson, Blind Lemon	"See That My Grave Is Kept Clean"	Paramount 12585
Johnson, Louise	"All Night Long Blues"	Paramount 12992
Johnson, Robert	"Come On in My Kitchen"	Vocalion 03563
Johnson, Robert	"Hellhound on My Trail"	Vocalion 03623
Johnson, Robert	"I Believe I'll Dust My Broom"	Vocalion 03475
Johnson, Robert	"Kindhearted Woman Blues"	Vocalion 03416
Johnson, Robert	"Love in Vain"	Vocalion 04630
Johnson, Robert	"Sweet Home Chicago"	Vocalion 03601
Johnson, Robert	"Terraplane Blues"	Vocalion 03416
Johnson, Tommy	"Big Road Blues"	Victor 21279
Johnson, Tommy	"Canned Heat Blues"	Victor V-38535
Johnson, Tommy	"Cool Drink of Water Blues"	Victor 21279
Johnson, Tommy	"Maggie Campbell Blues"	Victor 21409
Jordan, Frank, and a group of Parchman convicts	"I'm Going to Leland"	Library of Congress, 1936
Kimbrough, Junior	"Meet Me in the City"	*All Night Long* (Fat Possum), 1995

Artist	Performance	Release
King, B.B.	"How Blue Can You Get?"	Live at the Regal Theater, Chicago, 1964
King, B.B.	"Never Make a Move Too Soon"	*Midnight Believer* (MCA), 1978
King, B.B.	"Paying the Cost to Be the Boss"	*Deuces Wild* (MCA), 1997
King, B.B.	"Sweet Little Angel"	Live at the Regal Theater, Chicago, 1964
King, B.B.	"Three O'Clock Blues"	RPM 339
King, B.B.	"The Thrill is Gone"	Bluesway LP 6037
Lacy, Rube	"Mississippi Jailhouse Groan"	Paramount 12629
Lewis, Furry	"I Will Turn Your Money Green"	Victor V-38506
McClennan, Tommy	"Bottle It Up and Go"	Bluebird 8373
McDowell, "Mississippi" Fred	"61 Highway Blues"	Library of Congress, 1959
McDowell, "Mississippi" Fred	"Red Cross Store"	Capitol SM-409
Mississippi Sheiks	"Sittin' on Top of the World"	OKeh 8784
Nighthawk, Robert	"Friars Point Blues"	Decca 93037
Patton, Charley	"Banty Rooster Blues"	Paramount 12792
Patton, Charley	"High Water Everywhere"	Paramount 12909
Patton, Charley	"Mississippi Bo Weavil Blues"	Paramount 12805
Patton, Charley	"Moon Going Down"	Paramount 13014
Patton, Charley	"Pony Blues"	Paramount 12792
Patton, Charley	"A Spoonful Blues"	Paramount 12869
Patton, Charley	"Tom Rushen Blues"	Paramount 12877
Petway, Robert	"Catfish Blues"	Bluebird 8838
Reynolds, Blind Joe	"Outside Woman Blues"	Paramount 12927

Artist	Performance	Release
Rolling Stones	"Love in Vain"	Decca SKL 5025
Shines, Johnny	"Ramblin'"	J.O.B. 116
Smith, Bessie	"Empty Bed Blues"	Columbia 14312-D
Smith, Mamie	"Crazy Blues"	OKeh 4169
Spruell, Freddie	"Milk Cow Blues"	OKeh 8422
Stokes, Frank	"How Long Blues"	Victor V-38512
Thomas, Mattie May	"Dangerous Blues"	Library of Congress, 1939
Turner, Otha	"Shimmy She Wobble"	*From Senegal to Senatobia* (Birdman Records), 2000
Virgial, Otto	"Little Girl in Rome"	Bluebird B6213
Waters, Muddy	"I Be's Troubled"	Library of Congress, 1941
Waters, Muddy	"I Feel Like Going Home"	Aristrocrat 1305
Waters, Muddy	"I'm Ready"	Chess 1579
Waters, Muddy	"I'm Your Hoochie Coochie Man"	Chess 1560
Waters, Muddy	"I've Got My Mojo Working"	*Muddy Waters at Newport, 1960*
Waters, Muddy	"Mannish Boy"	*Hard Again* (1977)
Waters, Muddy	"Rollin' Stone"	Chess 1426
White, Booker	"Aberdeen Mississippi Blues"	OKeh 05683
White, Booker	"District Attorney Blues"	OKeh 05683
White, Booker	"Fixin' to Die Blues"	Vocalion 05588
White, Booker	"Shake 'Em On Down"	Vocalion 03711
Wiley, Geeshie	"Last Kind Words Blues"	Paramount 12951
Wilkins, Robert	"Rolling Stone"	Victor 21741
Williams, "Big" Joe	"Baby Please Don't Go"	Bluebird B6200
Williams, "Big" Joe	"Providence Help the Poor People"	Bluebird B5930
Wolf, Howlin'	"Back Door Man"	Chess 1777

Artist	Performance	Release
Wolf, Howlin'	"Evil is Going On"	Chess 1575
Wolf, Howlin'	"Killing Floor"	Chess 1923
Wolf, Howlin'	"Moanin' at Midnight"	Chess 1479
Wolf, Howlin'	"The Red Rooster"	Chess 1804
Wolf, Howlin'	"Smokestack Lightnin'"	Chess 1618
Wolf, Howlin'	"Wang Dang Doodle"	Chess 1777

for further reading

In addition to the books and articles listed below, readers will enjoy reading old issues of *Living Blues, Blues Unlimited, Blues World, Blues Revue,* and *78 Quarterly*—almost every issue contains worthwhile articles or reviews related to the Delta blues tradition.

Barker, Hugh, and Yuval Taylor. *Faking It: The Quest for Authenticity in Popular Music.* New York: W. W. Norton, 2007.

Bloomfield, Michael, with S. Summerville, *Me and Big Joe.* San Francisco: Re/Search Publications, 1980.

Calt, Stephen. *I'd Rather Be the Devil: Skip James and the Blues.* New York : Da Capo Press, 1994.

————, and Gayle Wardlow, *King of the Delta Blues: The Life and Music of Charlie Patton.* Newton, NJ: Rock Chapel Press, 1988.

Charters, Samuel. *The Bluesmen.* New York: Oak Publications, 1967.

————. *The Country Blues.* New York: Da Capo Press, 1975.

————. *The Roots of the Blues: An African Search*. New York: Perigee, 1981.

————. *Walking a Blues Road: A Blues Reader 1956–2004*. New York: Marion Boyars, 2004.

Chernoff, John. *African Rhythm and African Sensibility*. Chicago: University of Chicago Press, 1981.

Cobb, James C. *The Most Southern Place on Earth: The Mississippi Delta and the Roots of Regional Identity*. New York: Oxford University Press, 1992.

Cohn, Lawrence, ed. *Nothing But the Blues: The Music and the Musicians*. New York: Abbeville Press, 1993.

Davis, Francis. *The History of the Blues*. New York: Hyperion, 1995.

Dixon, Robert, and John Godrich. *Recording the Blues*. New York: Stein & Day, 1970.

Edwards, David "Honeyboy." *The World Don't Owe Me Nothing: The Life and Times of Delta Bluesman Honeyboy Edwards*. Chicago: Chicago Review Press, 1997.

Epstein, Dena. *Sinful Tunes and Spirituals: Black Folk Music to the Civil War*. Urbana: University of Illinois Press, 1981.

Evans, David. *Big Road Blues: Tradition and Creativity in the Folk Blues*. Berkeley: University of California Press, 1982.

————. *Tommy Johnson*. London: Studio Vista, 1971.

Fahey, John. *Charley Patton*. London: Studio Vista, 1970.

————. *How Bluegrass Music Destroyed My Life*. Chicago: Drag City, 2000.

Ferris, William. *Blues from the Delta*. Garden City, NY: Anchor Books, 1978.

Franz, Steve. *The Amazing Secret History of Elmore James*. St. Louis: BlueSource, 2002.

Garon, Paul. *Blues and the Poetic Spirit*. New York: Da Capo Press, 1978.

Gioia, Ted. *Work Songs*. Durham, NC: Duke University Press, 2006.

Gordon, Robert. *Can't Be Satisfied: The Life and Times of Muddy Waters*. Boston: Little, Brown, 2002.

————, and Bruce Nemerov, eds. *Lost Delta Found: Rediscovering the Fisk University–Library of Congress Coahoma County Study, 1941–1942*. Nashville, TN: Vanderbilt University Press, 2005.

Groom, Bob. *The Blues Revival*. London: Studio Vista, 1971.

Guralnick, Peter. *Feel Like Going Home: Portraits in Blues and Rock 'n' Roll*. New York: Bay Back Books, 1999.

————. *Searching for Robert Johnson*. New York: Plume, 1998.

Hamilton, Marybeth. *In Search of the Blues: Black Voices, White Visions*. London: Jonathan Cape, 2007.

Handy, W. C. *Father of the Blues: An Autobiography*. New York: Da Capo Press, 1991.

Keil, Charles. *Urban Blues*. Chicago: University of Chicago Press, 1991.

King, B.B., with David Ritz. *Blues All Around Me: The Autobiography of B.B. King*. New York: Avon Books, 1996.

King, B.B., with Dick Waterman. *The B.B. King Treasures: Photos, Mementos and Music from the B.B. King Collection*. New York: Bullfinch, 2005.

Kostelanetz, Richard. *The B.B. King Companion: Five Decades of Commentary.* New York: Schirmer, 1997.

Kubik, Gerhard. *Africa and the Blues.* Jackson, MS: University Press of Mississippi, 1999.

LaVere, Stephen. Accompanying biographical essay to *Robert Johnson: The Complete Recordings* (Columbia C2K 46222).

Leadbitter, Mike, ed. *Nothing But the Blues.* New York: Oak Publications, 1971.

Lomax, Alan. *The Land Where the Blues Began.* New York: Pantheon, 1993.

McGee, David. *B.B. King: There Is Always One More Time.* San Francisco: Backbeat, 2005.

Murray, Charles Shaar. *Boogie Man: The Adventures of John Lee Hooker in the American Twentieth Century.* New York: St. Martin's Press, 2000.

Nicholson, Robert. *Mississippi: The Blues Today.* New York: Da Capo Press, 1999.

Obrecht, Jas, ed. *Rollin' and Tumblin': The Postward Blues Guitarists.* San Francisco: Miller Freeman, 2000.

Odum, Howard W., and Guy B. Johnson. *The Negro and His Songs: A Study of Typical Negro Songs in the South.* Hatboro, PA: Folklore Associates, 1964.

———. *Negro Workaday Songs.* New York: Negro Universities Press, 1969.

Oliver, Paul. *Blues Fell This Morning: Meaning in the Blues.* Cambridge: Cambridge University Press, 1990.

———. *Conversation with the Blues.* New York: Horizon, 1965.

O' Neal, Jim, and Amy van Singel, eds. *The Voice of the Blues: Classic Interviews from Living Blues Magazine.* New York: Routledge, 2002.

Palmer, Robert. *Deep Blues.* New York: Penguin Books, 1982.

Peabody, Charles. "Notes on Negro Music." *Journal of American Folk-Lore,* 16 (July–September 1903), pp. 148–52.

Pearson, Barry Lee, and Bill McCulloch. *Robert Johnson: Lost and Found.* Urbana: University of Illinois Press, 2003.

Roberts, John Storm. *Black Music of Two Worlds.* New York: Original Music, 1972.

Sacré, Robert, ed. *The Voice of the Delta: Charley Patton and the Mississippi Blues Traditions, Influences and Comparisons, An International Symposium.* Liège, Belgium: Presses Universitaires de Liège, 1987.

Sawyer, Charles. *The Arrival of B.B. King.* New York: Doubleday, 1980.

Segrest, James, and Mark Hoffman. *Moanin' at Midnight: The Life and Times of Howlin' Wolf.* New York: Pantheon, 2004.

Spencer, Jon Michael. *Blues and Evil.* Knoxville, TN: University of Tennessee Press, 1993.

Sydnor, Charles S. *Slavery in Mississippi.* Baton Rouge: Louisiana State University Press, 1966.

Titon, Jeff Todd. *Early Downhome Blues: A Musical and Cultural Analysis.* Chapel Hill, NC: University of North Carolina Press, 1994.

van der Tuuk, Alex. *Paramount's Rise and Fall: A History of the Wisconsin Chair Company and Its Recording Activities*. Denver: Mainspring Press, 2003.

Wald, Elijah. *Escaping the Delta: Robert Johnson and the Invention of the Blues*. New York: HarperCollins, 2004.

Wardlow, Gayle Dean. *Chasin' That Devil Music*. San Francisco: Backbeat Books, 1998.

Waterman, Dick. *Between Midnight and Day: The Last Unpublished Blues Archive*. New York: Thunder's Mouth Press, 2003.

index

Page numbers in *italics* refer to illustrations.
Page numbers beginning with 401 refer to endnotes.